ABORTING LAW:
AN EXPLORATION OF THE POLITICS OF MOTHERHOOD AND
MEDICINE

In *Aborting Law* Gail Kellough examines the hegemonic processes concerning the control of women and reproduction. In doing so she illustrates how individual liberty and collective welfare are socially structured through the institutions of law and medicine.

The internal logic of reproduction discourses provides a framework for examining both the legal right of a woman to exercise reproductive choice and her ability to gain access to the medical resources needed to exercise such choice. Kellough focuses on the internal decision making of women active in the Ontario Coalition for Abortion Clinics. Through her association with the socialist-feminist group over the years, she is in the perfect position to note important parallels and contradictions between political strategies of feminist groups and the moral reasoning of women who contemplate abortions. Kellough emphasizes that although women's political choices, like their personal ones, are bound by relations of domination, they are not passive, non-reflective reactions of powerless subordinates.

Aborting Law is a call for an alternative model for discussing and thinking about human autonomy and social responsibility. Kellough argues that ideological discourses are strategic problems that the women's movement cannot afford to ignore in that the struggle for reproductive freedom is already structured and perceived in terms that take beliefs about women's powerlessness for granted.

GAIL KELLOUGH is an associate professor in the Division of Social Science at York University.

GAIL KELLOUGH

Aborting Law: An Exploration of the Politics of Motherhood and Medicine

UNIVERSITY OF TORONTO PRESS
Toronto Buffalo London

© University of Toronto Press Incorporated 1996
  Toronto Buffalo London
  Printed in Canada

  ISBN 0-8020-2971-x (cloth)
  ISBN 0-8020-7741-2 (paper)

Printed on acid-free paper

Canadian Cataloguing in Publication Data

Kellough, Gail
  Aborting Law

  Includes bibliographical references and index.
  ISBN 0-8020-2971-x (bound)
  ISBN 0-8020-7741-2 (pbk.)

  1. Abortion – Canada.   2. Abortion – Moral and
  ethical aspects.   3. Abortion – Law and legislation –
  Canada.   I. Title.

  HQ767.5.C3K45 1996   363.4'6'0971   C95-932843-2

University of Toronto Press acknowledges the financial assistance to its
publishing program of the Canada Council and Ontario Arts Council.

This book has been published with the help of a grant from the Humanities
and Social Sciences Federation of Canada, using funds provided by the Social
Sciences and Humanities Research Council of Canada.

For Doran, Trevor, and Kara

Contents

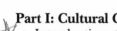

Acknowledgments

This book would never have been written had it not been for the activists in the Ontario Coalition for Abortion Clinics, who shared their time and knowledge with me. I thank them for giving me the opportunity to share their experiences. The intellectual influences are too numerous to mention, but I particularly want to express my gratitude to my adviser and friend, Richard Ericson, for his ongoing intellectual guidance and counsel. Other colleagues whose friendship I have valued are Ron Schriml, with whom I had many stimulating discussions about the issues raised in this book, Laureen Snider, whose comments and support provided me with encouragement when I most needed it, and Stan Cohen, whose writing inspired me to think about realities that are denied. I also thank all the faculty and staff at the Centre of Criminology, who on more than one occasion welcomed me and accommodated my needs. Within this hospitable environment, Dr Tony Doob obligingly provided his advice and assistance. The friends I met at the centre have extended numerous personal favours, and I am particularly grateful to Tammy Landau, Dany Lacombe, and Maeve McMahon for their ongoing support and advice. I also want to thank Cathy Matthews and the wonderful librarians at the Criminology Library, who provided invaluable assistance in securing media clippings and literature sources for my research.

I have been most fortunate in the variety of institutional supports that I have received. Saint Mary's University provided backing during the writing of earlier drafts, and York University gave me an intellectual home in which to complete the work. Many individuals within these two universities were helpful, but I particularly want to thank Marie Richard in the Sociology Department at Saint Mary's for the attention she devoted to my needs. Generous funding has been received from the Centre of Criminology, the Social Sciences and Humanities Research Council of Canada, the solicitor general of Canada, the Ontario Arts Council, and the Humanities and Social Sciences Federation of Canada. This institutional backing made the book possible, and the fine editorial skills of Robin Metcalfe, Beverley Endersby, and Carlotta Lemieux did much to improve it.

My thanks would not be complete without a mention of the dear friends who have been my Toronto family: Neil Webster, who has always been at the centre of my 'caring community,' the late Dale De Marsh, who inspired me with his courage and warmth, and the late Madeleine Varley, whose cheerful presence brightened my life. Others who helped me through the extended gestation of this book include the special 'co-op group' who share my daily joys and sorrows: Anne Bryden, Dell Wolfson, Gail Van Varseveld, Joan Lewis, and Lesley Silver. I owe them my heartfelt thanks.

Those for whom my gratitude is least often expressed but most often felt are the family members who allow me to take their love and support for granted. Particularly, I want to thank my children, Doran, Trevor, and Kara, for the concrete meaning they have given to the abstractions of care and diversity, as well as for their toleration of my often imperfect mothering. I also owe much to my generous daughters-in-law, Diane and Kelly, who find time to 'mother' me, and to my sister and brother, Ann and Bill Mitchell, who are my most consistent and loyal confidants. Finally, I thank Eric, Kirsty, Nicholas, and Caelin, not only for joy and laughter but for reminding me that some truths really are uncomplicated.

PART ONE

CULTURAL CODES AND SOCIAL ORGANIZATION

1

Introduction

The debate over abortion goes through cycles of intensity, but the magnitude of this intensity appears to bear little relation to the laws that surround the practice. When public conflict abates, as it periodically does, its decline appears to have less to do with actual legal prohibition than with other crises or other institutions that render the controversy moot for a time (Harrison 1983:4). An examination of formal legal prohibition does not capture the extent to which women have resorted to abortion in order to rid themselves of unwanted pregnancies. While the moral force of law places powerful constraints on reproductive decision making, there is little evidence to suggest that differences in the law of the land will eventually reflect the reproductive reality of a historical period.

To explain the disjuncture between legal formality and daily reality, some critical legal theorists have taken the position that legal discourse is a closed autonomous system of concepts with no direct reference to the 'real world' of personal and political activity. The more recent tendency, however, is to contend that social reality is itself culturally constructed and that legal discourse plays a role in this construction. For example, Boyle (1985) argues that the legal system encapsulates more than legal discourse and legal reasoning, since it relates also to discourses of the broader social world. The reality we understand in a cultural sense, he states, 'is composed of two inter-locking cultural codes, one social and one legal,' and at the point where these codes interlock, the meanings that are culturally available for understanding reality become limited. At the point of intersection a 'mind-set' is created that 'acts as the bridge between indefinite words and closure of a finite, albeit fuzzy, social world' (Boyle 1985:728). According to Boyle, the relationship between legal and social codes is not closed or one-way because each strand contradicts and relies on the other, and it is precisely because the legal code interlocks with the social code that law has ideological power in the construction of inequality.

The process by which power relationships are maintained or re-negotiated within an overarching ideological framework is most easily understood through Gramsci's elaboration of ideological hegemony. As Gramsci articulates the concept, hegemony is not simply a one-way shaping of institutional structures by prevailing cultural paradigms. Rather, relations of power are inscribed in a political process that is so all-encompassing that existing social relations seem to most of us to constitute the limits of possible human experience. Social and economic tensions are played out in the lives of individuals so that the role of power is integral to everyday cultural life, limiting the choices that can be conceived at any given time. Thus, ideas and the language that expresses them are always present in material structures, and material structures always presuppose ideas (Gramsci 1971; Williams 1977).

The concept of hegemony transcends the traditional debate on the relationship between base and superstructure; the structures of society are viewed not as fixed and static entities but as social processes bound up with individual experiences and with the language by which the experiences are interpreted. The emphasis on the importance of ideological frameworks is further extended in the work of a varied group of contemporary theorists (commonly referred to as 'poststructuralists' or 'postmodernists') who stress the importance of the way knowledge is itself structured within and across particular sites. Poststructuralists hold that social reality is ideologically based and that all social practices are inscribed with linguistic understandings.[1] This analysis escapes determinism in that, although ideological domination is a powerful constraint on an individual's activity, it can never be total; there will always be points of contradiction between the basic principles of site-specific discourses or between a particular discourse and the more generalized 'common-sense' understandings of the culture. What makes the systemic reproduction of the status quo possible is the concealment and suppression of these contradictions through a strict separation of the spheres (science, law, family, and so on) in which particular codes are meant to apply and by an acceptance that some discourses are more objective, rational, and truthful than others.

---

1 For example, Foucault (as a prototypical post-structuralist) describes our modern cultural heritage as derivative from 'a series of discontinuous discursive and disciplinary practices' (Yeatman 1990:292).

An analytical understanding of the inseparability of co
which they explain broadens our understanding of
which one group in society can systemically assert
another. The idea of distinct social and legal codes dire⌣⌣
the logical structure of concepts within particular discourses. How concepts are related to one another reflects unquestioned assumptions about
the nature of human reality and the appropriate responses for particular
situations. Where assumptions of one code are similar to those of
another, discourses that are otherwise dissimilar or contradictory will
have a potential point at which interlocking can occur. By describing the
parameters of the points where interlocking may occur, we can mark the
discursive boundaries of our culture's mind-set.

The notion of underlying discursive codes intersecting to produce
ideological hegemony is a useful one for understanding the abortion
struggle and for situating it within the broader institutional practices that
systematically reproduce gender inequality. Like all social practices,
reproductive practices are constituted by the discourses in which they are
thought, and thus a woman's decision to abort her pregnancy cannot be
fully understood without considering the discursive emphasis that a
culture places on the rights or responsibilities assigned to reproductive
activity.

Rhetoric about rights and responsibilities surrounds legislation wherever the practice of abortion is legitimated, regulated, or prohibited.
Indeed, one is tempted to suggest that the recurring abortion conflict will
always be with us because of an irreconcilable tension between individual
rights and collective responsibilities: the right of the individual to make a
private moral decision and the responsibility of the state to pass law in the
interest of collective well-being. However, an examination of legal regulation and reproductive practice in different historical periods and in various countries suggests that we should resist the idea that individual rights
and collective responsibilities are ultimately irreconcilable. Ideas about
rights and responsibilities are inherently inscribed with culture, but at
issue is whose culture? I hope to convince the reader that a belief in this
premise is created when dominant discourses appropriate and transform
the linguistic code that directs reproductive activity.

Legislated rights and customs concerning moral duties are site-specific
in form and content, but at the same time one can observe an ideological
continuity in the coding of the relationship between liberty and need.
While there is a wide diversity in the way concepts of rights and responsibilities are emphasized over time and across place, ideological closure is

naintained because the nature of their conceptualization (within both site-specific legal codes and the broader social code) provides a gendered point at which interlocking can occur. Although each institutional site will produce its own form of control and its own points of intersection, wherever there is hegemonic domination there will also be a cluster of beliefs common to both public-level discourse and the more particular discourses of the ruling apparatus. It is the deeper structure of these unified and often contradictory discourses that allows them to transcend the local and particular in order to create an androcentric mind-set that neutralizes and absorbs the challenges posed by acts of resistance.

Since political activities are constituted by the discourses in which they are thought, a recognition of the shared linguistic conventions of these discursive codes is also a prerequisite for understanding social movement dynamics. Because culturally embedded assumptions shape the kind of legal rights that may be claimed, that which is taken for granted permeates all discourses about power and inhibits political activities that otherwise would be effective strategies for confronting structures of domination. To understand the ideological force of abortion law and its divergence in practice is to uncover the way in which all hegemonic social and legal codes – despite opposition and contradiction – have variously interlocked on the basis of gendered moral assumptions about individual liberty and collective responsibility. Legal rulings concerning abortion and social understandings about the reproduction of human life imply distinctive discourses that are considered applicable to specific spheres of human endeavour, yet these often-oppositional discourses are interrelated aspects of an overarching mind-set. The deeper structure of this mind-set is crisscrossed with assumptions about individual rights or collective responsibilities that are rooted in common beliefs about the nature of reproduction, its relations, and its outcomes. Thus, hegemony is gendered; the closure produced at the point where legal and social codes intersect is logically possible because reproductive practices are discursively relegated to a taken-for-granted backdrop for human life and individual liberty.

The description of the political work and decision making of the Ontario Coalition for Abortion Clinics (OCAC) in part 4 exemplifies the difficulties women face in organizing within the boundaries of social and legal discourse, but it also presents a model for organizing according to the principles and equations of a logic that has the potential to resist absorption into the prevailing mind-set. There are connections between the co-optation of resistance at the political level and the elicitation of 'consent' to reproductive hegemony at the personal level; conversely, there is a sig-

nificant difference between the personal and political challenges to reproductive control. It is the nature of this difference that is important for the
construction of a revolutionary discourse. By understanding the discursive
and institutional context in which challenges are conducted, we can
understand not only how resistance itself becomes part of the hegemonic
process but also how it might withstand such co-optation.

To describe the political struggle of pro-choice activists without an
analysis that counters the current positioning of reproductive reality in
dominant codes is to remain locked within a mind-set that fabricates
reproductive relationships by defining the terms by which we can speak
about them. Only by decoding the structural characteristics of these terms
and tracing their evolution can we assess the relevance of pro-choice decision making for political struggles in general. Thus, before addressing
how political activity can be used to expose the inherent contradictions of
dominant forms of discourse, I shall describe the conceptual and historical context within which OCAC originated and operated. This exposition
of theory and practice forms the first three parts of the book. Historically
and comparatively, it provides a context for understanding the direction
and detours that the OCAC activists took in their attempt to combine
political mobilization with a legal challenge. Because the focus of this
background depiction shifts in a number of interrelated ways – from the
construction of legal theory to the reality of reproductive practice, from
law to medicine, and from historical to comparative analysis – I offer the
following outline as a guide to assist the reader in discerning the connections between seemingly disparate chapters. As it is a guide, it also pre-
figures the inferences with which I shall conclude the book.

Part 1: Cultural Codes and Social Organization

This first section (composed of two chapters) examines the logical structure of legal and social discourses, contrasting their coded assumptions
with the material reality of reproductive practice.

Chapter 2 sets out the basic characteristics of classical moral philosophy, describing the ways in which public discourse about abortion has
mirrored the logical equations made by legal and moral thought. In illustrating how the respective emphases of classical theory's oppositional discourses (deontology and teleology) are reflected both in law and in the
public articulation of the political positions of the pro- and anti-choice
activists, this chapter deconstructs the underlying structure of the legal
and social codes. Based on similarities in the kinds of equation that are

assumed, otherwise oppositional discourses accept the existence of an inherent clash between the right of an individual to pursue self-interest and the responsibility of the state legally to regulate this self-interest on behalf of the collective. Following from this preconception, the primary legal task is to determine the point on the continuum at which state intervention is legitimate in the balancing of liberty and need. Wherever this conceptual framework is accepted as an accurate model for describing opposing political or moral positions, there is ideological support for the contention that the law must periodically intervene in order to strike a new political balance between those who stress individual liberty and those who favour collective welfare. This intervention presumably will occur whenever one set of political ideas achieves prominence over another (the idealist perspective) or whenever changes in the productive relations of a society promote the adoption of some new legal accommodation (the materialist perspective).

Chapter 3 sets out the basis for my challenge of this causal model. I argue that, despite their differences, oppositional discourses within the legal and social codes take for granted certain assumptions about the nature of reproductive reality that are inaccurate in practice. The reality of reproductive practice is that, despite the conceptual tension between the exercise of autonomy and the need for welfare, individual rights and social responsibilities are more connected and allied than they are separate and oppositional. The hegemonic mind-set reduces its conceptualization of reproduction to a biological event, an interpretation that excludes a consideration of the human choices that are a universal aspect of the creation and empowerment of human beings. The logical result of this coded exclusion is that power is reified from a dynamic experiential process into conceptual categories that allow persons to be distinguished on the basis of independence and dependence. To comprehend how human life, individual subjectivity, and social power are created and sustained is to understand how a discursive distortion of experienced relationships can enable legal and social codes both to contradict and to rely on one another in effecting ideological closure. In excluding, suppressing, and distorting the material reality of reproductive relations, as these relations exist at the level of practice, legal and social codes intersect to justify practices that in turn make future connections possible.

Part 2: Legal Choice and Medical Access

The three chapters in part 2 provide examples of the various categories in the theoretical framework set out in part 1. This section of the book is intended to illustrate how shifts in discourse are themselves an integral part of the hegemonic process. I argue that, despite the existence of differences across historical and cultural sites, domination of some by others is made possible because the discourses that are inscribed in various practices have persisted in a misrepresentation of human reproduction and its related activities.[2]

Chapter 4 describes how the discursive misrepresentation of reproduction was established during the periods when medicine was being transformed into a professional practice, and it elaborates on the unevenness of this transformation during the development of colonial North America. Although my consideration of a Middle Ages shift in the relations of reproduction is extremely broad (and some might say highly speculative with regard to the historical 'truth' of the period), there is substantial evidence to suggest that early struggles over medicine transformed the way our culture thinks about reproductive practices.[3] Similarly, the shifts in medical practice in colonial North America, and the discourses with which they were inscribed, were site-specific, but they nevertheless augmented earlier discourses about the place of medical authority in the structuring of reproductive relations. Only when the control of reproductive activity was removed from those who were engaged in its performance did it become reasonable to exploit this work for the purpose of defining which legal subjects were entitled to autonomy and which ones would require control.[4]

While chapter 4 is concerned with a significant historical discontinuity

2 However, the tendency in recent poststructuralist theory is to reject all generalist categories as totalizing fictions and to focus primarily on multiple differences and site-specific explanations. I suggest that a more politically relevant way of approaching this is to consider how the very differences of certain forms of discourse are part of the process that allows a totalizing mindset to be reproduced. Focusing on diversity and discontinuity, without noticing how these shifts in discursive emphasis or differences in legal approach reproduce a mind-set oriented by opposition and hierarchy, is part of the process whereby we imprison ourselves within language. Within this prison, there is no subjective reality other than that which language has already created, and this privileging of language as the constitutive factor in the construction of subjectivity resonates with a new way of misrepresenting the reproductive work that is universally required for the creation of human subjectivity (Kellough 1992).

3 Although the discussion of medieval witch trials is based on a particular view of preliterate history, the analysis is given weight by the kind of shifts that have taken place in reproductive relationships wherever and whenever medical practices have been professionalized.

4 This is not to say that inequality did not exist before the professionalization of medicine, only that this historical process was an essential factor in establishing gendered activity as a taken-for-granted backdrop for the discursive justification of inequality.

in the logic underlying the practice of medicine, chapter 5 describes an example of continuity between contemporary legal reasoning and the classical reasoning described in chapter 2. A contemporary legal theorist, John Rawls, is said to have unhinged the opposition of self and other that is found within the opposing traditions of classical reasoning. In order that law might more objectively determine the appropriate balance of rights and responsibilities in any given situation, Rawls specified a method for distinguishing between legal subjects who are entitled to be free from state intervention and those who, in the interest of social justice, are not. A deconstruction of this achievement exemplifies how contemporary theory is able to structure different legal accommodations without undermining the ability of language seemingly to 'reproduce itself.' Although Rawls's work purportedly provides a way to bridge the political antagonisms between self and other within classical thought, I argue that the logic of his reasoning remains firmly fixed within androcentric boundaries. He achieved a veneer of political neutrality only by employing the implicit fiction that the reproduction of human life is simply a natural backdrop for the way human volition is to be exercised or regulated. At the same time, this theoretical deconstruction illustrates that the argument that women are written out of legal reasoning is misleading. The writing out occurs only at the surface level; the consciousness of the need for women to continue to provide for the welfare of others is a subtext without which the legal code would have no meaning.

As well as investigating discontinuity in medical practice and continuity in legal theory, part 2 also explores the interaction of medicine and law in the two countries of North America. Chapter 6 compares the different legal accommodations to abortion struggles in Canada and the United States, illustrating how different forms of institutional control and discursive emphases can interlock to effect similar outcomes for women. Although the two countries are characterized by different combinations of legal regulations and medical practices, and although these differences are important for understanding the range of reproductive options that were actually available to women in Canada and the United States, the reproductive concessions won from each state depended on a general affirmation of hegemonic thought. Different institutional practices delineated the boundaries where legal or medical codes were meant to apply, but, in each, these boundaries were mediated and renegotiated only at the point where their respective codes could interlock. From different kinds of legal accommodations, then, came the ideological endorsement that permitted existing asymmetrical relations to remain intact.

Part 3: Alienated Consciousness and the Reproduction of Medical and Legal Discourse

A discursive-code framework directs our attention to the relationship between conceptual building blocks within the logical structures of hegemonic discourse, but it also provides a way of thinking about counterhegemonic practice at both personal and political levels. The four chapters in this section provide the link between my theoretical arguments in parts 1 and 2 and the political struggle I describe in part 4.

Chapter 7 makes the argument that just as there are specific codes that structure the discourse of various sites such as law and medicine, there is a reproductive code that is inscribed in tasks that empower others. Common-sense understandings about women's work in general structures reality so that a woman who undertakes the responsibility of caring for others often appears to be 'consenting' to the disempowerment that is associated with the labour. This misrepresentation of reproductive reality is possible because the discourse already defines these activities in terms of the powerlessness of women and the deterministic nature of their responses to others. Although the work that produces people and relationships is usually (though not necessarily) performed by women, this fact then becomes part of the process through which discursive misrepresentation is made possible.

The appropriation of reproductive labour also includes an alienation of the moral consciousness that informs it and the linguistic understandings with which it is inscribed. Any articulation of the difference is transformed by a linguistic script that has already gendered its dichotomous points of reference. This script transforms experiential motivations, translating them in terms that affirm dominant-code assumptions about the nature of men and women and the work they perform. It is not just that dominant cultural codes demonstrate a gender bias in the way they misrepresent reproductive reality; they also appropriate and make use of the type of thinking that is itself created or shaped by performing activities that empower others. It is not that women are the only human beings who use a reproductive code to respond to the needs of others, and it is not only in the personal realm that such a code motivates activity; rather, the predominant forms of discourse shape the description of thinking itself to fit within the parameters of a mind-set that already assumes asymmetrical relations of power.

The reproductive code is relevant for all activities that enable rather than control, and it is therefore coincident with political responses as well as with personal ones. Thus, it is only by developing space for construct-ing an alternative moral paradigm that one is able, both politically and personally, to argue one's ends in one's own terms.

A moral consciousness and the code that informs it can only be alien-ated from those who practice its precepts by social processes that trans-form the motivations of the actors. In chapter 8 I describe how one such institutional practice shaped and distorted the motivations of Canadian women who sought access to abortion services to help them cope with their particular reproductive realities. The mechanisms established by the 1969 amendment to the Canadian Criminal Code provided a point for social and legal codes to interlock; according to the provisions of this law, doctors sitting on the mandated therapeutic abortion committees (TACs) operated within the confines of the law only when their provision of abor-tion services was accompanied by a justification that affirmed the logic of the hegemonic reasoning.

The TACs were sites where women lived out the contradictions between ideology and reality. The existence of these sites and the mecha-nisms they imposed created a tension between the immediate interests of a pregnant woman and the broader interests of women generally. Any woman who wished to make a responsible decision about her reproduc-tive capacity had little option but to consent to the transformation of her moral reasoning into hegemonic terms. Her consent was part of her resis-tance to biological determination in that her ability actually to secure an abortion symbolically reinforced the prevailing stereotypes about why a woman might require an abortion. In circular fashion, the ideological assumptions that these justifications perpetuated were the discursive material that doctors needed to emphasize their professional right to decide reproductive matters. A doctor who wished to respond to a woman's need was also required to participate with her in the endorse-ment of the interdependent assumptions that doctors are the real sub-jects of the life-giving process and women's bodies are the objects on which they work.

The Canadian law allowed moral questions about how reproductive relations could be organized in a socially responsible way to be removed from the public level and resolved at the private level of medical practice, where doctors had the discretion to construct justifications from the material of women's lives. Uncovering this process reveals that sexual hegemony is not just something imposed on passive and victimized women. Rather, the interaction of law and medicine channelled individual resistance along paths that in turn replicated the distorted interpretations of dominant discourse. Women who were actually resisting control of their personal reproductive capacity or whose decisions were motivated by a reproductive logic became part of the process that reaffirmed the very mind-set that dictated the imposition of medical control in the first place. The choices they made in coping with reproductive reality were, at one and the same time, involved in reproducing existing relations and resisting them (Marshall 1988).

It bears repeating that while ideological domination is a constraint, it can never be total. Its existence is not deterministic because points of contradiction exist between the basic principles of site-specific discourses and the more generalized understandings of the culture. The 1969 changes to Canadian law channelled women needing abortions into an institutionalized process that contradicted the law's precepts of equality and the premise that universal access to health care is a central aspect of what it means to be Canadian. This contradiction mobilized women in support of the illegal abortion clinics, a move that ultimately led to a Supreme Court challenge and the repeal of the law. Although it has been charged that legal struggles have the effect of diluting political dissent, in this instance it was the challenge to the law that permitted the political issue of abortion to be redirected from the private arena of medical practice to the public debate over a controversial legal issue; and, in the courtroom, it was not so easy to mask contradictions between legal ideology and medical practice.

Legal arguments defending the Canadian abortion law at the Supreme Court of Canada were given logical weight by the data which TACs were producing. Chapter 9 describes the state's defence of the abortion law, and chapter 10 analyses the points at which the gender-neutral language of legal discourse intersected with coded assumptions about the nature of men and women.

The narrative of courtroom argumentation (in the appeal courts where Dr Morgentaler's conviction for operating illegal abortion clinics was being reconsidered) exposes the kinds of contradiction that the abortion law had deflected to the medical arena, where they could be privately negotiated by women and their doctors. The 'text' of these legal proceedings provides an illustration of how the courtroom adversaries differentially incorporated the Rawlsian method for distinguishing between primary legal subjects (those with inherent liberty rights) and secondary subjects (those whose powerlessness qualified them for a state consideration of their welfare). The paradox of the discourse at the Morgentaler appeals is that in order to reaffirm the neutrality of the legal method,[5] the Crown had little option but to stress gendered presuppositions emanating from outside the boundaries of formal legal theory.

The legal 'text' of the Morgentaler appeal hearings, where the state was called on to defend its intrusion into the private lives of women, illustrates a particular reading of the contemporary legal code. A deconstruction of the Crown's arguments demonstrates how discourses applicable to medical and reproductive spheres coincided to provide a logical, albeit patriarchal, rationale for distinguishing between primary and secondary legal subjects. For the casual observer at the court, the legal terminology implied that the state was seeking to incorporate the welfare interests of particular legal subjects into the framework of negative law; that is, the lawyers were deliberating about the exceptional circumstances that would allow the state to interfere with a pregnant women's liberty. The language was deceiving. Despite the rhetoric of rights in which the Crown's argument was clothed, what was implicitly being discussed was the manner in which the (deontological) duty of women to care for others could be protected so that 'normal' legal subjects could continue to be guaranteed the liberty already assumed by the legal paradigm. Within a general framework that implied a norm of noninterference by the state, the Crown's arguments juxtaposed notions of responsibility and human connection to ideas about rights and self-sufficiency, and this juxtaposition reaffirmed the norm of independence and liberty even as it bypassed it.

Contradictions normally faced by women and negotiated with the help of ideological currency were revealed in statements made by the Crown attorneys. If the law was to be defended, the basic contradiction of legal theory – its discursive assertion of equality before the law and its coded dependence on the imposition of asymmetrical rights and responsibilities – had to be addressed. According to the contemporary legal code, which specifies a norm of autonomous individuals (with inherent liberty to be protected) and exceptional victims (whose powerlessness renders them deserving of protection), the state can legitimately intervene to protect those who are incapable of exercising autonomy. The dependence of women on their doctors and the asymmetry of reproductive relations were the interdependent 'facts' that provided the rationale for proclaiming the legitimacy of a law that restricted both liberty rights and universal

5 An essential aspect of legal methodology is that its users, the legal authorities, are to remain outside and above the social reality they are attempting to regulate.

health care. Common-sense understandings about the objectivity of medical science united with beliefs about natural female nurturance in order to provide the distinguishing point for deciding who, in Rawlsian terms, would enjoy the benefit of liberty rights and who would have to forgo this benefit in order to have their welfare protected. The discourse of both Crown and defence affirmed the rights granted by the law and the legal statuses that were implied. Their point of disagreement was simply whether, in this instance, it was liberty or welfare rights that should be paramount.

Legal and social codes are able to intersect on the basis of their common reification of power and independence; the work that women perform in the creation of these resources becomes the natural backdrop for their exercise. In the process of enlisting a 'woman's ethic' of care as the rationale for denying all women choice, the Crown's arguments at the Morgentaler hearings depended on the overarching assumption that a foetus already exists as an independent other, separate and apart from the activity and consciousness that creates it. By attributing values of care and responsibility to women *in essential ways,* reproductive-code beliefs are appropriated and framed in terms that justify the medical control of women in order to protect the values. Yet also implicit within the Crown's arguments was a recognition that the existence of life requires something more than noninterference. Otherwise, the need to control pregnant women would not have arisen.

The defence provided for Dr Morgentaler challenged the legal regulation of abortion by stressing a different ordering of priorities than the Crown did. Morgentaler's lawyer, Morris Manning, argued that the TAC procedures unnecessarily undermined the state's objective of ensuring women's medical welfare, but the framing of this contention itself affirmed the conventional legal method for deciding which legal subjects are to be entitled to liberty rights and which to welfare ones.[6] While the outcome of the court case was a repudiation of the current abortion law, the language in which the victory was sought reaffirmed the existing legal paradigm. It simply bypassed the reproductive understanding that the existence of life does require something more than noninterference, leaving the door open for future reverses of a right to medical responsiveness.

6 Whether arguments presenting the pro-choice case could have pushed the boundaries of legal debate beyond the liberty/welfare dichotomy is a question that ultimately distinguishes those who see legal struggle as a political activity from those who do not.

The first three sections of the book serve as an introduction to the fourth in that they contextualize the primary research into the political decision making that I describe in part 4. In chapters 11, 12, and 13, I provide a description and analysis of the political choices which the OCAC activists faced as they attempted to satisfy a short-term practical goal (repeal of the law) without losing sight of their long-term political vision (reproductive freedom for all women).

Just as one cannot truly understand the choices of a woman grappling with reproductive options within a particular society without understanding both the institutional context and the motivations of the actor, similarly one cannot understand the choices the OCAC activists made unless one understands the contradictory context in which OCAC operated and the vision that inspired its choices. In both the political and the personal sphere, the chosen activities appear ambiguous or contradictory only because they cannot be adequately explained by the abstractions of dominant discourses. Despite the public perception of pro-choice activities, the decisions made at OCAC meetings were motivated by issues that went far beyond the goal of repealing the abortion law. However, like the women who sought abortions within the confines of this law, the activists lived out contradictions between ideology and reality. To participate in the performance of reproductive tasks or in revolutionary politics is to encounter similar difficulties. When one listens to the OCAC deliberations about a particular course of action, a parallel emerges – that between the political organizing of a group seeking power for others (often at the cost of its immediate organizational aims) and the strivings of individual women who seek to do the same in their personal relationships (also often at the cost of their immediate interests).

Every 'practice has its theoretical assumptions, whether or not they are explicitly acknowledged' (Bartlett and Kennedy 1991:4). Although they may be conceptually eliminated from discourse, no individual or social practice can ever remain apart from the construction of the discourse itself. The contradiction between discursive context and reproductive reality that exists within all dominant codes affects and is affected by each new abortion struggle and the consciousness that motivates it. The key to OCAC's political organizing was both an explicit and an implicit understanding of this knowledge-practice spiral. While acknowledging that particular political decisions would have to be shaped by hegemonic processes, the OCAC activists consciously aimed their practical acts of resistance at the broader goal of changing the terrain of cultural hegemony. With the repeal of the law, the terrain has changed – partly through the efforts of these women – but equally important is the fact that the vision of reproductive freedom is still out of reach for most women. The analysis of the post-repeal era goes beyond what is attempted in this book, but the alternative discourse I have described will undoubtedly be an ingredient of any future struggle that aspires to the construction of a moral consciousness that is resistant to ideological co-optation.

Conclusion: The Contradictions

To explain the lives of women within conventional discourse is to find inconsistency and contradiction. Whether they are acting personally or politically, their motivations appear to be ambiguous and incoherent. Within conventional discourse, reasons are sought to explain why women act or think so irrationally, and there is much speculation about how female deficiencies of consciousness can be corrected. Despite the different solutions that are posited, oppositional discourses have traditionally assumed female inferiority in moral or political subjectivity and have advocated measures to aid women in casting off the 'outdated' attitudes and beliefs that have inhibited them from achieving the male norm. More recently, feminist theory has mounted a powerful challenge to this discourse, showing that a more intractable problem for reform is the very idea of a male norm that women must strive to attain.

Carol Gilligan's (1982) research into the way women approach decision making on abortion inspired an alternative frame of reference for thinking about moral consciousness and moral subjectivity. Rather than assuming that the inconsistencies and contradictions in a woman's stories were evidence of an immature or undeveloped moral sense, Gilligan challenged the model itself as a construct of male experience, arguing that women speak in a 'different voice.' Because she concluded that a woman's moral reasoning is more likely to centre on connectedness and responsibility than on autonomy and rights, some feminists have viewed this different voice as the same old feminine discourse, a male tool that encourages women to be passive and accept victimization rather than being active shapers of their own destiny (MacKinnon 1987). While I agree that human identity has been constructed from a male standpoint, my research indicates that the problem lies with narratives that equate the ethic of care and responsibility with passivity and victimization. The equation of responsibility with passive victimization is a primary assumption of all hegemonic narratives, and making the same equation does not allow us to escape the boundaries of the mind-set that encompasses it.

The most difficult aspect of describing a different voice is that, within discourse, the definitions of concepts and their relationship to one another are interpreted with reference to equations that are already assumed by hegemonic codes. Within this framework, to speak about responsibility and connectedness is to speak about powerlessness and the private world of personal relationships, equating them with the essence of femininity and with women's work. What Gilligan heard in the voices of her women respondents was, I believe, something very different from the interpretations of customary theorizing. To hear these voices clearly is to understand that the tasks that empower others are not essentially feminine; they have simply been defined as such by the language that explains them.

The basic conceptual problem is that dominance and subordination have been conceptualized from the perspective of the dominators, and this social construction has consequences not only for how we perceive power but for how it actually gets created, appropriated, and resisted. The underlying code of all hegemonic discourse depends on an alienation of reproductive work and the linguistic code with which it is inscribed. To appreciate the fact that revolutionary politics is confronted by dilemmas similar to those faced by women in their intimate lives is to understand that reproductive work is not essentially feminine, nor is it confined to the private sphere of personal relationships. These activities continue to be defined this way because institutional processes structure asymmetrical relationships between those who create human power and those who exercise it. Women at both the personal and the political level do not just speak in contradictory ways; they live these contradictions. To reveal the social process whereby power is created, reified, appropriated by others, and then used over and against those whose actions have helped create it would be to reveal a different understanding of the dynamics of power.

In my final chapter, I explore the way in which contradictions, resistance, and accommodation are part of the process by which our society's moral script is written. It is difficult to make inferences about the long-term implications of the events I have described; their relevance cannot be disentangled from what happens next. What makes the task of drawing conclusions about any particular political strategy or outcome so difficult is that even the interpretation of these facts has the possibility of altering the direction of future struggle. Changes in institutional practices may, on the one hand, be considered to be real gains for oppressed groups while, on the other hand, the way that any reform is interpreted within discourse may strengthen the ideological assumptions that allow future forms of domination to reverse the gain. While the repeal of Canada's abortion law can certainly be said to be a precondition for reproductive freedom, it is not solely determinate of the direction that change will take in the future. Thus, my final words seek not so much to draw conclusions as to become part of a process of constructing discourses that will counter the contradictions that are currently faced by all who seek transformation of the social order.

Juxtaposing the contradictions that women face at the personal level with those they face at the political level illustrates the need for a moral vision that will discursively challenge the opposition of hegemonic codes. Although hegemony derives its power through a discursive logic that creates dilemmas, reproductive logic implies that the empowerment of dependent others requires something more than a removal of these ideological constraints. It also requires the *construction* of a counterhegemonic moral vision that recognizes the meaning women have imputed to their various experiences of caring and being cared for. For theory to continue to ignore the manner in which women's work has been central to and invisible within the discourses that create our understanding of human subjectivity is to continue to create, within language, women who remain outside the power dynamic.

The construction of a moral vision that avoids misrepresenting the reality of some must always be a collective exercise. Just as life and subjectivity are social constructions, the construction of a new moral vision can never be a private exercise. Moreover, while a vision is necessary, it cannot specify strategies irrespective of actual contexts. It is possible, as Cohen (1990) has stated, 'to recognize the contingency of our values and language and yet remain wholly faithful to them.' The relevance of the political theorizing of OCAC is that resistance to domination requires a continual modification of our political vision as we interact with others whose experiences are different from our own. That these experiences will always be more than a matter of ideological victimization – are, indeed, part of a process for empowerment – is a necessary component of this construction.

2

Interpretive Codes of Legal and Social Discourse

I fully agree with many abortion opponents that we owe it to each other to shape our common life as effectively as possible around 'the moral point of view.' In any case, morality always enters into politics one way or another, and deep political conflict is always simultaneously basic value conflict about what constitutes human well-being ... Moral reasoning is inherently dialogical; it involves the effort to communicate to others ... [W]e eschew moral analysis at the risk of failing to understand what it is we are actually doing through political choices and social policies. (Harrison 1983:5–6)

Our theoretical goal might be best envisaged as a process oriented (not structure based) model which begins with a reflection of *how* specific social groups are organized in social praxis, and on the role of systems of meaning in this practical organization. (Valverde 1990:63)

'Autonomy' and 'Responsibility' within Moral Discourse

At the heart of all cultural discourses are moral assumptions about the relation between self and other. This self-other relationship is reflected in understandings about the nature of autonomy and responsibility, key concepts in classical moral and legal thought. Moreover, the oppositional discourses within different forms of classical reasoning are reproduced in popular discourse about abortion practices. This chapter elaborates on the nature of the self-other relationship that is assumed by otherwise contradictory discourses; it is this cluster of moral ideas that permits legal and social codes to interlock in the reproduction of ideological hegemony. As Harrison has so cogently pointed out, to ignore these moral underpinnings is to risk consenting to practices that create inequality and oppression.

Classical moral philosophy consists of two opposing schools of thought: deontology and teleology. Deontology is concerned with moral principles that specify duties and obligations; these principles are derived from a natural order that exists over and above the personal intentions of human actors. As Lake (1986) puts it, '[M]oral truths (or values) exist apart from individuals and can be discovered (but not created) by the studious person' (484–5). By contrast, teleology is individualistic and situation-specific, and is concerned with the promotion of individual autonomy rather than with duty to others. Whereas deontology requires the individual's absolute adherence to rules, teleology stresses that morality is relative and that when applying it to a particular situation, one must actively contemplate the problems at hand. From this perspective, 'the ultimate human responsibility is to listen to the immediate, unreduced claims of the hour' (Martin Buber, as cited in Lake 1986:486). In sum, deontology is concerned with 'right' action as defined by the rule, while teleology is concerned with the 'right' consequence of one's action (Duff 1976).

Although classical moral thought posits dichotomous systems for achieving the 'good society,' these opposing traditions share a belief in two inherent antagonisms: that between the individual and society, and that between social (volitional) activity and natural (determined) factors. Whereas the teleological tradition seeks to maximize individual autonomy in the pursuit of self-interest as an expression of moral social activity, the deontological tradition stresses duty to others as the expression of a natural moral order. Thus, teleology posits the existence of autonomous individuals creating their own reality and ministering to their own needs, while deontology presupposes a natural moral order providing rules for social well-being and for harmonious relations between individuals. In deontology, care for others is automatically identified with a natural prohibition against acting in furtherance of individual intentions; in teleology, the frequently unstated equation is between human volition and self-interest. Both take for granted that free will is equated with self-interest and determinism with responding to others. Where they differ is in the degree and nature of the control that is perceived to be necessary for promoting individual liberty and social well-being.

The assumptions of classical moral reasoning are the building blocks with which the classical legal code's and the contemporary social code's explanations of the moral positions of 'pro-life' and 'pro-choice' activists are constructed. Legal scholars who advocate the deontological position are frequently referred to as absolutists or proponents of a natural law. Since natural law is supposed to incorporate principles of justice, absolute compliance to the rule of law is the prerequisite for achieving the good society. Legal rules are fundamental because it is believed that they explicate the obligations and duties owed by one individual to another. Because legal rights and responsibilities are not viewed as social constructs, they are generally applicable, independent of the particular circumstances of any individual. Further, since the principles are morally sacrosanct, the onus is placed on the individual to sacrifice self-interest so that the fundamental principles of natural justice may prevail. Such absolutist conceptions of law have an authoritarian character; social compliance is secured by placing limits on individual autonomy.

Public discourse interpreting the abortion controversy interlocks with classical legal reasoning in its beliefs about the role of law. Anti-abortion activists are understood, in theory, to be individuals who accept the principles of natural law, with its implied determinism. They are said to believe that 'moral principles simply should be "obeyed," thereby terminating the process of moral reasoning. Hence, if this sort of moralist tells you always to honor the principle of respect for human life, he or she means that you stop reflection and act in a certain way, in this case accept pregnancy regardless of consequences' (Harrison 1983:255; cf. Falik 1983). Since existing reproductive relations are perceived as being part of a natural order, life itself is predetermined: foetuses will naturally develop into children, and women will naturally provide the support necessary for this development. The abstract principle of 'human life' supersedes any particular context in which life is created, and law is expected to conserve this natural order.

Responsibility for others is also an integral part of deontology, and this orientation to the other is echoed in the social explanations of anti-abortion activists. In describing the prohibitions required by a deontological morality, Duff (1976:74) notes that 'the Absolutist is other-oriented in his approach and [in his actions] considers the context of relationships, responsibilities, rights and duties.' Lake, in describing the 'pro-life' position, echoes this other-orientation: 'It is important to note that these duties are obligations toward others. The duty to keep one's promise is an interpersonal obligation' (1986:481; cf. Williams 1977); those who express anti-abortion sentiments frequently articulate a concern that women who choose abortion are putting their own needs above their concern for others.

In contrast, the legal scholars who draw on the teleological conception of morality (those referred to as 'utilitarians' or 'consequentialists') adopt an approach to the law that is directed towards maximizing human autonomy and free will. From this perspective of human reality, 'so long as individuals exercise self-determination, the dynamics of interpersonal relationships create a society amenable to the interests and perceived needs of individuals' (Falik 1983:43). Under teleology, morality is personal and individualistic, and 'no just concepts of morality or retribution independent of maximizing the utilitarian aggregates' exists (Richards 1981:254). Here, what is important is not an individual's adherence to duty, which upholds the collective good, but the protection of an individual's right to pursue self-interest. Those who advocate a pro-choice position are culturally understood to be motivated by this desire; since human volition is involved, the promotion of self is implied. Thus, pro-choice supporters frequently articulate the belief that women should be entitled to make personal decisions without having to consider the needs and desires of others.

Despite its emphasis on individual autonomy, the teleological tradition is not anarchic. It views law as being necessary to the ordering and prioritization of competing self-interests. With no natural law decreeing an absolute obligation to others, legal experts must balance the various competing self-interests, limiting any individual's activity only when its consequence is harm to the interests of another. Theoretically, then, teleological legal reasoning requires law to intervene only when the choices of one mature human being interfere with the purposes of another. Clearly, such intervention requires a consideration of particular circumstances.

Law is important for both classical traditions, but each posits a different mandate for law. Deontological reasoning stresses the fundamental duties owed within a just society and sees the moral order as a given rather than as something socially constructed. Law upholds this order. Teleological reasoning evaluates particular situations on the basis of whether the action of one party will constitute an intrusion into the right of another to act autonomously. The assumption is that 'normal' interactions between individuals will be consensual because, normally, individuals will choose to interact only with those whose interests complement their own or with whom they have entered into a mutually accepted 'contract.' Since individual responsibility is limited to noninterference with the private choices of others, law is expected to intercede only in circumstances where the interests of two legally equal subjects collide.

Public debate on the moral impasse in the abortion issue draws out the

cal equations common to both deontology and teleology (see figure 1 in chapter 4). As heuristic devices, the models of classical moral and
legal reasoning capture the manner in which the abortion debate is
understood within the political positions of conservativism and liberalism, and a common conclusion of studies contrasting these world views is
that the former is associated with an outmoded style of thought based on
deontological reasoning while the latter incorporates the logic required
by modern societies. For example, Falik (1983) portrays the ideological
difference between pro-choice and anti-abortion activists as a choice
between the traditionalism of deontology and the modernism of teleology. The opposing political positions concerning abortion are thus culturally understood according to the same logic that informs classical legal
reasoning, and each is based on the same antagonisms and the same
equations derived from moral philosophy. Deontological moral positions, natural-law legal principles, and anti-choice political positions form
one pole of the antagonistic stances of Western culture. Teleological
moral positions, utilitarian legal reasoning, and pro-choice political positions coalesce at the other pole.

While the antagonisms between free will and determinism and
between self-interest and response to others are well understood by those
who compare and contrast the different positions of moral and legal theory, the equations between free will and self-interest and between determinism and response to others are frequently taken for granted. The
language of public discourse about abortion illustrates the implicit equations of self-interested autonomy and deterministic responsiveness. On
the absolutist side, 'life' is an abstraction that exists over and above conscious human volition, and maternal duty to this natural fact is implicit.
Being 'pro-life' is culturally understood as absolutely upholding maternal
responsibility to life in the abstract. Circumstances do not alter this
female obligation, and the law is expected to uphold it. Being 'pro-
choice' implies giving primacy to human volition in seeking one's own
purposes according to particular circumstances. As a corollary, a woman
is seen to be acting independently of any particular relationships other
than those she has freely chosen, and self-interest is implicitly understood
to be the motivational factor for women seeking an abortion. To desire
control of the abortion decision is culturally understood to be putting
one's own needs ahead of those of others. From the teleological perspective, responsibilities normally accrue as one chooses one's set of social
relations, and the law may have to intervene to balance competing interests. Thus, within public discourse, a demand for 'no law' by pro-choice

activists can be portrayed as an extreme or anarchic rejectio
ests other than one's own.

The Social Code: Morality by Gender

Analytically, the social code – the underlying concepts and assumptions of popular culture, as distinct from the more abstract codes of legal and moral discourse – incorporates the same oppositional patterns of self-interest and social responsibility, but it involves a greater complexity than the codes of abstract theory do. As a guide to action in everyday life, the social code does not presume gender or class neutrality within context-free relations but is adjusted for situations involving these relations. The self-other opposition remains within the social code, but it is not exactly the same as that in the legal code. Neither is it identical to the opposition that exists in classical moral reasoning. Unlike teleology and deontology, the central concepts of self-actualization and other-response do not refer to opposing moral positions that presumably apply to all; rather, they refer to beliefs about appropriate gender behaviour and about appropriate relations within the public and private spheres of life.

The social code includes a number of assumptions that are presumably gender neutral. For example, beliefs about those who take pro-choice and pro-life positions on abortion are said to reflect a particular moral position rather than a position on appropriate gender behaviour. Nevertheless, all social discourse, including abortion discourse, is permeated by presuppositions about men and women or the value of the work considered appropriate for each. The most pervasive gender stereotypes invoke the self-other opposition that is embedded in classical moral reasoning, and this opposition is further saturated with notions of activity and passivity. We understand men's lives in terms of their independence from the actions and concerns of others. Within this state of independence, males are motivated either by egoistic self-interest or by a heroic concern for another. In either case, the masculine image is permeated with notions of free will and with the potential to 'use' power to force other people to accede to the choices of the actor. By contrast, we culturally understand women's lives to be connected to and dependent on the actions and concerns of others. The social code provides categories for understanding a woman in terms of either natural female passivity or victimization at the hands of hostile others. Commonly, the two images come together as women are perceived to be hapless victims of a socialization process that rolls over them and leaves them in a state of 'learned helplessness.' Whatever the implied cause, motivations disappear and women do not act but are acted upon. Where women are concerned, notions of determinism and powerlessness predominate.

Just as the variants of classical theory equate determinism with responsibility to others, so does the social code. The concept of male social interaction as a group of players freely competing to promote their own self-interest logically leads to the need for external control. If the social game of the public sphere is not to break down, it requires constant vigilance and control of the behaviour of the players, and hence the need for absolute rules of conduct or legal mediation. There is thus a correspondence between legal-code imagery and social-code assumptions about normal male behaviour. This intersection of the legal and social codes concerning the need to regulate self-interested individuality reflects the needs of capitalism in that individual competition is both encouraged and regulated in an orderly manner.

While, for men, this determinism is provided by legal regulation, popular beliefs about female behaviour imply no such need. According to the operative code of social discourse, women will normally act, think, and feel in a responsive manner as a natural part of being women. It is expected that a woman's inclination to form relationships will motivate her to perform acts of self-sacrifice whenever the maintenance of a private relationship requires such a response. At the same time, since the cultural understanding of the basic human nature does not equate altruistic behaviour with human volition, female responses to others are frequently discussed in terms of their irrationality or their lack of logical consistency. It has become almost an academic cliché to say that men are associated with rational thought and social activities, and women with irrationality and nature (Griffin 1983; Merchant 1983; Sydie 1987). Within this cliché – that both male and female nature are determined by biology – an inconsistency between ideological depictions and structural requirements is hidden: although the 'natural' female concern for others is considered irrational, it is male behaviour for which legal regulation is designed.

Traditionally, law has been expected to apply neither to women nor to the private realm, and this omission is culturally justified on the basis of the different natures of men and women. Because it is the male nature that is presumably aggressive, competitive, and self-interested, the development of legal regulation is intended to regulate male interests for the purpose of promoting collective harmony in the public realm. 'Normal' female behaviour, on the other hand, is naturally inclined towards promoting the interests of others and poses little problem for social harmony. Based on entrenched assumptions about female biology, law and criminology have largely been able to ignore women when *formal* methods of social coercion are considered (Naffine 1987).

Although they are ignored by the formal social-control apparatus, feminine characteristics are nevertheless part of the informal policing process that permits legal regulation to be kept to a minimum. Presumably lacking in anarchic spirit, the female psyche is the mechanism by which women are relegated to being the police within the *informal* social-control apparatus. Women are understood to be the essential core of the private realm, and it is here that wives, mothers, and sweethearts are implicitly held responsible for ensuring that male self-interest remains within acceptable limits. Traditionally, legal regulation within private relations has not been thought necessary precisely because women have been expected to shape and control male self-interest in a manner that will ensure a modicum of social responsibility. Only when this 'normal' social-control mechanism breaks down (generally termed 'family breakdown,' implying a failure in the organization of female responsibility) has it traditionally been thought necessary to invoke the legal apparatus as a reinforcement for the natural control mechanism of the private sphere. The degree to which women are perceived to have fallen down in the expectation of keeping male behaviour within appropriate bounds determines the degree to which they themselves are accorded the status of a victim in need of protection. Generations of victims of rape and domestic violence can attest to the fact that women's behaviour is the primary factor in this judgment.

The self-other dichotomy of classical moral and legal reasoning is preserved in the social code but in a manner that is thought to be *determined* by sphere and gender. Whereas the moral paradigms of classical reasoning involve a dispute over the best way to organize a moral society, the social code synthesizes the opposing poles along gender lines and between gendered spheres of activity. In this synthesis, presumably provided by nature, negative teleological principles of individual liberty are understood as primary within the public sphere (where men exercise choice), and positive deontological principles of collective welfare are understood as primary within the private sphere (where women naturally accede to the desires of others).

Traditionally, the social code has assumed another equation: that between masculine characteristics and public-sphere morality and that between feminine characteristics and private-sphere morality. On the one hand, public-level activities are expected to be based on a 'rational' distancing of the actor from the concerns of particular individuals – either to promote one's own interest or to evaluate whose interests should be limited to achieve a just result. Such expectations correspond to and are based on beliefs about the nature of men. On the other hand, private-level activities are expected to be based on emotional connection between individuals, so that particular needs may receive a response. These expectations correspond to and are based on beliefs about the nature of women. Within the social code, then, it is assumed that public life will be organized according to negative principles that objectively limit the autonomy of independent actors whenever necessary, but that private life will be organized according to positive principles of subjectively responding to the needs of interdependent others.

'Common-sense' discourse, unlike legal and moral reasoning, has presumed a different ordering of negative and positive principles, depending on the sphere of activity and the gender of the individual who is acting. The social code reflects the more varied reality of existing social circumstances, and the elements of common parlance reflect more accurately the elements of social life as it is lived at the daily level than the abstractions of legal and moral theory do. Nevertheless, the reality that is understood is a conceptual reality derived from a male standpoint. What is ignored in hegemonic discourse is the process by which the social organization of gender relations sets limits on a woman's ability to secure a response to her particular needs and to exercise autonomy in responding to the needs of others. The dominant abstractions of theory and of daily life do not incorporate an understanding of the ways in which social power is created and appropriated according to the social organization of productive and reproductive labour.

3

The Social Organization of Reproductive Labour

[Power] requires *noticing* – the word I chose when asked to name in one word the quality that most distinguishes women from men in patriarchy. Women *notice*; men can afford not to. (Morgan 1984; emphasis in the original)

Attention is a unique face-to-face resource, allocated and distributed much like economic wealth. Attention can be understood as an interactional currency subject to distributive justice or inequity ... The inequalities of face *are not simply interesting derivatives of economic and social power*, but an integral dimension of their very structure. Stratification systems create distinctions of social worth that are communicated, learned, and enforced in ordinary face-to-face processes. (Derber 1979:41; emphasis added)

A man whose relationships have always been maintained by women will remain unaware of and take for granted the activity and energy which goes into maintaining relationships. (Blum et al. 1976)

Women are threatening to remove certain key props from men. It is particularly hard to endure someone taking props away, but it is even harder if you have pretended all along that you did not need them in the first place. (Miller 1986)

Attention as an Invisible Power Resource

An interesting facet of the social code is the fact that only men are associated with power. There is no female equivalent for the erosion of power and autonomy. For example, 'emasculate' and 'effeminate' are both concepts that refer to the taking away of male power and making a man powerless, like a woman. The basic presumption is that only men inherently have power that can be taken away. Women, on the other hand, have no power to lose and can gain it only by taking it from men. The invisibility of reproductive labour and the distortion of reproductive reality are central to this common understanding about the relation of men and women to power.

Public discourse explains female subordination as being the result of women's dependence on men and of men using their power over women. Men have this thing called power and women lack it. To rectify this situation, social institutions concentrate on methods that will teach women 'self-assertiveness' so that they, too, may learn the skills necessary for accumulating or seizing power. What is missing from this picture of human reality is the work that society has assigned to women and the importance of that work for the creation of power resources. Although women's activities are more likely to include responses to the needs of those with whom they are related, the social code does not conceptually understand the recipients of female responses in terms of dependence. Moreover, women's work is associated only with powerlessness and external control. This conception glosses over the process by which power is created and appropriated, leaving the impression that power is something one can seize or achieve on one's own.

Within discourse, the association of male and female activity with independence and dependence, respectively, is directly related to beliefs about the reproduction of human life and the degree of human choice that reproductive labour entails. By reproductive labour, I mean work that produces human beings and human relationships, a labour that creates human value. Although, as O'Brien (1984:95) notes, 'there can be no human value without human labour,' the reproductive tasks that create human value and enable social interaction are not understood as involving socially structured labour relations. Because women's reproductive labour is understood primarily in biological terms, what is overlooked is the social process by which power is created, reified, appropriated by others, and then used over and against those whose actions have created it.

As popularly understood, reproductive tasks are tasks that mothers perform, presumably because they are women. These activities provide the care and nurture on which all human beings are initially dependent. Human infants need attention and response from others (usually their mothers) if they are to develop and grow, and this requirement goes beyond a detached meeting of physical needs. The emotional bonds created during early infancy are considered to be very important, but it is presumed that infants outgrow this dependence in the natural course of time. The prevalent model of human development assumes that as maturity is achieved, separation and independence from others increasingly supersede the early emotional attachments (cf. Kohlberg 1981). Within this frame of reference, the need for attentive care from another is a short-term biological and psychological requirement of immature beings.

Underlying social-code assumptions about the deontological nature of womankind is an apparently unshakeable belief in the naturalness of the maternal acquiescence to infantile demands for nurturance – a 'maternal instinct.' Seen as part of the normal maternal psyche, this acquiescence is further extended to all interactions involving women; 'caring' becomes an adjective describing women rather than a verb denoting an activity. The work that empowers all human subjectivity is assumed, in the natural order of things, to be a universally available resource unlimited by the vagaries of human choice. Where the supposed naturalness of female care is challenged, the other-orientation associated with women is generally identified as a problem of socialized passivity, an interpretation that views women and their work as part of the power relationship only in a negative or limiting sense. The reform message is that if women resist their socialized inclination to care for others, they will be in a position to compete for power on an equal footing with men.

Yet despite the acceptance of autonomy as the mark of maturity (which is culturally read as a decreasing human need for attention from others), 'mothering' activities in our society extend far beyond women's direct responsibilities for creating and caring for new human life. The responsibility for the care and nurturance of social relationships throughout the life cycle is implicitly assigned to daughters, sisters, and other female intimates. Moreover, the parallel extends beyond private relations to those that structure the paid work that women perform within the public sphere. Even a cursory examination of nurturing work demonstrates that scientific, political, and social development are dependent on the existence of female supportive activity. Arditti (1980:359) notes that the positions women occupy when they work within the academic and scientific sphere 'is suspiciously similar to the position we have in the nuclear family ... A woman in a research laboratory is often expected to perform "mothering" functions that nobody else will take on.' Similarly, Stehelin (1976:77) argues that the top 20 per cent of the scientific establishment who 'make science progress' are 'fed' by those who perform supportive tasks. These tasks enable the valued achievements of a society but are of little social value in themselves.

Although much of the liberation struggle for women has been oriented towards freeing women from their dependence on others, what has less often been noted (and is actually precluded within the hegemonic framework) is the degree to which all human autonomy is predicated on the responses of others to one's particular needs. Having the service of others oriented towards one's particular needs is a necessary resource for individual empowerment. This resource goes beyond the meeting of obvious physical needs. The attention one receives from others is the social basis that allows one to carry out particular intentions. Attention, as a resource, is not just a symbolic indication of status; it requires the giver to expend emotional energy and enables the receiver to take autonomous action.

Despite the supposed superior independence of men and boys, men develop and grow only within relationships, and a continuance of their autonomy is achieved through access to a mode of labour that is generally performed by women. From this vantage point, then, it is not female dependence on male responses that is at the heart of women's subordination; rather, it is women's relative lack of access to and personal control of the very resources which they provide for others. In other words, the 'products' of female labour are alienated, in the Marxian sense of being turned against the worker. Moreover, female 'consent' is integral to the process by which such labour is alienated.

Hegemonic codes are important in securing consent to the alienation of reproductive labour; cultural explanations of the nature of women provide a 'common-sense' justification for inequalities in the attention given to particular or situation-specific needs. Within the prevailing cultural codes, supportive work, when performed by women, is perceived not as real work but as a measure of one's womanhood. When women pay attention to the diverse needs of others in an ideologically satisfactory manner, their activities are virtually invisible as work. Bertelson (1986:60) describes how notions of appropriate femininity (what one is, rather than what one does) ideologically transform the activity of caring for others into something that occurs naturally rather than being consciously chosen:

The art of truly feminine supportiveness is to understand and accept such a male [one who feels that he is free to do as he wishes] and to harmonize one's relating to him so perfectly that he will have no sense of a will contrary to his own ... The basic logic of individualism ... calls not for a man to exercise conscious dominion over even an obedient woman, whose will is understood to be at least in some measure different from his own, but to share a relationship with someone whose will always harmonizes with his own ... A perfect wife sees to it that situations never arise in which her husband feels obliged to constrain her will to meet his own needs and desires.

What Bertelson is describing is not only an activity; it is one that provides a standard by which femininity can be measured. Caring activities are performed satisfactorily to the extent that they appear natural and do not involve conscious direction. Because this ideal is a measure of what a woman 'is,' the greater the visible effort, the more she has failed to demonstrate her worth as a woman. Invisibility is thus built into the activity of women caring for others in a way that it is not for men who do so, even in cases where the emotional work is virtually identical.

The characteristic that links the activity of all women to that of mothers is its emphasis on creating the conditions by which others may pursue their interests. 'Women's work,' whether in the so-called public or private sphere, is of a particular nature; its activities provide the relational networks and concrete supports that underpin the more individualistic and 'heroic' enterprises of the men in the women's lives. What we are looking at is not a public/private distribution of labour between the sexes but a type of interaction that is decidedly gendered whether it is performed at home or in the workplace. Women's work is about power, about the enabling and expanding of human choices through the meeting of human needs. As Miller (1987:5) notes, 'Another way to describe this activity ... is to say that traditionally women have been using their powers to increase the power of others – that is, to increase other people's resources, strengths and effectiveness in many dimensions – emotional, intellectual, etc. At first glance, such a statement may sound altruistic, idealistic or unrealistic. But it is not. It is what most mothers and other women try to do all the time, *although we may not always succeed*' (emphasis added).

It is important to note that women do not always 'succeed' in performing caring tasks and also that, in many instances, they may choose not to respond to externally imposed demands. Equally important for the creation of power is the fact that someone will have to perform the tasks that support 'independent' actions. The underlying cultural expectation is that women will naturally perform these tasks and that 'not succeeding' is never a matter of choice but always a measure of womanhood. Yet such work is not sex-specific. Reproductive labour involves activities that can be performed by men (and often are). In referring to the type of work generally performed by women, then, it is perhaps better to speak of a particular 'mode of activity'; for, as Rose (1983:83) notes, the production of people is ' qualitatively different from the production of things. It requires caring labor – the labor of love.' Nevertheless, despite the acknowledged importance of 'love' within the public culture, caring activities are rarely accorded the status of real work. This is because they usually require some form of emotional commitment, thereby obliging the workers to give something of themselves to those for whom they are caring.

The fact that women are stereotypically associated with emotion and men with reason is not related to any biological or psychological difference between the sexes; it is the result of a misconception about the reality of 'producing people.' As the term is culturally understood in our society, 'labour' involves the conscious directing of physical or intellectual energy towards the meeting of 'rational' objectives. Within the world of capitalist production, individuals are expected to separate and distance their emotional feelings from their physical or intellectual work; love is love, and work is work. If love is perceived as an emotion beyond one's conscious control, it is clearly a hindrance to the rational achievement of cognitive goals and a restriction of autonomy.

One common explanation for female subordination is that women oppress themselves by loving too much and by being too willing to consider the needs and desires of others. This perception of love as a hindrance to self-fulfilment is not simply a myth. Within an egoistic culture, love can erode one's ability to achieve one's goals. In the public world where self-interested individuals compete, it is dangerous to confuse emotion and activity. To feel is to take into consideration the subjectivity of the other and to impede the competition process. Conceptually, then, love and work are separated and are associated with private and public relations, respectively. If an activity involves love, it is not real work; and if it involves work, it is not real love. Because one's activity in the public realm is considered more valuable for the creation of social life, it is less common to suggest that the problem of gender inequality might more accurately be seen as a structured lack of responsiveness by men to women's needs.

Although women participate in the cultural discourse that explains caring activities as emotionally based (and therefore neither objective nor rational), the activities they regularly perform are ones that rarely allow them the luxury of splitting subjective feeling (being) from objective activity (doing). When one examines the nature of caring, it becomes clear that the concept is not simply a feeling (as in love), nor is it simply an activity (as in work). The expenditure of physical, intellectual, and emotional energy is indivisibly part of the practice of caring work (Graham 1983; Rose 1983; Hochschild 1983). As a labour that both ensures life and expresses love, caring is an inclusive activity that marks the boundaries between doing and being, between action and feeling. When one's tasks are oriented towards meeting the needs of others, volitional activity is not in opposition to personal feelings. Choosing to empower others is facilitated by intense emotional commitment. When satisfactorily performed, activities consciously intended to empower others involve empathy – the 'ability to imagine and be sensitive to the interior life of others' (Belenky et al. 1986:143). Such 'attentive love' (Weil 1951), or 'maternal thinking' (Ruddick 1982), involves much more than nonvolitional subjective reaction; it requires a concentrated giving of attention to others in terms of *their* definition of reality. Empowerment of another requires that one retains the right to participate in the definition of needs and priorities of any particular situation. Thus, whereas caring labour necessarily involves emotions regardless of the sex of the worker, the subjectivity involved is not solely that of self-interest. In this sense, the self-other relationship does not correspond to the dichotomy of autonomy (self-interest) and welfare (responsiveness to others) that is articulated in moral, legal, and social codes.

Although we can theoretically analyse the active and the feeling strands involved in most caring activities, in actual practice they are not separable. Graham (1983) illustrates well the problems that result when we attempt to reduce our analysis of female labour either to a psychological one, whereby women's feelings and consciousness are shaped by these caring activities, or to an economic one, which sees the activity as part of an obligatory transaction of goods and services. If we focus strictly on the emotional and subjective factors by which women *choose* to care, we come close to a biological determinism or essentialism that sees the nature of women as inherently different from that of men because of their ability to act while feeling and to feel while acting. If, on the other hand, we focus strictly on caring as a political and economic relationship (structured by a particular kind of society) that simply exploits women, we miss the moral implications of separating love and work and the importance of the symbolic bonds of 'love' for creating a society that would incorporate a reproductive understanding of self and other.

Nonreciprocal Empathy: The Alienation of Power

The structuring of emotional work along asymmetrical lines is an important factor in the access that any individual will have to the resource of attention. When other-responsive acts are transformed into a measure of natural femininity, their performance provides a justification for structuring social relations in a manner that imposes reproductive responsibilities on women while denying them the right to control the context in which these responsibilities will be undertaken. Within our society, women are called on to perform work that sustains and facilitates relationship. That this work appears natural for them, because it is socially required of them, obscures the fact that women work in an unreciprocated fashion at supporting others (Fishman 1978; Chafetz 1988). The lack of any reciprocal obligation to respond to others in their own terms reinforces the status differential, because caring labour is performed by one party and appropriated solely for the benefit of the other. In a nonreciprocal context where attention is given as part of one's natural being rather than as a conscious form of doing, the act of attending to the needs of others becomes part of the process by which one consents to and participates in one's own subordination.

Explanatory frameworks that ignore the interactional context reach the erroneous conclusion that women have not learned the skills required to exercise authority. There is much more involved here, however, than different patterns of socialization. Where emotional work is demanded and expected according to gender, 'neutral' job descriptions take on an added dimension whenever they are undertaken by women. Although both men and women perform emotional work (Hochschild 1983), the discursive asymmetry is so pervasive that similar types of behaviour are given different meanings depending on the gender of the worker. Even where the behaviour of men and women is virtually identical, those with whom they interact give them differential meanings. These, in turn, influence the range of emotions that may be legitimately expressed by any individual.

If, as Derber (1979) argues, 'attention' is a resource that bestows power on the recipient, then to view caring work as a natural part of being a woman means that women's demands for reciprocal attention to their particular needs as they define them can be invalidated or ignored. So long as the process by which female choices are structured remains invisible, women's willingness to consider the needs and concerns of others 'satisfies both patriarchal needs insofar as male authority is acknowledged and individualistic ones in that the relationship is voluntary as well as supportive' (Bertelson 1986:61). In performing this labour, women then 'consent,' in hegemonic fashion, to their own subordination. As Chafetz

(1988:122) notes, 'if women choose to do that which men want them to do, superior male power remains a male potential; it need not actually be used. Ironically, by not having to use their power, male superiority may be reinforced.' The result of this gender asymmetry of asymmetrical patterns of empathy is that males more frequently get to choose when to make the resource of attention available, and they tend to feel no moral responsibility to account for instances when they do not respond to the needs of others. For women, nonresponsiveness to another always requires explanation if one's worth as a woman is not to be called into question.

The Commodification and Privatization of Caring

The nature of caring activity has not been static and unchanging; it has responded to particular historical contexts and social requirements. Early in the capitalist period, attention to the needs of particular others was privatized and became the responsibility of women. During the contemporary phase of capitalism, activity involving personal service to others has increasingly moved from the private sphere into the marketplace. However, although emotional labour is becoming more and more commodified, it cannot easily be mechanized, and it has retained a 'feminine' character (cf. Hochschild 1983). The movement of these tasks into the public realm has not meant that they have been socialized; rather, there has been an intensification of individual responsibility for caring work. As various groups of professionals have introduced 'quality control' into the tasks of mothering, there has been a concomitant decrease in women's control of when and how they undertake nurturing responsibilities. While caring has remained both labour intensive and the specific responsibility of women, control of the activities involved has increasingly been transferred out of their sphere of influence and into the control of professional experts. The combination of this increase in responsibility and decrease in control has resulted in a situation in which the resources required to meet new and conflicting responsibilities are unavailable for more and more women.

Women in the twentieth century are caught in a 'squeeze' between abstract assumptions of expanding choices and a system of social relations that concretely limits available options. This contradiction has arisen from their struggle to claim both the right to be active sexual beings and the right to participate in the economic sphere. The change in public consciousness about women's participation in sexual and economic activity has not resulted in their having increased power to control

their lives; it has led to a privatizing of individual responsibility as a consequence of their assertion of their abstract right of autonomy.

While women have largely won the ideological right to be actors in the
public and sexual spheres, they have lost the traditional expectation that
they will be supported economically in return for performing nurturing
and reproductive tasks. The change in public consciousness that has
allowed for women's sexual 'liberation' has simultaneously allowed men a
greater independence from traditional constraints and from obligations
to support women and children economically (Ehrenreich 1984). Consequently, women are shouldering a double burden. As men escape from
the traditional expectation that they will be the family's sole breadwinner,
women have increasingly become responsible not only for the economic
support of themselves but also for their children – to the extent that
female-headed, absent-male families are becoming a growing feature of
modern society. At the same time, the right to have choice in sexual matters at the ideological level has not affected women's responsibility for
nurturing tasks. In fact, with expectations for fewer children, women are
now responsible for producing ever more perfect children (a development that has been exacerbated by the growth of new technologies).

At the level of day-to-day practice, women do not control access to the
resources that would allow them the male option of separating sexual
activity from parenthood. Only women bear children. Access to effective
safe contraception and abortion services has not substantially increased
their options for 'worry-free' sex. At the same time, women as a group are
facing an erosion of access to the economic resources that would allow
them the option of 'passively' accepting impending parenthood. The
resources required to meet increased reproductive responsibilities (such
as day care, contraception, and abortion services) are becoming less
accessible to the majority of women. While it can legitimately be said that
few women have ever had security of resources, it is equally true that as
women have gained the ideological right to be treated as autonomous
subjects, they have become less able to command support from the
fathers of their children. If anything, where the care and control of children is concerned, male choices are expanding as female responsibilities
are growing (Delorey 1989).

Women's work responsibilities have been further exacerbated by the
direct connection between reproductive tasks and productive tasks. Even
if such measures as 'equal pay for work of equal value' were to be
achieved, the responsibility of women as the sex that is 'naturally' responsible for performing nurturing tasks would continue to constrain their

ability to pursue and retain career opportunities. At the same time, increased responsibility for the economic support of children constrains their ability to meet increased demands for longer and more intense periods of nurturing activity. Taken as a whole, this generally has meant that women are more likely to be individually responsible both for nurturing and for the economic support of their children, while the symbolic expectations have increased with regard both to careers and to motherhood.

Women today are facing a crisis as they struggle to mediate the widening disjuncture between the ideological belief in their equality with men and their inequality in practice. While women are ideologically expected 'to become the men they previously sought to marry,' in practice they have to do so without the benefit of the attentive concern they are expected to provide for others. While, ideologically, men are assumed to achieve their own freedom, in practice it is women who have been given this unachievable task. The disjuncture between the public consciousness of what constitutes autonomy and what autonomy actually entails has given rise to the current reproductive struggles involving women, the state, and the medical profession.

PART TWO
LEGAL CHOICE AND MEDICAL ACCESS

Contemporary struggles over abortion are unique neither to North America nor to the twentieth century. Although women have always tried to control their reproductive powers and have been willing to go to considerable lengths to do so, access to the means of securing abortions has varied according to time and place. The relationship between the moral or legal right to choose when (or if) reproductive responsibilities will be undertaken and the access to needed medical resources is part of a broader history of political struggle over conceptual reality. Within this history, the periods when the material parameters of liberty (choice) and welfare (access to resources) were broadened for men have frequently been those when women had their social power eroded (Kelly 1984). While contemporary academics do not always agree about the degree to which women have historically had access to the means of fertility control, it is instructive to examine the gendered nature of medical relations across time and place. Such an examination reveals a variety of ways of regulating women's access to fertility control, but within this discontinuity there is a consistent pattern involving the intersection of law and medicine. Moreover, there is a relationship between the consistency of discourse and the varied practices across time and place.

The consistency of our cultural discourse on abortion has materialistic roots in the shifting practices of medicine and law and their relationship to one another. The historical struggles between women and a largely male professional class illuminate the contours of sexual hegemony and the process by which it has been reproduced and combated. Law is part of this struggle. However, the implementation of the formal code (whether emanating from religious or legal prohibitions) involves social interpretations that reflect existing power relations. Whereas major historical shifts in social relations (for example, the Enlightenment) have not resulted in similar shifts of power for women as for men, it is also true that legal or moral restrictions have frequently been at variance with the degree of power that women have been able to exercise in their daily lives. The relationship between the legal or moral codes of a period and the actual practices of that period is not a causal one, nor can the variation between code and practice be explained by the concept of historical lag. Symbolic rules forbidding abortion (as codified in religious or secular law) are more accurately viewed as a resource that may or may not be used at any particular time.

Before turning to contemporary legal theory and its relationship to abortion arguments, it will be instructive to look at medical practice before the Enlightenment (the period when classical reasoning was established as the legitimate knowledge base of Western society). My survey of feminist works on reproductive history suggests that despite significant shifts in abortion ideology and abortion practice, the general pattern of medical-legal control that emerged during the beginning of the modern period in Europe was reproduced within colonial North America. When situated within this broader historical context,contemporary abortion practices in Canada and the United States can be seen to follow the general medical-legal pattern of 'choice' and 'access' that is suggested by the reproductive practices of earlier periods.

4

The Medicalization and Professionalization of Reproduction

The story of the rise of the psychomedical experts – the doctors, the psychologists, and sundry related professionals – might be told as an allegory of science versus superstition: on the one side, the clear-headed, masculine spirit of science; on the other side, a dark morass of female superstition, old wives' tales, rumors preserved as fact. (Ehrenreich and English 1978:33)

[An] element of objectification is fundamental to the epistemological stance of masculinist science, a stance which demands distance, unemotionality, and cool observation. Within this framework, the relationship of science to nature is one of objectification, control and domination. In the interests of objective detachment scientists are trained to withdraw from the objects of their consideration, to view them dispassionately, 'if necessary take them apart to see how they're made.' (Beagan 1990:7, citing Bleier 1984 and Wallsgrove 1980:233)

In American medicine ideals of heroic achievement increasingly have overshadowed the value of nurturance and close personal affiliation. Technological advances have repeatedly been gained at the expense of the doctor-patient relationship ... the needs for power and achievement are counterposed to the need for affiliation. This antagonism generates an illusion that is particularly dangerous for the physician – the image that safety lies in success, and invulnerability can be gained through separation. (Gilligan and Pollock 1988:246)

Medieval Medicine: Men Define the Law but Women Control the Practice

The Middle Ages, particularly the early part of the period, was a time when both legal principles and church doctrines did not appear to coincide with the social customs of the day (Stuard 1976). If one were to deduce the position of women simply from the laws and statutes of the period, one would conclude that they lived strictly curtailed lives, unable to exercise the rights enjoyed by their fathers, husbands, and sons. However, a number of scholars have argued that despite the written Christian prohibition on birth control, the knowledge of various ways of preventing conception and aborting pregnancy was largely unrestricted during the medieval period (Noonan 1970; Beard 1976; Donnison 1977; Ehrenreich and English 1978, 1973; Heinsohn and Steiger 1982; Easlea 1980). These scholars conclude that women did not behave as if they accepted the laws of the period. Further, it appears that female 'deviance' was related to the social interpretations that were placed on moral and legal prohibitions.

Noonan (1970) has convincingly argued that European peasant families had fewer children per household during the years from A.D. 800 to 1300 than in the centuries that followed. Feminist interpretations of these demographics focus on the blurred boundaries that existed between the public and private spheres of life as well as on the general understanding that economic well-being was ultimately dependent on reproductive practice. Stuard (1976) notes that despite religious and legal restrictions, the reproductive practices of the day were in tune with the economic realities; the frequent wars and the slow communications inevitably threw a great deal of public responsibility on wives as the representatives of their absent husbands and although women were confined by laws and religious doctrines to the private sphere, this sphere encompassed the greater portion of the lives of ordinary men and women. Beard (1976) supports this argument, stating that the social relations of production and reproduction were intertwined and were largely undifferentiated by gender. As a result, men and women worked together and, for the most part, enjoyed similar liberties of choice.

One of the factors cited for the relatively stable population rate during the medieval period is the degree to which the average woman had access to the available medical knowledge and the degree to which she was able to control the use of contraceptives (Heinsohn and Steiger 1982; Noonan 1970). Midwives, and women of the medieval period in general, determined the use of a host of remedies and procedures that were designed to deal with the uncertainties of both illness and reproduction. A number of modern-day medicines are derived from early midwife knowledge, including ergot for the pain of labour, belladonna for a threatened miscarriage, and digitalis for heart problems.

Although no scholar has suggested that the medical knowledge of the period was highly effective in its degree of accuracy, the power enjoyed by women arose from the fact that the users of contraceptives were the same individuals who were knowledgeable about the risks of any particular remedy, and it was women themselves who controlled the level of their use. Whereas most instances of illness were viewed as matters outside human control, family size was an area in which women were expected to exercise conscious responsibility. According to Noonan (1970:24–5), the term 'medicine' was associated with a 'contraceptive drug,' and more than two hundred contraceptive and abortion methods (both vegetable and mechanical) were in common usage. Thus, health remedies were 'defined essentially through their use in preventing and aborting pregnancy' (Heinsohn and Steiger 1982:199). Regardless of the limited effectiveness and safety of the available remedies and contraceptives, Heinsohn and Steiger argue that a woman's reproductive capacity was less socially controlled than during any later period. According to this interpretation of the evidence, a woman's capacity to control fertility is related more to her ability to obtain the available medical resources than to the sophistication of the resources themselves.

Just as important for medieval women as their access to the medical means of regulating fertility was the nature of the medical relations themselves. In a number of feminist accounts of these pre-professional relations, the art of healing was linked to the everyday tasks and spirit of motherhood. Although healing activities were not exclusively the responsibility of women, providing for health needs was an activity generally associated with reproductive responsibilities rather than with productive ones. As a reproductive task, health care was informed by the activities associated with reproducing the species and with providing care for dependants. All but the most privileged women were expected to be knowledgeable in their practical care of others and to understand the relationship between healing, growth, and nurturance. In short, health care involved a form of reason derived from the requirements of daily life, and the practice of medicine attended to the particular conflicts experienced by the patients being treated.

While our knowledge of women's lives during the Middle Ages is limited, the reproductive prohibitions found within the religious law of the day appear to have been interpreted through reference to the actual reproductive requirements. Any contradiction between religious law and social understanding was mediated by a general societal understanding that moral prohibitions against birth control and abortion were intended to prevent complete childlessness rather than birth control in general

(Noonan 1970). The social meaning of parental responsibility included the view that parents should limit the number of children they brought into the world to the number they could support. One can therefore conclude that the law was a matter of social interpretation; the moral and legal codes were understood according to the general belief about the dependence of productive life on reproductive practices.

The Witch Trials and the Professionalization of Medicine

If the feminist interpretations of medieval reproductive practice are correct, female control of medical knowledge and access to medical resources has been substantially eroded with the passage of time. With this loss of control, knowledge about the realities of human life has shifted from its base within reproductive experience – to such an extent that reproductive experience is now associated with nonreason and superstition. According to a number of feminist historians, the major reason for the change in gender control, and the severing of medicine from reproduction, involved massacre and death on a grand scale (Ehrenreich and English 1978; Heinsohn and Steiger 1982; Donnison 1977). The shift occurred during a period when many women, especially midwives, were hunted down, tried, and exterminated for being witches. 'Many writers have estimated the total number killed to have been in the millions. Women made up some 85 per cent of those executed' (Ehrenreich and English 1978:35; cf. Jong 1981; Donnison 1977).

Some medical historians have argued that the male medical profession sought to eliminate the female healer from the ranks of the profession well before the beginning of the witch-hunts (Ehrenreich and English 1978). In its struggle for legitimation, the emerging professional group managed to turn the repressive religious codes to its advantage and apparently influenced new religious laws. While a religious decree of 1215 stated that all heretics were to be punished by death (Jong 1981), this proscription was expressly directed towards women in a religious treatise of 1486. This tract, *The Hammer of Witches*, decreed that 'the greatest injuries to the Faith as regards the heresy of witches are done by midwives' (36, see Heinsohn and Steiger 1982), and 'it explicitly defined witchcraft as practicing any means of limiting the size of one's family' (ibid.). At the heart of the hunt for 'practitioners of evil' was the religious principle that life is God-given and outside the realm of human volition. The traditional use of medicine to choose when and how life was created and cared for violated this principle and was therefore an act of heresy. According to Jong (1981), the document stressed that women's weak-mindedness made them unfit to have a profession. The women who were particularly in danger of being labelled witches were those who did not nurture men or children (Larner 1984).

The historical record of the witch trials indicates that the religious law of the period was used to transform the locus of medical knowledge. Despite the fact that the formal religious prohibitions were in direct opposition to the informal understandings at the level of practice, the religious rules became the justification for eliminating practices that stood in the way of the professionalization of medicine. The majority of the crimes for which witches were executed involved the use of medical knowledge for contraceptive purposes, for the performance of abortion, and for relieving pain during childbirth (Ehrenreich and English 1978). 'The proportion of women to men slaughtered as witches throughout Europe was about 80 percent, and as high as 95 to 100 percent in England and Russia' (Hale 1989:175, citing Larner 1984).

The wresting of medical practice from medieval midwives accomplished more than a change in the means of dispensing medical potions. The struggle exemplified by the witch-hunts also involved the control of public consciousness about the practices that created both life and relationship. Along with the extermination of witches and midwives, knowledge itself began to be professionalized and brought under hierarchical control (Donnison 1977). The knowledge of medicine came to be used as a kind of currency that could give the knowers a power over those they treated, thus establishing a hierarchical relationship between the treater and the treated. 'Under capitalism, the "art of healing" became the "science of medicine" practiced by men as a commodity to be sold at a high price' (Hale 1989:321). Ehrenreich and English (1978:34) describe the different social relations involved as follows: 'While the female lay healer operated within a network of information-sharing and mutual support, the male professional hoarded up his knowledge as a kind of property, to be dispensed to wealthy patrons or sold on the market as a commodity. His goal was not to spread the skills of healing, but to concentrate them within the elite interest group which the profession came to represent.'

In grappling with the contradictions of reproduction, women of the medieval period appear to have played an active social role, influencing not only their own reproductive power but also the kind of images and explanations reflected within the social code of the period. As Dorothy Smith (1987:19) notes, although most people in our kind of society 'do not participate in the making of culture,' the exclusion of women in the Middle Ages rendered invisible a mode of activity that was necessary for individual growth and social change. The intense intimidation of the witch trials detached the form of knowledge represented by the midwives from the social explanations of human reality. In gaining the power to control social thought, male scientists and medical men established themselves as interpreters of women's experience and eliminated female definitions from an understanding of all human reality. With the professionalization of medical thought, the 'universe of ideas, images, and themes – the symbolic modes that are the general currency of thought – have been either produced by men or controlled by them. In so far as women's work and experience have been entered into it has been on terms decided by men and because it has been approved by men' (ibid.).

It is important to understand that the witch trials and executions were not a struggle between rationality and irrationality (Easlea 1980). As Heinsohn and Steiger (1982) so eloquently point out, the knowledge of the witch midwives of the period was eminently more rational in its concrete effects than that of the professional medical class, and 'it was not until the last third of the 19th ccentury that these doctors achieved a level comparable to that of women in medieval society' (ibid.:194). At the time of the witch trials, doctors were students who rarely saw any patients at all. It was the midwives who had 'developed an extensive understanding of bones and muscles, herbs and drugs, while physicians were still deriving their prognoses from astrology and alchemists were trying to turn lead into gold' (Ehrenreich and English 1978:37–8).

Despite the reasonableness of midwifery techniques, the new discursive 'rationality' that was to become established within the realm of science was one that ascribed superiority to a knower who was separated from and emotionally neutral about that which was to be known. Unlike reproductive medicine, where knowledge was both politically and personally relevant, the type of thinking that arose within the professional establishment contended that knowledge was derived from the exercise of abstract reasoning (Beard 1976). Henceforth, it came to be understood that material reality could be explained, controlled, and changed only through a process of logical abstraction and scientific observation. Within the 'scientific' paradigm, reason came to be seen as the type of thinking that detached subjective experience from objective thought and subordinated lived reality to the cognitive categories that explained it.

While the beginning of the modern period has been hailed as a major advance for man in his quest to control the vagaries of nature, the same period brought women's reproductive capacity under the scrutiny of professionals. It began an intermittent process that gradually transformed the accumulation of medical knowledge from a reproductive task into a process involving male 'scientists.' The public executions ushered in a historical period that has been called the Renaissance of man, but for women it was not so much a period of rebirth as one that saw the systematic destruction of reproductive knowledge. The public executions had a strong moral content in that they clearly established for the general populace the dangers associated with disseminating birth-control information or otherwise controlling fertility. Although the scale and violence of the witch-hunts has not been repeated the overall pattern of the struggle to control medical knowledge and technology has been re-enacted at various times up to and including the present.

Colonial North America: The Struggle Continues

The struggle for control of medicine that began during the late Middle Ages did not result in a final and decisive victory. There is much to suggest that in their private lives, women continued consciously to limit their families as the larger political and economic context required. To the degree that women interpreted legal prohibitions according to reproductive realities, they kept alive a counterhegemonic consciousness, one that perceives a fundamental unity between individual autonomy and social responsibility. During certain historical periods, this consciousness has not only been tolerated but has been exploited for social purposes.

In colonial North America, female networks of mutual help were an important part of the development of both Canada and the United States. Ehrenreich and English (1978) document the role of American women within health care, including reproductive practices. Women who immigrated to that country brought with them healing lore from the old countries and integrated it with the native knowledge of the available herbs. Healing in the settlement period of the New World became once again a female responsibility, and the use of medical knowledge was again attached to personal relationships.

During the period in which British settlements were spreading across North America, extensive information about abortion methods was tolerated, and the use of this information went largely unregulated by the formal legal system, nor was it challenged by the medical establishment. Once again, women were left to their own devices, for 'no consistent policy of professional regulation was pursued during the early nineteenth century' (Kett 1981:191)). Throughout the first half of the nineteenth century, American women commonly resorted to abortion as a means of dealing with the economic and social realities of the New World. Mohr (1978) indicates that, until 1880, English common law established 'quickening' as the time when a women could legally terminate a pregnancy for whatever reason and that, until that date, abortifacient recipes were an accepted part of American culture. The fertility rates of the new settlements were related more to the degree of control that women exerted than to the actual level of reproductive knowledge (ibid.). Even where access to medical knowledge was minimal, women rarely accepted what nature and man handed out. 'Economically and sexually subject to the will of their husbands and lacking any effective or reliable contraception, women turned to abortion in an attempt to gain some control over how many children they would have and when they would have them' (Kaufmann 1984:219).

Although the therapies of the female lay healers of this period lacked a theory of disease causation, they were nevertheless as rational as those of the professional physicians. Whereas early-nineteenth-century doctors held that nature itself was the harbinger of disease, and advocated 'heroic' interventions in the form of such measures as blood letting, blistering, leeching, and laxative purges, the nonscientific knowledge of the women lay healers was geared to prevention and the use of remedies found in nature or in common household products (Ehrenreich and English 1978). But as scientific contraceptive knowledge became more widespread during the twentieth century, women once again lost their relative control over medical practice. The loss was not related to a greater degree of medical expertise; as before, it was part of a wider struggle over knowledge: how it should be used, who should control it, and for whom the benefits would be parcelled out (Kett 1981).

In the United States, anti-abortion rhetoric first emerged within medical literature under the influence of the American Medical Association (AMA). The AMA's campaign against the practice was part of a much larger strategy to secure a monopoly of control on medical technology and knowledge, a strategy that included medical licensing laws that would bar midwives and other 'irregulars' from practising medicine. As Gordon (1976) points out, the success of the medical profession's campaign blocked the average woman's access to the available information and technology of birth control, reinforced her image as a person naturally oriented towards motherhood and nurturance, and brought the 'feminine nature' of care for others under the control and guidance of the medical expert. When doctors gained the right to define the appropriate behaviour for pregnant women, they moved to extend their reach into the nursery and beyond.

The struggle for control of the reproductive process in colonial North America once again had a gender dimension in that the conflict revolved around whether medical knowledge and empirical understanding would be derived from reproductive practices or from scientific observation. Medical opinion sought to demonstrate that female understandings of pregnancy and birth were irrational and that, without regulation, pregnancy and birth would constitute an unwarranted danger to the life and health of mother and child. This 'new' struggle once again involved a clash between the reproductive motives of women and the power-seeking motives of the medical profession, the difference being that, this time, economic profit was central to the machinations of the profession: 'The North American female healer, unlike the European witch-healer, was not eliminated by violence. No Grand Inquisitors pursued her; flames did not destroy her stock of herbs or the knowledge of them. The female healer in North America was defeated in a struggle which was, at bottom, economic ... When the attempt to heal is detached from personal relationships to become a commodity and a source of wealth in itself – then does the business of healing become a male enterprise' (Ehrenreich and English 1978:41).

The available evidence about fertility control in the United States suggests that after the middle of the nineteenth century the public image of abortion began to undergo a transformation (ibid.; cf. Mohr 1978; Gordon 1976; Kaufmann 1984). This transformation involved scientific pronouncements on the point at which new human life exists as a distinct entity, apart from the mother, and on the necessity for medical intervention in order to prevent maternal tampering with the rights of the foetus. 'Citing recent advances in medical science, the American Medical Association declared that quickening had no significance as a stage in fetal development and launched a nationwide crusade against abortion' (Kaufmann 1984:220). The crusade was part of a general shift within social-code explanations of reproduction; human life was abstracted from its dependence on maternal nurturance and gained the status of a new patient with biological characteristics that could be manipulated and understood by medical science.

The American medical profession's quest for knowledge control had its parallels in changing medical relations north of the border. Although as Kett (1981:200) notes, 'we know too little about the development of medicine in nineteenth-century Canada,' the work of McLaren (1981) and of McLaren and McLaren (1986) illustrates the role women played in colonial medicine and their subsequent loss of control to the medical profession. 'Even a casual glance at the medical history of Upper and Lower Canada reveals notable similarities to American patterns. Both Canadas had long confronted quackery, doubtless intensified by pioneer social conditions' (Kett 1981:194). According to McLaren, the Canadian medical establishment's advocacy of abortion legislation had an added dimension: the fear of race suicide. He argues that 'the same fears of race suicide were expressed in Britain and the United States, but in Canada the anxieties of the middle-class English were exacerbated at the beginning of our period [1870] by both the fertility of the Irish and Quebec's successful "revanche des berceaux," and later by the influx of non-British migration' (McLaren 1981:286). Regulation in Canada 'always had a political as well as a purely professional goal. It meant not only safeguards for health but guarantees of stability ... Medical institutions in America seemed out of step with triumphant egalitarianism; in Canada they appeared to be guarantors of triumphant paternalism' (Kett 1981:195). Fears of race suicide and political order came together with the medical profession's desire to confront the expanding group of 'irregulars,' many of whom were involved in gaining a clientele through widespread advertisements for abortifacients (McLaren 1981).

In 1892 the Canadian Criminal Code was enacted, bringing into law restrictions against the use of contraceptives as well as prohibitions against abortion. The new code incorporated the British restriction against abortion,[1] and until the 1969 amendment, not only was it a criminal act consciously to terminate a pregnancy but the dissemination of birth control information also was made illegal. Section 179(c) of the 1892 Criminal Code (replaced with section 207 in 1900) restricted any public discourse on the subject: 'Everyone is guilty of an indictable offense and liable to two years' imprisonment who knowingly, without lawful excuse or justification, offers to sell, advertises, publishes an advertisement of or has for sale or disposal any medicine, drug or article intended or represented as a means of preventing conception or causing abortion.' Some historians have argued that despite this legal prohibition, the dramatic decline of the birth rate in Canada during the late

---

1 Under British law, abortion was not made a statutory crime until 1803, at which time abortions performed after 'quickening' were declared illegal. This law was strengthened in Great Britain in 1837, when the dividing line of 'quickening' was dropped, and again in 1861, when women having abortions began to be considered partners to the crime.

nineteenth century (particularly among English-speaking families), together with stable marriage rates and improving fecundity, can be taken as evidence that both contraception and abortion were in fact being employed. McLaren's (1981) essay 'Birth Control and Abortion in Canada' provides historical evidence that during the period 1870–1920 not only did Canadian couples have a fairly wide variety of contraceptive measures available, but abortion was a measure to which women frequently resorted.

McLaren and McLaren (1986), in examining the personal letters that Canadian women wrote to one another, also discovered that women used both contraceptives and abortifacients in their efforts to control the size and timing of their families. These women shared and used many 'home remedies,' and as they passed along 'recipes' they articulated the known risks, but they rarely distinguished between contraceptive and abortifacients (ibid.:32). In 'putting themselves right,' women – to the frustration of their doctors – continued to disregard legitimate medical opinion and to act as if they knew when antenatal life began:

Women and doctors had different views of antenatal life. Women remained true to the traditional idea that until the mother felt the foetus 'quicken' it was permissible to take whatever measures necessary to make herself 'regular.' Dr. Ballock asserted that 'I am not able to recall one who was ever particularly distressed over such an act, especially if it happened in the early months of pregnancy.' The thought that women rather than doctors should decide on whether life was present was what raised the ire of men such as Hodge. 'What, it may be asked, have the sensations of the mother to do with the vitality of the child? It is not alive because the mother does not feel it?' (Shortt 1981:300). Many women would have answered it is not. (McLaren and McLaren 1986:32)

Despite the restriction on contraceptive information and the life-threatening aspects of the available abortion methods, Canadian women of the period 'were not, as was frequently assumed, passive in relation to their own fertility: they wanted to control it and were willing to go to considerable lengths to do so' (McLaren 1981:293). During the nineteenth century in Canada, there was both a substantial drop in the birth rate and a drop in infant mortality rates, but maternal mortality remained high. McLaren (1981:293) argues that the high death rate for pregnant women was attributable not to the profession's lack of knowledge but to the profession's refusal to make abortion technology available to women.

Although relatively safe procedures for carrying out abortion were available by the 1890s, these operations were generally not employed by the medical profession. At the same time, there was a widespread public tolerance of overt information regarding the more dangerous commercial abortion methods. Newspaper advertisements of the period indicate that abortifacients were available and that their availability created competition between popular practitioners (or 'quacks') and the medical profession. However, this competition did not lead to more accessible and improved medical services; on the contrary, it resulted in professional attempts to have the state control the proliferation of 'popular remedies.' Rather than using the available knowledge to assist women, physicians argued for a greater degree of regulation over quacks and popular practitioners. While Canadian doctors, like their American counterparts, sought to control the practice of medicine by 'irregulars,' they also resisted any suggestion that they themselves should provide the services that women required.

In his examination of nineteenth-century medical tracts, McLaren found that doctors were seeking to instil, within public consciousness, a moral belief in human life from the moment of conception onward. Because this was a relatively new idea, arising from recent biological discoveries, the women of the period found it alien to their reproductive experience. In their lobbying for control over unlicensed practitioners, physicians linked the health of society to women's acceptance of their natural biological role. They took the position that abortion was both medically and morally wrong – a medical danger to the health of individual women and a moral danger to the health of society. Since 'health' was involved, they argued that doctors were the appropriate moral gatekeepers for the preservation of the social fabric. Their arguments included notions of a threat to professional autonomy if women were allowed to request abortion procedures as a medical service. As one medical tract put it, doctors could then easily become 'victimized' by any woman seeking relief 'from the social disgrace attached to her sin, or the selfish and degraded married female from the care and trouble naturally devolving on her' (McLaren 1981:288).

McLaren and McLaren (1986) provide further evidence that medical doctors considered themselves to be at grave risk in the contradiction between legal prohibitions and female practices. To assist a woman intent on abortion 'was of course out of the question, but even to see her, if she had already attempted to induce her own miscarriage, could put the physician in a position where he might be held responsible for the consequences' (McLaren and McLaren 1986:36). If doctors could be held accountable for women acting on their own understanding of birth, the solution was to challenge this understanding as irrational and to ensure legitimacy for professional knowledge and expertise. The professional argument stressed that life began at conception and that any suggestion of women consciously creating life was not only immoral but was unscientific and irrational: '[T]he moral conscience of the public, including that of some physicians, needs educating, and it should be someone's business to make it known that from conception the unborn child is a human creature whose destruction is equivalent to murder' (excerpt from a 1922 issue of the *Canadian Medical Association Journal* as cited in McLaren and McLaren 1986:39).

The medical establishment's acceptance of 'life from the moment of conception' was an important advance in the struggle for reproductive control. Medical expertise would henceforth be required to confirm the existence of new life and to specify its requirements. It is within this context of medical monopoly that contemporary legal reasoning has taken shape. This reasoning provides the ideological justification for contemporary legal rulings in the United States and for changes in the Canadian law.

5

The Contemporary Legal Code

The classical literature of political theory, liberty or freedom always had two reciprocal elements: a negative aspect which could be rendered by the idea of 'absence
of constraint,' and a positive aspect which could be rendered by the notion of
'opportunity to pursue purposes.' (Macdonald 1982:344; cf. Michelman 1973,
1979)

In a significant critique of pure utilitarianism, and, perhaps, unintentionally, of
the existing American social order, Rawls' theory also suggests the need for full
recognition of the equality principle, going so far as to suggest modified redistri-
bution of wealth to the least advantaged in order to rectify inherent inequalities.
(Matsuda 1986:615)

Paternalism ... holds out the power of security for the price of freedom. Utilitarian
individualism ... holds out the promise of freedom at the expense of security.
(Ursel 1992:45)

Classical Principles and Political Reality

Much of the abortion controversy in Canada has taken place within and
around legal sites, and the struggle has been waged by groups that have
very different visions of the place of law in society. According to the logic
of public discourse, the principles of contemporary legal reasoning
appear to favour the pro-choice forces. Since the time of John Stuart Mill
and the rise of the liberal democratic state, any state interference into the
private life of individuals has been considered legitimate only to prevent
harm, and legal theory has concerned itself primarily with negative prin-

ciples. Within all liberal democracies, freedom from externally imposed rules has been the central tenet of the legal code. Operating largely with principles of noninterference, the moral obligation to respond to the needs of others became a symbol of traditionalism that had no place within the modern legal apparatus (Falik 1983). However, positive principles did not disappear with the rise of liberalism; they were diverted to the realm of private relationships, where they were viewed as appropriate guides for relations within the private realm of family and religion. Thus, the moral requirement to provide for the welfare of others became a matter of private choice (or religious charity), and the private realm was theoretically off limits to state intervention and the coercive arm of the law.

According to the liberal model, individual liberty is the freedom to refrain from externally imposed obligations, and social justice is best served when the decision to respond to another's need – and how to respond – is left to the discretion of the potential helper. The liberal presupposition (and that of the teleological tradition on which it is based) is that all mature individuals have equal access to the kind of relations that enable self-fulfilment, and that all that is required of the law is to regulate private interests when they come into competition. Any affirmative distribution of societal resources by the state has been viewed as a political matter, outside the mandate of the legal arena. Just as an individual's response on behalf of another is to be left within the boundaries of private relations, state responses to need are to be left within the boundaries of the political arena.

At the same time, liberal theory has not been uniformly translated into practice within liberal democracies. As I shall demonstrate in chapter 6, its application has varied by country as well as by historical period. Generally, however, whenever a government has been pressured into taking a more affirmative stance in providing for the needs of particular groups, the logic of deontology has entered political discourse. Deontological challenges concerning state obligation result in a visible politicization of the boundaries of legal regulation, which in turn influences the particular pattern of legal logic that justifies new practices or policies.

Even before abortion challenges were raised in the Canadian courts, federal and provincial states were faced with demands from a variety of disadvantaged groups that their respective legislators address the unequal distribution of collective resources. These demands forced accommodations that obliged the state to move beyond its original lack-of-interference stance, and it became increasingly interventionist. As Reasons (1989:13) notes, 'the state has itself become an increasingly important interest group since World War II ... For example, affirmative action programs, legislation on equal pay for work of equal value, and human rights laws and tribunals show the active involvement of the state in these matters of social concern.' With increasing state intervention in areas previously regarded as private matters (either in compelling individual forms of behaviour for the benefit of a group or in providing collective resources to meet individual needs), the courts were called upon to evaluate the boundaries of this broader state interest. As a result, pure teleological principles were no longer adequate for accommodating a balance between individual rights and the developing state interest in affirmative action.

As the state was taking on new welfare functions, contemporary legal theory was itself experiencing a conceptual shift. New forms of legal reasoning purportedly could transcend the opposition of liberty and welfare within the different political positions of classical philosophy. This synthesis of contemporary legal reasoning permitted a rationale for deciding when and how the state should intervene in private lives, but it also allowed the law to claim for itself a greater political neutrality than was possible within a purely teleological framework. In going beyond the balancing of competing interests to include a rationale for state activity aimed at providing social justice and remedying inequality, the 'new' legal code could address and neutralize political criticisms from both the left and the right.

'Transcending' Classical Oppositions in Legal Theory

Contemporary legal philosophy has been greatly influenced by attempts to overcome the oppositions within classical reasoning and to make the legal code less tied to the political positions inherent in these oppositions. Most notably, John Rawls (in *A Theory of Justice*, 1971) has devised an analytic model that purportedly accomplishes this goal. In concerning himself with the need to provide greater equality in the provision of legal justice to disadvantaged groups, he addresses the relation between the individual and society. His basic premise is that moral principles are those standards of conduct that perfectly rational persons – in a hypothetical 'original position' of equal liberty, and acting not as altruists but from self-interest as representatives of themselves and their descendants – would accept as generally applicable. Since he is primarily concerned with developing a theory of justice, he introduces into the 'original position' the existence of conflicting claims to a limited supply of general goods, offering a specific set of principles that would regulate these claims (see Richards 1981:266–7).

In developing his model for legal justice, Rawls unhinges the equations implicit in classical reasoning: he elaborates a method for deriving abstract moral principles (deontology) by which individuals may pursue their own self-interest (teleology). His 'original man' contemplates situations involving 'competing rights' without knowing into which side of the competition he may be born. By abstracting himself from particular relations and then contemplating his needs in a variety of situations, this original man cognitively arrives at principles of justice for all. Since no individual can be certain of what his status will be, he must agree to a social contract that limits liberty rights if he is going to be able to ensure his own self-interest. Since he, himself, may be the person who will benefit from a limitation on autonomy, a just consensus can presumably be achieved by elaborating those situations that interfere with self-determination in the abstract. Law becomes 'natural' in the sense that it elaborates absolute rules (deontology) for providing the greatest amount of independent human volition (teleology). Since autonomy is maximized for all, the objective of social justice also is achieved.

By abstracting the individual from any particular set of social relations in order to arrive at a binding moral principle, Rawls is able to keep the abstract-principle component of the natural-law perspective. By creating the absolute principles necessary for a just society, he establishes an external authority for the practice of individual morality: because social justice is the intent of the legal principle, one is absolved from responsibility for any unintended or unjust consequences of one's responses or nonresponses. The certainty of deontology is achieved because one acts morally through adherence to the principle and not through contemplation of particular circumstances. In salvaging the fundamental-principle strand of deontology, however, Rawls has weakened the social connectedness stressed in that position. As Mensch (1982:19) points out, he 'postulates a hypothetical initial position of "rational" people who are essentially atomized monads with an interest in attaining their own private stock of social goods, but who demonstrated no interest in promoting the welfare of others or in building a society of true participation, equality or shared values.'

Drawing from the teleological tradition, Rawls contemplates situations that might affect self-interest. The proposed method for elaborating principles of social justice gives primary emphasis to abstract self-interest and relegates the particular relations that are required for original indepen-

dence to the realm of the private – where access to the resource of attentive concern may be taken for granted. Without reference to the *particular*
responses required for human contemplation to take place, the individual who represents 'man in general' is not dependent on reproductive
choices; he is already fully formed. In the logic stemming from the 'original position,' there is no consideration of conscious choices being made
in the reproduction of humanity itself. Without another who devotes
activity to the meeting of his needs, the original thinker could not have
come into being, nor could he have progressed to the state where independent contemplation is possible. Rawls takes reproductive activities for
granted as something universally available to human beings. Where life is
natural and nonproblematic, activities oriented towards meeting the
needs of others become part of a natural backdrop for normal human
volition.

By excluding a referent to the particular needs that have to be met
before independent thought and action become possible, Rawls makes
two key assumptions about human nature and human reality: that human
beings are essentially self interested, and that whatever is required to
establish human autonomy is naturally accessible on a universal basis.
One need only ensure that no impediments are placed in a person's path
and that no situation leads to an erosion of the original position. From
this 'normal' starting-point, the exceptional instance – where a supportive environment is lacking – requires the elaboration of general moral
principles. The initial position, that of independence and self-interest,
sets the boundaries for the conclusions that can be made. All that can be
contemplated within this frame are, first, the range of possible impediments (caused either by an abnormal state of nature or by the self-
interested activity of another) that might compromise this original state
of autonomy and, second, the social responses that will be required to
correct for the deviation from the norm.

A Separation of Liberty and Welfare Rights according to Individual Status

Rawls's synthesis theoretically separates the classical equations of determinism with orientation to the other and of volition with self-interest, but
he retains the traditional opposition between self and other. Two levels of
legal rights and two categories of legal subjects emerge. The primary legal
principles of contemporary legal theory remain those that will mediate
the competing liberty rights of autonomous individuals. However, sec-

ondary principles have been added in order to correct for social or natural imbalances. If some event or action has caused some individuals to 'fall' from the original state of autonomy, this 'dependant' can claim legal compensation. It follows logically, from the presumed norm of an independent self-interested human nature, that the legal rights one may claim will, first, ensure that the actions of one party do not encroach on the freedom of another and, second, provide for compensatory supports to victimized individuals whose natural independence has been compromised.

The contemporary legal code incorporates both negative and positive principles in a way that provides a basis for two classes of mutually exclusive legal subjects. The normal legal subject is a self-interestedly autonomous actor, who requires no particular responses except those universally available to all. His or her liberty rights involve noninterference in this private autonomy. Each of these legal subjects is equal before the law, and the right that each enjoys is the right of noninterference. The exceptional legal subject, by contrast, is one whose need for a response marks him or her as a victim. All legal responses on behalf of others are viewed as corrective in the sense of that they intend a return of the individual to the original position. Moreover, in order to gain a response to a particular need, the 'victim' must prove that he or she falls outside the norm. Response depends on the fitting of one's needs into the categories defined by the moral principles that provide for such responses. The legal right to a social response, therefore, denies its recipient the autonomy of the normal legal subject. Within this model, the antagonism between response and autonomy remains, but it has now become the basis for distinguishing between the rights that can be claimed by particular groups of legal subjects.

The importance of Rawls's justice theory for the contemporary legal code relates to the way that the welfare (positive) principles of deontology have been integrated with the liberty (negative) principles of teleology. The theory does not imply that freedom for all individuals will require a response to their particular needs; rather, it sets out a logic for determining who may legally lay a claim to a liberty right (freedom from interference in autonomy) and who can expect a welfare right (a response to need according the definition of the responder). While Rawls has unhooked the classical equations, his interpretive method continues the dualistic terms of classical theory. The terms then set the boundaries for the construction of legal subjects: either our identities are independent of the choices of others, leaving us totally free to make our own

TABLE 1
Internal Assumptions in the Logic of Discursive Codes

	Moral, legal, and social thought		Rawls's synthesis	
	Deontology Natural law 'Pro-life'	Teleology Utilitarianism 'Pro-choice'	Normal legal subjects	Exceptional legal subjects
Human autonomy (absence of fixed rule)	No	Yes	No	No
Maximizing self-interest	No	Yes	Yes	No
Determinism (adherence to general rule)	Yes	No	Yes	Yes
Maximizing human responsiveness	Yes	No	No	Yes

choices, or they are constituted by a relationship that is characterized by weakness and abnormality (see table 1).

The contemporary code elaborates a model for distinguishing between the interests of individual liberty and a state interest in the welfare of particular groups, thus providing a conceptual basis for distinguishing between groups of legal subjects. Liberty rights remain the primary area of concern in normal situations, and freedom from interference is the basic liberal right. In 'exceptional' instances, however, some individuals will be limited by their environment, and justice requires that they receive a response to their needs. In a model that categorically separates autonomy and response, an individual or group with unmet needs loses the right to define the need or the response required. Since the right to autonomy is based on the ability to demonstrate independence from others and to secure 'universal' resources without assistance, one loses this right if one lacks this ability. The interpretive schema from which Rawls begins equates the provision of justice with a compensation for inferiority. Because independence is the essential characteristic of the original position, it logically follows that justice involves compensating those who, by reason of victimization or abnormality, do not have the capacity of normal legal subjects.

Rawls's theory goes beyond the individualism of teleology: those whose independence has been compromised, either by biological abnormality or by harmful social activity, now have a legal right. However, since the receivers of supportive activity are, by definition, not fully autonomous, they cannot claim support for their needs as a matter of individual right. An objective determination of need is required according to the abstract principles of law. Responses promoting the welfare of others are brought within the framework of legal reasoning as a separate state interest, and in the ideological terms of cultural discourse the receipt of welfare is dependent on a qualified 'expert's' validation of the receiver's exceptionality.

Rawls's synthesis of the abstract principles of natural law and the situational principles of utilitarianism cannot be viewed as a politically neutral exercise. The legal code purports to be gender neutral, and in this it differs from popular understandings of male self-interest and female responsiveness. Yet the situations contemplated by Rawls's original thinker are dependent on a taken-for-granted assumption: that the resources required for life itself are naturally forthcoming, providing that no limitations are placed on this apparently human capacity to 'self-actualize.' Because societal institutions are not structured along gender-neutral lines, this thesis provides closure of the understanding of human nature and the relation between self and other. The initial position, of independence and self-interest, sets the boundaries for the conclusions that can be made. When the creation of human life is assumed to be natural, conclusions may be arrived at by contemplating how the actions of others might erode normal autonomy.

Foetal Autonomy: The Rights of Patriarchal Men

The contemporary legal code involves the same gender bias that permeates public discourse within a patriarchal society. In its original assumptions, Rawls's method for discovering principles of social justice relies on particular conceptions of human nature and scientific rationality that exclude female understandings of human reality. As its critics have suggested, the language of law ignores the reality of concrete social needs and the way these needs actually get met. However, there is a deeper structure within this reasoning, and the law's failure to address social requirements is based on a selective myopia rather than on a consistent blindness. On the surface, the labour performed by women is invisible, but underlying the acceptance of this is a deeper intent – the construction of a social order in which women are normally expected to meet the needs of two mythical human beings: autonomous man and rational man. Each of these images is part of our culture's depiction of human nature. Within this paradigm, man is naturally free from the concerns of others (with all the potential for harm that such a freedom brings with it), but he has the capacity to extend this inherent independence from others to an independence from his own interests as well. According to norms of objectivity, he can learn the skills necessary to transcend all feelings in order that he may, from a position of rational detachment, consider the needs of both self and other.

When 'acting naturally,' man (as depicted by Rawls) is both autonomous and self-interested. In his natural state (exemplified by the conditions existing in the 'original position'), he acts independently of the choices, needs, or desires of others, and he freely pursues his own interests with no concern for those of others. In this depiction of human reality, autonomous man uses material resources to further his own interest; and in the absence of interference, his access to these resources is restricted only by his own capabilities. The underlying presumption of this reasoning is that there is an inherent essence of independent maleness in the original position. To maintain this natural state of 'freedom,' however, there must be a mechanism that will ensure the absence of interference by other individuals who are simultaneously pursuing their own interests. Thus, the state is mandated to interfere in the interest of facilitating social interaction and promoting social order. The teleological quest of law remains its primary emphasis – namely, to determine what interference with an individual's inherent independence is legitimate and what is unnecessary or harmful.

If a synthesis between absolute principles of responsibility and situation-specific rights is to be achieved, negative law must make room for positive law, and Rawls suggests a process for accomplishing this. Concerned with more than specifying rules for expanding the autonomy of individuals (a utilitarian objective), he devises a method for specifying general rules for both state responsibility and individual obligation (a natural-law aim). By adding a right to claim welfare as a corrective measure, Rawls allows the state to intervene in the lives of 'exceptional' legal subjects in order to return them to the original position of autonomy. Although, in this conception of social justice, autonomy remains the fundamental right to be protected by law, the state can legitimately suspend this right in order to provide for the needs of dependent or defective individuals.

The manner in which this response to harm is forthcoming will be specified by a standard derived from rational detachment, and this standard will be applicable to all. It is here that we can see the emergence of a second mythical man. The second man in legal discourse is rational man, he who defines truth and justice. He is the legal theorist who has the capacity to transcend his own nature in order to specify the social organization that will best allow for all men to pursue their natural self-interest. From this position of detachment, Rawls's observer is expected to arrive at universal standards for responding to contexts involving need. In doing so, the rational man of law relieves independent man from having to take responsibility for his activities; if there are rules and standards about equality and justice, no individual will actively have to contemplate the desires of others or respond to their needs. By identifying a natural order and specifying the obligations that each member of society owes to another, rational man frees normal individuals from having to consider the effects of activities that are not regulated by law. Moreover, the resources he has – by natural right – are those that others must not interfere with.

In this patriarchal conception of the orginal position, women are already choiceless; the responses they make to empower independent man are those that he can normally expect. The interpretive schema already presumes that law will uphold and protect this expectation. The paradox is that while the code proclaims neutrality (all individuals to be assessed on their normality or exceptionality according to universal standards), the neutrality it proclaims is based on treating women differently so that they will continue to consider the consequences of their choices for natural man. Independent man is to be freed from the responsibility of having to make difficult choices, but the deontological emphasis on responsibility is absolutely transferred to women.

Although Rawls's method for achieving social justice relies on patriarchal assumptions about the nature of women, there is more involved here than the construction of an ideology about natural womanhood. This is more than misguided sexism. At stake in the ideological construction of female identity is the identity of man himself. Constructing the moral nature of women is not really about women. It is about what patriarchal man requires if he is to retain his ideological independence from others. Hegemonic discourse relies on the notion that women (at least, pregnant women) are the mothers of mankind, and that it is mankind's needs that define the responses which the state will legally be required to make.

Within all hegemonic discourse, reproduction is not seen in relation to men, and the omission of perspectives derived from the actual performance of reproductive labour has implications for the feasibility of societal aims and goals. A major goal of independent (natural) man is to reach a state in which he can transcend his connection with nature itself.

Without such independence, how can he achieve the detachment of rational man? Ultimately, then, the logic of patriarchal reasoning concerns the rationale by which males may justify their superiority and by which they can legitimate their knowledge as truth. If his withholding of response affects the very responsiveness on which he depends, how can the male be an observer of nature rather than a participant in its processes? By detaching himself from his dependence on a particular organization of the societal resources, rational man can ideologically convince himself and others that his superior position has been reached by merit and by his capacity to resist the power of others.

Despite the similar interests of independent man and rational man in ensuring that women remain responsive to their needs, there is an ongoing tension in the relation between rational man (science) and independent man (nature). Each of them depends on men's right to take female nature for granted, and the ideological opposition that characterizes the moral principles of deontology and teleology mediates this dependence. An examination of the different patterning of negative and positive principles (liberty and welfare) within North American law reveals that each depends on the opposition of the other to transmit the broader messages about gender that is embedded within their shared mind-set.

6

Legal Choice and Medical Access in North America

The abortion decision in all its aspects is inherently, and primarily, a medical decision, and basic responsibility for it must rest with the physician. (U.S. Supreme Court, *Roe v. Wade* 1973:166, quoted in Petchesky 1984:148)

The abortion struggle was not destroyed by legislative victory. Once abortions were universally legal, women still had to contend with the problems of availability and quality of abortion services. Abortion activists who had lobbied, counseled, or done illegal abortions before the liberalization of abortion laws, now found themselves pitted against a medical system which effectively had the legal sanction to determine all the aspects of delivery of abortion care. (Marieskind and Ehrenreich 1975:38)

The most important fundamental right for the majority of Canadians is not a right to be free from certain kinds of governmental activity, but rather the right to be free to benefit equally from the advantages that organized government fosters. (Macdonald 1982:344)

Liberty or Welfare, Equality or Difference?

It is precisely because the legal code is ideologically supposed to be neutral that liberal theory views law as having the potential for extending equality to women. From this perspective, the extension of liberty rights to women will put them on an equal footing with men. The liberal emphasis on negative law has led many socialist reformers to conclude that diverting energy into struggles over abstract rights allows the state to ignore the concrete needs of women – that is, to direct attention away

s that would provide the resources women need for their
welfare. Because legal struggles over abstract rights appear
to address only the concerns of women whose welfare is already assured,
they have been viewed as inherently elite.

Feminists have been divided on the question of legal reform. Some, in
a parallel of the socialist argument, have contended that the law is a
closed system based on principles of individuality and self-interest that
are central to masculine identity. In a male-oriented culture that eschews
social responsibility for the needs of women and prioritizes individual
rights over collective responsibilities, the struggle to extend legal rights to
women diverts the attention of activists from the political sites where
power is actually exercised. Despite the parallel between feminist and
socialist criticisms, however, feminists (socialist and radical as well as liberal ones) have been more likely to press for an extension of legal rights
to women on the basis that the law's traditional disregard of female liberty has left women vulnerable to the subjective whims of individuals in
institutions that are controlled by men. While legal struggles may not lead
to basic changes in the structure of hierarchical relations, those who are
most affected by a lack of formal rights often have little recourse but to
fight for legal protection, as flawed as this protection might be. Since law
does have an effect on daily reality, women who live with the consequences of law (or of its lack) cannot afford to ignore policies that have
the weight of the law behind them. As numerous feminists have pointed
out, the distinction between the public and private spheres – coupled
with the belief that law has no place in the latter – has more often than
not left individual women isolated in their oppression.

Abortion law is one area in which women have not been able to ignore
the abstract rulings of the court, and it is an area that demonstrates how a
determination of either liberty or welfare status can reproduce the original conditions of their subordination. In comparing abortion practices
across time and place, what is most obvious is that abortion discourse
alternatively shifts from issues of abstract liberty (a legal right to choice)
to issues of concrete welfare (the access to medical resources). Moreover,
within each of the different configurations, the resistance of women to
biological determination has significantly affected the process in which
these shifts have occurred.

United States Law: Abstract Choice in the Absence of Access

Since 1973, women in the United States have had a legal right to choose to terminate their pregnancies, a right based on the privacy of the doctor-patient relationship. At that time, the *Roe v. Wade* decision of the Supreme Court was publicly proclaimed as a victory for women. Although this court ruling ostensibly made abortion a 'private' decision for American women, the medical monopoly on the provision of abortion services (which also was enshrined in the ruling) meant that, in practice, a woman's right to choice was tied to a doctor's right to withhold access to medical services. The rights of women and physicians were both based on negative principles limiting state interference in the private exercise of choice. It soon became apparent that the medical monopoly made a woman's right of choice a hollow victory, especially for those with limited financial resources.

Although the U.S. Supreme Court decision in *Roe v. Wade* has ideologically been portrayed as upholding the right of women to 'abortion on demand,' the ruling itself did not give a pregnant woman the unqualified right to terminate her pregnancy or to choose when and where she would bear children. The wording of the decision certainly held more than a clue that what the court was considering was the right of the medical profession to control reproduction and not the right of women to do so. The Supreme Court ruled: 'The decision vindicates *the right of the physician* to administer medical treatment *according to his professional judgment* up to the points where important state interests provide compelling justifications for intervention. Up to those points, the abortion decision in all its aspects is inherently, and primarily, a medical decision, and basic responsibility for it must rest with the physician' (*Roe v. Wade* 1973:166, quoted in Petchesky 1984:148; emphasis added).

Subsequent rulings have reaffirmed the physicians' right to use or withhold their services without interference. Following *Roe v. Wade*, state legislatures and city governments passed a variety of laws intended to limit access to abortion services. E. Rubin (1987:126) notes that 'in the twenty-four months immediately following the Supreme Court's decision, sixty-two laws directly related to abortion were adopted by thirty-two states.' Certainly these laws affected women, but many of them also restricted the right of doctors to use their services as they deemed necessary. The majority of these laws were subsequently challenged, and the deluge of litigation involved such issues as hospital requirements, clinic regulations, parental consent, viability of the foetus, and government funding for the procedure (Lucas and Miller 1981).

In most instances where restrictions on access were struck down by the courts, a woman's interests coincided with those of her doctor. In *Planned*

Parenthood v. Danforth, the court emphasized that 'the viability determination must be left to the physician's discretion. This holding gives
physicians greater leeway when performing late second-trimester abortions' (Lucas and Miller 1981: 81). In *Doe v. Bolton*, a requirement that
first-trimester abortions be performed in hospitals was struck down
because this restriction was deemed an infringement on 'the woman's
right to receive medical care in accordance with her licensed physician's
best judgment and the physician's right to administer it' (*Doe v. Bolton*
1973:189, quoted in Petchesky 1984:148).

The city government of Akron, Ohio, passed an ordinance containing
a host of requirements surrounding the performance of abortions,
including the 'informed consent' of the pregnant woman, spousal and
parental notification, second-trimester hospital requirements, and
extended record keeping. The Akron ordinance, termed 'the toughest
law yet passed' (E. Rubin 1987), has been the model for similar local legislation in eleven other states. A distinctive feature of this type of legislation
has been the 'informed consent' clause, which forces doctors to give
women specific information, such as the physiological characteristics of
the foetus at different stages of gestation. The first level of the federal
court system rendered a decision that these 'requirements interfered with
a patient's right to consult with a physician free from state interference'
(Lucas and Miller 1981:104). This court decision, consistent with the predominant legal paradigm, identified the issue as one of upholding the
patient's right to interact within a 'private' relationship as she sees fit. In
Connecticut v. Menillo, regulatory provisions affecting the operation of
free-standing clinics also were tested in court. The Menillo decision
'upheld only a state law requiring a physician to perform the abortion.
This holding merely reaffirms the rule in *Roe v. Wade* that the abortion
decision during the first trimester be between a women and her physician' (Lucas and Miller 1981:94). The pattern that emerges is one in
which medical agents are not to be restricted in the practice of their craft
and yet are free to withhold their services. 'In regard to all these issues,
medical criteria and medical authority were the cutting edge of the decision. What the court was really objecting to ... was less the intrusion by the
state on the woman's abortion decision than its intrusion on the physician's autonomy' (Petchesky 1984:165, citing Greenhouse 1982). The liberty rights of 'rational man' were the overriding concern of the courts in
all these rulings.

While restrictive legislation continues to be passed and litigated in the
United States, women have generally been successful in overturning the

restrictions when their interests coincided with those of the medical profession; but where no commonality of interest existed, women have had their access eroded. The most successful state legislation restricting abortion services involves access to government funding for medical services. Although the United States does not have a universal system of medicare, it does have the federal Medicaid system whereby low-income earners can receive medical care which they could not otherwise afford. It is this system that has been closed to women who require medical services for the purpose of terminating a pregnancy.

In 1965 the U.S. Congress enacted the Social Security Act to provide medical coverage to those 'whose income and resources are insufficient to meet the costs of necessary medical services' (Lucas and Miller 1981:108). Under this act (commonly referred to as Medicaid), the federal government contributes funds to the states to implement medical assistance programs to low-income earners. 'Medicaid was the main source of funds for abortions for welfare recipients. By 1977 it accounted for nearly a third of the 1 million or so operations performed annually' (E. Rubin 1987:149). During the late 1970s, a series of state restrictions on Medicaid abortion funding was enacted and subsequently challenged in court.

Several judgments will suffice to illustrate the pattern of legal reasoning concerning the restrictions placed on state funding for low-income women. In *Maher v. Roe*, the court ruled that women had a constitutional right to decide to have an abortion but had no such right to receive state aid in carrying out that decision (Lucas and Miller 1981). In *Harris v. McRae*, the court argued that 'it simply does not follow that a woman's freedom of choice carries with it a constitutional entitlement to the financial resources to avail herself of the full range of protected choices. The reason why was explained in *Maher*: "although government may not place obstacles in the path of a woman's exercise of her freedom of choice, it need not remove those not of its own creation. Indigency falls in the latter category"' (*Harris v. McRae* 1981:316, quoted by Petchesky 1984:161).

The legal limitation placed on the public funding of abortions by state governments has had its counterpart at the federal level. During the late 1970s, Congress passed the Hyde Amendment cutting off Medicaid funds for women seeking an abortion, and the Supreme Court subsequently upheld the constitutionality of this amendment. In 1980 it ruled that the Hyde Amendment does not violate constitutional rights and that the U.S. federal government is free to refuse to fund abortions even where they are deemed to be 'medically necessary.' Since this ruling, 'Medicaid abortions have been virtually eliminated' (Lucas and Miller 1981:107).

The legal tying of female rights of choice to medical autonomy in providing access has meant that the rights won in *Roe v. Wade* have easily been eroded, particularly for women with limited financial resources. In saying that the state has no obligation to provide the means whereby abortion services may be attained, the courts have reproduced patriarchal relations within a market structure. In addition, the courts' denial of Medicaid funding for abortion services denies any state responsibility for providing equal access to this market. These rulings are based on a moral conception of the individual as one whose essential liberty is independent of the responses of others. At the same time, the distribution of power within the doctor-patient relationship is normalized and legitimated.

The right to choose that women 'won' in the 1973 *Roe v. Wade* decision was based on the liberal presumption of laissez-faire and the state's noninterference in personal relationships. However, the liberty in question involved the private rights of doctors, not those of women. In effect, the various rulings upheld the legitimacy of an unrestricted medical monopoly. The relations these rulings preserved can be seen as an extension of traditional patriarchy – asymmetry of husband-wife rights and responsibilities – into a more contemporary patriarchy – asymmetry of doctor-patient rights and responsibilities. In the 'privacy' of their professional relationships, doctors do not have any obligation to respond to the needs of their patients, but women can refuse their reproductive responsibilities only to the extent that they can elicit the necessary medical response, usually with dollars. The accompanying 'feminization of poverty' within the United States meant that more and more women were dependent on the benevolence of their doctors.

American women and physicians come before the law as equally autonomous people, both presumably able to exercise their private liberty rights in the absence of interference from the other. Women were granted the same abstract right as any other legal subject, but they were simultaneously denied the concrete conditions necessary for exercising that right. As Petchesky (1984:151) notes, this contradiction between abstract rights and practical access in the United States 'is structured into the present system of health care funding and delivery.'*Without the financial ability to elicit a response from the health-care system, women retain the ultimate responsibility for reproduction without the means of controlling how they will fulfil it. The result, in practice, has been that American women, unlike American doctors, do not have the right to reject societal responsibilities for the care of others, even potential others.

If American women have been unable to claim their abstract legal right of choice because of a lack of practical access to medical services, the question becomes 'What effect would access to professional medical services have in the absence of an abstract legal right of choice?' Would women in such a situation enjoy the same measure of reproductive freedom that they exhibited during earlier historical periods? Has the greater level of medical expertise been translated into increased freedom *despite* the existence of repressive laws? Or does the professional production of reproductive explanations set boundaries for the freedom that can be achieved? The Canadian model of health-care delivery, coupled with restrictions on choice within Canadian law, provide a means of examining these questions.

Canadian Law: Abstract Access in the Absence of Choice

Whereas the role of the American state has been essentially liberal in orientation, stressing the autonomous liberty of all individuals to secure their own resources, the activity of state actors in Canada has followed a somewhat different course. This is evident in Canadian society's view of the nature of liberty and welfare rights. In a number of areas, a 'shared responsibility' for meeting individual human needs has taken precedence over a lack of interference with the marketplace. One such area involves the organization of Canadian medical relations. The Canadian social code differs from the American one in the manner in which the societal response to health needs is understood.

The Canadian health-care system is unlike that of the United States in that it is based on the principle of universality – the right of all Canadians to enjoy equal access to medical care regardless of their ability to pay. This principle has been an established feature of Canadian life for more than thirty years. The universality enshrined in the Canadian health-care system goes beyond the notion of 'limitation of interference' to include a positive right to medical welfare for *all* citizens. The political organization of health care on a universal basis means that the right to medical care in Canada is not publicly perceived as a welfare right provided to the 'weaker' members of society; rather, it is taken for granted as a fundamental right of all members of our society. In this sense, access to medical resources is generally perceived in liberty terms, and publicly funded access to health care is viewed as a right not to be interfered with.

Despite the rhetoric of universal access, however, Canada's system of medicare remains an attempt to provide collective medical services within the larger negative-rights model of the marketplace. The basic assumption of the noninterference model is that collective needs are best met when each individual is free to pursue his or her individual interest unhampered by others. To offset unequal participation in this market – as a result of insufficient income – the Canadian state guarantees medical dollars. Because the provision of state funding for medicare gives each individual equal access to these medical dollars, each individual supposedly has an equal ability to gain access to the services that meet his or her health needs. Within this negative model, there is no requirement that the services should actually be made available above and beyond what is dictated by the market. In this sense, all medical services are provided on a welfare basis, with doctors defining the needs to which they, as a profession, will respond.

Whereas access to 'basic' medical services in Canada is clothed in liberty-rights discourse, the situation has been very different with regard to access to medical services for the purpose of procuring an abortion. Before 1969, Canadian women were legally prevented from securing a medical response to their reproductive needs; the provision of contraceptive information, birth-control devices, and abortions was a criminal offence. This situation was changed when the 1969 amendment to the Criminal Code established conditions under which women could legally secure a state-funded medical abortion. This legal 'reform' gave women unregulated access to contraceptive information and birth-control technology, but at the same time it placed abortion services within a legal framework that spelled out a general principle by which the need for an abortion could be assessed.

There is a widespread assumption in Canada that the amendment to the Criminal Code increased abortions and made them more readily available to the women who needed them. It appears, however, that the change in law was more a formalization of what was already occurring informally. Following the success of the nineteenth-century attempts to restrict the dissemination of contraceptive and abortifacient information by 'irregulars,' the medical profession had stepped in to fill the void it had created. By the middle of the twentieth century, the provision of both birth-control information and abortion services had become a part of established medical practice. In the decades leading up to 1969, contraceptive information and birth-control devices, though prohibited by law, were available in every drug store on presentation of a doctor's prescription. Meanwhile, doctors were performing abortions on a regular and informally regulated basis. Before the 1969 legislation, a number of hospitals had established abortion committees composed of doctors who met and approved their colleagues' abortion-related activities. As Larry

Collins (1982:2) notes, an 'informal abortion system had evolved within some Canadian hospitals where abortions were performed on a daily basis.' The informal committee system diffused personal responsibility from individual doctors while retaining the profession's right to act as a moral gatekeeper. Cognizant of the fears of earlier practitioners, doctors in the twentieth century also established strict quotas in order to avoid gaining a public reputation for being overly 'permissive' and to prevent 'victimization at the hands of desperate women.'

Anne Collins (1985) has suggested that the first indication of public dissatisfaction with the pre-1969 legal prohibition of all abortions came from the media. As abortion was placed on the public agenda, it became a source of news. Journalists began to report on the abortion situation in other countries, and Canadian women's magazines also picked up the topic. The emergence of abortion as a public issue, however, involved more than media entrepreneurship. It involved the same old antagonists: women and the medical profession. Certainly, the women's movement was not organized on the question at this time. Even so, the split between the public consciousness and the reality of the average woman was already an issue for feminists. Nevertheless, the change in law was a response less to feminist concerns than to the legally vulnerable position of the medical establishment.

As Larry Collins (1982:3) notes, 'fraud was often necessary' in Roman Catholic hospitals, and although no doctor operating within the hospital system had been charged with breaking the law, their informal abortion practices were threatened by the exposure to public scrutiny, an exposure that was certainly influenced by a growing feminist movement. Additionally, both sides of any abortion controversy represented a threat to the basic professional values of the medical establishment – values that involved 'its status as a free, autonomous, self-governing profession' (Blishen 1969:13). If the pro-choice activists were successful in removing abortion from the Criminal Code, the medical monopoly over the provision of services would be eroded as women 'demanded' abortion as a medical right; and if the anti-abortion forces prevailed, the 'privacy' of the doctor-patient relationship would be seriously undermined (Larry Collins 1982). In the first instance, a certain amount of decision-making power would be transferred to the woman involved; in the second, the decision would be taken out of the doctor's hands altogether.

In August 1961 the British Columbia branch of the Canadian Medical Association (CMA) was the first professional body to call publicly for abortion reform, and the abortion debate then became part of the internal politics of the national association. With media attention focused on the ensuing discussions, it became publicly apparent that although the abortion procedure was a common medical service, access to it depended on a particular doctor's or hospital's moral position. As the medical debate found its way into the media, the gap between the law on the books and the daily practices of doctors was increasingly opened to public scrutiny: 'During the eight years that passed between the first CMA motion and the 1969 legislation, eminent members of the profession regularly confessed in public that they were regularly breaking the law, and still no doctor was prosecuted for performing a "therapeutic abortion in a hospital"' (Anne Collins 1985:15–16).

By 1966, the CMA had officially taken a position that abortion should be legal. However, the resolution it put forward was simply a codification of what already existed in practice, a reaffirmation in law of the status quo. The resolution called for abortion procedures to be performed by licensed medical practitioners in hospitals, after approval by hospital committees, when the committees deemed that the continuation of pregnancy would endanger the life or physical health of the mother. In addition, the resolution argued for spousal or guardian consent whenever the committee decided this was necessary. Here again, the resolution simply affirmed what was already happening in practice. As Gavigan (1986b) notes, even without formal consent laws, Canadian doctors generally took into consideration the wishes of the male partner when deciding whether to support a woman's request for an abortion. In essence (although 'consent' is not mentioned in the law), the existing practices were the basis for the 1969 changes to the Criminal Code.

Research into medical practices before and after the 1969 amendment confirms that the legal change cannot be considered the basis for any actual change in abortion policy (Smith and Wineberg 1970; L. Collins 1982; A. Collins 1985). Copied from the 1966 CMA resolution, the new law was designed to formalize the current practices in order to provide legal protection for the profession. The new law, in its legitimation of doctors as moral gatekeepers, simply formalized a process that provided women with unequal access to health care. The informal system had been limited to meeting the needs of middle-class women rather than women generally, and the new law simply institutionalized this discrepancy. Rather than eliminating the class bias, the changes in legislation codified the existing inequalities and did little to expand the parameters of reproductive choice for women generally.

There is ample evidence to suggest that doctors did not simply enforce the new law on abortion, as it was written, but that they actively created it according to their own personal values. Shortly after implementation of the 1969 amendment, Smith and Wineberg (1970:279) conducted a study 'to discern whether there existed any objective standards by which these committees were making their rulings.' Their findings provide convincing evidence that the new law simply institutionalized the subjective decision making that had led to the previous social, geographic, and economic disparities. The procedures involved in the committee system ensured that access was controlled first and foremost by the decisions of individual doctors. Further, since this was a state-mandated process concerning matters of 'health,' doctors were the principal actors in the process. Pregnant women had no legal opportunity either to present their case directly or to appeal it. If a woman's request was turned down by her doctor, her only recourse was to find another doctor, one who might be more responsive to her need and might take the case to the hospital committee for approval. The problem of access to abortion services was exacerbated by hospitals that required the referral to be made by a specialist rather than a general practitioner or when they required more than one letter of referral. These access problems were further compounded by hospital quotas and by the fact that the law allowed no appeal of committee decisions. Although the Smith and Wineberg study as well as later ones (cf. L. Collins 1982) show that hospital committees rarely refused the abortion requests put before them, this was because the referring doctors were aware of the attitudes of particular hospital committees and referred only those 'cases whose acceptance would be consonant with the temper of the committee' (Smith and Wineberg 1970:292).

Women were thus wholly dependent on having access to a doctor who knew the informal rules that would make possible the committee stamp of approval. As one gynaecologist quoted in the Smith and Wineberg study put it, 'Knowing the right people will definitely help get a girl to the committee' (ibid.: 290). But even with women who had access to private physicians, the control of the service was still in the hands of the medical profession and could be withheld as any doctor saw fit. Thus, while the 1969 reform took some abortions out of the 'back rooms' and provided the service as part of the state medical plan, the cost was in terms of increased medicalization of women's reproductive choices. In order to receive a medical response to her particular reproductive needs, a Canadian woman, like her American sister, was dependent on the benevolence of her doctor.

The 1969 abortion law was a clear exception to the principle of universality within the health-care service generally. It permitted abortion services to be claimed only in 'exceptional' circumstances, as determined by the providers of the service. The extension of medical services to women who required an abortion was thus done on the basis of welfare-rights reasoning: in exceptional instances, a woman could claim access to the resources that would return her to the 'original position' of a normal legal subject; that is, a nonpregnant person. Whereas abortion became legal in the United States on the basis of a negative liberty principle, in Canada the 1969 amendment to the Criminal Code simply legalized the exceptional welfare status that abortion already had within the medical system of health delivery.

Conclusion: Legal Choice and Medical Access

Feminist research indicates that, during the Middle Ages, women directly controlled the resources required for limiting their fertility – to the degree that this knowledge was available. Further, the repressive religious and legal codes of the day were mediated by reference to a reproductive code, and these interpretations enabled women to cope with the conflicting responsibilities they faced in their daily lives. In an age when medicine was associated with reproductive tasks, medical activities and medical knowledge were directed towards responding to the needs of others in a manner that served to increase autonomy. So long as societal resources for health care were encompassed within reproduction, medical power was viewed primarily as an enabling force that allowed women to achieve a measure of control in coping with particular realities. The witch trials began a historical process that shifted medical practice away from its locus in reproduction. With this shift, medical knowledge and medical technology became commodities that could be used to assert power over those who were in need of these resources.

The process of medical professionalization was not an even development, and the access women had to abortion resources frequently did not correspond to the repressive moral and legal codes that were prevalent. For example, in colonial North America, women's self-help activities were allowed to flourish, and prohibitions against reproductive control were interpreted in a permissive manner. But as medical specialization increased, the 'law on the books' became a resource that the profession could use in its struggle for reproductive control. At the same time, the use of law as an instrument to control reproductive decisions was buttressed by medical 'knowledge,' which confirmed the exact time when life began.

The medical relations of any society permeate social-cod tions of human life and its reproduction. These interpretati effect on the development of legal codes, which in turn can resource to maintain the status quo. This interaction of medicine and law is demonstrated by the different legal approaches taken by the United States and Canada. As described above, major changes occurred during the 1960s and 1970s in the legal codes of each of these countries. Ideologically, women gained greater reproductive freedom through the legalization of abortion, as a liberty right in the United States and as a welfare right in Canada.

The abortion rulings in the United States were all based on 'the purely negative right to obtain (at a woman's own expense) an abortion free from state interference' (Appleton 1981:757). These rulings demonstrate that the extension of liberty rights on an abstract basis, without consideration of the existing power relations, creates a situation in which the right itself 'can equally be appropriated by more powerful sectors of society' (Brophy and Smart 1981:14). 'Choice' became a right won by physicians and not by women. By contrast, the 1969 Canadian legislation on abortion was passed within a different sociopolitical context concerning health-delivery services. If the law in this country had taken a strictly negative approach to reproductive rights, it would have given Canadian women a much greater capacity to exercise control over their reproductive lives than their American sisters had. However, the Canadian abortion law did not stress the liberty rights of women to privacy or choice as the American law did. Rather, abortion practice in Canada was governed by a more explicitly patriarchal law that stressed the right of a pregnant woman to medical services according to a legal standard interpreted by a committee of doctors. Unlike Canadian health care generally, access to medical abortion services was to be dependent on one's ability to satisfy a doctor that one's circumstances could be 'fitted into' legal categories.

The court judgments that followed *Roe v. Wade* illustrate that freedom from state interference (choice) without a corresponding right to medical services (access) is not much of a right for those without social power. In the absence of socialized medicine, the rights won by American women were illusory for those lacking monetary resources. In Canada, the legitimation of the medical profession as the appropriate judge of a woman's need for 'welfare' achieved a similar end result for low-income women. In the two countries the medical profession was legally granted the power either to restrict choice by regulating access or to restrict access by regulating choice.

In the United States, women won the *symbolic right of choice* without gaining the corresponding right of access to medical services. In Canada, women won a *symbolic right of access* but without the corresponding right to choose. In each instance the realities women face are rendered invisible. The legal rulings from U.S. federal and state courts demonstrate that the negative orientation of liberty rights masks the actual circumstances of women who require abortions, and the Canadian law serves the same ultimate purpose. The separation of liberty and welfare rights, and the overriding protection of the medical profession's autonomy, have provided an ideological framework for controlling women's reproductive activities in practice. The end product has been patriarchal control of reproduction in both countries.

A comparison of reproductive rights across time and between countries illustrates that the form patriarchy takes is historically specific. Over time, the authoritarian but informal and personal control exerted by husband or father has given way to a formal and bureaucratic style of public patriarchy. Patriarchy, as described by Ferguson and Folbre (1981), has moved 'from the classical rule of the father, through husband-patriarchy, to the current form of public patriarchy' (Marshall 1988:221; cf. Ursel 1992). The medical relations involved in the provision of abortion services illustrate Smart's (1981:43) point that quasi-legal agencies may take over and develop certain controlling functions. With the diminution of husband patriarchy, the medical profession has taken on a crucial role in the patriarchal control of women's reproductive power (Mitchinson 1979; Doyal 1985; Findlay 1986). In the United States, this control is more frequently asserted through the marketplace, and the medical monopoly ensures that the market is not 'free.' In Canada, the medical profession legally gained the right to determine the welfare needs of its pregnant patients and to dispense abortion services benevolently or restrictively as it saw fit, a more visible form of public patriarchy. In each instance, however, physicians have gained the right to act as gatekeeper in the definition of the reproductive needs of society.

My research indicates that the medical and legal realities faced by women vary substantially by time and place. However, while cultivating a sensitivity to such particulars is a vital component of the feminist political project, this diversity must not be allowed to mask the gendered nature of ideological hegemony. Although the research I cite for this historical period may be regarded as tentative, the patterns revealed by these medical struggles suggest that feminists need to be wary of any theoretical tendency to downplay the gendered aspect of the relations of domination –

particularly where medicine is concerned. For example, although post-modernists have done much to illustrate the widening influence of science over many spheres of life throughout modernity, what has too frequently been glossed over is the way the rise of scientific knowledge within modernist truth developed in and through struggles about the nature of medicine and its relationship to modern science.

The feminist objective in understanding social reality is, as Gayle Rubin (1975) put it, to account for the oppression of women in its 'endless variety and monotonous similarity.' Embedded within this desire to understand the subordination of women is a clash between providing better theoretical explanations of women's diverse social experiences and the political goal of changing the social structures that silence and subordinate women as a group. Where abortion is concerned, the interaction of law (including its various discourses about liberty and welfare) and medicine (including its various patterning of reproductive choice and access to medical resources) provides a mind-set that transforms the resistance of individual women into discursive 'facts,' which in turn structure the form that resistance will take at the political level. For feminists, to focus only on endless variety is politically and theoretically problematic: it means missing the way that discourse consistently justifies the subordination of women by shifting an issue from one pole of a dichotomy to another.

PART THREE
ALIENATED CONSCIOUSNESS AND THE REPRODUCTION OF
MEDICAL AND LEGAL DISCOURSE

If hegemonic practices are inscribed with a discursive logic that justifies their existence, one can speculate about a counterhegemonic logic. In this section of the book, I describe the code inscribed in reproductive practices and analyse the interaction of law and medicine that permits reproductive labour to be alienated. In speaking of the alienation of reproductive labour, I am referring to the social practices in which women's performance of socially needed tasks re-creates the conditions for their subordination.

The idea that caring for and nurturing the desires and needs of others is a form of labour, regardless of whether it is paid or unpaid work, links the realm of private relationships to the realm of public affairs. Moreover, just as there are specific codes that structure the discourse of various sites such as law and medicine, there is a reproductive code inscribed in tasks that empower others. The activities that reproduce people and relationships are themselves inscribed with linguistic understandings, but these are understandings that incorporate a different kind of logic, a 'different voice' so to speak. Although this reproductive code does not make the same conceptual equations that are made within other discourses, its radical potential can be diluted wherever institutional processes work to translate its terms into those that can be incorporated into the hegemonic mind-set.

Sexual hegemony is not simply something imposed on passive and victimized women; it involves the transformation of female motivations and understandings into language that denotes natural passivity and victimization. It is not just that dominant cultural codes demonstrate a gender bias in the way they misrepresent reproductive reality; these discourses also appropriate and make use of the moral consciousness that is itself created and shaped by providing the resources that empower others. When reproductive labour is appropriated rather than performed within a relationship of mutuality, alternative versions of reality are absorbed and their radical potential is neutralized. This neutralization is most effective when female resistance to ideological control remains at the level of individual practice, and it is this process of neutralization that can be seen in the work of Canada's therapeutic abortion committees (TACs).

So long as the Canadian abortion law was administered within the discretionary spaces assigned to the medical sphere in which the TACs performed their work, any decision made by any doctor was a reaffirmation of the gendered relationships that underpin the rationality of the legal paradigm and the neutrality of the scientific one. When access to the process was legally challenged, however, the issue became politicized in that the regulation of these relationships was brought out of the private spaces where it had been administered and was moved into the public court-room, where it was debated by legal adversaries. The legal 'text' of the Morgentaler hearings illustrates an attempt to mediate thecontradiction of legal discourse and medical practice through its juxtaposition of adversarial arguments over the allocation of liberty and welfare rights. Although the legal adversaries disagreed about the impact the law had on these rights, their differences remained within pre-established categories for determining which legal subject was entitled to which rights.

The theoretical problem for legal reasoning is that gender equality cannot coexist with the basic precept of the legal code – that life itself exists a priori, independent of human agency. Historically, this theoretical problem has been mediated by controlling women through an inter-section of legal regulation and medical practice. I argued in chapter 5 that the contemporary legal code is not so much an innovation in legal theory as a sophisticated attempt to save the core aspects of 'male-stream' thought and to legitimate the different forms of medical control of repro-duction that are characteristic of contemporary patriarchy. The flexibility of contemporary law allows it to intersect with culturally specific forms of medical practice, an intersection that will ensure that women's reproduc-tive lives reflect an ideological polarization of liberty and welfare; cross-culturally they have been able to claim either the abstract right to deter-mine their own reproductive responses (choice) or the abstract right to have a response to their reproductive needs (access).

The particular form that the legal polarization of autonomy and response has taken has not been random; it is related to particular forms of medical relations. As we have seen, the law in the United States granted women liberty rights as normal legal subjects, a logic that pre-sumes the essential equality before the law of all competing claims. Judg-ments of the U.S. Supreme Court have allowed women the normal legal right to enjoy the privacy of decision making until such time as these deci-sions come into conflict with others. Roe v. Wade recognized the right of private autonomy in the abortion decision, and the later rulings that undermined this decision were all based on 'the purely negative right to obtain (at a woman's own expense) an abortion free from state interfer-ence' (Appleton 1981:757). Under American law, then, the state resolved its theoretical problem by relinquishing control to the medical market-place, where women could not be assured of the medical responses they needed to exercise their abstract liberty rights. Without access to the required medical response, the legal right to make private abortion choices was more illusion than reality, and the right to choice became a hollow victory for those women who were unable to gain access to health services controlled by a medical monopoly.

The Canadian abortion law operated within a different sociopolitical context. Canada is culturally assumed to be a more 'caring' society than her American neighbour. The level of guaranteed social assistance in terms of unemployment insurance, old age pensions, minimum wage levels, and state-funded medical assistance are all assumed to be an indication that the Canadian culture is more collectively oriented than that of the United States and that 'Canadians have accepted an active role for the state in the promotion of economic and social objectives' (Jackman 1989:261). This welfare orientation has led to a structuring of medical relations that has not allowed the same kind of marketplace control of reproduction as that which is possible in the United States. To combine the socialization of medical resources with a guarantee of liberty rights in matters of reproduction would have given Canadian women a much greater capacity to exercise control over their reproductive lives than their American sisters have. However, the Canadian law was not concerned with liberty rights of privacy; rather, it stressed the right of a pregnant woman to be provided with medical services according to a legal standard interpreted by a committee of doctors. Thus, the theoretical problem was resolved by reversing the logic of liberty and welfare rights according to social-code understandings about the nature of women and the nature of reproduction. In 'normal' situations, women would be compelled to perform the reproductive tasks that create the conditions of foetal autonomy; and in 'exceptional' situations, they could claim a welfare right that would allow them to refrain from doing so. While American women were to be treated like autonomous men (without their taken-for-granted resources), the Canadian law recognized reproductive difference (as this difference was understood within dominant cultural codes) and accorded pregnant women the status of exceptional legal subjects.

Within reproduction, it is women who provide the resources that foetal life requires. If courts were to assign rights within reproductive relationships according to contemporary legal principles, any rights assigned to foetuses would be the welfare rights that the law makes available to 'exceptional' subjects, and those who provide the resources to these dependent subjects would automatically retain the inherent liberty right to withhold a response (Farrell Smith 1984). The conceptual problem for law is that foetuses require something more than noninterference if they are to achieve the independence of normal legal subjects. Abortion practices are ideologically problematic because, rather than noninterference, it is the withholding of a maternal response that jeopardizes the ordering of relationships assumed for the original position, an ordering that implies the normality of human independence and of reproductive determinism. Thus, any 'normal' apportioning of liberty and welfare rights within reproductive relationships would undermine the conceptual underpinnings of the legal code.

Although the law cannot treat pregnant women as normal legal subjects, the conceptual problem has traditionally been avoided by the systematic structuring of social practices that separate the liberty rights of women from the resources required to exercise them. But if women achieve both the option to withhold their reproductive responses and the means of doing so, the conceptual underpinnings of hegemony will be threatened. In an era in which private patriarchy is being eroded, the contemporary state has avoided this challenge by providing the medical profession with a monopoly in return for its participation in ideological renewal.

Public patriarchy is not monolithic, however. It contains its own contradictions (Marshall 1988; Smart 1986; Gavigan 1988). The imposition of patriarchal medico-legal structures did not mean that women passively accepted the structural dichotomization of choice and access. In fact, the effect of the laws, coupled with anincreased privatization of reproductive responsibilities, provided the impetus both for individual resistance and for new political struggle. While the 1969 reform strengthened medical control in Canada, it also sowed the seeds for further resistance, though the extent of resistance by Canadian women remained largely hidden from public view and outside the public frame of reference. At the personal level, resistance was mostly contained within the boundaries of therapeutic abortion committees. Confined to this site, attempts by individual women to control their reproductive capacity served to reproduce the gendered categories of hegemonic discourse.

The extent of female resistance to reproductive control in Canada was masked by an institutionalized medical process, but when the abortion issue moved into the courts, the resistance became a matter of public debate. The struggle that ensued involved the women's movement, the medical profession,[1] and the state. In their attempts to buttress the exist-

---

1 The medical profession's voice in this struggle was not a homogeneous one but the various positions taken by doctors were themselves tied in with the broader issue of health-care funding, a topic that I explore in more detail in part 4.

ing medical practices, state-employed legal actors who had to defend the law were forced into arguments that reveal the patriarchal underpinnings of legal reasoning in general. In the latter half of this book, I compare the similarities and differences of women's resistance at the political level with those at the personal level, but in order to demonstrate the process by which a mode of thinking can be alienated, I first need to describe the contours of what I have labelled a reproductive code and then to illustrate how medical and legal workers, each in their own way and at their own site, constructed women and their foetuses as particular kinds of medical patients and judicial subjects. The intersection of legal and medical practices demonstrates its potential for strengthening the conceptual categories of hegemonic discourse and fortifying public support for policies that promote and extend patriarchy. On the other hand, this pessimistic outcome is inevitable only if we ignore the integrity of relationships and discourse and fail to understand the contradictions that this integrity generates. As Maureen Cain (1994) argues, some political challenges have to be waged in legal arenas, because when we attempt 'to change relationships without changing the discourse, then the changes are vulnerable to attack as unprofessional or to co-optation.'[2] The difficulty is to identify those legal challenges that have the potential for expanding the boundaries of discourse.

2 I highly recommend the edited collection of articles in *Lawyers in a Postmodern World* (1994), edited by Maureen Cain and Christine B. Harrington. Maureen Cain's description of lawyers as 'conceptual ideologists' and Harrington's description of lawyers' ideologies as constitutive of relationships and institutions are relevant to my conclusion that while discourses and forums are integrally related, the intersection of law and medicine does not allow us to avoid what Fineman (229) termed 'the complex and difficult (perhaps impossible goal of introducing feminist theory into legal discourses).' The political activity I describe in part 4 of this book demonstrates that legal reform can be as politically relevant as any other challenge to inequality. Although the legal challenge of the Canadian pro-choice movement did not succeed in avoiding the conversion of its legal claims into the pre-established categories of the legal code, the courtroom discourse at the Supreme Court illustrates what the editors of this fascinating volume have suggested: 'that legal practice itself has to be transformed in order to be an effective prefigurative enterprise' (8).

7

Reproductive Consciousness and a Reproductive Code

For men, moral problems arise from *competing rights*, moral development requires the increased capacity for fairness, and the resolution of moral problems requires absolute judgments arrived at through the formal, abstract thinking necessary for taking the role of the generalized other ... In contrast, for women, moral problems arise from *conflicting responsibilities* to particular dependent others, moral development requires the increased capacity for understanding and care, and the resolution of moral problems requires awareness of the possible limitations on any particular problem resolution *arrived at through the contextual and inductive thinking* characteristic of taking the role of the particular others. (Harding 1984:55, citing Gilligan; emphasis added)

In contrast to obligations that generally specify what acts or conduct are morally required, permitted, or forbidden, responsibilities (in the prospective sense of 'responsibility for') specify the ends to be achieved rather than the conduct required. Thus, responsibilities require an exercise of discretion on the part of their bearers ... What I call 'the responsibilities view' of ethics takes the moral responsibilities arising out of a relationship as the fundamental moral notion ... Such relationships are not contractual ... In general, *relationships between people place moral responsibilities on both parties, and these responsibilities change over time with changes in the parties and their relationship* ... Each party in a relationship is responsible for ensuring some aspect of the other's welfare or, at least, for achieving some ends that contribute to the other's welfare or achievement. (Whitbeck 1984:79-80; emphasis added)

To treat others as you would be treated demands distance and objectivity. It requires disengaging oneself from a situation to ensure that each person is treated equally. In contrast, to work out the least painful alternative for all those involved means to see the situation in its context, to work with an existential reality and ensure that all persons are understood *in their own terms*. These two ways of perceiving others and being in relation to them are thus central both to a way of describing the self and to thinking in moral choice. (Lyons 1983:133; emphasis added)

Moral Consciousness: Where Concepts Meet Reality

If those who perform reproductive labour experience social reality differently from those who do not, then one can say that our consciousness of human reality has been constructed from the standpoint of male experience. In O'Brien's (1981) terms, our culture is based on 'male-stream thought.' This phrase is part of a broader feminist critique that suggests that the codes with which we structure our conceptual reality are based on a language that women understand but that is not their working language (French 1985; Harding 1984; Schaef 1981; Smith 1987, 1979; Miller 1976). At the day-to-day working level, the meanings assigned to particular activities may be expressed in the same words but are nonetheless at variance with the abstract concepts articulated at the level of social discourse.

It has often been noted within social science literature that there is a world of difference between what one says and what one does. Although reality is experienced differently from the way it is interpreted within the totalizing voice of dominant culture, this is not a simple distinction between words and actions. Rather, there are actually two levels of consciousness or two levels of culture, a public one where values are articulated for public consumption and a private one where actual activities require a different kind of explanation (Gusfield 1981a; Ericson 1985). At each level, our understanding of concepts and the reality they describe come to involve divergent meanings.

Lacking a reproductive referent, the discourses of the dominant culture all presume an antagonism between one's self-interest and one's responsibility for others. To the extent that women participate in public discourse, they come to understand the dominant cultural discourses that pose self and other in oppositional terms. At the level of reproductive practice, however, an experiential consciousness persists. At this frequently unarticulated private level, women appear to understand that the autonomy and 'independence' which children acquire, and which men aspire to, is not something that evolves on its own but is directly dependent on their own attentive responses. However, because the subjectivity of a woman who chooses to respond (or not) to the concerns of others has been eliminated from hegemonic discourse, the concepts of dominant codes do not allow her to express her reality in her own terms.

'Speaking' from a standpoint inside the 'reproductive sphere' of daily life, where reproducing people is the main order of business, women conceptualize and explain their own experiences of caring for others in different terms from those of public discourse. Because the characteristic that defines a woman's identity is her capacity to empower and nurture others, responsiveness is not an activity she will reserve for those less powerful than herself. Nor is it an activity that excludes the perspective of the individual to whom she is responding. At the level where women perform nurturing tasks, responsibility and autonomy coexist as part of a larger interactional whole; responsiveness to the welfare of others means a continual modification of one's intent in order 'to accommodate the experience and feelings of those one's action affects' (Pepinsky 1987:7). This private-level consciousness of reproductive workers can best be understood with reference to a reproductive code, a code that expresses a different relationship between concepts rather than the use of different words.

The 'Different Voice': Conflicting Responsibilities and Particular Circumstances

A generation of psychologists has consistently found that women have an 'inferior' capacity to distinguish boundaries between themselves and others. Although most male-stream thinkers of the past accepted gender differences in reasoning as part of a natural difference between the sexes, more contemporary explanations have focused on the process by which girls are 'inadequately socialized' to participate in cognitive activities and to express their own subjectivity and interests. Within all manner of discourse, women are exhorted to become less concerned with the opinions and interests of others and more concerned with fulfilling their own needs. The failure to distinguish and separate one's own needs from those of others is perceived to be, and is labelled, a source of oppression for individual women. The tendency to ensure that others have the resources they require even when such provision works against one's own interests is a characteristic that contemporary professionals often go to great lengths to correct in women. This focus on changing women into more assertive beings is part of the larger cultural emphasis on 'self-development,' an emphasis that shifts attention from the kinds of relations that create the conditions for this development to take place.

While conventional understandings of gender difference in moral reasoning have stressed female inferiority and have advocated measures to help women reach a male norm, the work of Carol Gilligan (1982) has inspired an alternative frame of reference within feminist circles. When Gilligan found that her female subjects had difficulty in applying abstract principles to concrete problems of relationship, she did not ascribe these difficulties to an immature or undeveloped moral sense. Instead, she argued that when women consider questions of social justice or resolve moral dilemmas, they 'speak' in a 'different voice.' Specifically, she argued that the moral reasoning of women is more likely to be based on an ethic of care, concerned with the conflicting responsibilities one has for the welfare of others, while male reasoning is more likely to be based on a justice ethic, concerned with finding a fair balance between competing rights.

The most significant aspect of Gilligan's description of women's 'different voice' is her re-evaluation of the norms and behaviours that are traditionally viewed as essentially feminine. It is the capacity for nurturance and care that dictates the moral terms in which women construct their social relations with others; that is, 'women view the morality of actions against a standard of responsibility to others, rather than against a standard of rights and autonomy from others' (West 1988:18). Unlike the abstract and deterministic slant of classical understandings of collective obligation, however, the female sense of moral responsibility 'requires awareness of the possible limitations on any particular problem resolution arrived at through the contextual and inductive thinking characteristic of taking the role of the particular others' (Harding 1984:55).

In challenging traditional understandings about moral reasoning, Gilligan's description of gendered frameworks of thought has captivated feminist legal scholars. Much has been written in critique, support, and revision of Gilligan's initial theorizing. Some critics have suggested that the female voice Gilligan is describing is a voice that expresses traditional feminine virtues. MacKinnon (1987), in particular, has argued that the state of connection that purportedly illustrates the subjective experience of women is simply part of a false consciousness resulting from male domination. She views any discourse that equates values of care and responsiveness with female thinking as a technique for legitimating patriarchal practices that victimize women.

This reading of Gilligan's work suggests that the 'different voice' of her female subjects is simply a reaffirmation of the patriarchal social code in which men and women are linked with teleological and deontological visions of reality. The problem with this critique is that it remains firmly within a conceptual paradigm that opposes autonomy and responsibility, a paradigm that rests on male versions of what women do and why they do it. If, however, women's own analysis of what they are doing and what they value is taken as a frame of reference, it becomes clear that the basic difference between Gilligan's different voices is not that one stresses individual autonomy while the other stresses social responsibility; nor is this difference in conceptualization based on the free will – determinism dichotomy found between teleology and deontology; nor is it based on characteristics associated with active masculinity and passive femininity, as the social code implies. The difference between gender modes of thought lies in their differing perceptions of *the relationship* between the concepts of autonomy and responsibility.

One essential difference between the gender-differentiated paradigms that Gilligan describes is in the relationship between negative and positive principles and the relevance this difference has for the conceptualization of both power and intimacy. The rights framework (theoretically associated with men) grounds human morality in a set of general rules designed to limit negative interaction between individuals. Power is conceptualized negatively as 'power over' and as being external to the interaction. As a coercive resource, it regulates harmful activity by limiting the autonomy of the one whose actions are problematic. Within the rights paradigm, individuals have the general right to choose their own path in life and not to have their lives interfered with by others unless they themselves are interfering with another's self-interest. In short, the male paradigm posits that moral principles exist to provide a guide for regulating the expression of self-interest within social interactions. As such, it is a more or less direct reflection of dominant cultural codes.

In contradistinction, the responsibility framework (theoretically associated with women) grounds human morality in internal values intended to promote positive interaction between individuals. Power, in its positive sense of 'power to,' involves response, is internal to a particular relationship, and meets needs by expanding the autonomy of the one who needs. Following from this, individuals have particular responsibilities to consider the effect of their responses, or lack thereof, on the lives of others. In short, the responsibility paradigm posits moral principles as a guide for performing responsive activity. These principles are intended to increase the capacity of social actors to be able to respond to the needs of one another. Thus, the consciousness thatarises in a reproductive context is based on a reality where any maximization of autonomy requires a reciprocity of care.

Whereas classical morality, classical legal reasoning, and the social code all rely on a perceived antagonism between autonomy and responsibility, the 'conflicting responsibilities' paradigm does not. Dominant codes all approach the provision of social justice through some form of external coercion: laws prevent individuals from harming one another by enforcing deterministic principles that limit autonomy. Power is always negative in the sense that even where one is expected to respond to another's need, the process involves the imposition of an external control that limits autonomy. By contrast, the 'conflicting responsibilities' paradigm approaches social justice as a means of empowering others by responding to needs as the recipient defines them. The paradigm elaborates, in moral form, the conditions necessary for performing reproductive work.

Obligations or Responsibilities

Because what is being conveyed in the alternative discourse of the reproductive code is a different relationship between self and other, 'words like "obligation" or "responsibility" cannot be taken at face value' (Lyons 1983:137). Just as an examination of the activities undertaken in fulfilling 'caring' tasks illustrates the fallacy of opposing activity to feeling, an examination of the understandings of reproductive workers reveals that the reproductive code conceptualizes responsibility as something other than an obligation to limit one's own desires and interests. Within the logic of the reproductive code, there is no automatic link between responsibility and a deterministic limiting of human autonomy. In describing sex-differentiated ways of using language, Schaef (1981) defines the different meanings placed on the concept of responsibility by her male and female subjects. Within the different paradigms, which she calls the 'White Male System' and the 'Female System,' the concept of responsibility is seen as either (1) negative and/or limiting of human well-being or (2) positive and/or enhancing of human well-being:

In the White Male System, responsibility involves accountability and blame. The responsible person is the one who is blamed if something goes wrong. The dictionary describes responsibility thus: 'the state of being answerable or accountable as for an obligation.' From this perspective, the 'responsible' person is one who is

TABLE 2
Internal Assumptions in the Logic of Discursive Codes (including Reproductive Code)

	Moral, legal, and social thought		Rawls's synthesis		
	Deontology Natural law 'Pro-life'	Teleology Utilitarianism 'Pro-choice'	Normal legal subjects	Exceptional legal subjects	Reproductive code
Human autonomy (absence of fixed rule)	No	Yes	No	No	Yes
Maximizing self-interest	No	Yes	Yes	No	No
Determinism (adherence to general rule)	Yes	No	Yes	Yes	No
Maximizing human responsiveness	Yes	No	No	Yes	Yes

'accountable, morally or legally for the carrying out of a duty, trust or obligation.'
In the Female System, however, responsibility means the ability to respond.
A responsible person is one who *does something* when it needs to be done, and
blaming never enters in. (Schaef 1981:135, emphasis added)

The 'female' mode of thought described by Gilligan and Schaef is based
on an organic conception of society where dependence is not a sign of
victimization and where each individual is dependent on the attention of
others. But contrary to the deterministic slant ordinarily associated with
organicism (and embodied in absolutist conceptions of morality), in the
reproductive code, interdependence absolutely requires an exercise of
free will. If one is to be able to respond to the needs of another, one must
remain a part of the decision-making process, applying principles of care
according to the particular circumstances in which one finds oneself.

Whitbeck's contrasting of the passive and active characteristics of obligation and responsibility is also useful for understanding the difference
between male articulations of female responsiveness and women's own
understandings of what they do and why they do it. Whitbeck argues that
women, as workers who empower others, develop an ethic that focuses on
the desired aims of one's responses within the actual relationship rather
than focusing on the requirment of a particular form of conduct. Within
this frame of reference, relationships cannot be contractual; they require
an exercise of reciprocal discretion. It is the particular form of relationship that places 'moral responsibilities on both parties, and these
responsibilities change over time with changes in the parties and their
relationship ... Each party in a relationship is responsible for ensuring
some aspect of the other's welfare or, at least, for achieving some ends
that contribute to the other's welfare or achievement' (Whitbeck 1984:
79–80).

Responsiveness rather than obligation is the motivational aspect of the
reproductive code, and essential to its achievement is reciprocity. Without reciprocity – care provided by one to another according to particular
circumstances – the ability to perform reproductive tasks adequately
breaks down. The practice of empathy that characterizes the reproductive code is unlike the ideas of pity and welfare of dominant discourses in
that it does not relegate the person seeking a response to a status of weakness based on needs that differ from those of the responder. Unlike sym-
pathy for an inferior other who differs from oneself, empathy requires
that one consider differing needs and desires from the perspective of the
other. In addition to the emphasis placed on positive principles of

empowerment, there is, therefore, a second major difference in the reproductive code: the degree of attention given to the way particular individuals experience concrete circumstances. This difference is also integral to the different conceptions of power within the contrasting paradigms. The power created by empathy is a 'power to,' not a 'power over.'

The 'competing rights' perspective, on which the legal code is based, assumes that there is normal equality between individuals and that diversity of circumstance is the exception. Because equality is generally assumed, varying degrees of power in different contexts do not have to be considered in achieving a solution. By contrast, the 'conflicting responsibilities' paradigm, on which the reproductive code is based, points towards meeting concrete needs in diverse situations. Because diversity of need is the norm and not the exception, the authority of an abstract rule can never be paramount. A just result can be derived only by considering the relative power of those who are most affected by any particular set of circumstances. General relations of power cannot be ignored in any consideration of their particular effects.

The Radical Potential of the Reproductive Code

It is not a particularly radical notion to argue that women think differently from men. Within popular and academic discourse, female thought processes are commonly referred to as intuitive rather than rational, emotional rather than cognitive, and expressive rather than instrumental, and these differences are frequently used to argue that there is a natural difference between the sexes. The gendered nature of these categories is the 'working currency' of patriarchal discourse (Smith 1987). This discourse is 'masculist'[1] to the extent that 'choice' and 'need' are dichotomous concepts whereby nonreciprocal relations are structured through the linking of responsiveness to the nature of women.

To attribute a qualitative difference to the manner in which women morally understand the world, however, does not necessarily commit one to an essentialist position; rather, the best evidence would suggest a materialist explanation based on a division of labour between the sexes. Both world views are potentially available to either sex, but they vary by gender as a result of the different social relations embedded in reproductive

1 Penelope (1986) argues that masculist is the appropriate antonym of feminist in that it refers to cultural differences rather than biological ones. A male who actively resists the conditions by which he is permitted to exert power over women would not be masculist by virtue of his biology.

practice. Although Gilligan found a gender differentiation in the voice of her subjects, the paradigms I have contrasted are not essentially male or female, and further research has demonstrated the lack of any fixed gender boundaries (Lyons 1983; Johnston 1988).

Despite social-code understandings about differences between men and women, the difference between the two gender-related systems of thought is unlike the differences that exist between teleology and deontology. The reason that it is perceived and articulated along gender lines results from a social division of labour rather than from any difference in the biological capacity of men to attend to the needs of others. Because both men and women participate, to varying degrees, in the labour of empowering others, there is no absolute polarization between the way men think and the way women think. But they are differentially rewarded or penalized for thinking and acting in particular ways.

If the dominant cultural explanations do not fully describe women's reality and the choices they make, the omission of their lived reality also distorts cultural explanations of male reality. Since male activity is not conducted in isolation from the labour of women, the available explanations of human reality are no more an adequate reflection of male reality than they are of female reality. When cultural explanations of human reality are derived from a male standpoint within asymmetrical relations, the result is a mystification of reality for both sexes. As Derber (1979:96) notes, 'The prolonged dependency of children, as well as the needs of infants for continuing special attention, necessitates on the part of the caretaker a transcendence of the egoistic mode; the needs of children are one of the major species considerations which powerfully counteract narcissistic tendencies and create in every society the need for some measure of other-orientation. Since child-care roles are defined in patriarchy as female, this creates constraints only against female narcissism and permits the self-orientation of the male to remain relatively unfettered.'

If women as a group understand human reality according to a different code from that of the dominant culture, this can be sociologically explained by reference to the intersection of the tasks for which they are responsible with the discourse that explains them. The idea of a female nature characterized by responsiveness is not simply a conceptual trick played by men. Rather, it is an idea about female nature that is consented to and generally agreed with by persons observing the nature of those living within capitalist patriarchy. The satisfactory performance of caring tasks is facilitated not by one's biological make-up but by particular social arrangements that are justified by gender. While reproductive tasks are also affected by such things as class and race, women generally have a different experience of care than men have. This is not, however, an experience that men cannot or do not occasionally share.

Discourses that equate nurture with feminine identity are oppressive to all women, not just those who undertake reproductive tasks. They create a set of rewards and penalties that affect any woman regardless of the choices she makes or whether she adopts a moral consciousness that employs the reproductive code. It is therefore important to note that the categorization of thought processes as 'male' or 'female' is simply a way of describing the different social experiences of men and women in a world that structures human choice and human responsiveness in an asymmetrical manner. When one approaches responsibility from a negative and restricting point of view, rules become the restrictions necessary to keep autonomous individuals from harming one another when they interact. Following these principles limits one's accountability to the minimum required to keep from encroaching on the freedom of other independent beings. The minimum required then becomes the obligation that is absolute – the abstract morality one is bound by in the social contract. Once this social contract is in place or 'natural law' acknowledged, individual self-sufficiency is presumed possible so long as another does not intrude into one's own private space.

In contrast to the conservatism of dominant cultural codes, the reproductive code has within it a radical potential for bringing about social change. If one approaches responsibility from a positive and interdependent point of view, then rules are not restricting devices; rather, they enable one individual to respond to another individual's dependency and needs. The principle of concrete difference, rather than an abstract norm of equality, links the concept of autonomy to that of responsiveness as part of an integrated whole. The reproductive code thus reflects a practice that seeks to empower 'dependants' so that they may interact with others to shape their destinies. When satisfactorily performed, reproductive labour involves concern for another's needs as the other experiences them. It is this integration of difference and autonomy that is a distinguishing feature of the reproductive code and has possibilities for the construction of discourses that avoid the totalizing tendencies of modernist thought.

If one assumes that reproductive tasks are part of a process that creates the conditions for individual empowerment, the 'feminine' characteristics of social-code discourse are not simply 'false consciousness' but are hegemonic distortions of acts of power creation and the consciousness that such acts generate. These distortions are possible because power is appropriated from its creator by the belief that it is essentially present or absent according to the gender of the individual. There is a distortion of reproductive reality when attending to the needs and desires of others in their own terms is taken to be an indicator of both femininity and power-lessness while attending to the needs and desires of others in one's own terms is taken to be an indicator of both masculinity and power. Although our cultural codes suggest otherwise, women do not exist out-side the power dynamic; the powerlessness they experience results from social relationships that deny them access to responses to their needs as they define them, and also give them less control over the terms by which they respond to the needs of others. In short, the powerlessness lies in the nonreciprocity of the process by which individuals are empowered.

Partial Victories and New Oppressions

In their political mobilizing, feminist movements do not work in a vac-uum. Alternative models of social organizing become more relevant as a result of changes in the social structure itself. Despite the fact that the feminist movement has repeatedly pointed to the maleness of our cul-tural paradigms, it has had a marginal effect on the current assumptions and conceptual practices of the social code. This is partly because of the demobilizing effect that hegemonic explanations have on women. Because hegemony is not ideology imposed from above, it is difficult to penetrate without rejecting part of one's own experience. For example, in the hegemonic discourse surrounding abortion, the choice of posi-tions is frequently understood as opting for social responsibility or for individual autonomy. Women can choose to be their traditional respon-sive selves or they can choose to pursue their self-interest irrespective of others. The frame itself suggests either a continuation of nonreciprocal relations or a liberation from interdependence – a practical impossibility.

Within hegemonic discourse, the terms of the debate are posed in such a way as to invite women to choose between the oppression of patri-archy or the oppression of capitalism (Robinson 1979). There is a link between the feminist literature on 'women's culture' and the Marxist method for knowing the world. Despite 'common-sense' explanations of the working of female minds, the seemingly instinctive (and apparently perverse) thought processes of women are underpinned by a logic that is as internally consistent as those of the dominant culture, but the code implies dialectical thought rather than oppositional reasoning. This logic arises because reproductive practice involves dialectical relations: one's ability to respond presupposes a degree of autonomy and one's autonomy presupposes access to the responses of another. It is not incidental that the reproductive-code insight of self-other interdependence is a dialectical one. The practice of caring for others, regardless of the gender of the carer, requires a type of moral reasoning that is based on understandings of human interdependence and reciprocal responsibilities. Here, social justice is built not on structures that *balance* zero-sum notions of autonomy and responsiveness but on structures that *integrate* these concepts.

Our cultural rhetoric tends to preserve the status quo because the conservative option speaks directly to a woman's reproductive experience of social connectedness, whereas the option of independence revolves around an individualistic ethic derived from the capitalist mode of production. The distortion of reproductive reality within discourse means that as women perform reproductive work, they simultaneously reproduce the grounds of their own subordination. As long as the labour that produces an autonomous 'self' is seen as an inherent or natural part of womanhood – rather than being recognized as an activity that is consciously performed and is often chosen – the socially necessary tasks that each woman performs will continue to be conceptual bricks in the reproduction of the social code. Because various discourses provide the justification for social institutions that limit reciprocity, when women successfully resist limits on their autonomy at the individual level, their 'success' becomes part of the ideological justification for limiting social responses to their welfare.

The contradiction of patriarchal capitalism is that in the contemporary historical context, women have found it increasingly difficult to consent to their part in the reproduction of hegemony, and at the same time their individual acts of resistance have served to recreate its conceptual terms. At the level of concrete practice, where social responsibility is not reciprocal (as far as the needs of women are concerned), to choose the ideological alternative of independence is not a realistic option for many women, and for a growing number of them it is becoming impossible. Moreover, women's struggle for 'independence' has been part of the process that has led to an increasing privatization of caring tasks. As women fought for and gained the ideological status of subjects deserving of liberty rights, men became increasingly 'liberated' from their traditional obligations towards women and children (Ehrenreich 1984). With women being under increasing pressure to succeed 'like men' and with the increasing privatization of caring tasks and the erosion of the support necessary to perform such work, the gap between hegemonic discourse and daily reality has precipitated ever greater pressures on women to control their fertility. During the 1970s and 1980s, these pressures caused Canadian women to resist reproductive control in the medical arena at the personal level and in the legal arena at the political level. However, to understand the institutionalized nature of modes of thought and the problems these discursive codes pose for changing the nonreciprocal structuring of autonomy and responsibility, it is important to uncover the manner in which Canadian law and medicine turned the acts of resistance into facts that further confirmed the dominant discourses.

8

Therapeutic Abortion Committee Practices: Reproducing Medical 'Subjects' and Immoral Women

The purpose of the 1969 Canadian legislation was
(1) to allow relief from criminal sanction where there was a reliable independent and medically sound judgement that the life or health of the mother would be or would be likely to be endangered, and
(2) to insure that the developing life of the fetus would not be casually destroyed but only destroyed in cases where there was such a reliable independent and medically sound judgment. (Oral Submission to the Supreme Court of Ontario by Crown Attorney Pennington, 7 May 1985)

Where women resort to law, their status is always imbued with specific meaning arising out of their gender. (Smart 1989:9)

[T]here was more than medical judgment contemplated in his categories of women for whom he would and would not be prepared to perform an abortion based on the threat to their mental health. Thus the spurious distinction between 'virgins' and 'whores' ... came to be understood to be a medical distinction in the practice of abortion. (Gavigan 1986a:309)

Legally Protecting the Right of Medical 'Choice'

The 1969 amendment to Criminal Code provided doctors with reasons for their decisions to respond or not respond to the reproductive needs of particular women. The law provided for a panel of doctors to determine whether the health of a woman would be best protected by a termination of her pregnancy. If the panel determined that it would be, an abortion was lawful. Although the therapeutic abortion committee (TAC) process legitimated what was already occurring in practice, it placed doctors in a somewhat anomalous situation. The abortion techniques then available meant that abortion was safer than pregnancy, so a consideration of medical 'health' alone would have led to the aborting of the pregnancies of all who requested this. On the other hand, rising standards of living meant that carrying pregnancies to term posed no significant medical risk, so the need for an abortion based solely on medical criteria was relatively rare. Clearly, the abortion decision could not be solely a matter of the health of women patients, but if the law was not to be completely meaningless, physicians were obliged to make decisions that involved responding to the concrete social position of their pregnant patients. At the same time, the law specified that providing abortion services was not to be based on a woman's consideration of her own needs. Her reasons were to be validated by her doctor, who in turn required the TAC stamp of approval. Doctors, individually and as a group, were legally obligated to make judgments about the morality of abortion decisions.

Implicit within the process of deciding about the health of individual women was the notion that physicians were responsible for the health of society. Since the law did not define the term 'health,' this determination was left to the discretion of individual doctors. The legalization of medical discretion left the door open for doctors to consider a wide range of circumstances that were unrelated either to their medical training or to the actual wording of the law. Faced with the reality of abortion need, doctors generally recognized that the decision could not be reduced to medical criteria alone, so they expanded the criteria for health to include issues of lifestyle. The distinction between the subjective reasons for granting abortions and the justifications used was not a simple case of hypocrisy. The standard of legitimacy at the public level determined the boundaries in which actions at the private level would be considered legitimate. The lack of a legal definition for health indicated that a medical one should be employed. Idiosyncratic decisions could be justified on 'medical' grounds precisely because the health of any woman is in fact related to the social context within which she lives her life.

The legal frame within which the TAC process operated recognized the relation between lifestyle and health, but it reinterpreted it according to abstract and generalizable criteria based on social-code assumptions. A doctor's medical diagnosis could be accorded a legal status so long as it was explained in terms derived from the symbolic level of public discourse. The result was that doctors could make decisions based on social-code assumptions and these decisions would in turn be legitimated by reference to legal principles involving a woman's right to welfare.

The requirements of the abortion law could be fulfilled by selecting appropriate facts on a case-by-case basis. A woman's life circumstances became material to be organized in a manner that would satisfy legal criteria. Once a doctor had subjectively weighed the circumstances of a woman's life, she or he selected from them a fact that would satisfy the terms of the law. In the process, not only were women's motivations for seeking an abortion transformed, but if a particular woman was to receive the response she required, she had to participate in the creation of distorted explanations for why abortions were necessary and why law and medicine should collude in providing them.

The moral decisions of women would be considered legitimate if they could be moulded and shaped according to the prevailing notions about women and about reproduction. The process reaffirmed a status quo in which 'normal' women accepted biological dictates to provide nurturing responses. However, if a doctor agreed that any particular woman's circumstances were exceptional, he or she could grant her the medical responses that she required. The TAC process ensured that the actual requirements for undertaking nurturing work would remain invisible because the need for an abortion was judged according to social assumptions about healthy womanhood. The process involved an active negotiation between women and their doctors, and hegemonic assumptions were the only currency that women were allowed.

Psychological Justification

Doctors did not change their decision-making practices following the 1969 law (Smith and Wineberg 1970; L. Collins 1982). The 1969 law simply provided a means for legitimating the decision making of individual physicians – investing the doctors involved with the power to enforce their own particular values concerning women and reproduction. The institutionalized committee system meant that moral questions about how reproductive relations could be organized in a socially responsible way were removed from the public level and were resolved at the private level of medical practice, where doctors had the discretion to construct justifications from the material of women's lives.

By requiring that doctors set down 'good' reasons for providing a woman with an abortion, the hospital committee system simply shifted the emphasis to documentary justification. Justifications had to be encompassed within the parameters of law; that is, abortion was legal if the mother's life or health was endangered by a continued pregnancy. 'Health' proved to be a principle of such ambiguity that justifications could be made for almost any decision. Although the medical profession remained largely unconcerned about the implications of a broader understanding of health when it allocated dollars and skills, for the purposes of providing the legal rationales for abortion services, it selected from all possible aspects of physical and mental health.

The way in which 'medical facts' were used to justify individual decisions at the day-to-day level of the hospital abortion committees meant that a woman had to convince the doctor that her case could be justified for reasons of health, even though the particular fact used to justify her need bore little relation to the need itself. She had to select from among the various events in her life a rationale that would fulfil the criterion laid down by law. The broader the definition of health used by a hospital committee, the more likely it was that psychiatric justifications would be required. If any woman had difficulty in forcing her life into the legitimate categories that would allow her abortion services, a psychiatrist would help her. He would organize her experience by selecting the medical 'fact' that would make the abortion procedure a legal one.

Health was an enabling principle in that it allowed doctors to consider reasons not specifically laid down in the law, and this was especially so where mental health was concerned. The psychiatric evaluation of a woman's mental state was an important factor in transforming a variety of personal circumstances into legal facts. At abortion tribunals held in Toronto, one woman told a story that illustrates the importance of psychiatric interpretations in dropping out the flaws and ambiguities of a woman's life that did not fit the law on the books:

Kathy: I was told I had to see a therapeutic abortion committee and they would decide whether I was medically unfit and could therefore have an abortion ... The last person finally that I was to see was a psychiatrist and I was looking forward to this, as a matter of fact, because I felt that with the nature of his business and his relationships, he would be very human with me considering my predicament. He would assure me that I was making a responsible decision and his participation in the decision was just as much red tape. I also wondered if he would find me normal! I went to see him, determined to be very positive and responsible. And he was very cold and impersonal and technical and he would not meet my eyes or my mood or anything like that. He asked me technical questions, facts, things like that. So I told him about my life and when we got to the part about my father dying in a car accident (and I didn't go the funeral because it was enough for my mother to face it herself without all of us kids) he asked if I had ever been to the grave and I said no, actually I hadn't and he said, 'Aahh,' and proceeded to write on his forms. He would not answer my silent plea as to what was going on until I finally asked him and he said, 'Well, I think we've found our reason: you have not accepted your father's death and therefore you are not ready for a responsible relationship with a man.' (Oral testimony of abortion patient at Toronto tribunal, March 1986)

In this account of the psychiatric reinterpretation of the circumstances that made it impossible for Kathy to carry out the responsibilities of motherhood, one can perceive an ideological circle at work. The particular – her father's death – is picked out and reflected on to reach a conclusion of emotional instability. The psychiatrist's selective sensitivity towards what is legally important allows him to construct an account that will enable the woman's doctor to grant her the right to an abortion. As a psychologically unstable person, Kathy qualifies for a welfare right. This assumption of psychological ill health then becomes part of the 'universal' for why women require abortions, thus recreating the ideology on which the law was based in the first place. Within this circle, Kathy's 'responsible' motivations were rendered invisible.

The transforming of pregnancy and abortion into medical events did not fit with the experiences of individual women, but it helped to reinforce the stigma of abortion and the immorality of those who required them. Although Smith and Wineberg's (1970:299–300) study of Canadian hospital committees found that virtually every one of the abortions granted on psychiatric grounds was done for reasons of socio-economic or personal circumstances, doctors understood that such decisions had to be justified as posing a danger to the physical or mental health of the woman. In this circular process of reproducing reproductive hegemony, the justificatory process was an important link between the symbolic level of reality and the actual practice of abortion. Each situation, justified in terms of 'health,' reaffirmed the public perception that abortion is legitimate only where the mother's life or health is endangered. Pregnancy and its termination could continue to be understood as medical events requiring medical decision making.

In a circular fashion, the process by which women obtained an abortion under the TAC system symbolically reinforced the prevailing stereotypes about why any woman might require an abortion. In turn, at the committee level, these ideological assumptions enabled doctors to make decisions that would solve the problems of the women who managed to get before them.

'Welfare': The Deserving of Pain and Humiliation

By selecting out the appropriate facts to justify the procedure, psychiatrists, simply in doing their job, reinforced social-code assumptions about the kind of woman who would require abortions. While the committee system 'spread responsibility across the medical institution, psychiatrization went one step further. It blamed the victim at the same time that it exonerated participating physicians' (Davis 1985:72). In this process, women had to consent to the mystification of their lives and of their motivations for terminating their pregnancy. Caught in the ideological circle, women who sought to control their reproductive capabilities had to prove that they were irresponsible, immature, or emotionally unstable. If they 'proved' this and accepted the shame or immorality of their circumstances, they could then be provided with the 'help' they needed. This symbolic interpretation of their experience involved women as co-conspirators in producing in themselves the emotional trauma that was already assumed by the diagnosis. As Kathy's account of her abortion experience explained, the psychiatric assessment of her irresponsibility 'did nothing to alleviate the emotional turbulence I was going through. As a matter of fact, it made me feel all the more confused, made me *feel guilty, inept and upset* but it was a problem I had to put aside at the moment.'

While a woman had to put aside 'at the moment' her feelings of guilt and shame, many of those who responded to her need seemed determined to ensure that she would associate the experience with pain and humiliation. A woman who chose to seek an abortion was treated as a double failure. The very fact that she needed an abortion demonstrated her failure as a mature adult to act without depending on others, and it also demonstrated her failure as a woman. She was rejecting her 'feminine' capacity to nurture others and to put their needs ahead of her own. The provision of abortion services was an indication to the doctor that 'shame' and 'guilt' were called for. It signified that she was immoral in her choices, careless in her sexual activity, or otherwise a passive victim of circumstance. The circumstances that would allow her to be helped were implicitly designed to create the type of emotional trauma that would indicate to her and to others that her decision was an immoral one. Her emotional unfitness for motherhood marked her as an 'unnatural woman.'

Stories from women who had had abortions before and after the Criminal Code amendments illustrate that legalized hospital abortions often did not change the labelling dynamic. The law simply legitimated a morality play based on condemnation and resulting in emotional trauma. The following accounts demonstrate that the legal service provided by the head gynaecologist in a major Toronto hospital paralleled, in pain and humiliation, that provided by illegal abortionists before 1969:

Pat: I went in the room and was going to have the internal examination. It was a very young intern, very nervous. I was quite tense. She couldn't complete the exam so they called in the head doctor, who is supposed to teach doctors how to be a doctor and to treat people. He proceeded to brush her aside, 'Move, move, move, you're not doing this correctly,' and he rammed a speculum up, I think, as hard as he could. You almost had to peel me off the ceiling because the pain was so bad. I literally remember my hands on the walls, gripping it and I began to scream and cry quite hysterically. He looked at me and said, 'Women like you are just pigs. And you come in here all the time and you want an abortion. Can't you learn how to use birth control?' And I'm lying on this table, sobbing hysterically, thinking, 'What kind of a monster is this treating me?' Then he threw his instruments down and said, 'You have an infection and its called trichinosis,' and he said it in a really loud voice and I thought, 'My God, am I going to die of this, what is this?' I didn't know at the time that it was a minor infection. That really disgusted him; I was, I think, a very piggish person then. Then he left and the nurses came in and were very comforting and I realized that they knew that this doctor did this to women all the time. Because they said, 'Oh, he's done it again' or 'Another poor woman lying there crying.' And I just couldn't believe that a doctor like this was allowed to touch women or get near them. (Oral testimony of abortion patient at Toronto tribunals, March 1986)

Diane: On the way back to my hotel, the contact person ... said, 'I have to stop at my apartment for a moment and make a phone call. Just come in.' ... I was feeling very sick and very disoriented. He took me into the house, said, 'Just a minute, I have to make a phone call.' He then came out of his kitchen, handed me a drink and said, 'Here, have a drink, you'll feel better.' I said, 'No, I just want to go and lie down.' He said, 'Listen, have a few drinks. We'll have a good fuck and then it'll happen faster' ... [Following the abortion] I started bleeding very heavily; by midnight I thought I was haemorrhaging and I had never seen so much blood or felt so much pain. I couldn't do anything. I couldn't scream so I held a pillow over my head and screamed into that. I spent the night on the toilet, or on the bed, or on the floor, bloodying all the sheets and towels in the hotel room ... About 7 o'clock in the morning I passed a lot of blood and I was very frightened and I thought I should go to the hospital because I couldn't stand. I called this man, and I said, 'I'm very frightened, I'm haemorrhaging and I don't know what to do.' And he said, 'Is it over yet?' and I said, 'I don't know, I don't know, what should I do?' He said, 'You stupid bitch, didn't you look?' and I said, 'There's just a lot of blood and I don't know what to do.' He said, 'Then it's almost over and don't call me again and don't call the police.' (Ibid.)

A woman who found herself in a situation requiring abortion was frequently assumed to be sexually immoral and therefore fair game for exploitation. Whether legal or not, abortion was treated as a guilty secret, and the woman who resorted to it was irresponsible and immoral. 'The overall administrative strategy for hospitals had the effect of politically immobilizing individual abortion patients. Patients experiencing inept or brutal treatment, poor service, enforced sterilization or psychiatric or mental health labels could hardly bring demands on a system that barely tolerated them in the first place' (Davis 1985:85). The ideological message that a woman received when she claimed her welfare right was one that called into question her moral capacities. The resulting psychological trauma confirmed that abortion was 'unnatural.'

Providing 'Welfare': Doctors as the 'Real' Subjects of Reproduction

As doctors performed their job within the legitimate parameters of the committee process, it was a natural step for them to see their profession as a front-line defence of both individual morality and the social health of society. Legalizing abortion was a measure designed to concentrate control of abortion decisions in the hands of the medical profession; as such, it intensified the feeling of objectification and estrangement that women experienced in the process. In this moral drama, doctors were the real subjects and women were the objects of their work. The relations between them curtailed women's agency and reaffirmed the belief in their essential passivity.

The major effect of hospital abortions on women was not pain and humiliation, however, for not all doctors treated women in the cruel fashion described above. In fact, many of the procedures appeared to be designed to 'protect' women from the whole abortion experience. The process was one of structured passivity, where women did not choose to terminate their pregnancies but had something done to them. As beneficiaries of medical expertise, they were categorized and responded to in assembly-line fashion. The following account of a hospital abortion illustrates how medical procedures had the effect of transforming the patient from a decision maker into a medical category:

Pat: I went to a clinic at the Wellesley Hospital. There was a whole bunch of us that were there that day. It was the abortion day at the hospital so there were maybe 10 of us. We were called T.A.'s. 'T.A., could you come over here. T.A. could you go down to that room.' I kept thinking, 'What is a T.A.?' And then I had to fill out this form that said, 'Are you sure you want an abortion and what is the reason?' and I saw T.A. written there and it stood for 'therapeutic abortion.' And I thought, 'They're calling me a T.A.' and it seemed very stupid to call a person a T.A. (Oral testimony of abortion patient at Toronto tribunals, March, 1986)

Objectification of their experience was common both to women who had their abortions before 1969 and to those who had them legally after that date. Once a doctor had given a woman his permission to have an abortion, she was expected to place herself completely in his hands. From the women's own accounts, it is clear that doctors frequently assumed that providing for a woman's medical welfare was the business of the medical expert and that women did not need to know what was happening to them. Whether the abortion was performed in a hospital, as in Julie's legal experience, or by an illegal 'professional,' as in Diane's pre-1969 operation, women were not regarded as active participants in the termination of their pregnancy; they were viewed as the objects of the doctor's professional administrations:

Julie: When I saw the Dr. I wanted to ask questions; I wanted him to explain the procedure to me and I wanted to know exactly what was going to happen to me. And he said that as far as he was concerned there was no questions, it was a standard procedure, and that was *all* I needed to know. So I paid the money, and he booked the appointment for five weeks later. (Ibid.)

Diane: I was asking questions about what he was going to do because I had no idea about what he was doing or about what was going to happen. He said not to worry, he had performed thousands of abortions ... He treated it in a very cavalier fashion ... he wouldn't answer my questions. He said, 'Just lie there quietly and don't worry, everything is going to be fine.' (Ibid.)

According to the legal principle by which a woman could claim an abortion, she was '"psychotic," "hysterical," "depressed," "neurotic" or "guilt-laden."' She therefore 'was considered to be in an unfit mental state to evaluate her own treatment' (Davis 1985:73).

Social-Code Assumptions and Reproductive Reality

Although the 1969 amendment was a formality that legitimated practices based on social inequities, it exacerbated the problem women faced at the symbolic level. The requirement that doctors justify their decisions through recourse to 'ill health' (whether physical or psychological) reinforced the common belief that abortions were required by women for medical reasons only. For the medical diagnoses to be granted a legal status, they had to be explained in the terms by which the standard was defined. 'The concept of "medical necessity" or "therapeutic abortion" defines nonmedical abortions as "elective," meaning they are somehow frivolous, *merely* "personal," "unnecessary." This bifurcated view distorts reality, denying that familial, economic, and sexual conditions as well as physical health create genuine, pressing needs that justify abortion. It also reduces the meaning of "health," ignoring the extent to which medical problems themselves are related to social, economic, and family-sexual conditions' (Petchesky [1984:289]).

When the abortion issue was organized around the medical procedure required to terminate a pregnancy, the public perception of abortion as a medical procedure, legitimate only in cases where the mother's life and biological health were endangered, was reinforced. The legalization of abortion set up an organized method for dealing with problem pregnancies, but in doing so it institutionalized basic assumptions about what sort of woman would require an abortion, assumptions that had little basis in material reality.

In their selection of the 'facts' necessary to legitimate the abortion, the hospital committees participated in a process whereby 'flaws and ambiguities could be "dropped-out" in the interests of clarity and certainty' (Gusfield 1981a:71) The 'facts' as they were presented were then given as an appropriate representation of the entire situation, rather than as facts that had been selected from the woman's entire life situation. By narrowing the focus, the committees avoided inquiring into the relevant social and economic factors that formed the context within which women sought abortions.

The narrowed focus created by medical decision making at the level of private professional practice reinforced moral stereotypes about abortions and those who sought them, and these stereotypes in turn provided the basis on which doctors could justify their decisions. By narrowing the scope of the debate to include only a portion of the women's reality – the need for a medical procedure – the hospital committees functioned to convert a social problem into instances involving individual women. The morality of the system itself could not be addressed at this level, only the morality of the pregnant woman. This individualization of morality resulted in 'the old eugenic idea of childbearing as a "scientific" undertaking for which only certain women are "fit." Thus it can allow abortion in some cases because in those cases women are seen as too poor, too young, or too mentally or physically incompetent to bear children; or some foetuses as too defective to be born ... In this way, therapeutic-eugenic discourse about fertility control, including abortion, allows the liberal state to accommodate without at the same time legitimating feminist demands' (Hubbard 1983, workshop presentation at Women in Law meetings, Ottawa).

· In terms of the social relations of reproduction, the ideological process created a power resource for the medical profession. The 1969 amendment to the Criminal Code expanded and solidified the existing monopoly of the medical profession. The law legitimated the physician's right to make moral decisions about who was fit to have children and who would be allowed to choose not to do so. Because the medical profession administered this welfare benefit, the decision no longer belonged to the woman involved. Since it was a technological event, she no longer needed to concern herself with the details. At the same time, the legal criterion of mental health provided doctors with an ideological resource that allowed them to implement their own moral values and then to justify these decisions by activating explanations that already existed within popular culture.

When one examines the medical site at which legal regulations and medical practices intersected, it is possible to understand the reproduction of hegemony as a process that moves from the public realm to the private realm. In the process, 'women consent to the ideology and practice of patriarchy' (O'Brien 1984:98). Although the legal 'explanations' did not reflect the realities experienced by women, their choice was to consent to the 'legitimate' medical interpretation or to lose the right to the medical responses they required. The TACs were a site where women lived out the contradictions between ideology and reality. The choices they made in coping with reproductive reality were at one and the same time involved in reproducing existing relations and resisting them (Marshall 1988). Although the choices did not necessarily conform to the norms and values of the dominant culture, the distorted explanations of why women consent to patriarchal control both draw on and reproduce assumptions about the nature of women and the social relations that exist between doctor and patient, woman and foetus.

9

Assessing Liberty and
Welfare Rights Status

The 1969 amendments are all designed for the *protection of the developing human life* in the womb against any casual or convenience destruction at the instance of the pregnant woman. (Statement of Fact and Law filed on behalf of the Attorney General of Canada to the Supreme Court of Ontario)

The law protects women. When putting aside the state's interest in protecting life, the state cannot then ensure the women's consent to the procedure and protect them from the psychological problems the decision could bring. (Oral submission to Supreme Court of Ontario by Crown Attorney Pennington, 7 May 1985; cf. Statement of Fact and Law filed on behalf of the Attorney General of Canada)

It is in error to focus on Parliament's emphasis on health since the primary intent is protection of life. It is not fundamentally or primarily a matter of the health of women. The *intent was to inject a third person into the decision- making process.* (Oral submission to the Supreme Court of Canada by Crown Attorney Wein, 9 October 1986)

With regard to a doctor's right to assist a woman ... I submit that this argument is not important ... Doctors are not mandated beyond that given in the section of the Criminal Code ... There are *provisions which allow doctors **not** to participate ... The absence of coercion and constraint is the important factor.* (Oral submission to the Supreme Court of Canada by Crown Attorney Wein, 9 October 1986)

A Social-Code Transformation of Legal-Code Logic

In making Canadian abortion policy, law and medicine intersected to invent the categories within which women could achieve their reproductive objectives. Cain (1994) has noted how lawyers do translation work as a matter of routine, showing how the facts of a particular case either falls within a rule or does not. At therapeutic abortion committee (TAC) sites, doctors were engaged in a similar kind of translation work. In effect, the legal work had been relegated to the medical profession. The interpretive tasks undertaken at the Supreme Court in the Morgentaler appeals involved a different level of justification. At issue here was the right/responsibility of the medical profession to undertake this translation work on behalf of the state, and it was now the lawyers' turn to perform work that would justify established boundaries of discourse. Each of the legal adversaries working to defend or challenge the law's structuring of abortion services implicitly argued about whether the law was an aid or a hindrance in securing normal liberty rights for doctors and exceptional welfare rights for pregnant women. In the juxtaposition of arguments, both sides reaffirmed the ideological boundaries of the legal mind-set, but it was the Crown's defence of the law that most clearly unmasked the gendered assumptions on which the legal code is built. To justify the law required a more explicit use of social-code assumptions about the exceptionality of women than was necessary for defending the actions of a particular doctor.

If the law were to be administered in a gender-neutral fashion, according to the principles of contemporary reasoning, women would have liberty rights; and foetuses – if they were to have any rights as independent individuals – would have welfare ones (Farrell Smith 1984). But such an apportioning of rights undermines the logic on which the legal code is based, exposing the contradiction that is masked by the lack of a reproductive referent. This theoretical lack means that legal practice has a problem whenever it is faced with issues of reproduction. If both human autonomy and new human life result naturally in the absence of interference, then two competing liberty rights are involved: the right of a woman to choice and the right of her foetus to life. The contradiction is that foetuses require something more than noninterference if their liberty rights are to be exercised. Envisioning choice and life as competing liberty rights allows no resolution, because it is based on a false conception of reproductive reality. When women exercise the right of choice, the 'harm' they cause is the *withholding* of the responses necessary for a foetus to reach the original position where its liberty right can be exercised. As Farrell Smith (1984:271) notes, 'the right to life is primarily a welfare right, a right to well-being that imposes positive duties of care and nurture upon a particular person. It calls for much more than noninterference in the sense of not killing.'

To make an assessment about which liberty rights accrue to which legal subjects is understood to be making assessments about 'human institutions and relationships in terms of whether those institutions and relationships conform to principles of obligation and duty that guarantee to each person equal concern and respect in exercising autonomy' (Richards 1981:263). But the social code already makes assumptions about the gender of the person whose duty it is to provide for the needs of others and whose right it is to exercise autonomy. The legal discourse surrounding the challenge to the Canadian abortion law provides an example of how legal discourse, in its articulation of images and words, can produce a pattern of normalized rights and responsibilities based on the status quo of asymmetrical relations between the sexes. In undertaking their legal task of defending the law, the Crown attorneys were forced to abandon the abstract legal-code assertions of gender neutrality and to stress the differences that exist between men and women in the performance of reproductive work. By contrast, the arguments that defended Dr Morgentaler's rights before the law (and presumably those advocating on behalf of the pro-choice movement) had only to rely on the court's understanding of abstract legal reasoning. Morgentaler's lawyer, Morris Manning, was therefore able to refrain from discussing the theoretical underpinnings of legal discourse in a way that was not possible for the lawyers whose job it was to justify this particular abortion law.

The legal 'text' of the Crown discourse at the Morgentaler appeal hearings illustrates a particular reading of the contemporary legal code, a reading that qualified legal precepts by contextualizing them according to perceptions of the morality inscribed in various practices. An examination of the argumentation at these court hearings exposes the way in which legal reasoning implicitly differentiates liberty rights and welfare responsibilities according to the more explicit misogyny of the social code. Social and legal codes interlocked within this courtroom discourse so that decisions about a person's legal status could be made on the basis of social-code stereotypes about the effect of gender on practices directed towards the empowerment of others. This intersection of legal principles and social interpretations of existing practices allowed the state to justify a gendered inversion of formal legal principles even as it affirmed the Rawlsian method of apportioning rights and responsibilities.

In identifying the rights to be considered, the Crown attorneys – who defended the social organization of abortion practices through therapeutic abortion committees – sketched a pattern of reproductive relationships involving three distinct sets of rights: a foetal liberty right, a maternal welfare right, and a medical liberty right, the last named to be qualified by the responsibility of the medical profession to ensure a balancing of women's welfare and foetal liberty. This apportioning of liberty and welfare rights was justified in Crown rhetoric through a selective and interwoven patterning of legal-code principles and social-code assumptions. Different images and meanings were juxtaposed to reaffirm both the social organization of reproduction and the logic of legal discourse.

Normal Foetal Rights and the Exceptionality of Women

Normal legal distinctions between those entitled to liberty and those entitled to welfare are based on the degree to which legal subjects require responses from others in order to achieve their goals or purposes. If, in Canadian legislatures and courtrooms, this determination had been made without reference to social-code understandings about gender, foetal dependence would have led to the foetus's right to life being viewed as a welfare right. Although the state's interest in and responsibility for future generations would have had to be delegated to pregnant women, the normal legal assumptions would have upheld the liberty right of responders to decide in any particular instance how best to fulfil these tasks (Farrell Smith 1984). Further, the recognition that foetuses require something more than a lack of interference would have obligated the state to ensure that the responding party (a pregnant woman) had the resources necessary to make meaningful decisions about her capacity and willingness to undertake these reproductive responsibilities. Instead, the Canadian law (and the discourse of those who defended it) assigned welfare-right status to the pregnant woman and sought to ensure that the responding party (a medical doctor) retained the right to choose when and how to carry out the obligations of the medical profession for the welfare of women.

The fundamental assumption of legal reasoning is that normal legal subjects exist apart from any particular set of social relations and that state intervention is required only in exceptional situations. Beginning with this presupposition, the 1969 amendment to the Canadian Criminal Code implied, without having to articulate, a natural foetal liberty right that preceded the state's interest in providing for maternal welfare.[1] Although neither the Canadian law nor the courtroom discourse that

---

1 The normal autonomy assumed for foetuses is the metaphoric basis that permits the depiction of 'autonomous man' within contemporary legal theory (see chapter 5 for an articulation of this characterization).

defended it explicitly assigned foetuses an inalienable right to life and liberty, the right was already implied by the legal framework that defined access to abortion services as an exceptional health requirement. The normal allocation of medical services in Canada was the background within which this exceptionality was ascribed to pregnant women.

Whereas the role of the American state has been essentially liberal in orientation, stressing the liberty of all individuals to make private decisions and privately secure their resources, the activity of the Canadian state has followed a somewhat different course. In a number of areas, a 'shared-responsibility' orientation towards the meeting of individual human needs has taken precedence over a lack of interference in the marketplace. One such area involves the organization of Canadian medical relations. The political organization of health care on a universal basis means that the right to state-funded medical care in Canada is not publicly perceived in welfare terms. Rather than being a state response to the 'weaker' members of society, access to health care is viewed as a basic service with which the state ought not to interfere.

The 1969 abortion law was a clear exception to the Canadian conception of the universality of health care. By qualifying the general Canadian right to medical services, the process for allowing a woman access to abortion services made this health benefit a welfare right. Unlike medical services generally, women could claim abortion services only by fulfilling the legal standard's definition of need. The Crown's presentation to the Supreme Court of Ontario succinctly outlined the state's objectives that provided the frame in which courtroom argumentation took place:

The purpose of the 1969 legislation was
(1) to allow relief from criminal sanction where there was a reliable, independent and medically sound judgement that the life or health of the mother would be or would be likely to be endangered, and
(2) to insure that the developing life of the fetus would not be casually destroyed but only destroyed in cases where there was such a reliable independent and medically sound judgement. (Oral Submission to the Supreme Court of Ontario, Crown Attorney Pennington, 7 May 1985)

Despite the order in which the state's aims were presented, the Crown left no doubt that the law was designed, primarily, to ensure that the inherent foetal right would normally encounter no interference and, secondarily, to protect a woman's reproductive health through a provision of medical welfare.

Within legal theory, welfare rights are meaningless without an existing liberty right, and only by negating the social aspects of women's reproductive labour could the law give foetuses a right normally associated with autonomous actors and give women the derivative right that is normally associated with immature or victimized individuals. Without the initial intent to protect the presumed autonomy of foetal development, it would have been legally unnecessary to give women a derivative welfare right. Throughout the various court hearings, the Crown made clear that 'the primary intent of the law is protection of life. It is not fundamentally or primarily a matter of the health of women' (oral submission to the Supreme Court of Canada by Crown Attorney Wein, 9 October 1986).

Because notions about the fundamental essence of life and independence are derived from a fallacy about the nature of reproductive relations, legal reasoning could not focus on maternal liberty and foetal welfare without undermining the basis of legal theory itself. Any state interest in autonomy and equality for women had to be discursively transformed. In accomplishing this transformation, the various Crown attorneys at the Canadian hearings used words which suggested that they were addressing female liberty and foetal welfare, but they used a logic that posited the reverse. In doing so, they summoned the same social-code assumptions about gender and power that informed Rawls's synthesis of teleology and deontology: in the original position, 'everyman' retains the inherent autonomy characteristic of teleological reasoning while female nurturance becomes a deontological obligation imposed by natural law.

Unlike Rawls, the Crown, in responding to the legal challenge, was forced to provide an implicit consideration of the relationship between foetuses and women; but like Rawls's prescription for social justice, Crown submissions proceeded as though the existence of a foetal liberty right was not in question. Because law is expected to intervene to protect individuals in adversarial situations, the first priority of the law, the Crown attorneys argued, should be to determine if any particular pregnant woman's actions could be said to be an inappropriate interference with another legal subject's right to achieve independence. One of their briefs stated that 'the 1969 amendments are all designed for the protection of the developing human life in the womb against any casual or convenience destruction at the instance of the pregnant woman' (Statement of Fact and Law filed on behalf of the Attorney General of Canada to the Supreme Court of Ontario). From the original starting position, any withdrawal of 'natural' support was thus construed as an act of infringement on inherent liberty rights. If such 'violence' was required to offset the powerlessness of women, it had to be legitimated by the rule of law.

By articulating a legal subtext based on a social-code interpretation of normal gender relations, the task of providing *explicit* welfare rights for women could be addressed in relation to the *implicit* liberty rights of potential human life. By transferring the actual maternal capacity for purposeful reproductive activity to the abstract essence of foetuses, the protection of maternal health became a state interest only to the extent that foetal activity was itself the probem. A foetal right to life could be legally qualified, like any liberty right, if the exercise of this right created harm to a dependent or powerless other. In transferring agency from women to foetuses, the state could then be said to have an interest in protecting a woman if the activity of her foetus potentially caused harm to her health. This inversion of agency depended on invoking ideas about natural femininity, and the Crown's argumentation drew heavily upon the conception of human life as the spontaneous product of the biological responsiveness of women. Any infringement on female autonomy, the court was told, lies not with the law but with the laws of nature: '*In this instance*, it is not the legislation but nature that *denies men* the right to bear children – it is biologically mandated ... *All* of these women are denied the right to choose – even those entitled to legal abortion ... Parliament achieves a balance by giving *exemptions* to women, such exemptions are proportional to the diametrically opposed interests involved' (oral submission to the Supreme Court of Canada, 9 October 1986; emphasis added).

In stressing the conditions by which the state would step in to exempt women from performing services for others, this presentation was clearly at odds with normal legal reasoning, but it mirrored social-code understandings about when a woman might expect a charitable response to her needs. The judgment of the Ontario Court of Appeal made clear that it concurred with Crown arguments that legal intervention is legitimate when a woman's choices correspond to conventional expectations of womanliness: 'Some rights have their basis in common law or statute law. Some are so deeply rooted in our traditions and way of life as to be fundamental and could be classified as part of life, liberty and security of the person. The right to choose one's partner in marriage, and the decision whether or not to have children would fall in this category ... We agree with Parker A.C.J.H.C. that ... it could not be said that there is a right to procure an abortion so deeply rooted in our traditions and way of life as to be fundamental' (judgment of the Court of Appeal, Supreme Court of Ontario).

Clearly the judgment of the Court of Appeal was stating that the option of caring for others is a normal choice for women and that abortion is not. Crown arguments at the federal appeal court picked up this theme as they stressed the social importance of ensuring that pregnant women accept the responsibility for considering the interests of others. Rationalizing why a pregnant woman's right to medical resources must include a regulation of her liberty, they contended: 'Abortion is different ... it involves not just a matter of individual choice because it affects other interests. It also affects foetal life of the unborn. Society has an interest; the father may have an interest' (oral submission by Crown Attorney Wein to the Supreme Court of Canada, 9 October 1986).

In this emphasis on the other interests with which women are to be concerned, the legal paradigm of normal human autonomy is being affirmed even as it is bypassed. It is precisely because the exercise of choice is normally equated with self-interest that reproductive tasks can be considered exceptional. And if reproductive activities (and, by extension, the nature of women) are always exceptional, then abortion is different because it constitutes an exception to this general exceptionality of women. It is at this point that the legal and social codes intersect. According to both codes, to exercise choice involves human volition but human volition is equated with self-interest. Because female responsiveness is equated only with passive determinism, for women to choose whether they will provide the responses necessary for new life to develop is for them to act selfishly – for the sake of 'instantaneous convenience,' the Crown suggested. The pursuit of one's own interests in one's own way is a fundamental principle of liberal law, but it is not the behaviour that is culturally expected from mothers.

The reasoning used to defend the law variously selected from and contradicted aspects of the legal code, but it did so on the basis of social-code interpretations of actual practices. According to the legal code, all individuals come before the law as equal subjects, each pursuing his or her own self-interest. To explain gender-differentiated labour that empowers others within a discursive frame that equates autonomy with self-interest, one must first surmise that all women are inherently powerless, a condition that can then be addressed through the benevolence of the state. By invoking generally accepted beliefs about the powerlessness of women and the naturalness of their reproductive responses, legal reasoning allowed the state to address the medical well-being of women by providing them with 'exemptions' from their maternal role in exceptional circumstances. But neither code provided any rationale for changing a woman's normal obligation to create the conditions by which others might enjoy life or exercise their liberty.

The Crown argument has hegemonic force because, in the real world, women do make choices that are cognizant of the differing interests of those to whom they are related. Within a framework that dichotomizes self and other, these practices create the social-code understanding that abortion is a self-interested practice which normal women will resort to in exceptional circumstances. Abortion is therefore not different from legal-code expectations of normal human beings, but it is different from social-code expectations that women will care for the needs of the social collectivity. For a woman to make a decision not to respond to the needs and desires of others goes against the presupposition that women will inevitably and naturally sacrifice their interests so that others may be allowed the opportunity to exercise legal rights of autonomy.

Legal Code Meets Social Code: 'Choice' Meets 'Responsibility' and 'Protection'

Although the public's understanding of the abortion debate is framed in terms of a competition between the rights to life and choice, within the Canadian courtrooms this competition was played out against a backdrop of maternal responsibility. Despite the legal rhetoric of a state interest in balancing competing liberty rights, maternal choice – in the negative sense of freedom from state intervention – was notably absent from both the legislation and the discourse that defended it. For the casual observer at the court, the words used suggested that the court was seeking to balance interests within the framework of negative law; that is, it was deliberating about the exceptional circumstances that would allow the state to interfere with a pregnant women's liberty. The language was deceiving. Where maternal choice was concerned, the Crown arguments evoked relational reasoning that would have been more suitable to a reproductive discourse than to a legal one. Within a general framework of negative rights, notions of responsibility and human connection were juxtaposed to ideas about rights and self-sufficiency, and this juxtaposition reaffirmed the operative mind-set even as it bypassed it.

The Crown's assertion that 'the issue before the court is choice' was contextualized in order to give the word an exceptional meaning. When discussing pregnancy decision making, terms usually associated with negative rights were used to refer not to the right to be free from state interference but to the option to seek state intervention. The problem, the argument went, was not the liberty principles of 'choice' and 'privacy' but that they should abstractly be applied to reproductive relations. Ironically, while reproduction has traditionally been equated with an individual's right to be free from state intervention within the private sphere, it was here argued that 'where pregnancy is concerned, there is a problem with "privacy" in that it allows rights of the unborn child to go unsupported. There is [then] no "balance of interests" ... Privacy, in this instance, puts aside the state's interest in protecting life, including the woman herself ... a pregnant woman cannot be isolated in her privacy' (oral submission to the Ontario Court of Appeal by Crown Attorney Pennington, 7 May 1985).

Social-code assumptions about gender difference rather than legal-code assumptions about gender equality provided the rationale for explaining why principles involving privacy and choice could not be straightforwardly applied to the issue of abortion decision making. In stressing the difference of the court's task, the Crown argued that 'in this instance' the Supreme Court justices had to determine what liberty meant. It was also the Crown's contention that the question had been answered satisfactorily by the Canadian legislature.

Although the legal answer had qualified the usual meaning of liberty, the Crown asked the court to consider that the limitation placed on the universality of health care was actually necessary for protecting female liberty. Various Crown submissions asserted that the state had an obligation to intervene in instances where foetal development could lead to a deterioration of maternal health. Because the state was protecting physical and psychological well-being, argued the Crown, the law could not be said to be interfering with maternal choice. If biology restricted female liberty, it was the law that would give women some choice. As Crown Attorney Pennington put it, '*The law protects women.* When putting aside the state's interest in protecting life, the state cannot then ensure the women's consent to the procedure and protect them from the psychological problems the decision could bring. It also protects the women's right to safety and requires that a medical judgement is necessary. Her liberty is not really constrained if safety and consent are being protected by the legislation' (oral submission to the Ontario Court of Apppeal by Crown Attorney Pennington, 7 May 1985).

Within courtroom discourse, female liberty was given an exceptional meaning: the freedom to apply for an exemption from reproductive obligation if that obligation impaired reproductive health. This shift from 'choice versus life' to 'health versus life' was an important one..If repro-

ductive labour had been considered a social activity subject to female volition, normal legal logic would not have allowed state intervention into
private decisions concerning one's care of others. The Crown reasoning
reversed this logic: it was the exceptional circumstance that would allow
women to be absolved of their maternal responsibility to nurture. If, for
reasons of health, a woman could not undertake her reproductive tasks,
the state would permit the medical establishment to respond to her
needs. In normal circumstances the foetus was to continue to be entitled
to its enjoyment of maternal health, but in exceptional circumstances a
woman could apply for a state-sanctioned welfare right.

By equating social justice with the benevolent protection of powerless
subjects, contemporary legal reasoning can provide a method by which
these subjects can 'consent' to the suspension of normal liberty rights so
that they may be 'helped.' If nature has made all women powerless during pregnancy, the role of law is to compensate them for this biological
handicap; only a welfare right can ensure that women will not be unduly
harmed by the liberty rights of those who are not so handicapped. The
various Crown attorneys at the Morgentaler appeals picked up this social-
justice theme of legal reasoning by arguing that providing abortion services on a welfare basis was an important component in providing assistance to women in danger of victimization. They reverted to social-code
assumptions, however, in order to equate pregnancy with maternal powerlessness. Here, it was proposed that a woman's physical and psychological make-up during pregnancy made her an easy victim of the misguided
intentions or inferior skills of others. It was because a woman is vulnerable to victimization that her liberty was viewed as being best protected
when law steps in to ensure that her decisions are not manipulated.

In turning the decision-making power over to the medical profession,
the law gave it the responsibility to assess when women were in danger,
even from themselves. At each of the appeal hearings, the various Crown
attorneys portrayed women who sought abortions as individuals who, acting against their natural inclination, were apt to make 'irrational' or emotionally based decisions. At both the Supreme Court of Ontario and the
Supreme Court of Canada, it was emphasized that 'a medically sound
opinion is needed if women are not to risk psychological problems.'
Without the law, a woman's emotions made her decisions suspect, and
without the law, she would be at the mercy of incompetent abortionists.

Speaking in the language of autonomy and stressing concepts of
choice and privacy, the Crown arguments retained the gloss of a neutral
consideration of liberty rights, but it is clear that liberty for potential

mothers meant something very different from that intended by the legal norm. Selecting from both contemporary legal reasoning and social-code stereotypes, the Crown contended that the TAC process gave women a right to a greater degree of protection than a liberty right would allow.

According to the court, women had a great deal to be protected from. Not only did they themselves and incompetent medical practitioners pose an ever-present threat, but foetal activity also could leave them vulnerable. If pregnancy could be dangerous to a woman's medical welfare, only the professional expertise of medical science could reliably assess the danger and weigh it against the rights of foetuses. Thus, the law was really protecting women from the 'deviancy' of others in that it provided 'relief from criminal sanction where there was a reliable, independent and medically sound judgement that the life or health of the mother would be or would be likely to be endangered' (Statement of Fact and Law filed on behalf of the Attorney General of Canada to the Supreme Court of Canada, no. 27).

By referring to the normalcy of female responsiveness, the exceptionality of female autonomy, and the deviancy of those who would subvert this natural law for self-interested purposes, the discourse established the state interest as its obligation to protect foetal autonomy by ensuring the reproductive health of the prospective mother. Within this discursive framework, a pregnant woman had both her decision-making rights and her access to resources restricted in a way that was unlike that of other Canadian citizens: while her health was to be protected by a restriction on her liberty, her liberty was protected by a limitation on her access to medical resources. This double restriction could only be accomplished by speaking about maternal choice as something that preceded the state's obligation to provide welfare. In the picture of reproductive reality that is provided, women have 'choice' in the decision to enter into a relationship that might lead to pregnancy, and they have a further 'choice' to seek medical advice about their health. Because of the potential of adverse consequences arising from these decisions, the state provides a standard that will protect women and ensure 'quality control.' At the same time, the law will protect them from the adverse consequences of these personal options. In other words, the state affirms a woman's right to protection from blatant victimization at the hands of those whose primary rights are liberty rights. However, the particular patterning of rights that were allocated by Crown discourse were said to be protecting something more than the health of women. They also protected the health of a moral order that was concerned with values of community and caring.

To Protect Morality Is to Control Women

Underlying the Crown arguments for a law that would enable medical science to protect the health of women was a deeper structure that tied the protection of women's reproductive responsibilities to the protection of the essence of morality itself. This underlying concern was most explicitly argued in an oral submission asking the Supreme Court of Ontario to consider carefully the consequences of making reproductive choice the right of women and not of doctors: 'There are problems created by handing this right over to the unrestricted power of women ... Far too often we see some who find themselves in financially or psychologically poor circumstances ... [Such a right] would result in some who would decline their natural motherly inclinations. To give this right is legitimating this kind of response and life is abandoned to their arbitrary decision. If threat of punishment is removed, [it] is dangerous in that societal morals will be impaired' (oral submission to the Supreme Court of Ontario, 7 May 1985).

From protecting women against choosing 'instantaneous convenience' over their natural disposition for sacrificing self-interest, it was an easy (if surprising) step for the Crown to invoke feminist arguments about the nature of liberal theory. In an unexpected twist, Crown Attorney Jablonsky buttressed his argument for controlling women by referring to the socialist-feminist critique of capitalist relations, going so far as to cite the work of a Canadian pro-choice advocate, Shelley Gavigan, to support his contention that 'not just individual interests are involved but there are social interests to be considered' (oral submission to Supreme Court of Canada by Crown Attorney Jablonsky, 10 October 1986).

In following this theme of collective responsibilities, the Crown also made the case for linking the Canadian abortion law to social-code understandings about the distinctive nature of Canada as a national community. Stressing that Canadian culture embodies a greater degree of concern for community than the United States does, the Crown asked the court to reject the American solution and articulated a version of community characterized by female self-sacrifice. Some Crown arguments were more explicit in their focus on the importance of ideas about community and collective well-being, but all implicitly linked female self-sacrifice and obligations to that preservation. The tenor of the Crown argument suggested that if the law were to allow women the right to choose when and where they would reproduce, this would promote a situation detrimental to the distinctive fabric of Canadian society. The tacit plea was that the court had the power to prevent the sacrifice of motherhood at the altar of rampant individualism.

Despite the fact that the legal terminology of courtroom discussion continually invoked a surface frame of prioritizing, balancing, and accommodating the competing rights of all individuals, the relationships that were being organized depended on the conception that women are the preservers of a humane society. If men have to be coerced into acting towards others with care and concern, the regulation of the capacity of women to nurture would seem to be necessary in order to preserve any semblance of love and intimacy in an otherwise hostile world. Implicit in all of the Crown's arguments was this underlying fear that allowing women the normal legal right to decline to empower others would ultimately lead to a loss of all care and concern.

While many have commented that this gendered division of labour rests on the separation of the public and private spheres of life, interwoven with this division of tasks is an equally important separation of moral imperatives, a separation that is captured by the difference 'between a man's cultural world and a women's cultural world' (Miller 1987:347). Although the latter has been distorted and undervalued in most discussions about social control, the ongoing maintenance of a women's culture is an important aspect of reproducing hegemony. While women have been conceptualized primarily as victims of social control, it is clear that they have also participated as agents of it (Miller 1987). The Crown submissions seem to have recognized this role while simultaneously depicting it in deterministic terms. On the one hand, aspects of women's culture are valued in the abstract, as is motherhood, while, on the other hand, they are portrayed as part of a moral framework that is naturally associated with women rather than being part of a world view that is socially constituted. Where social action is then thought to be necessary is in the control and protection of communitarian values through state policies that will regulate and protect women.

The appeal to community came through loud and clear in the oral arguments of both the federal and provincial Crown attorneys. In various ways they submitted that if reproductive activities were to be judged on the same basis as productive ones – if pregnant women (and by extension all women) were to be allowed the same rights as men – then Canadian society would be set on the road to either fascism or moral anarchy. The fears articulated by these Crown submissions cannot be said to be idiosyncratic; they have a well-established base not only in popular culture but in moral and legal reasoning. As Boyle (1985:704) notes, 'Centrist and right-wing scholars ... have always nursed dark, Hobbesian fears of [this] slippery slope to anarchy or fascism, a slippery slope that is at present walled off by a fragile belief in a government of "laws not men."' But the logic of law is itself built on the belief that regulation will normally be unnecessary because the general existence of a women's culture has eliminated much of the need for formal moral regulation.

The moral order, as we know it, depends on the generally unspoken expectation that normal women will not act as men are supposed to act. The supposed essence of womanhood is presumably the one natural force that will keep human selfishness and irresponsibility under control. In becoming synonymous with notions of moral care, women's activities within the private world of family have been viewed, both in popular culture and in academic theory, as necessary for keeping the self-interest of the marketplace within clearly demarcated boundaries (Lasch 1977; Elshtain 1982). If, in the contemporary context, women cease to perform the activities that preserve the moral order, and if the male human nature is naturally self-interested, then either moral anarchy will prevail or law will have to step in to override the liberty rights of all individuals, an alternative leading to fascism. Thus, those who adopt either teleological or deontoligical world views have a stake in ensuring that female responsiveness continues.

In the various Crown arguments, emphasis was placed on the protection of social connection and moral responsibility, but the social and moral interests that were to be protected became synonymous with a protection of the existing structure of heterosexual relations. Because reproduction is not taken to be essential to the legal code, the problem of abortion could only be addressed through some kind of intersection of social- and legal-code assumptions. Adversaries in the Canadian court chose to do this in different ways. In challenging the Crown's position and the unfairness of the law, Dr Morgentaler's defence lawyer, Morris Manning, did not address the underlying belief that female nurturance within heterosexual relations is the bedrock of a moral society. He did, however, feel called upon to address the threat that overturning the abortion law would undermine women's willingness to carry out the responsibilities of care and concern for their families. In his address to the court, Mr Manning refuted the assumption that, left to their own devices, women might choose self-interest over family responsibilities. He cited evidence from a Hawaiian study, which showed that the decision of women to terminate their pregnancies was 'not a rejection of motherhood but actually improved family situations.' Further, he argued that a Czechoslovakian study illustrated a corresponding detrimental effect on family life when-ever abortions were refused to women who requested them. Whereas Crown Attorney Pennington's argument explicitly revealed the underly-ing patriarchal assumption that it is necessary to control and dominate 'natural' maternal nurturance, Mr Manning's brief did nothing to chal-lenge the equally patriarchal idea that responding to the needs of others is primarily the responsibility of women. It simply sought to illustrate the fact that not only is state control unnecessary but it undermines the tradi-tional nurturing role of women. The difference of opinion was related to questions about the role of law and not the role of women.

The belief that human nature is essentially self-interested – combined with a fear that women, if given the choice, might opt for this human self-ishness – provided the discursive space for grounding the liberal argu-ment that while the law should interfere in family functioning only in exceptional instances, any breakdown in female responsiveness consti-tuted such an exception. The state has an interest, according to the Crown, in ensuring that the nature of reproductive relationships remains distinct from those that characterize 'normal' public interactions.

Although the symbolic images presented by the Crown are based on the actual experiences of individuals within families (women have largely been responsible for the collective requirements of their families), it is also based on a belief that public-sphere competition is unavoidable and that an aggressive and self-interested male subjectivity is equally inevi-table. For many women, this argument has hegemonic force precisely because they experience heterosexual relations in the manner described by the Crown.[2] Those experiences, however, are interpreted within a par-ticular mind-set where the nature of women is synonymous with love, fam-ily, and community. The message received is that to allow women the self-interested autonomy of a liberty right undermines the morality of all that human beings hold dear, so a law that protects the 'natural' order of gen-der relations safeguards personal and community relationships from assault by the marketplace. Such interpretations create ambivalence because they offer women the option either of freedom without caring or of caring without freedom.

Step by step, the Crown set out a gendered explanation of why, *in*

2 Surveys conducted in the United States and Canada have asked women about the way men generally act within heterosexual relationships. In each case, a majority of women agreed with the description of men as predictably selfish and lacking any motivation to consider the wishes and interests of their female partners.

this instance, women need to be treated differently. First, reproductive activity is different from the norm of human activity. Human activity is self-interested, and, where pregnancy is concerned, there are other interests to be considered. Secondly, while pregnancy is different from normal human activity, abortion is itself an exception: to make an abortion decision does not sacrifice self-interest for the good of another. Thirdly, because women are essentially powerless, they require a legal welfare right to protect them from their own irrationality as well as from the self-interested actions of others. Finally, the state accepts an obligation to protect women and, by extension, to protect the moral order itself. The regulation of abortion through the therapeutic process 'assures to the female person some quality control in the performance of this medical procedure' and, most importantly, ensures that societal morals will not be impaired by the 'lack of standards' that abortion on demand implies.

Doctors: The Responsibility to Determine Necessity and the Right to Withhold a Response

Under the 1969 amendment to the Criminal Code, the medical profession was granted both a monopoly on the provision of abortion services and the legal liberty to refuse particular women access to that service. According to the law, women had a welfare right to the health services necessary to terminate their pregnancies, provided that doctors determined that this exemption was warranted. Health became a welfare right available to those women who could prove one of two propositions: their powerlessness or their lack of femininity. If their powerlessness had resulted in their being victimized or if they lacked the capacity to provide nurture to others, they could be exempted from the responsibilities expected of them. The proving of one of these propositions asserted their essential femininity, while the proving of the other asserted their lack of it, but each reaffirmed the normal pattern of gender relations.

Whether a woman seeking an abortion was a 'good' woman or a 'bad' one, the right to determine the responses that would meet her needs was denied her. In gaining a welfare right, a legal subject must forgo the normal liberty right because the principle that distinguishes welfare-rights logic and links it to liberty-rights reasoning is the premise that if a person provides a response to another, that person will retain the right to determine when, how, or whether to respond. As long as the responding party is not compelled to respond, the belief is that no liberty rights are being undermined. Because autonomy and need are conceptually polarized, being visibly in need of a response or a resource that another controls brings with it the loss of the right to define both the need and the response required. Thus, when one speaks of state-provided welfare – the formalization of a response to need – it is assumed that the person in need will not be given the right to define either his or her own need or the response that will alleviate the need.

According to welfare-rights logic, the state's obligation is to determine a general standard for response to need and to appoint a neutral arbitration process to determine whether the circumstances meet the criteria of the standard. According to the Crown, it is incumbent on the state to set down the standard by which need can be assessed. In the words of one brief filed with the court, to leave an abortion decision up to 'the mother alone, the aborting physician alone, or both ... would for practical purposes have amounted to condoning "abortion on demand," "abortion on request," "convenience abortion," or "abortion as a method of birth control" (as it has been variously described), and would in effect have been tantamount to *eliminating any standard whatsoever*' (Statement of Fact and Law filed on behalf of the Attorney General of Canada to the Supreme Court of Ontario, vol. 1, no. 34; emphasis added). In this statement, the Crown not only sets up the basis for arguing that regulation is necessary, but it implies that without a legal standard abortion decisions will be made irrationally. Although this is a prerogative of liberty rights, it is not one of welfare rights. Further, the statement groups together a number of situations on the basis of the automatic equation of human volition with self-interest. Treating convenience and birth control as equivalent presumes that using contraception or seeking an abortion is something that women do, not as part of fulfilling reproductive responsibility but as a convenience for themselves; and that abortion may be a more 'convenient' alternative than any other means of contraception. If the law does not specify a medical standard, what, the Crown asks, will prevent a woman from taking the convenient but immoral and medically dangerous path of requesting or demanding an abortion for a frivolous reason?

In most instances, the medical profession is culturally presumed and legally mandated to be the 'expert' body best equipped to define and respond to health needs. By linking abortion need to health, the Criminal Code amendments recognized this expertise and granted the medical profession a monopoly on the provision of abortion services. Medical expertise was the criterion that allowed doctors the sole right to define whether a woman required an abortion and to respond accordingly.[3] Because health was the standard by which a woman could claim the medical services required to secure an abortion, it comprised the entire definition of reproductive need and doctors became the agents responsible for assessing the degree of need.

The medical monopoly on the provision of abortion services implied that the profession had both a collective right to exclusive medical practice and a public responsibility for determining the line between legality and illegality. The rights and responsibilities of the medical profession as a whole were interdependent within the terms of the law. Because doctors were designated the agents responsible for promoting 'the state's interest in balancing maternal health and foetal life,' the exclusivity of their right to provide abortion services equipped them with the resources to carry out the task of determining what circumstances interfered with foetal liberty and maternal welfare.

The legal obligation of the profession to define need and the legal right of individual doctors to decide whether they would respond to any particular need were two separate issues, involving a collective obligation of the profession and an individual right of doctors. The professional monopoly on determining reproductive need was not in question during the court hearings. Rather, the court was being asked to determine whether the rights of individual doctors were being limited by the procedures required by law and, if so, whether this resulted in unequal treatment of women. Although the collective right of the profession was not at issue, there was a clear tension between the profession's mandate to act as an agent of the state and the autonomy of individual doctors. Of concern was whether the liberty rights of individual doctors were being compromised by the collective responsibility of the profession.

Whereas the balancing of foetal and maternal rights was the primary focus of the abortion law, the central concern of the courtroom debate was the effect of this law on the rights and responsibilities of physicians, collectively as a profession and individually as practitioners. The question of whether the law put the welfare of women at risk brought to centre stage the parallel issue of a physician's liberty right to define health in his or her own terms and to respond accordingly. The ensuing debate focused on whether the legal procedures involved in fulfilling the profes-

3 The normal rationality assumed for the medical profession is the metaphoric basis that permits the depiction of 'rational man' within contemporary legal theory (see chapter 5 for an articulation of this characterization).

sion's obligation hampered or enabled individual doctors to deal with actual situations of medical necessity. If women could not secure abortions without the provision of a medical response, the problem for the court became, To what degree does the law infringe on the right of the profession to fulfil its responsibility to women? Does the law itself impair the doctors' right to determine their own responses to situations of need?

Although the law highlighted the health of women, whether this was in fact achieved was not the issue as far as the Crown was concerned. According to the statement of one attorney, 'It is in error to focus on Parliament's emphasis on health since the primary intent is protection of life. It is not fundamentally or primarily a matter of the health of women. The intent was *to inject a third person into the decision-making process*' (oral submission to the Supreme Court of Canada by Crown Attorney Wein, 9 October 1986; emphasis added). In redirecting attention to the 'third person in the decision-making process,' the Crown shifted the major focus to a question of whether the legal process by which a doctor undertook the professional responsibility to determine reproductive needs constituted an undue infringement on the right of individual doctors to determine the parameters of their own activity. Once the Crown had discursively disposed of a woman's right to choose by turning her liberty right into a welfare one, its attorneys turned their attention to the main point of contention, which was the reason for the hearings in the first place: the relative primacy of Dr Morgentaler's medical responsibility for upholding the state's interest (to protect morality by balancing foetal liberty rights and maternal welfare rights) and his private right to exercise professional autonomy.

The Crown held that the primary intent of the law was to protect foetal life, but it nevertheless disputed the charge that the law constituted an infringement on the liberty rights of individual doctors. Its counsel disagreed that a doctor's right to respond to health was being limited by the legal standard. In order to claim a welfare right, there must be a legal standard or, as the Crown stated, 'when one deals with necessity, there must be an objective standard of whether necessity actually exists' (oral submission by Crown Attorney Blacklock, 19 October 1986). In providing doctors with the standard of health, the Crown insisted that the law had also provided them with the means for dealing with a large variety of circumstances involving need. Therefore, it was the law itself that allowed doctors to attend to a woman's health requirements whenever her circumstances, in their professional opinion, made abortion a necessity. Because the law was the instrument that gave the medical profession a way to respond to cases of need, a doctor could not then claim to have broken the law for reasons of necessity. According to this position, then, the law did not hamper doctors from performing their professional duty or exercising their liberty rights; it was in fact the law that *enabled* them to exercise their liberty right and, in the process, to assist women.

Liberty Rights and the Professional Responsibilities of Medical Practitioners

A number of interpretations have been posited concerning the work of legal advocates in the courtroom. The image of a lawyer acting as a 'hired gun' doing the bidding of a client has been contrasted with the image of lawyer as 'double agent' playing a confidence game in order to secure client acquiescence to existing institutional processes (Harrington 1994). Dr Morgentaler's defence lawyer (and by implication the advocate for women) presented himself to the pro-choice community as the 'hired gun' who could translate their political issue into legal terms and thus challenge the existing institutional process. Despite his discursive opposition, however, Defence Lawyer Manning was performing the ideological task of illustrating how the performance of reproductive work fitted within the rules of the legal paradigm. To achieve this, he called on presuppositions about medical relationships.

The core of Manning's challenge to the law – on behalf of Morgentaler's right to perform abortions without going through the TAC process – was that the legal process for determining the need for a medical response frequently worked against a doctor's actual ability to respond to that need, for legal constraints on individual doctors led to an inequity in the provision of health care to women. Manning argued that the procedures set down by law served to erode the main objective of the legislation which, in his legal opinion, was the protection of a woman's health. The problem of access, he charged, was not a result of a lack of medical concern for women's needs; rather, it was caused by the legal infringement on a doctor's right to respond to any particular woman when she or he chose to do so. In his words, 'The issue is not access per se but the denial of access by law. It is a denial of rights ... Once Parliament enters the field it must do so in a way that doesn't create inequalities' (oral submission to the Supreme Court of Canada by Morris Manning, 10 October 1986). From this side of the courtroom, the problem of inequity was created by the state's encroachment on the liberty rights of individual physicians, specifically, the 'doctor's right to assist a woman' (Manning Factum, presented to the Supreme Court of Canada, no. 37). In other words, the defence argued that the law not only interfered with Dr Morgentaler's liberty right but it also interfered with his professional responsibility to protect the health of women.

In contesting the process through which doctors could legitimately respond to abortion needs, Manning drew the court's attention to the fact that no other criminal law required a panel of experts to determine the legality of a particular action before its performance. The requirement that the professional expertise of individual doctors be subordinated to the collective obligation of the profession was, in his terms, an undue interference with a doctor's liberty right. The conflict, as he saw it, was between the collective responsibility of the profession and the liberty rights of individual doctors. His defence of Dr. Morgentaler clearly came down on the side of the latter because, he argued, this autonomy was required in order to fulfil the medical responsibility satisfactorily. His conceptual logic did not stray beyond the boundaries of the legal paradigm of differentiating between primary and secondary legal subjects; it simply illustrated how the law encroached on normal medical liberty, thus diluting the profession's ability to carry out the primary intent of the law – to provide for the welfare of patients with exceptional needs. State patriarchy, he might have said, depends on ensuring that its agents have the tools to carry out its tasks.

Although the various Crown attorneys certainly did not agree with Manning that the primary objective was a welfare one – the protection of a woman's health – their consensus was that the law did in fact accomplish this secondary objective even as it protected what they viewed as the primary intent – ensuring the foetus's right to life. Unlike Manning, who depicted doctors as primary legal subjects and women as secondary ones, Crown reasoning revealed that the law intended to preserve foetal liberty and protect maternal welfare. Moreover, each Crown attorney pointed out that the state's interest was served by the same process that allowed an individual physician to determine whether or not to respond to a woman's request for an abortion. Since physicians had been legally given a monopoly on both defining and responding to need, the Crown pointed out that nothing within the law prevented a doctor from either giving or withholding medical services. Simply by asserting their collective professional responsibility to define health, doctors were invoking their private right to exercise medical autonomy. The rationale for giving the medical profession the right to determine necessity in the first place was deemed to be sufficiently broad to allow an individual doctor to exercise a private liberty right without infringement in practice. The breadth of autonomy open to doctors was emphasized by Crown Attorney Jablonsky, who stated, 'The World Health Organization definition has been used; it is a wide definition and should be. [The breadth of] the definition is an indication of the flexibility of the law' (oral submission to the Supreme Court of Canada, 10 October 1986). Because the law ensured that the health standard was flexible enough to accommodate any particular doctor's definition, it was stressed that the collective responsibility of the medical profession to provide abortion services corresponded with the individual right of any doctor to give or withhold his or her professional responses. Thus, the Crown concluded that there can be no conflict between the rights of the collective and the rights of the individual.

Because the law gave doctors the exclusive right to make abortion decisions and to determine their own responses, the Crown argued that meeting the criteria of the law was demonstrably within any doctor's professional capacity. First, the justification for any abortion had to be framed in terms of the standard of 'health'; that is, a woman could be exempted if she was declared physically or mentally unable to perform her biological role. This rationale was easily met by any doctor, since it was the law itself that allowed doctors to make this determination according to a definition that encompassed a wide range of circumstances. Second, rationales had to be framed in terms that conceptually posed foetal and maternal needs in opposition to one another; that is, the foetal requirement of a response from its prospective mother posed a threat to the life or health of that woman. Inasmuch as there is always some risk involved in undertaking any pregnancy, and considering the broad parameters of health, a doctor could always frame the justification in terms that implied that a woman would be victimized if 'foetal activity' was allowed to continue. Thirdly, the determination of necessity had to be derived from an 'objective' medical judgment; that is, there should be no suggestion of 'abortion on demand' according to the 'subjective' interpretation of the woman involved. The Crown concluded that the law simply prevented a woman from making an independent decision concerning her own need; therefore, a doctor's capacity to pursue his or her self-interest was unaffected.

The Crown concluded, with considerable justification, that it was not the law that prevented individual doctors from performing abortions. Although the structure of hospital committees often resulted in a limitation of a particular doctor's ability to perform an abortion, the law itself did not limit an individual doctor's liberty right to decide that an abortion was necessary. According to the reasoning of the Crown's attorneys, all that the law had limited was the range of rationales that doctors could give for their actions, and Crown submissions stressed that the legal requirement to provide official rationales could not be viewed as a restriction on medical autonomy inasmuch as the justifications for responding or not responding were already allowable within the law. They consistently reiterated that it was not law that victimizes women but law that provides for the welfare of women, even when women themselves do not understand what is good for them. Although the Crown attorneys sought to illustrate that the state's primary interest was in ensuring a foetal liberty right, they also argued that, by protecting foetal life, the law was also protecting a woman's welfare right to health. The arguments they used to justify this position often slipped into rhetoric that was overtly paternalistic.

The Crown contention that Dr Morgentaler's own liberty rights were not really at issue had a great deal of substance. Any particular abortion performed by Dr Morgentaler could abstractly have qualified for a TAC stamp of approval. Providing he had been willing to subordinate both a woman's choice and her health to the requirements of the law, his own freedom was not restricted. So long as he had participated in the reproduction of hegemony, no infringement on decision making concerning his self-interest would have occurred. He was not compelled to respond to the interests of another: he had a choice. In reality, it was the medical obligation to restrict women's choices that Dr Morgentaler was defying. According to patriarchal codes, such responsiveness to the concerns of others is an obligation of women and not of normal legal subjects.

Once again, the Crown was contextualizing legal theory to what was occurring in actual practice. Solid evidence exists to illustrate that therapeutic abortion committees did not in effect limit any individual doctor's decision to perform an abortion. The concept of 'health' as the allowable justification meant that there was rarely any limitation of a physician's discretionary powers.[4] The implication of the Crown's description of the 'flexibility' of the law was that Dr Morgentaler could legally have responded to any circumstance that he believed involved necessity. What he could not legally do was to allow that necessity to be defined in his patient's own terms.

4 A number of studies have demonstrated that the 1969 amendment to the Criminal Code did not significantly affect medical practice; rather, the law simply institutionalized what the medical profession was doing while providing a defence against prosecution (see in particular Smith and Wineberg 1970). The shortage of committees and hospitals with committees affected medical decision making to a greater degree than the change in legal regulation did.

The Crown attorneys made clear to the court that where doctors were concerned, negative law took precedence over any obligation of the state to safeguard the health of women. They contended that the sole issue to be determined by the court was whether any doctor was compelled to respond to the demands of others. Unlike their discussions about the rights of pregnant women, their depositions concerning medical autonomy stressed the lack of compulsion to care for interests other than one's own, and they sought to demonstrate that nothing in the law's requirements compelled any particular doctor to respond to any particular abortion need. In protecting liberty rights, the compulsion to respond to others or a constraint of one's own self-interest are the primary factors to be avoided, and legal precedents were cited to the effect that it is 'the absence of coercion and constraint that is the important factor' and that 'the real issue is not whether a doctor should assist ... Doctors are not mandated beyond that given in the section of the Criminal Code ... [T]here are provisions that will allow doctors *not* to participate' (oral submission to the Supreme Court of Canada by Crown Attorney Wein, 6, 9 October 1986).

According to the Crown's logic, the law has said that there is no necessity if a doctor has not determined that there is one. But once a doctor has determined that need does in fact exist, the law provides the means for that doctor to escape sanction regardless of whether she or he decides to respond. The provisions of the law have taken care of all possible situations of necessity, so necessity cannot be used as a defence for breaking the law. Doctors themselves always have a choice, but women never have a need for an abortion unless doctors so determine. Thus, no necessity can exist for which a legitimate response is unavailable.

The Crown's reasoning is tautological in that the law sets the framework for defending itself. Under the law, women need abortions only for reasons of health, and doctors have been given the monopoly in defining the health needs that necessitate abortion. Thus, a woman's health needs can never be violated by the terms of the law. Since, under the law, physicians are the only individuals allowed to determine when abortions are required, it is the law that provides a doctor with a choice: to respond according to prescribed procedure or to withhold medical services. In either case, doctors may make a choice without fear of sanction, so their liberty rights cannot be said to have been violated. The logic concerning medical rights of decision making is clearly different from that used in discussing the rights of pregnant women. In contrast to a pregnant woman's responsibility to support foetal rights, nothing in the law compels a doctor to support women's rights. Inasmuch as the state does not compel the responses of particular doctors, there is no infringement of liberty rights involved. In this, a doctor's rights correspond to the legal norm, and this strand of courtroom argument does not have to concern itself with specifying exceptional instances whereby a doctor might refuse access to abortion services requested (or demanded) by a woman.

Despite their opposing positions, lawyers on both sides of the courtroom were acting as 'conceptive ideologists' (Cain 1994) on behalf of the legal paradigm. As they translated the opposing political positions into appropriate legal terminology, their opposing arguments affirmed the legal code's portrayal of reality – namely, independent life upheld by a patriarchal control of female nurture. In defending Dr Morgentaler, Mr Manning did not explicitly question the underlying asymmetry of welfare and liberty rights.[5] The evidence he presented to illustrate that both a woman's welfare right and a doctor's liberty right were compromised remained within a frame that guaranteed women and doctors different kinds of rights; that is, women could be exempted from responsibility for foetal requirements only in exceptional circumstances, but individual doctors were under no compulsion to respond to women's health requirements. The distinction between a doctor's rights and responsibilities and those of a woman rests on the belief that male responses are socially structured, involving human volition, whereas female responses are biologically mandated, involving passive acquiescence. The Crown's reasoning relied on a gendered subtext: for women, responsiveness to others was the important consideration while, for doctors, the exercise of choice in the pursuit of self-interest took precedence. Unlike the welfare-rights logic used to discuss a pregnant woman's exceptional right to evade responding to her developing foetus, the Crown's rebuttal of Manning's position – that a doctor must have the right to determine need –

5 A continuing issue is whether Manning could have done otherwise. Fineman (1994:223) has noted that 'the transformative potential of feminist thought is blunted because in order to even have a chance to be incorporated into and considered compatible with legal theory, feminist thought must adapt, even if it does not totally conform, to the words and concepts of legal discourse. Feminism may enter as the challenger, but the tools inevitably employed are those of the androphile master.' This is, in fact, what happened. Manning was hired to adapt feminist thought into the words and concepts of legal discourse. I am not so sure, however, that such incorporation is inevitable, that one cannot construct prefigurative discourses. As events described in part 4 of this book suggest, Manning did not share the standpoint of women and was thus not the best person to attempt this creative work. On the other hand, it can also be argued that Manning's strategy was the one most likely to achieve the pro-choice objective of overturning the law.

was posed within the negative framework of liberty and self-interest. Dr Morgentaler could not claim that his rights were violated when it was women's liberty rights that he was championing. In reality, his crime was the breaking of the medical obligation to ensure that women were denied choice whenever they were provided with welfare. This medical obligation, the Crown implied, was necessary if women were to be adequately protected. Dr Morgentaler was being legally held accountable for his failure to uphold the patriarchal order of society. His practice was legitimating a woman's own interpretation of her need, and in doing so he was challenging the ideological underpinnings of structural inequality.

Private/Public Statuses: Natural Maternal Sacrifice and Self-Interested Human Nature

Privacy is the underlying principle on which liberty rights are based. Privacy provides the climate in which individuals supposedly can pursue their purposes free from the hindrance of others. In the public/private split around which human social relations are organized, family functioning constitutes a basic example of an individual's freedom from state intervention. At the abstract level, family privacy is generally viewed as a unitary concept, whereby all family members are assumed to share a single reality of shared interest (Eichler 1983). With a legal status similar to that of a single individual, the family is guaranteed privacy by the same logic as that which guarantees autonomy to any single individual. Based on this conception of the family as one unit, law traditionally has refrained from interfering with the private structuring of relationships within the family. In this sense, the family is conceptually synonymous with a private realm where individuals may be free from outside regulation.

Court traditions have been notoriously reluctant to accept that women might have interests that differ from those of the family unit. However, the Canadian abortion law was built on the presumption that, in exceptional cases, they might. The arguments of the Crown in defence of the law assumed an adversarial relation between a pregnant woman's interest and the presumed interest of her foetus, a relation that was apparently unlike the relations of normal families. In response to the challenge that the legal requirements constituted an exceptional intrusion into the privacy of the doctor-patient relationship, the Crown reiterated its contention that 'there is no other procedure like an abortion – so a panel is justifiable and explainable' (oral submission 10 October 1986, Jablonsky).

Because abortion is 'different,' Crown counsel emphasized the moral and medical necessity for overturning a woman's right to make private decisions, but where doctors were concerned, they stressed that the TAC process was not an encroachment on private decision making. They contended that the law actually enhanced a doctor's liberty rights because the twin issues of autonomy and response had been rendered compatible by its standard. Just as they had previously reasoned that 'choice' and 'life' were rendered compatible by the standard of 'health,' they implied that the medical profession's responsibility to ensure a moral social order and a doctor's right to individual autonomy were enhanced by this standard.

It was the 'unnatural' possibility that a prospective mother would not put the welfare of her foetus first that led the Crown to argue that the state has a 'compelling interest' which – in this instance – overrides the privacy rule. Because the decision of a pregnant woman to abort is an intrusion into the developmental interests of the foetus, the privacy normally accorded the family unit will no longer apply. The activities women perform in support of their families are subsumed under the interests of the family unit only if these activities appear to support the interests of others within that unit. For a woman to choose abortion is to withhold her body and her emotional energies from those who can naturally expect this support. Because reproductive choice implies a deficiency in female responsiveness, the Canadian abortion law can be seen as a legislative attempt to protect the mythical independence that is legally assumed for human beings in the original position. As the Crown noted, 'the 1969 amendments are all designed for the protection of the developing human life in the womb against any casual or convenience destruction at the instance of the pregnant woman' (Statement of Fact and Law filed on behalf of the Attorney General of Canada to the Supreme Court of Ontario).

Because liberty rights are based on notions of self-interested individuals, being pregnant and providing nurture are the defining characteristics of the legal otherness of women. Normally, then, women within the family setting will fall outside legal regulation and legal protection. The key word is 'normally.' The abnormal situation that brings women into the competing rights framework is the decision to withhold reproductive labour. Women who seek an abortion are rejecting a passive determination of their fate and therefore are undermining the patriarchal rule which family privacy protects. For a woman to refuse her acquiescence to biological determinism is to place herself in an adversarial relationship with her foetus, and legal reasoning requires that the state then step in to mediate the opposing interests.

In recommending state intervention in family decisions concerning pregnancy, the Crown was not challenging the idea that the interests of all family members are normally unitary in nature. By insisting that private family decisions 'cannot *always* be considered inviolate,' the various Crown attorneys did not venture outside the ideological frame where women's interests are naturally synonymous with those of their families. Indeed, in reaffirming the belief that abortion is unnatural, they were upholding the metaphor of normal maternal self-sacrifice. Within a negative-rights paradigm, it is only when women refuse to accept the normality of passively acceding to the demands of others that the state is expected to intervene. The public/private distinction remained intact even though it was to be qualified in 'exceptional' instances; the Crown defended intervention in pregnancy-related decisions as being necessary only where abortions were contemplated.

The assumption that reproductive activity is nonvolitional and biologically determined is a vital component of this logic. A woman who requests an abortion is refusing to accept her biological destiny. Since such a refusal involves an act of human volition, it is then, and only then, that the state has an obligation to consider the relative primacy of the opposing motivations. The Crown is ultimately arguing that if women do not wish to accept a biological determination of their reproductive labour power, the unity of interests (on which family privacy is based) has been broken. In such instances, the foetus may gain the status of a distinct legal subject with liberty rights of its own. The reasoning involved depends on the unstated assumption that a human essence pre-exists and is independent of the reproductive labour of women.

Within the ideological frame of patriarchal capitalism, a decision not to be pregnant rescues a woman from her status as other. It brings her out of the realm of the private unitary family unit and subjects her choices to legal regulation. The decision to reject the presumably passive self-sacrifice of maternity then suggests a need for general standards – where the liberty rights of individuals compete.

When one equates the relationship between self-interest and response to others with the conceptual dichotomy between activity and passivity, the consequences of allowing reproductive choice is to leave 'wholly unprotected' (ibid.) the care and concern that supports individual initiative. According to this logic, women do not have conscious standards for determining their responses of care and concern; these responses are natural to their being. Other-oriented behaviour is presumably based on emotion and is therefore outside the scope of conscious human volition. The language of the Crown argument draws on and reaffirms the androcentric belief that all volitional activity is essentially self-interested and that the responses that support it may be left unquestioned as part of a naturally accessible environment.

A contradiction runs through the liberal ideal that women should be allowed to exhibit the human nature that is implied by the legal norm. If human nature is self-interested, and if women demand to be counted as human, who will perform the taken-for-granted activities that attend to human needs? Who will ensure the continuation of the species if any and all women are allowed to claim the right not to be interfered with when they choose not to respond to the wishes of others? The Crown argument implies that the question need never be answered because the very essence of a woman's nature is other; since women provide the conditions that enable the interests of others, female self-interest exists only in relation to those so served. A woman's decision to refuse self-sacrifice is the abnormality that must be controlled.

The legal arguments put forth by the Crown imply a hierarchy of differences. The primary model is the human norm of self-interest. Presumed female nature is exceptional to this norm. In turn, the act of choosing to abort is again different from normal female behaviour. Thus, women are naturally different from the norm of active self-interest, but abortion is different from natural female behaviour. It is this difference from difference that allows the Crown to argue the necessity for an independent mechanism to establish just which difference is involved in any given instance. If these various distinctions are to be 'objectively' determined, the law must set down a generalizable standard.

10

Legal Rationality, Medical Objectivity, and Patriarchal Logic

The embryo can be transferred from one woman to another, demonstrating the unique separateness of the unborn from its mother ... After embryo implantation into the uterus, the woman provides the environment for growth ... A woman's body ... [is similar to] other life support systems ... like a kidney dialysis machine. (*The Plain Truth* 1985:4)

Such independent certification [as provided by therapeutic abortion committees], it is submitted, is often found in many widely disparate human activities: for example, a mechanic may certify as to a vehicle's roadworthiness ... If the certificate of fact is not issued by the therapeutic abortion committee, the applicant is not thereby deprived of any rights or privileges, and indeed is at liberty to continue applying to as many therapeutic abortion committees as she may wish; just as one might apply to a second or third mechanic for a certificate as to a vehicle's roadworthiness. (Statement of Fact and Law filed on behalf of the Attorney General of Canada in defence of the Canadian Abortion Law, vol. 1, at nos. 79, 80)

'The Silent Scream' ... treats the issue of personhood as a scientific question. Its appearance as a medical document both obscures and reinforces a coded set of messages that work as political signs and moral injunctions. The viewer's impression is of an autonomous fetus (as person) and an absent and peripheral woman. (Eisenstein 1988:186, citing Petchesky 1987:267, 270)

The Gendering of Positive and Negative Rights

The assurance of equality before the law is as important for liberal legal theory as the right to pursue self-interest without interference from

others. While, at the level of social practice, individuals make moral decisions by considering the particular backgrounds of the persons involved,
liberal thought has traditionally assumed that the superiority of law lies in
its capacity to mediate abstractly between competing interests without reference to the particular status of the interested parties. In the theoretical
terms of the legal code, equality requires the identical treatment of all
legal subjects, so particular power relationships are considered to be irrelevant considerations for those whose task it is to apply the law.

In recent years, the notion of equality as sameness has come under
increasing attack. Concerned solely with individual interest in the
abstract, a system of prohibitions cannot, it is argued, address the collective societal responsibility to provide a concrete response to problems
that are experienced differently by the powerless. Various legal scholars
have demonstrated that a legal reliance on negative principles makes
legal intervention an ineffective mechanism for bringing about social
equality. Because negative law abstracts the pursuit of individual interest
from the context that enables it, the legal guarantee of individual liberty
does nothing to help those who do not have the social resources to act for
themselves. The U.S. abortion law, as it is experienced by poor women, is
simply one more illustration supporting this contention. The practical
result of extending the right of 'choice' to American women in a country
that denies poor women medical access demonstrates that guaranteeing
choice without attending to need qualifies freedom according to status.

The favoured solution for addressing social inequality by legal means
has been to call for a greater stress on positive principles (Michelman
1973, 1979). For this reason, Rawls's salvaging of deontology's social-
responsibility ethic is widely viewed within the legal community as a theoretical corrective for the inability of negative law to address issues of
inequality. By articulating a method for intervening in unequal power
relationships, Rawls's work has substantially undermined the hold of teleological reasoning on liberal law. Nevertheless, his basic tenets not only
remain in the liberal mind-set but are entrenched in 'a hypothetical original position of *equal* liberty ... [where normal human beings] are not
altruists but act from *self-interest* as representatives of themselves and their
descendants' (Richards 1981:266–7; emphasis added). While this contemporary variant of the liberal legal code promises legal redress to those
who do not prosper or who are victimized by the acts of others, Rawls
does not question the naturalness of a social order characterized by motivations of self-interest. Instead, his method for differentiating between
different classes of legal subjects is based on an equation of the norms of

liberalism with normalcy. Unlike social-code reasoning, however, it is dependence (rather than gender, race, or class) that is supposed to determine the applicability of positive or negative principles in any particular instance.

Legal practices in Canada afford a means of examining the effects of adding positive principles into the primarily negative framework of liberal law. Canadian legislatures have tended more towards the use of positive principles than their American counterparts, but these principles have been incorporated into the liberal framework without substantially changing the lack-of-interference nature of liberty-rights reasoning. To examine legal practice is to reveal how lawyers use the law to support social discourses about how gender relations should be. As Lees (1994: 125) has noted, '[i]t is important to be clear about the criteria which courts use to differentiate between individuals.' It is important because gender relations are constituted by these differentiations and the differentiations are dictated by the terms of the applicable laws.

The 1969 amendment to the Criminal Code (in contrast to abortion rulings in the United States) is a good example of the incorporation of positive principles into the negative frame of liberal law. According to what was popularly known as the abortion law, medical services for terminating pregnancy were available to women on the basis of the logic associated with welfare reasoning, and the rationale behind the law, and the arguments used to defend it at the Morgentaler appeal hearings reaffirmed Rawls's core assumption that human independence and individual subjectivity are inherent in the 'original position.'

The paradox of the discourse at the Morgentaler appeals is that in order to reaffirm the neutrality of the legal paradigm with which they worked, the Crown attorneys were forced to rely on gendered presuppositions emanating from outside the mind-set of formal legal theory. In theory, all legal subjects are to be judged without regard to their station in life, and women are to have no greater restrictions placed on the pursuit of their own interests than men are. However, while one's legal claim to a liberty or welfare right theoretically relates to the degree to which one is dependent on the response of another, the Crown portrayed reproductive relations in a way that negated foetal dependence on maternal response and highlighted the dependence of women on medical responses.

The lack of a reproductive referent within both social and legal codes creates a unity of discourse that provided an opening for the state attorneys to link abstract legal reasoning with the 'real' world of hegemonic practice and conservative political rhetoric. Whereas, in the legal code, response is exceptional and independence is normal, in the social code all normal women respond and care for the needs of potential life. The assumption that responding to the needs of others is essentially a maternal characteristic and not an activity requiring women to make choices provided a juncture along which the legal and social codes could intersect to discursively resolve the contradiction between theory and practice. What made the logic of the Crown argumentation plausible is that legal reasoning infers that the responses necessary for exercising liberty rights are a universally available resource that is not normally affected by human agency, while the social code images pregnant women as a conduit through which a new human life will emerge – also not normally affected by human agency. Both hegemonic codes rely on the unstated supposition that the other-oriented consciousness of women is characterized by passivity and victimization and is naturally gender-specific.

The Nurturing Womb as Universal Resource

Any consideration of a foetal right separate from a maternal one allows for a discussion of these rights within the primary legal framework of self-actualizing individuals. In giving women a welfare right, the Canadian law automatically gave foetal life the status implied by liberty-rights theory. A reproductive exemption based solely on preventing foetal infringement on maternal health bestows a right on that foetus which only independent entities are philosophically entitled to claim: the right to pursue one's purposes free from the interference of others. However, in order for law to accord to each and every human being an inherent liberty right – on the basis of some essential individuality – a basic resource is necessary. The resource that must be available is women's bodies. To consider social justice for a foetus – separate and distinct from a consideration of social justice for women – is logically possible only if potential life can expect that woman's bodies will *normally* be available for their use. Thus, any desire to protect foetal autonomy within this framework automatically precludes a consideration of reproductive choice for women; the assumption that life will develop in the absence of interference logically invokes the parallel assumption that the creation and nurturing of new life will occur irrespective of female motivation.

Within the boundaries of the liberty-rights framework, the granting of subjectivity to foetuses can be accomplished only to the extent that female subjectivity is simultaneously suppressed. In order to safeguard the foetus's right to develop – irrespective of the motivations of pregnant women – the Crown at the Morgentaler hearings set out to prove that the subject of reproduction is the foetus. Because medical science has taken on a central role in shaping contemporary relations of reproduction, 'proving' that a woman's body is simply the natural environment for foetal activity required the making of distinctions between the responsibilities of women and doctors within reproduction.

In the legal discourse of the courtroom, three sets of rights and responsibilities were readily discernible: foetal, maternal, and medical. In this triangle of interlocking rights, the state representatives depicted doctors as human subjects capable of making rational decisions and entitled to the liberty to do so; foetuses as potential human subjects who will autonomously self-actualize; and women as objects to be tested by doctors for their fitness to respond to foetal requirements. The best illustration of this deeper structure of legal discourse is found in the federal Crown's analogy between the Criminal Code amendments and administrative laws that require car owners to have the safety of their cars routinely certified by a qualified mechanic. In oral submissions to the Supreme Court of Ontario, as well as in the federal brief to the court, Crown Attorney Pennington stressed that a state requirement for women to obtain a therapeutic abortion committee (TAC) certificate was no more onerous and constituted no more of a disadvantage than the legal requirement that drivers have their cars certified before the vehicles are allowed to be driven. As he put it, 'The applicant is at liberty to continue applying to as many therapeutic abortion committees as she may wish, just as one might apply to a second or third mechanic for a certificate as to a vehicle's roadworthiness' (oral submission to the Supreme Court of Ontario, cf. Statement of Fact and Law filed on behalf of the Attorney General of Canada, vol. 1, at nos. 79, 80). According to this argument, doctors – like mechanics – are professionally qualified to judge the level of 'safety' that the law requires. Just as society does not expect car owners to determine the safety level for themselves, neither should it expect women to be knowledgeable about their own 'roadworthiness.' In the Crown's metaphor, doctors are equated with mechanics, and women become the vehicles in which their foetuses ride. The foetus becomes the subject who sits in the driver's seat, and the woman is the vehicle that may be exempted from providing it with transportation whenever her doctor finds her to be in an 'unsafe' condition.

As archaic as the above metaphor appears to our contemporary sensibilities, it fits well within the legal paradigm. According to legal logic, it is generic 'man' who is privileged by the ascription of a liberty right; it is humanity that drives the vehicle, but it is women who are expected to provide the transportation. In patriarchal terms, women are subsumed within the concept of humanity, but at the same time they are differentiated from normal humanity. Women's bodies are different from those of men, and this difference means that their bodies are unquestionably available to be driven by human foetuses (representing 'men' in the generic sense of person). As vehicles, women's bodies require judgments to be made concerning their individual suitability for responding to the needs of humankind. What is needed in this metaphor is a neutral party to apply the standard that certifies roadworthiness.

If the health of the vehicle is the paramount consideration in determining whether or not it will be driven, then, logically, doctors are the mechanics. They presumedly are the experts equipped to make decisions concerning the health of human bodies and human minds. In the Crown's analogy, if a doctor determines that a particular woman is biologically, emotionally, or morally incapable of performing the nurturing role for which her biology has destined her, she may be exempted from the task of getting humanity to its destination. According to this metaphor, law is necessary if defective nature is to be properly identified and affixed with an 'unsafe' sticker. It is the responsibility of the medical profession to provide the technology and the expertise for ensuring that nurturance can normally be taken for granted. Until such time as technology can arrange for a 'replacement vehicle,' the only legal option is to provide a standard for limiting the liberty of particular foetuses in the interest of all.

In the space within which legal and social codes intersect, practices that allow the medical profession to assess the motivations and reproductive capacities of female patients can be legally justified within the contemporary legal paradigm. If the normal human subjectivity in the original position (embodied in the foetus) is both auotonomous and self-interested, doctors represent a superior form of being, their professional neutrality allowing them to adhere to Rawls's method of transcending human subjectivity. In stepping behind the veil of ignorance and neutrally assessing the conditions that erode the relations of the original position, doctors can both protect and transcend normal self-interest. In gaining legal support for its monopoly on assessing and protecting reproductive health, the medical profession gained the authority to determine when the inherent liberty of a particular foetus would have to be limited in the interests of reaffirming the essential responsiveness of all women.

Although Rawls assumed that natural human subjectivity is self-interested, he proposed a method for getting beyond this self-interest in order to ensure that all will have an equal chance of exercising the inherent right of autonomy. Within this frame, actual social practices made the medical profession the logical body to have the authority and responsibility of assessing when a woman does not have the capacity to perform the tasks normally expected in the original position. In short, women could be granted the 'choice' of normal human subjects if a medical expert determined that they were not capable of the 'responsiveness' of normal women. As noted above, one successful applicant for abortion services attested to the manner in which a doctor could grant women the freedom of a normal legal subject by symbolically defining her motivation for wishing to do so as one that involved 'irresponsibility.' She explained: 'He would not answer my silent plea as to what was going on until I finally asked him and he said "well, I think we've found our reason: you have not accepted your father's death and therefore you are not ready for a responsible relationship with a man"' (oral testimony of abortion patient at Toronto tribunals, March 1986). By setting out legal justifications for responding to a woman's request for an abortion, the doctor was simultaneously re-creating the gendered underpinnings of law. Each doctor was fulfilling the dual mandate of granting a foetus the legal status of an individual in the original position and of 'protecting' a woman's status as the responsibile nurturer of human relationships. Preserving independence as the norm of human subjectivity requires that, at the very least, pregnant women will continue to be perceived as 'other.'

An essential aspect of law is that it views itself as outside and above the social reality it attempts to regulate. By attributing the same disinterested neutrality to medical science, the Canadian law made the health of the foetal environment the standard that would permit the state to intervene for the protection of foetal liberty and maternal welfare. Abortion could then be justified because the state has a duty to limit the implicit liberty right of any particular foetus in order to protect the 'welfare' of womanhood, a right that presumably coincides with the health of society.

Social beliefs about autonomous foetuses and female bodies as life-support systems – 'like a kidney dialysis machine' – constitute the conceptual basis of the original position within law. If all women are biologically incapable of exercising reproductive autonomy, maternal responsiveness is both socially normal and legally exceptional. The incorporation of positive law into the contemporary legal code allowed the Crown arguments to link theory and practice discursively because the contemporary code obligates the state to intervene on behalf of women who are unable to act independently of medical responses.

The 'data' created in medical practice provided the Crown attorneys at the Morgentaler hearings with the basis for a logical argument – without the intervention of medical science, women cannot make choices about their reproductive lives. The law exists to protect the inherent rights of the original position and, as the Crown deduced, 'all ... women are denied the right to choose,' so the law cannot take away from them what nature has denied them. If women are biologically unable to exercise reproductive choice, argued the Crown, how can the abortion law be viewed as a restriction of female liberty? Indeed, by injecting the neutrality of medical science, it argued, the law was actually providing a means of ensuring female welfare. Thus, according to the Crown, a law that forbids a woman from making reproductive choices without medical approval is not a state infringement on her liberty rights because, unlike normal legal subjects, she has none. Since legal reasoning decrees that women in the original position are choiceless, the state cannot be said to be infringing on a right that does not exist. What the law can do, however, is compensate women for the consequences of their biological exceptionality.

In the Crown vernacular, when a vehicle is un-roadworthy, the state is obligated to override the normal legal protection of a driver's liberty in order to ensure that the vehicle is made roadworthy. The metaphor is consistent with legal reasoning because a foetus developing its own life is a normal legal subject, but the state can, according to normal legal principles, intrude on the inherent liberty if this intervention is necessary to prevent a breakdown of a social contract based on female responsiveness.

Institutional practices prescribed by the 1969 law provide a good example of the hegemonic process at work. In their justifications of this law, the Crown attorneys uncovered the process by which distortions of reproductive labour can be used to construct a reality where women will consent in their own subordination. It is only because this driver/vehicle/ mechanic analogy is so blatantly sexist that the nonsense of the subject/ object inversion is easily revealed. In practice, it is the woman (vehicle) who must actively seek and convince a doctor (mechanic) that she is unhealthy (unroadworthy) and unable to fulfil the purpose for which the law decrees she is intended (drivability). In the Crown's analogy – in which vehicles apply for certificates – a pregnant woman is still the acting subject, though her options have been limited by the medical process that the law has mandated. It is precisely because a woman has a particular motivation that she will consent to the bending of her intents into a judgment of her moral worth as a woman (roadworthiness). Legally required to place herself in the hands of her doctor, a woman's 'problem' then becomes a medical property, excluding her from any further decision making.

It is because the law considers a woman to be a nonthinking vehicle that she is legally and socially put into a position where she must consent to the process of proving that she fits the criteria of unroadworthiness. To refuse her consent to this myth would render her roadworthy when what she desires is the option to refrain from being driven. Only by consenting to the judgment of her doctor can she exercise her options. The responsibility of the medical profession becomes identical with an individual doctor's liberty right of providing responses in his or her own terms and according to his or her own inclination. The motivations and desires of the person receiving welfare become irrelevant to the decision-making process. In the words of a woman whose pregnant body became the property of her doctor, 'I wanted to know exactly what was going to happen to me. And he said that, as far as he was concerned, there were no questions. It was a standard procedure, and that was all I needed to know. So I paid the money, and he booked the appointment for five weeks later' (oral testimony of abortion patient at Toronto tribunals, March 1986). In this woman's experience, the doctor had gained the right to tell her that she need no longer concern herself with what was being done to her. The medical responsibility to oversee the relations of reproduction 'scientifically' transforms a woman's desire to terminate her pregnancy into an abnormality that can be determined and fixed by a qualified expert. Once law and science have decreed her dependence on the responses of the medical profession, her only hope of securing the response she requires is to give up the right to determine how and in what way her reproductive needs will be met. In the process, her motivations are transformed into the categories that permit legal and medical intervention.

Professional Responsibilities and the Liberty Rights of Doctors

Within the legal text of the 1969 abortion regulations, foetuses were implicitly granted the status of primary legal subjects with rights that could be limited in exceptional circumstances. The deeper structure of courtroom discourse, however, demonstrated more than an abstract concern for deciding when foetal liberty rights could legitimately be limited. Despite the liberty-rights language of the courtroom, the state's arguments were not primarily directed at assessing and balancing the competing rights of foetal life and maternal welfare. The Crown submissions had as much to do with the undertaking of social responsibilities as with preserving individual rights.

The Crown's deviation from a purely negative framework did not conform with the reasoning one would have expected if maternal and medical responsibilities had been approached in an identical way. Although the rights of women and of doctors were both tied to an implied responsibility to attend to the need of some 'other,' the choice of responding (or not) was explicitly reserved for doctors. Embedded in the Crown discussions were dual sets of beliefs about femininity and medical science. These beliefs provided a symbolic context for defining the meaning of responsibility and determining the contingency of liberty rights within reproduction. The maternal responsibility to respond to foetal requirements, and the medical responsibility to define what these requirements would be, meant that a woman's liberty right (choice) remained conceptually tied to her doctor's right to respond in his or her own terms, but that the foetus's liberty right (life) was not considered similarly contingent on maternal responsiveness. In short, a patriarchal asymmetry of feminine duty and medical authority provided the context required for understanding the responsibilities that the Crown argued must accompany any claiming of rights.

Implicit within the different forms of discourse used to discuss different patterns of rights and responsibilities was a recognition that the existence of life requires something more than noninterference. If accepted by the court, the Crown submissions would serve to ensure the continuance of this 'something more' without actually having to identify it as a purposeful activity that a woman might choose not to undertake in circumstances which she herself defined as undesirable. This recognition of the contingency of human subjectivity was submerged within an explicit reliance on cultural understandings which were at odds with the legal code's gender-neutral frame of reference but which coincided with the implicit gendering of Rawls's original position.

A symbolic re-creation of the legal status of the mythical original position provided the crucial underpinning for Crown reasoning. The status of legal subjects in relation to liberty and welfare rights provided the frame for arguing that a medical determination of normal reproductive requirements did not constitute discrimination of women or their doctors. Although the Crown admitted that the law was treating pregnant women differently from normal legal subjects, it submitted that 'not all distinctions are discrimination. Discrimination can only be said to occur if it involves the bringing of irrational distinctions' (oral submission to the Supreme Court of Canada by Crown Attorney Wein, 9 October 1986). In the Rawlsian formula for addressing problems of powerlessness, differential treatment with the intent to provide welfare is legally rational because the model requires a standard that will return legal subjects to their status in an original position where subjectivity is fixed by nature.

Although Crown arguments did not identify the various legal rights as welfare or legal ones, the Crown attorneys used their distinctive logic to assess the pattern of rights and responsibilities that legally accrue to foetuses, women, and doctors. According to the contemporary legal code, whenever individuals are dependent on another's help in order to assert independence, the state has an obligation to devise the standard and process that will correct for eroded autonomy. Since the schema takes reproductive responsiveness as a given, extending to women the resources required for independence is problematic because such an extension undermines presuppositions of the essential autonomy and independent subjectivity of normal human subjects. When combined with social-code understandings about gender characteristics, however, Rawls's method for achieving social justice provides a means of submerging the theoretical problem. Since women (in their reproductive capacity) are not 'similarly situated' in the original position, resources can be provided to them in order to compensate them for their essential powerlessness. Welfare-rights reasoning ensures a continuance of 'normal' female nurturance because the provision of resources is subject to a universal standard that re-creates the relationships of the original position.

In addressing the biological contingency of foetal life on maternal decision making and the socially imposed contingency of maternal choice on medical decision making, the legal argumentation focused principally on 'proving' that the legal responsibility of the medical profession did not contravene the normal right of individual doctors to determine their response to pregnant women. Although the law gave doctors the right and responsibility to 'repair' any breakdown in the norms of maternal responsiveness and foetal autonomy, this authority was given to them as members of a social category and not as individuals. Because liberty rights remain paramount in the legal frame, at issue for both the Crown and defence lawyers was whether the medical profession's collective responsibility to assess reproductive health impeded the liberty rights of any particular doctor.

The Crown was concerned to demonstrate that just as the law did not give women autonomy which they did not biologically have, neither did it take away from doctors the freedom to make choices consistent with their own consciences. The Crown attorneys cited a number of studies to illustrate that nothing prevented a doctor from providing abortion services when he believed that the protection of a woman's 'health' merited this response. They pointed to the flexibility of the 'health' standard, arguing that this flexibility was necessary to protect the right of a doctor to determine his or her own response. According to their submissions, the collective responsibility given to the medical profession was not problematic in an individual sense, because the legislation did not compel any particular doctor to provide abortion services. As the court was told, a legal protection of autonomy does not include any right to act on the basis of an altruistic motivation. Thus, according to the Crown, it was the law's lack of compulsion on any particular doctor to respond to any particular woman's need that provided the legal assurance of the medical liberty right. A violation of individual freedom would take place only if the law compelled doctors to perform their mandated responsibility, and the Crown took care to illustrate that this was not the case.

The Crown went further than arguing that the law did not interfere with individual liberty rights. In demonstrating that the law did not prevent any particular doctor from exercising his or her inherent liberty right, the various Crown submissions pointed to the medical monopoly which the law protected. Because it was the medical monopoly that gave individual doctors the right to decide whether or not an abortion was necessary in any particular instance, it was the existence of the law that enabled a doctor to remain free from any compulsion that a 'desperate' woman might exert. As for the responsibility to respond to that desperate woman, Crown Attorney Wein noted that liberty rights are not concerned with providing responses to others. Since responding to need is the obligation of the state, there is 'no fundamental right that would allow doctors to assist women beyond that which the law gives them.' Wein reminded the court that 'it is the absence of coercion and constraint that is the important factor' (oral submission to the Supreme Court of Canada, 9 October 1986); although the law permitted women to be exempted from their maternal responsibilities, it also allowed doctors to define whether this exemption was legitimate. Because a doctor could decide that any or all abortions were illegitimate, the law could not, it was claimed, be said to constitute an infringement on a doctor's freedom of choice.

Although the trilogy of rights being considered by Crown actors at the

Morgentaler appeals was addressed as distinct kinds of rights, the form of discourse provided the context in which meaning was assigned in any given instance. Although only foetuses were considered within the purely individualistic model that one normally associates with liberty rights, this abstract 'right to life' gained meaning only in reference to the type of welfare that a pregnant woman could claim. By linking maternal need to the powerlessness associated with the nurturance women provide for others, the conceptual basis of law could be preserved. By making doctors the benefactors who would dispense welfare rights while simultaneously protecting their liberty right to refrain from this dispensation, the abortion law provided the necessary link. Contemporary legal theory could in turn be used to pronounce the legitimacy of the law, but what the Crown arguments could not acknowledge was the circularity of the process that was set in motion.

The legal monopoly of the medical profession, coupled with its responsibility to transform abortion motivations into acceptable categories, created the data that reaffirmed social-code assumptions about law and its relationship to power within relationships. In turn, social understandings about benefactors and recipients form the basis for legally regulating autonomy and compensating victimization. The intersection of assumptions ensures that neither the nature of power relationships nor the paradigms that justify them ever get addressed. By selectively drawing from legal and social codes concerning the rights and responsibilities of recipients and benefactors, the Crown could present a logical case that explained why legally entrenching the medical monopoly on reproductive decision making was necessary for the protection of a moral social order.

The 1969 Canadian law enlisted the medical profession's help in defining women as different from the legal norm; that is, as essentially powerless and naturally responsive. By proposing a health standard as the basis of a woman's welfare right, the state allowed the medical profession to provide a woman with resources whenever she consented to these definitions. Because the law proclaimed a medical monopoly on abortion services, a woman and her doctor had different requirements placed on the right to claim a liberty right; pregnant women required an actual medical response in order to qualify, but doctors were required only to clothe their responses in the symbolic terms of the social code. By fulfilling this ideological responsibility, a doctor could address the concrete requirements of human independence while still reproducing common assumptions concerning the gendered social world and the gender-free legal arena. The delegation of the state's interest in reproduction to the medical profession thus allowed the law to preserve its gender-neutral veneer.

The medical monopoly provided the background for the Crown to distinguish between primary and secondary legal subjects in a 'rational' manner. Within this context, women could be exempted from passively responding to external compulsion provided they were duly certified by medical experts as abnormal women. Since the medical profession presumedly has the technological expertise to define both healthy womanhood and autonomous life, doctors logically became the appropriate agents for overseeing the state's interest in protecting developing life and in compensating women for their defects or victimization. Because the law made a pregnant woman's liberty right synonymous with the 'right' of her foetus to a healthy environment, courtroom discourse could point both to the dependence of women on the decisions of their doctors and to the independence of doctors from legal compulsion.

The 1969 abortion law furthered both the collective interests of the medical profession and those of the state. The legal articulation of the state's interest in foetal life and maternal health coincided with the medical profession's interest in expanding and consolidating its monopoly on health care. The law formalized the cultural belief that a pregnant woman's doctor had two patients for whom he or she should care. It also specified that the care of each patient brought with it a legal obligation to determine objectively whether a maternal or foetal right would take precedence in any particular situation and to act accordingly. A pregnant woman could claim a right to a medical response provided that her doctor determined that a state of necessity actually existed. Conversely, the foetal right to life was not to be interfered with unless the same state of necessity was deemed to exist. Implicitly, then, foetuses had gained the rights of normal patients while pregnant women had their normal medical rights restricted to those exceptional instances where foetal activity was deemed to be causing a deterioration of reproductive well-being – as such well-being related to the capacity for nurturance.

In the context of the 1969 law, maternal health cannot be secured without a medical response, but neither can foetal independence be realized without the responses of women. Despite the parallel (within reproductive and medical relations) of a connection between autonomy and response, the Crown attorneys framed their discussion about the effects of reproductive responsibilities differently from when they had been talking about maternal choice. Although a woman's capacity to nurture life was portrayed as 'a right that nature has denied to men,' the Crown acknowledged that the protection of a doctor's liberty right might actually impair a woman's ability to claim her welfare right, and it submitted that such adverse effects should not be a concern of the courts, since 'the function of the law is to give general abstract principles rather than to respond to pragmatic circumstance' (oral submission to the Supreme Court of Ontario by Crown Attorney Pennington, 7 May 1985).

Following Rawls's synthesis of the classical opposition of deontology and teleology, the reasoning of the Crown implies that principles derived from the original position take on the character of natural law. Within this frame, the court's role is not to be concerned about actual problems experienced in gaining access to the resources necessary for a woman to claim her right. Because the state cannot compel doctors to respond to women without undercutting its primary mandate of protecting liberty rights, such problems will 'occur in any event' (ibid.).

Abstract Principles, Pragmatic Circumstances, and Rational Objectivity

At the heart of the conservative discourse of the Crown attorneys at the Morgentaler appeals was the degree of 'subjectivity' that the hegemonic mind-set bestows on different social actors according to their gender. By subjectivity, I mean the ability both to act and to secure a response in one's own terms. The degree to which one is accorded ideological subjectivity depends on how much integration or opposition between personal autonomy and collective response is considered legitimate. The deeper structure of the discourse at the Morgentaler appeals was concerned with two levels of 'acting' subjects – foetuses and doctors – both of whom related to a maternal object in terms of her health.

In the Crown's arguments, reproductive relations were reduced to the activity of a self-actualizing foetus, whose primary interest is to retain the supportive and nurturing responses of its prospective mother. Although the foetus has no voice to express these terms, the state undertakes to act on its behalf, defining and responding to foetal requirements in the terms of every 'man' who exists in the original position. In this interpretation of the reproductive relationship, foetuses stand in for the normal legal subject who independently pursues the self-interest that is so central to liberty-rights precepts. Despite the fact that it is women (as reproductive workers) who are required to provide the response, they are not accorded a legitimate voice in interpreting the relationship or specifying its terms, because they are not similarly situated at the point of legal abstraction. In the legal metaphor, pregnant women are different from every 'man.'

Where women's needs are concerned, autonomy and response remain conceptually separated. A response to women is legally allowable only when their autonomy has been disallowed. The logic of welfare rights provides the rationale for the retention of a distorted version of human reality. At the centre of legal discourse – from which the Crown's argument concerning foetal rights and medical rights and responsibilities emanated – is the implicit belief that the highest stage of humanity is characterized by independence from the needs and desires of others. However, by adding a consideration of welfare rights to the legal equation, the state is able to ensure that, ideologically, foetal life can continue to take its enabling supports for granted. The result of this asymmetry of legal rights is that, where foetal needs are concerned, the right to act and to secure a response are integrated. Thus, in the Crown's interpretation of the maternal-foetal relationship, it is foetuses that retain the inherent subjectivity of essential humanity, and it is women who must respond to the 'choices' the foetuses make.

The subjectivity accorded to doctors belongs to a different order of human activity than that accorded to foetal life. The legal mandate of the state – to keep self-interested human activity in check and to bring order to the chaos of competing self-interests – has been delegated to the medical profession. As an agent of the state, the doctor's responsibility is to represent the state's dual interest in preserving foetal autonomy and protecting maternal health. The physician is the rational (disinterested) subject; the degree of his or her rationality depends on the ability to stand apart from the interests of those about whom he or she must make judgments. As individuals, doctors are entitled to the same liberty rights as foetuses, but as members of a profession they are expected to act as 'objective' scientists, and they carry out the law in its 'neutrality.' In return, the state undertakes to ensure that those doctors who faithfully carry out its mandate will lose neither their right to pursue self-interest nor their monopoly on medical decision making. In other words, physicians claim the rights of normal legal subjects and also the authority to help define those rights.

According to Crown Attorney Blacklock, it is 'rationality' that provides society with a method for articulating the universal principles that can differentiate between those instances when liberty or welfare is the appropriate right to be protected. The legal rationality of which he speaks depends on some individuals separating themselves from the 'irrational' feelings of those who have a stake in the outcome of decision making. As he argued, 'we expect courts to give us principles – to reason, not to feel' (oral submission, 10 October 1986). In the legal world, it is detachment, not empathy, that provides order. But the order that is provided by this rationality includes the assurance that women will continue to feel and to respond empathically.

Legal Code 'Rationality' Excludes, Depends on, and Controls the 'Irrationality' of Social and Reproductive Codes

Exclusion, dependence, and control characterize the relationship between the abstract legal code and the more situation-specific social and reproductive codes. The relationship parallels that existing between the sexes. Women and the system of thought that is created in the performance of their work have been excluded from arenas where direct power is exercised. At the same time, those who exercise power (including intellectual power) depend on women to perform the labour that sustains individual initiative (Smith 1987). This gendered asymmetry – between a right to participate in decision making and the responsibility to perform the tasks that enable this participation – gives rise to a conceptual framework which, in circular fashion, justifies societal control of women and their work: the justification itself depends on the gendered nature of reproductive thought processes.

The Crown argument involved a logic that is central to conservative political philosophy concerning both gender and medical relations. Although the dispersion of state power to the offices of doctors has allowed some women to have their reproductive needs met, the TAC process legitimated and strengthened the hegemonic power of legal discourse and ultimately of anti-choice depictions of the reproductive process. Similar discourses have emanated from the courtroom and the doctor's office, and each feeds into and depends on the abstract images that are ideologically prepared for public consumption.

The driver/vehicle/mechanic analogy which the Crown used to legitimate medical power over reproduction in the courtroom involved a mind-set that builds on and reinforces the type of anti-choice reasoning that likens women's bodies to technological life-support systems. These conservative messages draw their hegemonic power from the medical practices that law has structured. When such social processes as those of the Canadian therapeutic abortion committees become law, they bequeath subjectivity to foetal life and systematically deny it to women. Whether the metaphor being applied to the maternal-foetal relationship is a portrayal of woman as a vehicle or as a kidney dialysis machine, it draws on the usually unstated expectation that women can always be counted on to provide the resources required by others. Behind these analogies are not only cultural expectations about who will give care and who will receive it, but also cultural beliefs about the neutrality of medical science and the ability of technology to identify and eliminate unhealthy practices.

Common-sense understandings about female nurturance and scientific 'objectivity' provided the Crown attorneys with a basis for justifying the distinctions the law made between foetal autonomy and female dependence. Despite its veneer of neutral rationality, the logic by which the Crown differentiated between foetuses and pregnant women as autonomous and dependent legal subjects, respectively, depended on the same social-code assumptions of conservative ideological tracts: the naturalness of female nurturance and the socially acquired detachment of medical science. Within this mind-set, it is the rationality of medical science that provides the justification for granting doctors the right and responsibility to define autonomous personhood and to protect responsive womanhood.

There is a subtle but important difference between the neutrality of the law and the objectivity of medicine. In developing abstract universal principles, law is to be gender neutral; its precepts are considered applicable to all. In administering these principles in practice, however, medical science is called on to interpret the principles in a way that considers the particular competing claims of each of the gendered parties. The law structures a situation whereby gender can enter into law by the back door; social-code assumptions about foetal independence, maternal nurturance, and medical rationality structure the medical interpretation of supposedly neutral principles in gendered ways. Dr Morgentaler's response to women in their own terms upset this asymmetrical ordering of rights and responsibilities. In forcing the issue back into the courts, the illegal clinic strategy required the Crown to articulate how the principles of legal equality and the right to pursue self-interest were to apply to pregnant women.

Contrary to the assertions of some critical legal scholars, law does not function as a closed system of thought without reference to the social world it seeks to direct and regulate. Assigning implicit liberty rights to foetuses ignores the work that creates independent self-interest, but the legal paradigm also depends on the continuation of this work. Moreover, social-code understandings about reproductive relationships are central to legal texts and discourses. The asymmetrical rights discussed at the

Morgentaler appeals could be presented as reasonable because the rights themselves are based on patriarchal assumptions about the gendered nature of autonomy and response. The TAC process was portrayed as an intrusion on foetal autonomy, albeit a justifiable intrusion, through a combination of normal legal logic and social-code understandings about actual reproductive practice. The welfare and liberty rights under discussion constituted a reflection of the patriarchal order itself: foetal activity cannot be allowed to harm the very environment on which it depends, and the concept of liberty cannot be allowed to erode the gendered structuring of reproductive practice.

The depiction of reproduction that is implicit within legal reasoning is a distortion of reproductive reality. However, this reasoning is more than a perverse reflection of reality, for it provides the framework for regulating and controlling reproductive labour. Legal discourse does more than simply reflect contemporary power relations; it also constructs them (Eisenstein 1988). The legal reasoning by the Crown attorneys at the Morgentaler appeals retained its logical thread because, on the one hand, the legal framework within which the argument was placed had no referent to the actual relationship between a woman and her foetus, and yet, on the other hand, reproductive practice had been legally structured to ensure that female autonomy was contingent on a regulated medical response. 'Dependency,' as a legal concept, gains meaning through social-code stereotypes about the nature of women and reproduction, but any provision for maternal welfare can in turn be granted legitimacy only by reaffirming the normalcy of foetal autonomy. This method of reproductive control is hegemonic in that it requires women to consent to their own subordination.

An Alienation of Reproductive-Code Principles

The courtroom discourse at the Morgentaler appeals was not the gender-neutral reasoning that the legal code demands. It relied on generally accepted cultural understandings about foetal independence, maternal nurturance, and medical expertise. In the Crown's arguments, a woman's need for an abortion became a symbol of the ill health of society, a sign of the breakdown in the presumedly normal gender asymmetry of individual autonomy and response to others. Doctors who could sufficiently remove themselves from the subjective feelings of their particular patients could address the illness, curing even the 'abnormal' attitudes of their patients. Although welfare rights stress a positive state responsibility to address need, the specific needs of pregnant women (and of reproduction generally) were not viewed as something to be addressed in their own terms but as something that required protection by an objective expert. Protection, in this instance, becomes the means of perpetuating the gender asymmetry of authority and responsiveness that underpins the subordination of all women.

Intersecting with the social-code assumption – that women are normally the gender responsible for maintaining the moral social order – was the appropriation of reproductive-code values. Based on the legal-code assumptions (1) that women's wombs are a universally accessible resource and (2) that foetuses spontaneously self-actualize, the Crown argument emphasized that an ethical stance of 'care' was more appropriate for resolving reproductive dilemmas than one of 'justice,' and that the law was therefore needed if this alternative stance was to be protected.

Although women in general are more apt to exhibit an ethic of care than they are of justice, an understanding of both orientations is available to either sex (Lyons 1988; Gilligan 1982). By attributing values of care and responsibility to women *in essential ways*, however, the Crown appropriated reproductive-code beliefs to justify systemic gender injustice. In the portrayal of reproduction as different – because it requires women to be attentive to 'other interests' – the moral value of one's responsibility for others was both romanticized and distorted. The Crown's romanticization of reproductive relations negated the possibility of mutual concern for another's autonomy and transformed it into gender hierarchy. In this way, the discourse subordinated female ethical principles of responsibility and also used women's existence to justify the continuation of unequal reproductive relations.

Although it was a maternal-foetal relationship that was being discussed in the courtroom, the reasoning used was not that required for reproductive work. Despite the appropriation of a 'female ethic,' the Crown's description of the autonomy-response relationship differed significantly from that which informs the reproductive code. In hegemonic discourse, maternal responsiveness is rendered invisible as conscious human activity while the foetus takes on a subjectivity that it cannot attain without the performance of such labour. The Crown's invocation of the reproductive code was based on a partial and distorted interpretation of women's private-level understandings of the activity of care.

Care for the needs of others, in the other's own terms, creates and is sustained by a discourse that does not separate autonomy from response. Although response to another is a central element of the reproductive code, its logic presumes that autonomy is a necessary component of any authentic response to the needs of another. Further, the reproductive code does not abstract morality from the context in which it is practised; a foetus could, therefore, never be granted the status of a human person irrespective of the motivations of the pregnant woman.

The discourse in defence of the Canadian abortion law ideologically transformed the active care involved in performing nurturing tasks into a form of deontology; that is, an obligatory unthinking response according to the dictates of natural law. In this mind-set, the oppositional moralities of deontology and teleology are preserved along the gender lines of the social code; normal women are required to respond to others according to a natural law, while humankind retains the right to pursue self-interest according to particular circumstances.

Because the understandings of attentive labour are mystified and gendered in the process of producing cultural knowledge, the activities of women disappear into the taken-for-granted backdrop of 'real' history. 'When one is an object, not a subject, all of one's own physical and sexual impulses are presumed not to exist independently. They are to be brought into existence only by and for others – controlled, defined and used ... [In this way] inequality enlists some of a woman's own marvellous qualities in the service of her enslavement and degradation' (Miller 1976:63). Because women's subjectivities of their own experience have been excluded from the dominant depictions of human reality, the choices women make and the activities they perform get interpreted as a passive response to a deontological value system. Without an understanding of the motives behind their choices, women come to be perceived as biologically determined or culturally oversocialized. The distortion in the social code is that women 'are in fact different. But we are not as different FROM men (as false consciousness claims) as we are different FROM THAT WHICH men claim that we are' (Guillaumin 1982:43, as quoted by Eisenstein 1988:89). Women's own understanding of their difference from men is used to delegitimate their claim to the normal rights of humanity.

In the process of enlisting a 'woman's ethic' of care as the rationale for denying all women choice, the Crown's discourse depended on the overarching assumption that a foetus already exists as an independent other. If women can be convinced that the foetus is a separate human person, the reproductive code implies that its 'need' for life requires an attentive response. In this discourse, pregnant women cannot be considered to be acting responsibly unless they grant their foetuses the subjectivity of independent humanity. If maternal responsiveness is a natural part of being a woman, then withholding life-supportive responses is not an act of care. To accept this mind-set is to depend on the continuance of the reproductive labour of women while simultaneously rendering such labour invisible.

An androcentric mind-set, which dichotomizes autonomy and response, allows for a co-opting of the responsive choices women make in the performance of their work. It then uses these choices as evidence that a woman is naturally responsive but that her need for a response from others precludes a claim to the autonomy that is the mark of legal personhood. A rationale has been created for treating women unequally. In a Marxist sense, reproductive work has been alienated from those who perform the tasks. A fetishism of the 'commodity' created by reproductive labour (life and independence) endows the recipient of the labour with a subjectivity that can then be used to compel the labour itself. If women can be convinced that their foetuses are 'other' to themselves, then the reproductive code itself can be used to justify a law restricting abortions. In the process by which unequal gender relations are justified, women are alienated from their own power – both from the empowering work they perform for others and from the ethic of responsibility for others that is associated with this work.

Women face a dilemma when resisting structures bounded by an androcentric mind-set. If they opt to be considered by the standards of the norm – by proving that they are 'exceptional to the exception' – they can be denied the responses that are allowed to the 'exception' (that is, to those who are dependent). If they are judged according to the male norm of autonomy, they must give up the claim to the kind of responsiveness they provide for others. Each time a woman acts to secure a response, she proves her 'difference' by exhibiting an inability to meet her own needs. As she proves her difference by consciously choosing the response that will allow her a measure of autonomy, she is taking part in the process that suspends her right to participate in the definition of social need. In the same process, she retains the primary responsibility for providing the often invisible support that others will require.

To solve the dilemma created by the discourse of male hegemony, some radical feminists have argued for separatist strategies and the development of alternative resources. Other feminists, who have not understood the masculine nature of the legal norm (usually liberal feminists but also some Marxist feminists), have argued that all that is required is more access to state resources. While both solutions may offer some short-term relief for resource-poor women, neither addresses the basic problem – that social responses are directed towards needs as they are understood through male experience. What is needed are alternatives that challenge the norm itself. Although there is nothing essentially feminine about the logic of the reproductive code, when understood in its own terms it can provide the ideological basis for alternative forms of political activity. Just as Gilligan found her female subjects to be using a different moral voice when they engaged in personal decision making, I think we might find that some forms of political decision making engaged in by the feminist movement are also oriented by an ethic of care, which refuses to separate individual autonomy from concern for others.

Conclusion

The legal discourse used to defend the Canadian abortion law illustrates the interdependence of three ideas that are central to the maintenance of patriarchal relations: (1) that life exists independently of the context in which it is created, and law provides a protection of this normal 'liberty'; (2) that a woman's reproductive responses are natural, but in exceptional circumstances of defective or impaired femininity her 'welfare' also requires the protection of law; and (3) that the neutrality associated with science is the best method for deciding which protection the law should provide in practice. In the Canadian courtroom, lawyers worked on the law to recreate these coded assumptions, and in performing this work they stressed the very 'facts' that were created by medical professionals within the confines of therapeutic abortion committees.

In its intersection with medical authority, the law made women complicit in reproducing ideological hegemony. Unlike Canadian health care generally, the 1969 Criminal Code amendment made access to medical abortion services dependent on a woman's ability to satisfy conditions set down in law. Because the legal standard set the terms of justification according to the logic of a patriarchal social code, the intersection of legal regulation with medical practice preserved both the primacy of liberty rights within legal-code and social-code reasoning and the 'normal' equation of women's powerlessness with their nurture of these liberty rights. Women consented to this ideological process in the sense that personal autonomy could be achieved only by participating in a process that discursively denied all pregnant women the status of normal legal subjects. Whenever a woman claimed her welfare right to abortion services, her claim could be allowed only if it was justified in terms of a discourse that made abortions a service which only irresponsible and abnormal women desired but which was nevertheless needed to help and protect victimized or weak women. In short, the reform of the Criminal Code gave pregnant women a right to medical welfare.

PART FOUR
RESISTANCE AND CONTRADICTION

11

The Struggle for Choice and Access

To live in our culture is not (despite mythology to the contrary) to participate equally in some free play of individual diversity. Rather, one always finds oneself ·located within structures of dominance and subordination – not least important of which have been organized around gender. Certainly, the duality of male/ female is a discursive formation, a social construction ... [A]s such each of these dualities has had profound consequences for the construction of experience of those who live them. (Bordo 1990)

Medical and legalistic models of abortion ... always pictured women as victims ... never as possible shapers of their own destinies. And these models implicitly suggested that women were incompetent to act as moral agents on their own behalf. (Petchesky 1985:145)

The history of restrictive abortion legislation is also the history of women's resistance to it. (Gavigan 1986a:284)

A Federal Regulation of Choice and a Provincial Responsibility for Access

A major point of contention for activists seeking to eliminate class or gender inequality is whether the law can be used as an instrument for achieving social change. Many socialists, for example, conclude that legal reasoning is a closed system of thought and that its philosophical abstractions prevent the addressing of concrete human needs. Where the emphasis is placed on protecting individual liberty rights from intrusion by collectivities, disadvantaged groups will be denied access to needed resources so that the liberty interests of the powerful can be maintained. To seek equality of legal rights, it is argued, is to legitimate capitalist forms of organizing rather than to undermine capitalism's class structure.

Feminists have been divided on the question of legal reform. Some radical feminists, in a parallel of the socialist argument, have contended that the law is a closed system of thought that focuses on the principles of individuality and self-interest that are central to masculine identity while it ignores the ethic of social responsibility that characterizes feminine identity. As the antithesis of deontological thought, liberal law has traditionally had little to say about the responsibilities that individuals owe to others within society. Despite their differences, there has been agreement among some radical and Marxist feminists that legal struggles serve only to divert activists from the political sites where power is actually exercised.

Despite the parallel between feminist and socialist criticisms, socialist and radical feminists have been more likely to join their liberal sisters in pressing for an extension of legal rights to women. Although they may disagree about the role of law, there is a general feminist consensus that the law's traditional disregard of female liberty has left women vulnerable to the subjective whims of individuals in institutions controlled by men. As numerous feminists with diverse political positions have pointed out, the distinction between the public and private spheres – coupled with the belief that law has no place in the latter – has more often than not left women individually isolated in their oppression. Legal struggles may not lead to basic changes in the structure of hierarchical relations, but those who are most affected by a lack of formal rights often have little recourse but to fight for legal protection, as flawed as this protection may be.

My research into the legal and medical context surrounding the contemporary abortion controversy indicates that while the law is primarily directed towards protecting the individualism that underpins both capitalist and patriarchal relations, its role in conserving deontological beliefs about natural obligations is not insignificant. In fact, legal ideology itself depends on the capacity and willingness of women to undertake social responsibilities, and it actively constitutes and structures both their behaviour and consciousness. Since law does have an effect on daily reality, women who have had to live with the consequences of the abortion laws have not been able to avoid personal and political struggles with the policies and practices that these laws have generated.

Despite the ideological condemnation of abortion within cultural discourse, in practice, Canadian women did not passively accept the bureaucratization of medical control over abortion services. Individual Canadian women, like their counterparts elsewhere, continued to struggle consciously to limit their families as required by the larger political and economic context. This personal struggle was paralleled at the political level, and there are significant similarities between the contradictions faced at each level of activism. Just as individual women have personally been forced to opt for a liberty right of choice or a welfare right to needed resources, so has the political struggle traditionally been fragmented by the necessity of shifting its focus between legal and medical conflicts.

In Canada, the federal-provincial distribution of powers has played a role in the ongoing abortion struggle. Where abortion is concerned, the federal level has sole jurisdiction over the criminal law. But although federal politicians are the ones who pass the legislation that determines a woman's legal right to choice, it is the provincial governments that have the responsibility for providing the health services that women need. Structuring a legal right to choice through the therapeutic abortion committee (TAC) process meant that governments at the provincial level were responsible for ensuring the conditions whereby a woman could claim her 'welfare right' to a legal abortion. This division of powers allowed the two levels of government to throw the issue back and forth whenever political pressure became too intense at one level. This had a significant impact on the directions taken by the pro-choice movement.

The Abortion Law: A Matter of Federal Jurisdiction

Shortly after the passing of the Criminal Code amendments, women began to organize against the law. In May 1970 an Abortion Caravan descended on Parliament Hill in Ottawa. This action, 'where a group of women chained themselves to chairs in the Parliamentary Press Gallery demanding abortion on demand and forcing the House of Commons to adjourn its sitting' (A. Collins 1985:7), was a political articulation of the frustrations being felt by women's groups that were attempting to provide abortion referrals and counselling to individual women. Although the specific event – the demonstration and act of civil disobedience by 'women who had never done anything like this before' (ibid.:23) – attracted media attention to the cause, the organization of the caravan sparked something with a great deal more staying power. Out of the mobilization efforts of a small group of Vancouver women, a fledgling cross-country movement was born. Various women's groups across Canada began quietly to organize themselves politically and to translate this organization into not so quiet political actions.

1970s - women's groups

Within two months of that first national protest, feminists in Vancouver had forced a meeting with Prime Minister Trudeau and had demonstrated against the law. Winnipeg women had disrupted lunch at the Canadian Medical Association's (CMA) conference and had later presented their demands to a specially convened meeting of the CMA's board of directors. In Toronto, abortion activists challenged the then health minister, John Munro, while, nationally, the pro-choice network 'launched a telegraph campaign on Ottawa to support a man who was to become very important to them – Dr Henry Morgentaler' (ibid.:25–6).

The first practical challenge to the 1969 Criminal Code amendment came in 1973. At that time, Dr Morgentaler 'admitted performing over 5,000 abortions for poor people on request in his clinic [in Montreal] and published his practice openly in the *Canadian Medical Association Journal*' (L. Collins 1982:11). Although Dr Morgentaler was doing nothing more than other doctors were doing across the country – namely, providing abortion services based on his own subjective assessment of the need for these services – he was doing it publicly. His subsequent legal battles in the Province of Quebec made legal history. Although acquitted in three separate jury trials, he was imprisoned following a Supreme Court decision that overturned the first jury verdict, and he remained in custody despite two more jury acquittals.

Never before in the history of Canada had a jury verdict been reversed by a higher court. This could not have happened under British or American law. The issue became something other than abortion. The court's reversal of Dr Morgentaler's acquittal struck at the heart of the legal system: the right of an individual to be tried and acquitted by a jury of his or her peers. The public outcry from the legal community resulted in the Canadian Parliament passing the 'Morgentaler Amendment,' an enactment that ensured that higher courts would thenceforth be unable to overrule the decisions of juries. The legislation came too late to be applied to Dr Morgentaler himself, thus assuring him of a place in legal history. Further, in the light of his unique imprisonment, the Quebec government's persistence in charging him for each separate abortion became a political embarrassment.

When the Liberal government was defeated in Quebec, the Parti Québécois dropped all remaining charges against Morgentaler, claiming that the law was no longer enforceable in the province. The new government officially tolerated the continued operation of Morgentaler's clinics to the extent that although these services were provided in defiance of the law, the provincial health plan began to pay the medical costs of his patients. The national law was still in existence, but in one province this law was now openly being broken without formal repercussions. Although women in Quebec had no more legal right to make abortion decisions than women in other provinces, in practice the continued operation of the illegal clinics gave them both choice and access. The irony of the situation was that reproductive freedom was more readily accessible in a largely Catholic province than anywhere else in Canada.

The existence of visible clinics operating outside the law in Quebec had broad repercussions that were difficult for the federal government to ignore. By threatening to open the door to abortion 'on demand' throughout the country, the continued operation of the clinics posed a threat to medical autonomy and state control. Professional autonomy was threatened by the possibility of pregnant women demanding a medical service for which the profession could be held criminally liable. State control was threatened by the possibility that such blatant lawbreaking could spread throughout Canada. The situation also meant that Canadian women who could afford to travel to Quebec had access to the most sophisticated technology for securing abortions.

Instead of changing the national law to reflect the situation of legal nonenforcement in Quebec, the federal government appeared initially to adopt a strategy of containing the illegality in the Province of Quebec while reinforcing the bureaucratic process elsewhere. This approach brought the state and its agents of reproductive control, the medical profession, into open conflict. The Quebec situation brought increasing medical pressure on the federal justice minister, Otto Lang, to act to resolve the situation. Mr Lang's response came in the form of a memo to the medical profession. He demanded that doctors apply the law 'strictly: that social and economic considerations were not to be taken into account in determining whether a pregnancy could be lawfully terminated' (A. Collins, 1985:29; cf. L. Collins, 1982). Many in the profession interpreted these 'orders' as an encroachment on their right to make medical decisions about the health of their patients. Doctors now found themselves facing an erosion of the professional autonomy which the law initially had been meant to protect.

Mr Lang's memo opened up a heated exchange between the medical profession and the federal government. The increasing political pressure on members of Parliament led to the establishment of a federally appointed Committee on the Operation of the Abortion Law, chaired by Dr Robin F. Badgley. 'To be credible, the Badgley Committee could not deny the obvious social problem caused by the government's elite-permissive abortion policy. A considerable struggle occurred over exactly how it could explain the abortion problem without implicitly criticizing the abortion law ... The formula to resolve the difficulty for the Committee came in the form of a national patient survey which detailed the epidemiological nature of abortion, but blamed medical, hospital and provincial obstacles for preventing the law's equitable operation' (L. Collins 1982:13). Since, under the law, the provinces had the sole authority to accredit hospitals and to provide health services, the Badgley Committee's report blamed the provinces for their failure to provide the facilities necessary for dealing with the problem. The implication was that it was not the law – and its allocation of moral authority to the medical profession – that was the problem; rather, the report focused attention on the provincial implementation of the law.

While the official status of the Badgley Report (and its intensive documentation of the inequities created by the committee system) generated even more intense political pressure for something to be done, the report itself accomplished something further: in its identification of provincial responsibility for inadequate medical services, it took the pressure off the federal government and reoriented the struggle towards the provincial level. It turned attention from the negative aspects of the criminal law and focused it on the lack of positive response by those responsible for implementing health policy. The welfare status of women under the law was not challenged, but the availability of resources to judge their need was deemed to be lacking.

The reallocation of political responsibility to the provinces had implications for the direction of the future struggle and for the women's movement as a whole. Its main effect was to split the movement into separate provincial groups organizing to improve access in their respective regions, thus turning attention away from the federal law that underpinned the lack of access occurring at the provincial level.

Medical Services: A Matter of Provincial Jurisdiction

In the years immediately following the Badgley Report, the federal government generally abdicated responsibility for the abortion situation, leaving it to the provinces to define what would constitute a 'hospital' for the purposes of providing legal abortions. As the struggle for reproductive choice moved into English Canada, it took the form of a fight to establish free-standing abortion clinics in provinces outside Quebec.

Public challenges to medical and state control during the 1980s were an attempt to extend and consolidate the gains made during the 1970s in Quebec. Just as the earlier Quebec challenge to the law involved Dr Morgentaler as the central political figure, the challenge within the rest of Canada again involved the legal status of his activities.

Dr Morgentaler stepped into the limelight once more when he opened clinics in Winnipeg and in Toronto during the spring of 1983. Each was immediately raided and new criminal charges were laid against him. The manner in which these cities were selected differed, as did the clinics' degree of success in remaining in operation. Each clinic was opened within a particular political and a particular social context, and the difference between the two had implications for the way the struggle was able to proceed in each of these provinces. Anne Collins (1985) argues that if need alone had determined the area where new clinics were to be built, the sites chosen would have been in Newfoundland or Saskatchewan. Other activists, however, have suggested that the situation in Manitoba was among the worst in Canada, and Manitoba women's groups had been attempting to improve access in a variety of ways for a number of years. This was true as well for activist groups in Toronto. However, the decision to open clinics in Manitoba and Ontario was not made strictly on the basis of necessity or lack of access to services. These were political choices that took into consideration the necessity for ideological change and the ability to mobilize public support. These political choices were not made in the same way, by the same people, or in the same political context – a factor that helps explain the different outcomes in Toronto and Winnipeg.

The opening of the two clinics occurred only a month apart. Each was raided almost immediately, but the ability of the movement to keep them operating during the lengthy legal process was very different in each case. The continued operation of the Toronto clinic was a focal point in the mobilization of supporters. The closure of the Winnipeg clinic was part of a process of demobilization. It would be a mistake to believe that the women's movement in Ontario worked harder or chose better strategies in its fight to keep its clinic open. Just as the Ontario situation differed from and had different outcomes from the earlier Quebec strategy, the political and social contexts within Ontario and Manitoba were different. Further, the decision in Ontario was arrived at as part of a political process in which the women's movement participated, whereas Manitoba was chosen by Dr Morgentaler.

The Clinic Challenges: A Struggle for Both 'Choice' and 'Access'

Ontario: Mobilizing the Struggle

With the 1969 amendment to the Criminal Code, the abortion issue had lost pre-eminence at the ideological level, but the institutionalization of the informal committee system had created new obstacles of access for those with the least resources. Although, ideologically, the new law was publicly perceived as having fairly addressed the needs of any woman who really required an abortion, this was not in fact the case, and pro-choice activists faced the task of illustrating this fallacy while also addressing the actual problems of gaining access to the legal process. For health-care workers and those working with poor and immigrant women, the obstacles created by the law were a continuing source of frustration and outrage. The women they dealt with required abortions for other than medical reasons, and their legal access to safe medical abortions was severely limited. They needed the legal right to make reproductive decisions if they were to cope with their daily lives – a liberty right – but the availability of the services that would allow them their legal welfare right presented an obstacle course that was difficult if not impossible for these poorer women to traverse.

In Toronto, the women's movement had been quietly organizing around the issue of abortion ever since the days of the Abortion Caravan of 1970. From the very inception of the new law, women working in the women's health movement in Ontario had been frustrated by the legal and medical 'hoops which women were compelled to leap through,' and they concluded that the bureaucratic maze created by the 1969 amendments was making access more difficult rather than easier (Egan 1985). The Criminal Code amendments had not changed what doctors had been doing on an informal basis, but as the Badgley Committee had documented, the lack of access to the legal process made the difficult problem of finding a doctor willing to perform the procedure even more intolerable. The TAC process had given doctors protection from the threat of prosecution, but it required their patients to participate in what came to be described as the 'abortion lottery.'

The publication of the Badgley Report created a 'space' for challenging the public perception that the law provided an abortion to any woman who really needed one. The TAC process was restricting access, not facilitating it. In taking advantage of this space, the energy of pro-choice activists was redirected from the lack of *choice* women had in making reproductive decisions, a liberty right, to highlighting the problems women faced in gaining *access* to the medical resources required to exercise the welfare right to which the law entitled them. Because it was within provincial jurisdiction to ensure that medical services were made available, the shift in focus turned the struggle from the federal political scene towards the provincial level of government.

In 1975 several Ontario women's groups began lobbying the provincial government about its responsibility to provide medical care for all its citizens. In 1977 representatives of the Women's Health Organization (WHO) met with the minister of health, Dennis Timbrell, to persuade him to accredit a women's clinic which they wanted to set up. A women's free-standing health clinic, they argued, could alleviate the access problem that was created by the province's failure to accredit sufficient facilities to meet the demand for abortion services. In their discussions with the Ministry of Health, they pointed out the obstacles which Toronto women encountered in getting abortion services. They noted that the law did not require hospitals to establish TACs and that, where these committees did operate, they met infrequently and established quotas on the numbers allowed in a given time period. Since a hospital did not have to divulge its particular system of rules, many women experienced lengthy delays in getting their cases before the committee and consequently failed to meet the arbitrary time limits during which an abortion could be performed. These problems were compounded for poor women in that only gynaecologists were permitted to perform abortions in Ontario, and many of these doctors had opted out of medicare and demanded their fees in cash in advance (A. Collins 1985).

The documentation of the WHO was impeccable. Its research into the Toronto situation confirmed the findings of the Badgley Report. The limited choice allowed by the abortion law was further reduced by the access problem. The recommendation of WHO – that a women's health clinic be accredited by the provincial government – followed logically from the federal report. Moreover, this arrangement would save the provincial government a substantial amount of money, since there was extensive evidence that free-standing clinics were considerably cheaper than hospital-provided services. Nevertheless, the proposal was turned down. Again, what was at stake was the medical profession's control. Although WHO's proposal would clearly have provided women with better health care, Timbrell accepted the assurance of the Ontario College of Physicians and Surgeons that the problem was being addressed and that those of its members who put cash before care had been suitably chastised (A. Collins 1985:74).

In 1978 a new proposal was drafted, this time by the Toronto Women's Health Clinic. It proposed a health clinic for women that would provide them with a full range of health services. Architectural plans had been drafted, budgets prepared, and broad community support solicited. Again the proposal was blocked. The problem for the provincial government was that a women's health clinic would not only increase a woman's access to welfare resources but would give her a say in how and for what purposes these resources were to be used. Establishing women's health clinics, democratically controlled, would have been a step towards providing women with both choice and access. Such a step would have undermined the professional monopoly on decision making that doctors enjoyed.

Blocked by the medical lobby from securing increased access to abortion by legal means, the Ontario activists felt that it was time to consider illegal options. Predictably, they looked to Quebec, where they had a ready-made model for illegal action. As the Ontario Coalition for Abortion Clinics activist Carolyn Egan (1985), explains,

We looked at what had happened in the Province of Quebec, where CLSCs (community health clinics) and Centres de Santé des Femmes (women's health centres) were providing women with free abortions in their own communities. A lesson was learned from our sisters in Quebec, and we modeled our strategy on theirs. This strategy was the combination of a doctor willing to challenge the law by opening a clinic in defiance of the criminal code, and a broad-based alliance (led by the women's movement) willing to defend the clinic and fight for the necessary changes. We realized that we needed to organize a campaign which would include the trade union movement, immigrant communities, lesbian and gay organizations, anti-racist groups, riding associations, etc. We knew we were up against state and powerful right-wing organizations and we knew we wouldn't win it alone.

If broad public support was to be marshalled to the cause of illegal clinics, one needed a doctor who could provide the most up-to-date technology for safe abortion procedures, for public credibility required that the procedures should meet the most exacting scientific standards. Of course, such a doctor would have to be prepared to be charged by the police and subjected to the full range of harassment that could be expected from both the state and the organized right. In short, the women's movement needed a Morgentaler.

In the summer of 1982 nine members of the Committee for the

Establishment of Abortion Clinics (CEAC) met with Dr Morgentaler to ask him to act as medical adviser and to recommend a doctor to operate the illegal clinic they were proposing. In the fall of 1982 the Ontario Coalition for Abortion Clinics (OCAC) was formed to do the necessary mobilizing work. Before the doors opened on the Morgentaler clinic on 15 June 1983, the movement had begun to gain its public constituency. Its members worked among New Democratic Party and labour groups as well as professional and civil libertarian associations, and they also had their foot in the door at Queen's Park, lobbying and gaining MPP support for at least the idea of a free-standing clinic (A. Collins 1985).

The women involved in these mobilizing efforts viewed abortion clinics as a first step in reaching their larger goal of publicly funded clinics oriented towards a whole range of interconnected reproductive health services. Although the long-range goal of the women's movement was at odds with the idea of private doctor-controlled clinics operating outside medicare, the abortion activists felt that such a clinic could become the focal point for a political challenge to the existing system. Attempts to pressure the federal government to repeal the law, attempts to achieve greater hospital access at the provincial level, and attempts to establish legal women's clinics had all been rebuffed. In order to penetrate medical control and media control, the counterattack required medical expertise and a media personality. Although the opening of illegal free-standing clinics was a conscious political choice, for the most committed activists it was a choice of strategy in a long-term campaign. Their ultimate goal was to link choice and access through a repeal of the law and the establishment of free women-controlled health clinics.

The choice of the clinic strategy was, however, a double-edged sword. Its disadvantages were to become only too apparent as the abortion question was transformed in the public mind into the Morgentaler question, and as the right of women to control their own reproduction became Morgentaler's private right to provide a medical service in the manner he saw fit.

By contrasting the pro-choice struggle in Ontario and Manitoba, it is possible to see how the medical monopoly allowed physicians, as a group, to manipulate access in order to consolidate their own power position. In Ontario their manipulation involved a decrease in access in order to strengthen the profession's position *vis-à-vis* the state, and in Manitoba it involved an increase in access in order to strengthen the profession's position *vis-à-vis* the women's movement.

*Ontario: Maintaining Professional Autonomy by
Decreasing Women's Access*

All Canadians are entitled to state-funded medical care, and health services
authorized by a doctor, as medically indicated, are covered by medical
insurance. Under the 1969 amendment to the Criminal Code, abortions
authorized by doctors (and required for 'therapeutic' purposes) became
eligible for public funding. Following the enactment of the law, women
were in a position to secure funding for the abortions that doctors had
informally been supplying for some years. At the same time, however, the
ability to secure access to medical services was generally made more difficult by the law. Although doctors still made the abortion decision, the law
placed restrictions on where such services could be dispensed; abortions
could be performed only in hospitals or 'accredited facilities.' Further,
under the federal-provincial split of jurisdictional power, it was the provincial health ministers who had the authority to determine what constituted
an 'accredited facility' for performing abortions. Physicians, therefore,
could provide abortion services only in facilities accredited by the province,
but no such facility was compelled to provide abortion services or even to
set up the required therapeutic abortion committees (TACs). For Ontario
women, this meant that they were dependent on doctors who had access to
the hospitals that operated these committees. Because doctors and hospitals set informal quota systems, and because abortion services were 'time-
dependent' for pregnant women, the process ensured that these services
were by no means universally accessible, even at the best of times.

Under the Canadian health plan, physicians are not compelled to provide a service, but it is expected that the market for a service (together
with the 'peer policing' of professional associations) will ensure that all
legitimate health needs are met. Because health matters fall under provincial jurisdiction, the particular manner in which the Canadian medical
insurance plan is implemented can vary from province to province. During the 1970s and early 1980s, Ontario allowed the medical profession to
operate outside the health plan and to extra-bill its patients, charging
them more than the negotiated health-insurance rates. Although the
potential to extra-bill could give wealthier patients access to a greater
range of more expensive doctors, universal access to basic health care was
not expected to be affected; given the fact that all citizens had access to
dollars for purchasing medical services, supply-demand reasoning suggested that the medical market would ensure that basic needs would be
met by the demand for them.

During the 1980s the ideological principle of universal access to state-funded medical services was increasingly undermined by the practice of extra billing. Because extra billing was not distributed evenly across the spectrum of medical needs, the resulting disparities involved more than an inequality of access to the most expensive doctors. It meant that certain services were available only through the payment of money over and above state funding. The provision of abortion services was one such area where the principle of universal health care was visibly at risk.

The standard procedure of extra billing for abortion services illustrates the inequities produced by the market – where the provider of service maintains a monopoly on the rights of decision making while the consumer bears the responsibility for the results of these decisions. Because Ontario hospitals had restricted the performance of the abortion procedure to gynaecologists, and because gynaecology was a specialty with a high ratio of extra billing, the first hurdle that a poorer woman faced in achieving a 'response' to her abortion-related needs involved finding a gynaecologist who would perform the operation within the Ontario Hospital Insurance Plan (OHIP). Abortions were therefore heavily dependent on one's ability to pay for the services of an opted-out gynaecologist, many of whom demanded that their fee be paid 'up front.'

It was not, however, the problems arising from abortion-related services that forced the state to act to end extra billing. These problems only surfaced publicly when the provincial government faced a fiscal crisis involving its ability to maintain its previous level of medical funding. This crisis was precipitated by the actions of the federal government: on 1 July 1984 the Canada Health Act was enacted by Parliament. Under the provisions of this act, provincial governments would lose federal dollars if doctors continued to bill their patients above the negotiated health-insurance rates. Since it was estimated that 12 per cent of all Ontario doctors extra-billed (with a substantially higher rate in the larger centres and for certain specialties), the new federal legislation meant that the Province of Ontario risked losing approximately $50 million a year in transfer payments from the federal government.

Before the election of Ontario's Liberal government in 1984, extra billing had become a political issue in the province. The Liberal Party was elected as the result of an accord made with the New Democratic Party, and a major plank in this accord promised an end to extra billing. In order to keep this promise, the Ontario government introduced the Health Care Accessibility Act on 19 December 1985, whereupon the Ontario Medical Association (OMA) began a concerted effort to defeat it.

The physicians claimed that to take away their power to extra-bill would infringe on their autonomy as private professionals and would turn them into civil servants. The major danger they perceived was the threat to their liberty right to define what services they would provide and where they would provide them.

Doctors in various parts of Ontario protested the threat to their professional power in a number of ways, including both a general strike and a work stoppage in 'nonessential' services. The law that gave women a welfare right to an abortion provided a resource for physicians to use in their fight. The first area of work stoppage used to pressure the provincial government involved the operation of the TACs; in Sarnia, doctors protested the forthcoming legislation by resigning from all hospital committees, including the therapeutic abortion committee. This committee was the only TAC in that part of the province. Thus, the resignation of the doctors effectively cut off all access to abortion services in what was already a tightly controlled situation.

The action of the Sarnia doctors proved to be a tactical error, for it sparked a major mobilizing effort in support of the Health Care Accessibility Act. The response of the pro-choice movement was immediate, and it succeeded in organizing outraged women from a large number of organizations into one loud voice. The Sarnia doctors resigned from the TAC on Friday, 21 February 1986, and by the following Monday the members of the Ontario Coalition for Abortion Clinics (OCAC), the National Action Committee on the Status of Women (NAC), and the Canadian Abortion Rights Action League (CARAL) had called a news conference to respond to the resignation. The major points made at this press conference centred on the impact of extra billing on the well-being of all Ontario women. The spokespersons for the groups noted that women were at a special disadvantage because they constituted a majority of those living below the poverty line; that the specialties pertaining to women's health care were those with the highest ratios of extra billing; and that the resignation of the Sarnia doctors only served to illustrate how the existing law on abortion allowed women to be used as pawns in the furthering of medical interests. Their message was clear: the professional freedom sought by the medical profession was another term for professional 'licence' to exploit the medical needs of women.

The action by the Sarnia doctors brought immediate censure on the entire medical profession in the province. As the chairperson of the Social Development Committee (an all-party committee formed to hear submissions and briefs on the proposed act), MPP Richard Johnson stated that this action by doctors in one city 'was not a maverick action. They did so with the tacit approval of the OMA, which did not chastise them.' Further, the withdrawal of TAC services as part of a withdrawal of 'nonessential' services demonstrated the degree to which doctors could define what services would be covered by public funding, and it showed how vulnerable other groups were to such definitions. If the OMA would not police its own members, access to any medical service could become problematic.

Recognizing the importance of the extra-billing issue for abortion access, OCAC and NAC took the opportunity to organize and mobilize a diverse group of organizations into a new grass-roots political alliance. After the press conference, they approached other groups who were vulnerable to the power held by the medical profession in the province, pointing out the implications the actions of the Sarnia doctors had for medical relations in general. The result of this political organizing was a coalition of forty organizations. The Alliance to End Extra Billing involved a broad spectrum of the general public, including senior citizens, labour unions, women's groups, nurses, teachers, and the disabled. The alliance was described in the *Toronto Star* as a 'new social force' and indeed its establishment brought with it a heightened understanding of the fact that women's reproductive needs were most susceptible to manipulation by individual doctors.

The Social Development Committee provided the pro-choice movement with a new forum in which to push for the legalization of free-standing clinics as provincial facilities. Anything to do with the medical strike was news, and the actions of the Sarnia doctors had made abortion access an important part of that news. The hearings of the Social Development Committee provided another avenue for the pro-choice movement to gain media attention and initiate public discussion about the way in which the choices of all women were bound up with the medical access issue.

The Ontario Coalition for Abortion Clinics' brief to the committee challenged the state's commitment to universal access where medical abortion services were concerned. It pointedly addressed the contradiction and irony of the fact that doctors in illegal free-standing clinics wished to 'opt in' to OHIP while doctors performing abortions in hospitals had largely 'opted out.' The abortion issue exemplified the fundamental problems of the market model for providing medical services to women, especially abortion services:

[E]xtra billing is a matter of fundamental principle, the principle of universal access to quality medical care ... Women are the primary users of medical care and the majority of the poor are women ... The practice of extra billing places a major obstacle to abortion in an already overcrowded obstacle course. The majority of doctors who perform abortions privately extra bill ... Gynaecologists, who are the only doctors permitted to perform abortions in Ontario hospitals, charge as much as $400 over the Ontario health insurance plan rate, often demanding cash in advance ... Not only must a woman pay the gynaecologist, but if she is given a general anaesthetic, she must often also pay the anaesthetist. (OCAC brief to the Social Development Committee)

Whereas the experience of women in the United States demonstrates that the lack of a welfare right to medical resources erodes the liberty right of choice, the experience of Ontario women demonstrates that a legal right to medical services can also facilitate 'the development of new sources of control over women' (Doyal 1985:237). A welfare right, in the absence of a liberty right, makes the recipient of services vulnerable to being used to further interests that are not her own. However, the contradiction illustrated by the actions of the Ontario doctors is that where the medical profession sought to increase its own autonomy by decreasing access to its services, its strategy increased its vulnerability to the actions of politically organized groups. In fact, the tactic served as a catalyst for further mobilization of the pro-choice forces.

In a number of ways, the Ontario medical strike increased the power of pro-choice activists to affect the course of future events. Although the actions of the Sarnia doctors clearly had negative repercussions for individual women seeking an abortion, at the political level the pro-choice movement was helped enormously in its mobilization efforts. Months and years of work by pro-choice activists had not accomplished public visibility for the problems of access; and now, in one fell swoop, the work stoppage in Sarnia had brought instant access to the media while serving to forge networks of support from many other groups.

The problem for those who would challenge asymmetrical medical relations is much more difficult when the medical profession seeks to retain control of the reproductive decision-making process by actually increasing access to its services. The political struggle in Manitoba provides an illustration of this medical strategy for retaining the professional monopoly on decision making.

Manitoba: Mobilizing the Clinic Struggle

Although Manitoba women had been at work on this issue for at least as long as their counterparts in Ontario, the breadth of public support was quite different and the political relations also were of a different nature. As well, the establishment of the illegal free-standing clinic came at the initiative of Henry Morgentaler, and, from the beginning, the women's community was put in the position of reacting and supporting his decisions.

Morgentaler had chosen Winnipeg (as part of a plan to open two clinics simultaneously) because of his perception of probable political support from the newly elected New Democratic Party (NDP) government. As a party, the NDP had policies supportive of the rights of women, and at both the national and provincial levels, party policies favoured women's control of reproduction and an unfettered right to publicly funded abortions. However, the newly elected Manitoba government's support for official party policy was tempered by the political and personal interests of the caucus members.

The decision to open the clinic in Winnipeg was more a Morgentaler decision than part of an overall strategy of the Manitoba women's movement. Morgentaler hoped that NDP party policy would translate into the actual practice of giving accredited status to the free-standing clinic. As events were to prove, the choice of an NDP province, on the basis of its party platform, was unwise. The implications of the lack of organized support might have been more clearly noted if the Manitoba women's community had been more involved in the decision and early planning for a clinic. The Manitoba activists were in close touch with the realities of the political situation (including the personalities involved) and were aware of the difference from the official party line.

The NDP in Manitoba had always exhibited a more progressive stance on economic issues, than on social issues and this was very much a reflection of the political culture in the province. Although the women's caucus of the party had developed – over time and with a great deal of effort – a fair amount of organized power (evidenced by the number of women the party managed to get elected in 1981), their issues had not been translated into the consciousness of the old guard who controlled the caucus. Within the NDP caucus, many potential supporters of the pro-choice movement were wary of creating a rift over a 'women's issue.'

In many ways, the fact that the NDP formed the elected government worked against support for women's health clinics and free-standing abortion clinics. Because their party was in power, the women faced a stronger resistance to freedom of choice from within their own party ranks than was the case in provinces where the NDP did not form the government. Years of work by NDP women had paid off when they were nominated to and elected in winnable seats. They had a whole range of interconnected demands, all of which had secured support at party conventions and which now appeared to have some chance of being translated into practice. But support for this larger agenda was threatened by anti-choice supporters within the caucus. This conservative group hoped to defuse the political situation by increasing access to hospital abortions and using whatever means were necessary to keep Morgentaler out of the province. To achieve this objective, they used their support for other women's issues as a resource to divide pro-choice support within the party. Although the anti-choice faction was never successful in changing party policy, it was able to ensure that Morgentaler's clinic would not be accredited as a facility within the terms of the law.

The split between grass-roots activists (who perceived the NDP as a movement) and elected caucus members (who perceived the NDP as a party) was not a new one on the prairies. It had surfaced more than a decade earlier when the NDP first held office in Manitoba. Despite the NDP's commitment to having its party policy derived from convention debate at the grass-roots level, several of the elected elite were determined not to be bound by this with regard to abortion. Because Manitoba pro-choice activists could expect little support from the Conservatives on the issue, there was less organized political support for a clinic in Manitoba than there was in Ontario.

One reason for Morgentaler's optimism in opening a clinic in Manitoba was the expectation that legal action against the clinic might be avoided, because the attorney general, Roland Penner, was one of the most progressive members elected and was on record as being a strong pro-choice supporter. However, in addition to the political realities involved in being the elected government, personal commitments within the elected caucus were extremely polarized. Moreover, Penner was not the most influential actor in the internal political drama; the person who could approve the proposed facility as a hospital was not the attorney general but the minister of health, Larry Desjardins. Desjardins was a Roman Catholic and an anti-choice supporter, and he represented a largely Catholic riding. In addition, he adhered to a political philosophy that supported professional medical control over all health-related issues, going so far as to stake his political future with the party on the retention of all abortion services within the established hospital system.

Both Desjardins' and Penner's personal beliefs were clear from the beginning, and both held political clout within the elected caucus. However, Penner's left-leaning proclivities had put him at a disadvantage in the control of his department. A long-standing animosity existed between Attorney General Penner and the local police department, and new provincial legislation had exacerbated the conflict. As former chairperson of the Police Powers Committee of the Manitoba Association of Rights and Liberties (MARL), Penner had made a pre-election commitment to bring in a Law Enforcement Review Act to curtail police powers in the province. His fulfilment of this commitment strengthened the police animosity towards him. Certainly the situation was different from the informal ties of cooperation that existed between the police department and the attorney general's department in Toronto. As one Manitoba NDP party activist and longtime worker for abortion rights stated,

The tactics of the movement to focus anger on Penner rather than Desjardins was foolish. Larry is the one who could have legalized the facility. These tactics take one of the few pro-choice supporters in Cabinet and turn him against us ... The police were out to get Roland and the clinic provided them with one way to get at Roland and the NDP at the same time. Every time there is a decision to be made, they throw it back at him. He takes the flak for them raiding the clinic. People don't distinguish between him and the police. I believe that Roland probably advised the police that it was not a good idea to raid the clinic, and I believe that the police would have raided it anyway because they were so angry about the external review of police powers ... The only out for him would have been to resign. The approval or non-approval of the clinic was not his decision. He is faced with a situation in which the clinic is unapproved; it is clearly operating in violation of the law, the police have raided, the senior crown prosecutor has advised that there is evidence to lay charges. (Personal interview)

Whether Penner could have refrained from prosecution, as his counterpart in Quebec had managed to do, is both a legal and a political question. However, the context within which Penner might have been persuaded to use his ministerial powers to intervene with the police was lacking. Almost from the beginning, Morgentaler and Penner were at loggerheads. In February 1983, Morgentaler addressed a crowd of sixteen hundred people in Manitoba and made the statement that his clinic had performed an abortion on the girlfriend of a son of a Canadian attorney general – an attorney general who lived in a province where he planned to open a clinic. Since Morgentaler had publicly proclaimed himself to be considering only Winnipeg and Toronto, the remark led to an angry response from Penner: ' "It wasn't this attorney-general," Mr. Penner said angrily, noting that the audience was probably left with the impression that it was him. "I find this kind of manoeuvring intolerable" ' (*Toronto Star*, 3 February 1983). As each man reacted to statements of the other, Morgentaler again challenged Penner, in a statement that was guaranteed to make headlines. He accused him of being a coward who would sacrifice principles for pragmatism if he did not stay any charges laid by the police. The women in the Manitoba pro-choice movement attempted to smooth over the developing animosity between the two men by arranging for a private meeting between them, but their worries that neither of 'these two men with their huge egos' would bend proved to be accurate (previously cited personal interview).

Lacking any undivided organizational support for its cause, the Manitoba pro-choice movement attempted to keep the Morgentaler clinic open in a climate in which its own supporters had divided loyalties. The situation was not helped by the fact that the movement was in the position of reacting to Morgentaler initiatives. In the end, the concerted efforts of government and the medical establishment forced the clinic to close.

Manitoba: Maintaining Professional Autonomy by Increasing Women's Access

The pro-choice movement in Manitoba was in a reactive position almost from the beginning, and this generated a certain amount of hostility from women who were expected to support the clinic through their mobilization efforts. One Manitoba pro-choice activist explained:

I have felt extremely frustrated: two groups of men and they are both trying to tell us what to do. One of them sits in the legislature and says we have to sacrifice ourselves for the party and this government and social democracy and we shouldn't hold this up over one issue. On the other hand, there is Henry Morgentaler telling us what's best for us. He bloody well comes to Manitoba, opens the clinic with no prior consultation, reopens the clinic with no prior consultation. He is no more ready to let women take the leadership ... than the government is. His whole style is to tell us what he is going to do and he ignores the impact this had on all of us. When he decided to reopen the clinic, how many women had to dedicate themselves to getting escorts, to making sure there was security for women going in and out of the clinic! Just like the government knows that we're going to vote for them anyway (because we have no other real options), Henry knows that we are going to come through for him anyway. Even when the leadership of the women's coalition says, 'No, don't do it, we're not ready,' he does it anyway because he knows that he can rely on us. And I have frankly had it with all of them who tell us what to do! (Personal interview)

Such expressions of anger were generally kept guardedly closed from public view, and with good reason. They provided grist for the mill of an opposition that portrayed Morgentaler as just another victimizer of women. However, the above expostulation about lack of control for the direction the struggle would take (both in actual terms and in symbolic ones) should not be taken out of context. It is an example of the ambivalence that existed within the movement over the role of the Morgentaler clinics in both personal and political terms. There was a genuine acknowledgment of the fact that the movement needed a Morgentaler, that the structure of the system required a Morgentaler to challenge it, and that the consequences of illegal actions would be borne by Morgentaler personally. The Winnipeg pro-choice women recognized this from the beginning, and far from rejecting the idea of opening a free-standing clinic in the city, they welcomed it as a way out of the impasse they had arrived at in their attempts to establish health clinics. There was and there continued to be a feeling of heartfelt gratitude to Morgentaler and a recognition of his contribution. As the above 'angry' activist noted, 'If the clinic hadn't opened, we wouldn't have forced the provincial government to improve access at the hospital. As mad as I am, I recognize that' (ibid.).

This Manitoba activist put her finger on the dilemma faced by women in the pro-choice movement. Men controlled access to the political arena, just as they controlled access to medical services. Dr Morgentaler was, at one and the same time, the movement's greatest asset and its greatest liability. His involvement was vitally important for the struggle waged by pro-choice activists, and his medical expertise and willingness to challenge the system were crucial in opening up access to abortions for women across the country. Medical support was required, but gaining this support often meant that female participation in the decision-making process was eroded or bypassed whenever the males involved exercised their 'right' to control decisions. Still, male support was necessary if access to both medical and ideological resources was to be achieved, and women were grateful for the personal sacrifices made by Dr Morgentaler on their behalf.

The opening of the Morgentaler clinic in Winnipeg did make a significant difference in the level of access in Manitoba. Like their Toronto counterparts, the members of the women's movement in Winnipeg had been lobbying and proposing women's health clinics since the mid-1970s. In their lobbying for a free-standing clinic, the pro-choice activists had been turned down in 1977 by the then minister of health, Bud Sherman (Conservative). In 1979 things had looked more hopeful when two doctors from the Health Sciences Centre (the Winnipeg hospital where 98 per cent of all Manitoba abortions were performed) made a proposal for the opening of a clinic affiliated with the centre. These doctors were apparently motivated by statistics which showed that Manitoba had the highest second-trimester abortion rate – a fact that reflected badly on the hospital and its doctors. In the end, however, the doctors' proposal was dropped. The feeling within the Winnipeg women's movement was that the hospital had been bought off: the proposal had quietly disappeared following a provincial grant of $1 million for the upgrading of the hospital's existing facilities.

The years of fruitless effort by women in Winnipeg meant that they were highly receptive to Morgentaler's offer to open a clinic in the city. All the statistical information the movement had provided about the number of women leaving the province to seek medical help had been ignored and passed over until the Morgentaler clinic was opened. The opening focused public attention on the failure of the Manitoba Ministry of Health to provide adequate health services for women. Manitoba women in the pro-choice movement credit Morgentaler with taking a courageous stand on their behalf, and they are well aware that without this stand the government would not have moved to increase services in the hospitals. And move it did: 'The day the first charges were laid against Morgentaler and his staff, Larry Desjardins stood in the legislature to admit that abortion services in Manitoba were inadequate. He proposed to extend operating funds to the Health Sciences Centre to allow for nine hundred more abortions' (A. Collins 1985:64). According to one Winnipeg activist, the lobbying of the NDP government to ratify the Morgentaler clinic as a hospital facility resulted in an increase of 35 per cent in the number of abortions approved by existing committees. Yet the increase in access was a mixed blessing. Since the Morgentaler clinic was operating outside the law, abortions performed there were not eligible for coverage by medicare; but when publicly funded abortions became more easily secured, support for the movement's efforts to gain control of the decision-making process was undercut.

The state's strategy to depoliticize the abortion issue in Manitoba was assisted by laws that purportedly regulated the medical profession. The relationship of Manitoba's private medical clinics to the Manitoba College of Physicians and Surgeons meant that it was substantially more difficult to keep the Winnipeg clinic open. Although the provincial government could have licensed the Morgentaler clinic as a hospital, the clinic also required certification from the Manitoba College if it was to be allowed to operate. The college refused to grant this certification – not for medical reasons but for legal ones – arguing that it could not license a clinic performing illegal procedures. Considering that Morgentaler had not yet been convicted in a court of law for operating this clinic and that he had been found not guilty by four separate juries for operating similar clinics in Quebec and Ontario, the college was, in effect, making a finding of legal guilt where none yet existed. When Morgentaler persisted in operating the clinic in defiance of the college, it revoked his licence to practise medicine in Manitoba. Because no other Manitoba doctor was prepared to step in and risk the personal consequences of breaking the law, the revocation of Dr Morgentaler's licence had serious implications for the continuation of the clinic's operation in the province. With their alternative source of access thus cut off, the pro-choice women were put in the position of welcoming the increased hospital access offered by the government.

The actions of the medical governing body in Manitoba provide an interesting contrast to those of the Ontario Medical Association. The doctors in Sarnia were not censured for *withholding* the responses that women required. In Manitoba, however, Dr Morgentaler's licence to practise was withdrawn because he *provided* the required responses. Both measures were within the spirit of a law that allowed physicians to withhold abortion services as they individually chose but prohibited the provision of abortions outside the professional structure of legitimation. In each instance, the right of the profession as a whole to control medical resources was at issue.

As the Manitoba government moved to increase access to abortion services within hospitals, it reinforced the ideology perpetuated by the TAC process. In this version of reality, only women who face life-threatening consequences require abortion services. Anything else is seen as elective surgery – abortions of convenience, which do not require an expenditure of public funding. Just as the TAC process reinforced the belief that women seeking abortions were either victims or immoral women, increasing hospital access reaffirmed the state's obligation to provide welfare to the former and protect the moral order from the latter. By increasing access to the legal TAC process – however precarious that access was in actual fact – the state was able to undercut the mobilization of public support for a woman's right to make her own decisions about the kind of response she was prepared to make at any given moment.

A Contradiction of Choice and Access

The political dilemma for women is that they are caught in a structural contradiction. Giddens (1981:231) defines a structural contradiction as 'the existence of two structural principles within a social system, whereby each depends upon the other but at the same time negates it.' For women, the principles of welfare and liberty are structured in such a manner that while each depends upon the other, achieving one negates the other. When the pro-choice movement achieved an expansion of the medical responses necessary for women to control their reproductive potential, the movement simultaneously eroded its capacity for political mobilization. The federal-provincial division of powers within Canada contributed to the maintenance of the structural contradiction at both the personal and political levels of the struggle.

The division of governmental powers allowed federal and provincial politicians to shift political responsibility for the abortion 'problem' from one level to another. When the federal government was under pressure to address the illegal practices occurring in Quebec, it tossed the political ball into the provincial court. Because health is a provincial responsibility and because the provinces were responsible for accrediting facilities for the performance of abortion, problems of access could be blamed on the provincial government's failure to respond to the welfare needs of women. Similarly, when the provincial government was under pressure to authorize women's health clinics or to accredit free-standing clinics, it shifted the responsibility back onto the federal legislation that prohibited women from asserting such a choice. Thus, the political separation of law and medicine between the levels of government shaped the course of women's resistance to the 1969 legislation just as surely as the law shaped the manner in which individual women resisted compulsory motherhood.

When a fundamental contradiction is involved, the behaviour of individuals or groups may be shaped, but it can never be totally controlled. Despite various government attempts to frame the issue in terms of either law or medicine, the struggle between the movement and the state was not at any time a simple struggle over the legal right to choice or the medical right to access. The pro-choice movement did not control the terrain on which its resistance took place, but it resisted the dichotomization of options. As the pro-choice activists chased the political ball from one level of government to the other, the strategies they devised simultaneously addressed issues of liberty and welfare. When lack of access to hospital resources was highlighted as the source of the problem, they pressured provincial politicians to establish democratically controlled women's health clinics. When this solution was rebuffed – on the grounds that it would shift decision making from the medical profession's to women themselves – the movement, by providing illegal access, challenged the profession's right to control choice. The degree to which the movement was successful in providing individual women with choice and access was based on its own access to political resources and its degree of participation in the decision-making process.

The political struggle between the state and the women's movement in both Ontario and Manitoba involved the state's attempt to maintain and reinforce the structural separation of choice from access, whereas the women's movement attempted to devise strategies that would fuse them. The underlying factor that shaped the different outcomes in these provinces was not the degree of motivation and commitment of the activist in the respective movements; it was the differing political contexts with respect to control of political resources and political decision making. From this initial strength, the continued operation of the clinics in Toronto enabled the Ontario movement to enhance its resources and undermine those of the state and the medical profession. When the movement was able to keep the clinics operating, it prevented the provincial government from using hospital access as a resource for undermining political mobilization and it diminished the medical profession's monopoly of reproductive decision making. Conversely, when the Manitoba government simultaneously closed the clinic and increased hospital access, it undercut the ability of the movement to mobilize political support.

The structural contradiction faced by the women's movement was paralleled at the personal level of hospital committees. At this level, however, opportunities for resistance were minimized. Without the operation of the illegal clinics, individual women continued to be faced with the alternative of fitting their decisions into medical criteria or of forgoing their access to medical resources. By choosing to participate in the deception, individual women were able to have their abortions; but, in the process, they participated in reproducing the abortion ideology that justified medical control in the first place. The diversion of the abortion problem to the individual level allowed the medical aspects of abortion to be selected out as reasons why women required abortions and justified medical decision making. The social-code assumption that abortion is an exceptional requirement of women with physical or psychological problems remained intact, and the public debate ignored the larger political issues of power and morality. Although similar contradictions were involved at the political level, collective action brought these issues into the public domain and provided a challenge to the ideological basis of the medical control of decision making about abortion.

A Contradiction of Ideology and Practice

The legal structuring of abortion as a welfare issue of health (rather than a liberty issue of choice) has another contradiction built into it, one involving ideology and practice. As Petchesky (1984) has pointed out, the concept of 'medical necessity' as applied to abortion 'cuts in different ways.' On the one hand, it focuses the issue on technical questions requiring medical expertise. As such, the perception of abortion as a medical necessity restricts the consideration of abortion to a narrow medical model. On the other hand, however, it broadens the criteria of 'health needs,' thus having the contradictory effect of mobilizing women to achieve in practice what the principle of universality promises ideologically. When abortion is viewed as a health issue in a country that has socialized medicine, it is difficult to argue for its exclusion from medicare funding. Conversely, if abortion services fall within medicare and the market does not provide access to these services, this undermines the legitimacy of the medical profession's right to determine the medical services that will be provided.

The contradiction between abortion ideology and abortion practice is embedded in the medical profession's legal responsibility to define the need for abortion services together with its legal liberty right to withhold such services. When taken together, this responsibility and right become a resource for the profession to retain control of reproduction. When women are politically organized, however, the resource can be a dangerous one for doctors to use. The extra-billing issue publicly highlighted both how a woman's access to welfare rights could be eroded by the political interests of the medical profession and, conversely, how the welfare right itself can become a resource with which women can challenge medical control. The withholding of abortion services by the Sarnia doctors, and the implicit support of the Ontario Medical Association for their action, became a catalyst for political activity that ultimately undermined the profession's attempts to solidify its power base.

The continued operation of free-standing clinics was important in penetrating ideological perceptions about the relationship between self-interested autonomy and social responsibility for others. Without the Morgentaler clinics, the pro-choice movement had been faced with a dilemma, for the gaining of ground in the area of practical access for individual women would have meant that the mobilization of support for structural and ideological change would decrease. In the selective version of abortion reality that was produced by the TAC process, only women who faced life-threatening consequences were perceived as requiring abortion services. Anything else was seen as elective surgery, abortions of convenience, and not requiring public funding. In a circular manner, the committee system was then portrayed as the appropriate mechanism for determining abortion need.

The free-standing clinics represented an important stage in the historical struggle for reproductive freedom. Control of medical services is a significant resource in controlling the political power of women, and the operation of illegal clinics was a means of shifting the dilemma – where one cannot 'escape one horn without impaling oneself on the other' (Kellner 1981:261) – from women to the state. These clinics were a means of providing services to women at the individual level while mobilizing support to repeal the law that had polarized a pregnant woman's rights of choice and access. They created an opening to challenge social-code assumptions while still allowing the needs of individual women to be met.

The ultimate victories of the Canadian pro-choice movement were grounded in a strategy that challenged the legal and political mind-set which separated individual rights from social needs. Illegal clinics simultaneously raised questions involving individual rights and social needs as well as the relationship between the two. During the Ontario medical strike, political organization, which had been built up around the operation of the illegal clinics, enabled the pro-choice movement to raise uncomfortable questions about the medicalization of choice and access: If abortion was a moral or legal issue involving individual liberty, on what basis could the medical authority make such decisions? If abortion was a medical issue involving social welfare, why were abortion services not included in the rhetoric of universality? These were also questions that the operation of illegal clinics forced on the Supreme Court. Crown attorneys could answer them only by explicitly arguing that reproduction involves a 'different' kind of social relationship from that which the law is normally expected to address. Therefore, lawyers who defended the law had to portray pregnant women as 'exceptional' legal subjects in need of the state's protection, a portrayal they could not sustain whenever the issue of differential access to hospital committes was raised.

State efforts to maintain the ideological gap between what is believed at the level of public consciousness and what occurs in actual practice were undermined by the operation of the clinics: the abortion 'problem' could not be contained at the 'private' level of doctor-patient relations but was instead pushed into the public arena of political decision making. Attempts to contain the problem by legal means further highlighted the contradictions of addressing abortion within a model that takes female responsiveness as a given.

The Contradiction of Challenging Private Professional Control through Private Doctor-Controlled Clinics

Before the opening of the Morgentaler clinics, the pro-choice movement was faced with structural and ideological barriers that it could not penetrate. But the impact of an established media celebrity expanding his legal challenge was profound. Months and years of organizing and mobilization by women's groups across the country had not focused public attention on the issue as effectively or as quickly as a single pronouncement by Dr Morgentaler did. Whereas the national media had largely ignored the movement's national campaigns, Dr Morgentaler's name became synonymous with abortion rights in Canada. In the words of one activist, 'Henry has been a focal point that the media cannot ignore. He allows himself to be the link for the movement across the country' (CARAL annual general meeting, 1986).

The irony of a male physician carrying forward the struggle of the women's movement against a law 'designated to protect the interests of medical practitioners' (Gordon and Gavigan 1975:9) has not been easy for the movement to live with. Dr Morgentaler's willingness to provide abortion services to women as the women themselves defined the need was a challenge to the status quo. However, the strategy also made it difficult to change the frame of the ideological debate at the public level. Just as the dependence of women on the medical profession for access to abortion services at the individual level has distorted the public perception of women's reproductive labour in creating human life, so has the dependence of the movement on Dr Morgentaler distorted the abortion issue and the role of the movement in creating political change. The ideological identification of abortion with Morgentaler's activities and choices perpetuates the notion of independent heroes accomplishing social change through individual effort.

The fact that it was Dr Morgentaler's freedom that was at stake meant that he retained control of the legal and political decisions affecting the course of the struggle; yet his success depended on the strength of the movement. The movement's dependence on Morgentaler placed it in a position in which it had to negotiate with him over how the political struggle would proceed. The activists were thus grateful for the sacrifices he made in giving them control over their personal decisions, yet they were further inhibited from participating in the larger agenda of political decision making. The ambivalent feelings produced by the movement's dependence on Dr Morgentaler were not unlike those felt by women for male benefactors in other areas of their lives – or indeed by any party who receives 'welfare' as decided by another. When the resources that one requires are outside one's ability to influence, gratitude can be expected when the resources are forthcoming, but underlying this gratitude is an anger at one's lack of participation in the decision-making process. Dr Morgentaler allowed women personal choice at the individual level, but at the political level the movement often felt that it was reduced to manipulating decisions that had been made on its behalf.

The abortion struggle in Canada demonstrates that structural change and ideological change, as well as personal and political activity, exist in a dialectical relation with each other. The process by which responsibility for others and autonomy are ideologically separated reproduces the status quo of gender relations. The invisibility of women's work, politically as well as personally, is part of this process. In an effort to make the work of an important part of the Canadian pro-choice movement visible, the next chapter examines the internal workings of the Ontario Coalition for Abortion Clinics. This examination demonstrates how the pro-choice activists, in attempting to achieve their objectives, sought to mediate conflicts between themselves and those with whom they shared common cause.

12

OCAC Strategies: Mediating the Contradictions of Sex and Class

Just as Marxists posit that it is the alienated but interdependent relation between dominated and subordinated classes that leads to contradiction, struggle and change ... structurally it is the alienated but interdependent relation between dominant (productive) and subordinate (reproductive) modes that leads to contradiction, struggle and change. This assertion is not meant to be a simple addition to the Marxist proposition of class struggle but rather a restatement of that proposition, synthesizing class and gender structures into a dialectical materialist analysis. (Ursel 1984:260)

The relatively clear distinctions ... drawn between different strains of ideological thought have often not been so strictly drawn by movement participants themselves. In the flux of social movement activity, ideological assumptions and strategical implications that may seem contradictory in the abstract often appear together with no felt sense of contradiction. (Buechler 1990:124)

During the years the Morgentaler clinics operated illegally in English Canada, the pro-choice movement's involvement with them was analysed and criticized by a variety of feminist and socialist observers. Since the activists who formed the Ontario Coalition for Abortion Clinics (OCAC) were instrumental in initiating the clinic challenge in Ontario and provided the ongoing support of the Toronto clinic, much of this criticism was directed at the strategic choices they made. During 1985 and 1986 I was actively involved as a participant-observer with this group, and at the outset I shared many of the concerns expressed by the critics of the movement. But as I reflected, from inside the movement, on the choices made by the pro-choice activists, it became increasingly clear to me that theoretical prescriptions for change, including evaluations of any particular reform strategy, cannot be abstractly considered from a point outside the change process. When one analyses the efficacy of a particular social movement from a vantage point outside the movement, one remains within the frame of hegemonic discourse, thus missing the importance that the discourse itself has for shaping the actions of the movement as well as the way in which particular movement strategies will influence and shape any shifts in discursive frameworks.

The basic difference between OCAC activists and their socialist-feminist critics was not based on opposing political positions. The most active members of OCAC described their political objectives in the discourses of socialism and feminism, and where differences arose, they involved issues of strategy. From a vantage point within the movement, however, one can see that particular choices were affected by the context of the struggle itself, a context where class and gender interests were frequently posed in oppositional terms. However, the decisions taken could rarely be characterized as simply a reaction to external stimuli at the expense of either socialist or feminist principles of organizing.

When one is examining and describing the capacity for a social movement to initiate social change, the important questions include, 'How and in what way are the actions and ideological positions of movement activists shaped by the social context in which they act?' And, conversely, 'How and in what way is the social context affected by the perceptions and activities of the movement?' In answering these questions, it is important to reiterate that the vantage point from which one examines a social movement – and its decisions or actions – alters the way in which social change is understood. Within the cultural framework of social-code discourse, political motivations are distorted and structural contradictions are glossed over. Its abstractions distort our understanding of how social change is actually achieved because they render invisible the active decision-making process of those directly involved in the struggle, the reality of the constraints they face, and the kind of impact that these decisions have on the overall social context. The degree of 'success' or 'failure' of any particular strategy is not solely or necessarily determined (and may even be obscured) by a comparison of political objectives with the results of a particular strategy. What is needed is an examination of the ongoing decision-making process as it is interpreted by those making the decisions.

The Socialist and Feminist Critiques

Within socialist theory, it is commonly understood that the rule of law in capitalist societies serves to hide the way various social institutions work in tandem to reproduce unequal and hierarchical relations. According to this argument, any acceptance of law as the social institution that protects individual rights gives legal rhetoric its ideological power to mask the underlying structural nature of inequality and oppression. Legal discourse thus serves to turn social problems caused by unequal distributions of power into narrowly defined legal problems of discrete individuals. As White (1985:17) argues, 'to struggle for rights on legal terrain means that social issues are often separated from one another. The ideological boundaries placed on debate means that questions of power and interests are seen as being issue specific rather than in terms of an integrated framework.' As inequality comes to be popularly perceived as the result of individual inadequacy or an unfortunate aberration, psychological and legal solutions are preferred and political dissent is defused. For some socialist theorists, this analysis leads to the conclusion that law is simply a tool of the powerful and that those interested in social change should avoid diverting their energies into legal struggles. From this general orientation of law as an ideological tool of powerful elements in society, Canadian scholars have challenged the belief that the Canadian Charter of Rights and Freedoms can be used as an instrument for bringing about social change. For example, Samek (1982:762, 769) draws on the general critique of legal rights and argues that the use of Charter challenges focuses public attention on the symptoms of social malaise and suppresses the underlying disease. Thus, he argues, the system 'insulates against any criticism with which it cannot cope.'

The socialist criticism of the abortion clinic strategy (and of the pro-choice support given to Dr Morgentaler) also is based on the belief that struggles in the legal arena divert attention from issues of class inequality, focusing political dissent on the interests of an elite group of women. At an international socialist forum on reproductive rights held at the University of Toronto in 1985, this criticism was expressly directed against the pro-choice defence of illegal abortion clinics in English Canada. In a comparison with the earlier struggle to achieve abortion services in Quebec, the efforts of the English Canadian movement were said to be class neutral and hence of a reformist nature. In referring to the pro-choice movement's lack of unity with the broader struggle of the working class, the speaker, Nancy Nichol,[1] maintained that the choices made by abortion activists (such as those made by OCAC) were essentially motivated by bourgeois and middle-class concerns. She argued that whereas the Abortion Caravan of 1970 had been modelled on the On-to-Ottawa Trek of the unemployed during the 1930s, this working-class orientation was no longer the basis for the contemporary strategies of the pro-choice movement. Acknowledging the gains made in the Caravan campaign, Nichol went on to state that it had not achieved its objectives:

The reason: there was no building on the gains made. Those who remained in the struggle went into the establishment of alternative services. The general orientation in English Canada was one whereby abortion was viewed as a single issue, that is, to change the law. There was no recognition of the establishment of the movement within the working class as an important goal. While the orientation of the Abortion Caravan was socialist, the women in CARAL [Canadian Abortion Rights Action League] and the rest of the English pro-choice movement has concerned itself with the single issue of repealing the law. The notion of 'choice' is at the heart of the confusion. It is abstract and makes the assumption that we live in a free and equal society. The notion of choice obscures the class relationship within the society. Without day care, jobs, etc., women do not have choices and are determined by the material conditions of life. Anything less than abortion on demand does answer the problem. The movement does not talk about abortion on demand. The struggle is not just a battle to change the law and getting rid of it does not ensure reproductive freedom and this is not recognized within the abortion rights movement. It is not just that the working class suffers most from the current situation but the greatest gains have been because of mass-based working-class struggle, for example, the movement in Quebec. (Forum on reproductive rights, University of Toronto, 1985)

Nichol maintained that the 'success' in Quebec was related to the way the movement was organized and that 'the struggle in the rest of Canada needs to be rebuilt, not just around the legal issue but upon a firm working-class orientation.' Whereas much of Nichol's criticism was expressly directed towards the activities of the CARAL, she also characterized the work of OCAC activists as reformist, saying:

1 Nichol was a member of the International Socialists. At the time of the seminar at the University of Toronto, she was in the process of developing a documentary film on the abortion struggle in Canada. When the film, *The Struggle for Choice* (produced by Horizontal Forest Productions) was released, its description of the motivations of the pro-choice movement in English Canada was contested by OCAC activists.

[T]hey are really just talking about defending the clinic ... They feel that maintaining the clinic and fighting the battle in the courts is their most important priority and then they move to possibly open other services ... This focus on the
clinic doesn't allow for the building of a movement. It is a restrictive strategy ...
OCAC's obsession with the legal battle is siphoning off support for the movement
... In Ontario, as in the rest of English Canada, the movement is defensive and
even here, nothing has really been done to actively defend. They need to mobilize
more people to stand in front of the clinic. The arguments have to be taken to the
workplace ... Also the Community Health Clinics in Montreal talk about free
'abortion on demand,' not so in the rest of Canada. They do not make the necessary links. There has been no sustained discussion of access to hospital services.
There isn't a mobilization around access ... The major services that women need
are hospital services ... The movement in English Canada comes out of a bourgeois feminist analysis which tends to obscure a socialist analysis. (Ibid.)

Nichol's criticism of the English Canadian pro-choice movement is
consistent with the stream of socialist thought that views law as an ideological system of concepts about individual freedom which has no direct
referent to the societal structures that distribute resources. Because this
analysis remains within a mind-set where theory and practice, individuality and collectivity, are dichotomous rather than dialectical, the concept
of 'choice' is viewed as being essentially liberal and individualistic. Thus,
Nichol came down on the side of gaining access to the medical structures that dispense abortion services – an achievement, she argued,
that needed to be located within the broader working-class agenda of
demands on the state.

While OCAC activists came under attack from some Canadian socialists who rejected strategies involving the law, the Morgentaler strategy
drew a different kind of criticism from some women activists within the
feminist movement. The alternative strategies suggested from this quar-
ter were in direct opposition to those suggested by the socialist critique.
Rather than focusing on pressuring the state to increase access to medical
services, this group of feminists argued for developing services that would
bypass the state-mandated medical monopoly and be controlled by
women themselves. The problem of pressing for increased access to state-
provided services, they argued, is that it ignores the fact that male power
is not exercised over women solely through the activities or nonactivities
of the state and state agencies. Because control of women is situated
throughout civil society, in nonmarket as well as market relations, the
problematic relations are ones of patriarchy rather than capitalism.

· If patriarchy can be understood as 'any kind of group organization in which males hold dominant power and determine what parts females shall and shall not play' (Rifkin 1980:83), then control over reproductive capacity has progressively become concentrated in the medical profession. Although this control may be increasingly dictated by market concerns, the patriarchal nature of the control goes beyond economic relations to involve relations between the sexes with respect to reproduction and sexuality. Because medical relations are key aspects of reproductive decision making, any demand for increased access to medical services will not challenge the patriarchal nature of the relationship itself but will actually reinforce it.

A section of the Canadian feminist movement opted for the strategy of establishing alternative abortion services to those that the state provided within accredited hospitals; indeed, the clinic strategy was developed by women who not only deplored the unequal access to abortion services but were appalled by the conditions under which women were able to have legal hospital abortions. Rather than being fully supportive of the clinic strategy, however, a number of feminists from within the women's health movement had, in varying degrees, become critical of the direction in which pro-choice energies were being directed. Instead of supporting the active defence of the Morgentaler clinics, these women argued that the clinic challenge did nothing to undermine the root cause of unequal access: the medical profession's increasing control of all aspects of reproduction.

During the early to mid-1980s, a number of publications in the 'alternative' media articulated the concerns of activists within the women's health movement about the Morgentaler strategy. Adamson and Prentice (1985:6) argued that 'the strategy adopted by the pro-choice movement is one of near-total reliance on doctors and corresponding validation of the medical model.' This medical model, they said, 'is one which focuses on illness and its cure by medical doctors. Medical doctors, traditionally male, are the experts who have colluded with the state, and more recently with the pharmaceutical industry, to control women and our bodies by monopoly of the definition and treatment of health and illness. In addition, the medical model has denied connection between our health and our social, political and economic situations, and thus the links between mental and physical health and our material situation' (ibid.: 3). In a 1983 article in *Healthsharing* magazine entitled 'The Case for Lay Abortion,' Clement had argued: 'Abortion is among the simplest medical procedures performed, demanding far less range of knowledge and skill than attending births. The safety and cost-effectiveness of abortion provision by training paramedics has been proven in the Third World. Clearly it is possible to go one step beyond this and provide abortion by trained lay women in non medical settings' (Clement 1983:10).

Although, as Clement noted 'Canadian feminists didn't consider moving outside the law by providing abortions without doctors' (ibid.), an experiment of this nature had been attempted in the United States (Bart 1981). Clement argued that part of the reason why the Canadian abortion movement did not opt for nonmedical access was because of the influence of socialist activists on pro-choice strategies:

The Young Socialists, a Trotskyist organization dominant in the early 70s which heavily influenced the development of the Canadian abortion movement, also steered us away from taking abortion 'into our own hands.' The YS believed that to build a political movement demands must be made on the State. 'The radical feminist demand was "Free Abortion on Demand." The YS slogans were "Repeal the Abortion Laws" and "A Woman's Right to Choose,"' remembers Sue Genge, a Toronto feminist and former member of the YS. 'The focus was too narrow. We never discussed how abortion fit into the total oppression of women.' (Clement 1983:10).

Whether the pro-choice movement's focus on the legal right of choice (with its liberal implications) came from feminists interested in 'alternative medical services' (as Nichol suggests) or from socialists (as Clement suggests), one can readily see that a major difference in their criticism of the clinic strategy and the 'choice' slogan concerned whether the movement should directly challenge the lack of state-supported medical services (access) or whether it should challenge the medical monopoly itself (choice). On the one hand, Nichol castigated the movement for its lack of links with the workers' movement and the separation of abortion from issues of capitalist production. On the other hand, Clement argued for a coalition of the abortion movement with those sections of the women's movement that were concerned with the control of reproductive power. The major link that needed to be made, Clement argued, was with the midwifery movement and its challenge to the medical establishment.

While both the abortion movement and the midwifery movement are based on conceptions of reproductive freedom, each has had somewhat different relations with the medical profession. Although it is clear that the midwifery movement directly challenges medical control over reproduction, doctors themselves 'have been in the forefront of the world wide liberalization of abortion laws that has taken place over the past three decades' (McDonnell 1984:96). However, despite the fact that doctors figured prominently in the challenge to state regulation of abortion, this challenge did not undermine the medical power to define the reproductive needs of women. It was, feminists argued, simply an extension of the medical profession's belief in its right to determine who should or should not have an abortion (Cole 1983; McDonnell 1984). The feminist critics thus considered that activities in defence of the clinics were in fact legitimating the medical establishment's right to define and dispense the services necessary for undertaking reproductive responsibilities.

In their book on feminist organizing, Adamson, Briskin, and McPhail (1988:50) noted that 'the split between socialism and feminism was to be the major challenge' for the socialist-feminist stream of the Canadian women's movement. As will be evident from the dilemmas faced by the OCAC activists, this split was of particular concern to women who worked specifically on issues of abortion. The priority placed on class and gender inequality led to different positions about which side of the choice/access polarity should be attacked. Where the socialists were arguing for an emphasis on increased access to publicly funded medical services, the feminist critics sought to challenge the legal right of doctors to define the scope and nature of abortion services.

Despite their different concerns about choice and access, the feminists had a criticism of the clinic strategy that had much in common with the socialist critique of the law. Criticisms emanating from the women's health movement cohered with those emanating from socialist factions in that both viewed the whole concept of liberty and equal rights as an ideological abstraction from reality. The feminist criticism of law and legal discourse goes farther than the socialist one in that legal abstractions are viewed as perceptually biased precisely because they are derived from an androcentric male consciousness of reality (Polan 1982; Rifkin 1980; MacKinnon 1983b). This argument draws on a more general feminist epistemology, which views our culturally accepted ways of thinking as beginning from a conception of the self-other relation that is distinctively male. Feminist legal scholars argue that this is particularly important where a consideration of individual rights is concerned because law begins with an orientation that separates and individuates self and other rather than perceiving the relationship between individuals as one of attachment.

It follows from this feminist critique of the legal code that law can politically demobilize because the ethical frame of legal discourse leads to an ambivalence on the part of women. During 1984, a book written by a Toronto health activist, Kathleen McDonnell, developed the theme that the rights rhetoric of the legal arena was distorting women's experience of reproduction and, in the process, was creating ambivalence among the women who would most benefit from a pro-choice victory. McDonnell outlined some of the concerns of the women's health movement regarding the increasing medicalization of women's lives, but she did so within the broader perspective of the feminist analysis of the self-other relationship. Specifically, she argued that the Canadian pro-choice movement was not giving enough weight to women's personal experience with abortion and that it had not dealt with the grief and doubts that the women concerned felt about the issue:

Like no other dilemma that women face, abortion pits our desire to care for others, to protect others and avoid hurting them, into stark and seemingly irreconcilable conflict with our desire to protect and take care of ourselves, to act in our self-interest. This is the choice – self versus other – that women are faced with when contemplating abortion. And since all our upbringing, all our socialization, all the cultural messages we receive lean toward putting others' needs ahead of our own, toward nurturance rather than self-actualization, it is no wonder we approach the prospect of abortion with such profound ambivalence. For how can we be women and choose ourselves at the same time? (McDonnell 1984:30)

The contemporary legal code is built on assumptions of human nature that are particularly 'male' in the sense that a response to the needs of someone other than oneself is defined as an exceptional activity. As I have sought to demonstrate, Rawls's 'man' in the original position is not particularly concerned about promoting the plans of others unless there is a possibility that he might be one of those others. McDonnell's argument was that since women value activities that provide care for others and since equality of care giving is not a matter for legal consideration, women do not see abortion services as something that may be legitimately 'demanded' either from the state or from men. Moreover, any demand to extend individualistic rights to the area of reproductive practice is interpreted, in the legal mind-set, as a lessening of the social connectedness that women have learned to value. The question for McDonnell, then, was 'How much are these "nurturant" qualities a fundamental part of feminism?' (ibid.:25). If they are, she argued, mobilizing women on behalf of the pro-choice struggle must mean giving more credence to the ambivalence that women feel concerning their own abortion experiences.

Each of the socialist and feminist critics to whom I have referred was strongly pro-choice, and each understood the need for readily available abortion services. Yet each had strong reservations about the 'choice' slogan adopted by the movement and the ideological association of this term with the acquisition of formal legal rights. Although all were activists in promoting the rights of women, they differed about the best way to accomplish this, agreeing only that the clinic strategy was problematic. If the policy statements made by OCAC women had been taken at face value, there would have been little reason for either socialists or feminists to disagree with the group's political motivations. What is of greater interest for social movement theory is whether the clinic strategy was, in Nichol's terms, a 'strictly legal strategy' and therefore of a reformist nature. Did the necessity to defend the clinic drain off energies from grass-roots organization, as Nichol suggested, or was it a vital component in that mobilization, as OCAC argued? Did the clinic strategy reinforce overall control by the medical profession (as feminist critics worried), or is it better to characterize it as a short-term step in the achievement of the responses necessary for real reproductive freedom? Further, what factors in the political context shaped OCAC efforts to address class and gender concerns in concert?

Political Struggles with Social Contradiction

Where 'women's issues' are involved, the reform/revolution dilemma (with which political activists must always struggle) is complicated by a class/gender contradiction. Each of the critiques of the English Canadian pro-choice movement touched on a portion of the reality that women have to operate under capitalist patriarchy. Any organization that is both socialist and feminist, operating in a society that is at one and the same time capitalist and patriarchal, must inevitably mediate the contradictions that are 'expressed through the tension between domestic labour and wage labour, the role of the state, and the relation between the public and the private' (Adamson, Briskin, and McPhail 1988:97).

Contradictions between class and gender issues were at the root of many of the dilemmas that pro-choice activists faced in their attempt to mediate the short-term needs for abortion reform with their long-term objective of changing the social relations of reproduction. The task for activists seeking revolutionary change at the political level is remarkably similar to that facing individual women when they make choices about their reproductive lives. These choices are made within a cultural context that discursively dichotomizes the personal and the political, subordinating the diversity of actual human experience to the tyranny of cultural absolutes. Yet in practice each decision ideally requires strategies that will allow for a response to immediate short-term demands or immediate problems without significantly compromising one's long-term objectives or moral commitments.

Reproductive options have been structured in a context where challenging systemic class inequality in the provision of medical services has meant a strengthening of ideological myths about the exceptionality of pregnancy and the natural powerlessness of women. Contradiction cuts two ways, however. The 'fact that patriarchal capitalism is by definition committed to the continuation of unequal class, gender, and race relations, while the tradition of liberal democracy is one of concern for liberty, justice, and equality of opportunity' means that 'fault lines' are created whereby new conflicts can be generated (Giddens 1981:151, 237). Because OCAC's political choices were criticized from an 'outsider' standpoint (from a vantage point outside the process where the actual political decision making was occurring), theoretical debates about the pro-choice movement's clinic strategy frequently failed to understand the kinds of contradiction that arise in the practice of making social change as well as the way that these contradictions can afford new opportunities for resistance. From the perspective of OCAC, its critics could only see the limitations of a 'choice' strategy and failed 'to recognize its potential for mobilizing women initially around its demands but eventually going far beyond' (Adamson, Briskin, and McPhail 1988:52).

The ideological commitment of the state to liberal democratic principles uneasily coexists with the principles of patriarchal capitalism, and this underlying conflict presented a means for OCAC activists to push contradictions to their advantage. For example, the events surrounding the Ontario doctors' strike (discussed in the previous chapter) provided the opportunity to demonstrate the interlocking of patriarchal medical control with the state's allocation of collective resources on the basis of gender and class. Although conflicts generated by such contradictions can be viewed theoretically (and retrospectively) as new opportunities for challenging the status quo, the pro-choice activists often perceived this fact only in hindsight. In the midst of a conflict, they frequently faced the difficult dilemma of choosing between strategies that would accommodate only one of two desired objectives. Choices had to be made, and it was often only possible to choose the path that would do the least harm in the short term or that would allow some space for further manoeuvring in the long term.

Leading activists in OCAC consciously sought to avoid the trap of coming down on one side or the other of the systemic contradiction between political theory and personal experience. They viewed Nichol's stance as falling within the abstract principle side of the ideological opposition, while they perceived strategies built on experiential models as representative of a retreat from the struggle to change overall societal structures. Faced with a contradiction between practical reality and hegemonic interpretations of that reality, they sought to devise strategies that would help them integrate (rather than choose between) their ability to control the direction of their struggle and their responsibilities for the effects of their choices on the welfare of others. Members of the organization constantly referred to the need to mediate the tension between its long-term goals and short-term strategies. Considering the overall effect of OCAC's activities, projects that were 'aborted' (both early and late, in terms of the amount of energy exerted) are as important as those that were carried to fruition. In the overall struggle to effect ideological and structural change, the former cannot be considered failures of responsibility but should be seen as part of the process of responding to one's own needs and to those of interconnected others.

The strategy OCAC chose to deal with the opposition of choice and access was the establishing of illegal clinics. To understand the contradictory nature of the strategy and the events it precipitated, it is important to remember the course of events that led to the birth of the OCAC group and subsequently shaped its interaction with other actors and movements. During the 1970s, those in authority had repeatedly rebuffed attempts to pressure the federal government to repeal the law and to get provincial governments to increase medical access or establish women's clinics. Faced with deteriorating conditions of access to legal abortions and blocked in their efforts to achieve change through political avenues, the pro-choice activists felt that they 'could not choose or wait for the ideal conditions but needed to act to bring those conditions about through active initiative' (OCAC activist 1985).

Events occurring in Quebec suggested a possible strategy. Contrary to McDonnell's (1984) contention that the women's movement simply reacted to the actions of Dr Morgentaler, the clinic strategy in Ontario was initially set in motion by women's health activists, a number of whom went on to become the founders of OCAC and ongoing activists within it. From the perspective of these women, the clinic strategy would provide needed services to women in a way that highlighted the crisis of access that was occurring in the hospitals. It was thus perceived as a strategy that would not only address structural problems with access but could provide an entree for challenging hegemonic beliefs about the women who required such services.

The feeling of those who initiated the strategy was that the clinic would provide a focus for movement building by making the politics of the abortion issue more visible to the general public. It would bring these politics out of the doctor's office and project them into the public arena. In this way, they hoped to 'bring the legitimacy of the law into question and thus force a repeal of that law' (OCAC meeting, 5 March 1985). Without an overturning of the law, increased access left women dependent on the benevolence of their doctors. In order to challenge the law, however, the political activists required a political benefactor who would be prepared to put his medical power in jeopardy. Because he already had credibility as a 'martyr' to the cause and because he possessed the most advanced abortion skills, Dr Morgentaler was the obvious choice.

Although the clinic strategy ideologically upheld the right of the medical profession to define when and how abortion services would be provided, it included within this right an opportunity for pregnant women to define their own reproductive needs without subjecting their decisions to the authority of a therapeutic abortion committee (TAC). In the long term, OCAC viewed the clinic as a strategy for changing structural and ideological relations of reproduction, but, in the short term, the attempt to provide women with individual reproductive control brought with it difficulties that required constant attention if the broader political objectives of socialism and feminism were not to be eroded.

Although the Morgentaler clinics allowed women an opportunity to exert autonomy at the personal level where abortion decisions were made, the strategy compromised the political autonomy of the movement. The support that pro-choice activists gave to a cause identified with and controlled by Dr Morgentaler did not allow them political control of the direction their struggle would take. The resulting lack of autonomy meant that OCAC was often in a position of having to convince Morgentaler of the movement's political needs. Ironically, this often paralleled the ways in which women persuaded sympathetic doctors to respond to their personal reproductive needs under the TAC system.

The contradiction involved in a solution that provided individual women with access to resources for making reproductive choice but at the same time eroded the movement's ability to challenge ideological assumptions and control political decision making was not unheeded by the organization. Further, the organization's internal discussion of the problems generated by its choice of strategy demonstrates that it did not dismiss the criticisms being made by its socialist and feminist supporters; rather, its involvement in the practice of mediating the contradictions inherent in patriarchal capitalism meant that politically unorthodox solutions were sometimes called for. In discussing each new dilemma, the existence of socialist-feminist principles provided OCAC with 'a framework within which to situate the myriad of issues and details that often threaten to overwhelm feminist activists' (Adamson, Briskin, and McPhail 1988:126). In short, OCAC did not regard its socialist and feminist principles as a blueprint that precluded any particular strategy, but these principles did help to prevent the group from choosing the kind of separatist and isolationist strategies that experience by itself would have suggested.

Defending the Clinics

Although OCAC members were often painfully aware that their decisions were shaped by the structural contradictions inherent in patriarchal capitalism and by the conflicting responsibilities to which these contradictions gave rise, the discourses they constructed out of their experiences ensured that these influences were not unidirectional. The initial decision – to adopt a strategy of support for illegal abortion clinics – changed the political context in a way that presented new opportunities for expanding the movement while restricting the possibilities for achieving success through old options.

From the outset, the pro-choice activists intended the operation of an illegal clinic to address both structural and ideological problems. While providing access to abortion services, it would publicize the problems of hospital access; and as an illegal service, it would command media attention as long as it was able to stay open. Because the founders of OCAC also believed that a jury would ultimately give an aquittal, based on the evidence of discriminatory and unequal hospital access, they viewed taking the issue to court as a way of challenging the legitimacy of the federal law. In the words of one activist, the operation of the clinic would 'face the state with a contradiction between its regulation of woman's bodies and woman's labour through its broader imperatives to maintain the overall legitimacy of the legal and justice systems. At the same time it would allow us to begin to work out a concrete model for delivery of health services where control would be in the hands of the consumer' (discussion at socialist forum, January 1985).

Once in operation, a great deal of time and energy was required to defend the clinic and keep it open. Whereas the anti-choice forces could draw on bodies and dollars from institutional church sources, similar institutional support for the pro-choice position was initially unorganized. The availability of institutional resources allowed the anti-choice forces to mobilize numbers, primarily by bussing supporters from across the province. The importance of the right's use of tactics more familiar to radical social movements was explained by an OCAC activist as follows:

We have had a big success here in Ontario in the fact that we have held off the government's rage; we have held off further arrests. But, at the same time that we are getting some initiative now, the Right-to-Life is reacting and they are trying to build their campaign bigger and bigger too. And what are they doing? They're going for increased visibility. They've started demonstrating in Quebec in front of the clinic where they haven't demonstrated for a long time. ... And they are certainly mobilizing in the streets here. And look at them in Washington, thousands of them out there with Reagan cheer-leading for them. Why are they doing this? I think they learned it from us. They know that building a mass movement can work and they have seen that it can work for us. It has worked in other mass movements that some of us have participated in building. After the big rally in front of the clinic, one of the reporters came up and said, 'Is this basically a numbers game – you have 7000 out here – is this a numbers game?' 'Oh no, no, it's not basically a numbers game,' I said. But thank God, we got more than them and I think that we have to keep that up. Its very important. (Educational forum, March 1985)

Both groups realized that numbers, through their capacity to command media attention, were politically important in applying pressure on the state. On the part of OCAC, this notion was not based on a liberal conception of the state as a neutral arbitrator of group interests; rather, it was derived from the socialist principle that state 'responsiveness reflects the government's need for public credibility and legitimacy, which in turn relates to the fact that its power rests, to a significant degree, on the consent of the governed, however heavily that "consent" may be manipulated' (Adamson, Briskin, and McPhail 1988:153). There was plenty of evidence to suggest that various levels of government did respond differently to similar situations and that varying responsiveness was related to the ability of opposing sides to mobilize visible support. Reporting on one large pro-choice demonstration, an OCAC activist noted that 'the numbers mean that it will be very difficult for the government to move to close the clinic before the appeal is settled' (OCAC meeting, 5 March 1985).

At times, the need to compete with its adversaries in the matter of numbers was a major drain on the movement's energy. Ironically, though, it was often the actions of anti-choice advocates that made the clinic a focal point for organizing visible support and for raising funds. As long as the clinic was under attack, self-mobilization occurred with increasing frequency. Whenever harassment at the clinic was publicized, a wide range of irate supporters would call the OCAC office asking why demonstrations were not being organized on the pro-choice side. In a peculiar way, the mobilization efforts of the movement depended on the anti-choice harassment of women entering the clinic. The ongoing operation of the clinic, coupled with the attacks by its opponents, provided opportunities for mass mobilization that had hitherto been missing. Political opportunities to heighten public consciousness increased with the problems that were caused for individual women, and fund-raising was also made easier during these periods. At the height of one 1985 anti-choice mobilization, it was noted at an OCAC meeting that 'the contradiction is that harassment of the anti-choice focuses support on the clinic and brings in dollars.'

Although the anti-choice activities helped push the issue into the public arena and further mobilized the pro-choice forces, the calling of a pro-choice demonstration was not a straightforward matter of organizing supporters. While such tactics as the Catholic Church's bussing of its congregations from around the province enraged pro-choice supporters and provided opportunities for mobilization, OCAC's commitment to mass demonstration as a basic strategy had to be continually negotiated, varied, and reaffirmed as events required. These decisions frequently involved questions of responsibility and morality about whether other strategies would be more effective or more responsible alternatives in particular situations. The following comments, extracted from the deliberations of OCAC meetings during February and March 1985, illustrate the conflicting responsibilities felt by the members of the group as they worked their way to consensus on the strategies to be used in countering a major anti-choice demonstration:

'CARAL has organized an honour guard. The question is whether such a small number would only be demoralizing ... It is also important that we support actions initiated by CARAL' ...

'To do nothing will be more demoralizing for our supporters. There is an importance to symbolic actions. They get picked up by the media and can outweigh the number factor'...

'Symbolic actions can help to mobilize for future actions BUT there is also a
question of safety in putting a small group of choice activists into a crowd of
10,000 anti-choice' ...

'To counter at the clinic makes the situation more difficult for clinic staff and
for women themselves ... Also any polarization in the street in front of the clinic
erodes support from the business people in the area. They are already facing
enough problems at the hands of our opposition' ...

'We also have to remember that such polarizing conflicts could put pressure
on the state to move to close the clinic and ultimately play into anti-choice
hands' ...

'To use the church as a focus for countering is tricky because it can feed into
anti-Catholicism' ...

'We also have to consider that the need for a profile is great at this point in
time. We get calls from supporters who want to register their protest.'

Such comments by no means exhausted the range of persons and groups
that members felt needed to be considered whenever they chose a particular course of action. Like Gilligan's research subjects, the women in
OCAC demonstrated their recognition that the decisions they made
would affect other people, and they stressed that the nature of the effect
should be a factor in the conclusions they reached. Of particular concern were those who sought out the clinic's services. If anti-choice activity had benefits on the political side, it was clearly detrimental to the
patients, who were forced to run the gauntlet of harassment on entering
the clinic.

In order to provide personal support for women entering the Morgentaler clinic, OCAC organized a diverse group of volunteers to escort the
women when they came for their clinic appointments. The escorts not
only provided support for those seeking an abortion, but their presence
made it difficult for the anti-choice activists to distinguish between the
patient and the escort. In addition, the organization quickly came to recognize the escort service as an important mobilizing tool in its own right,
for it provided new avenues through which individuals could become
active in the movement, and the program elicited a high degree of commitment to the pro-choice cause from those who took part in it.

The escort program is a good example of problems that can be created
by even the most advantageous strategies, for the service had to be suspended for a time. Its suspension and subsequent reinstatement demonstrate how OCAC was constrained by the fact that doctors controlled the
clinics and defined the use of clinic resources. To train and coordinate

escorts required an enormous amount of time and eventually expanded into the equivalent of a full-time job. The project had to be suspended when it became impossible to organize escorts solely on a volunteer basis. The comments of activists at a meeting in January 1985 illustrate the tenor of the discussion that led to the suspension of the service:

'I do not agree with this move. As an escort, I see the value we provide to women using the service. Those who need the service don't get to vote' ...

'There is no question in the Coordinating Committee of the value of the service. But the staff at the clinic have not seen this as a priority with the result that coordination has become chaotic. There is less harassment at the moment and this makes it more difficult to argue for the service' ...

'The escort service is a political mobilizing tool as well as a direct service to women. Coordination is a full-time job in terms of hours. But we need to apply more pressure on the clinic to hire a coordinator.'

Despite its effectiveness in bringing together personal and political objectives, the operation of the service and its suspension highlighted the problem that the movement faced in not having control of the clinic and its resources. Nevertheless, the movement's relationship to the medical profession should not be viewed in unitary terms. The ability of OCAC to achieve its objectives depended in large part on the underlying willingness of particular doctors to share the decision making. Whether this willingness was forthcoming or not hinged on whether the doctor in charge saw the clinic as part of a collective struggle and, if so, whether this then called for participatory decision making.

The political relationships between OCAC and the doctors who operated the different clinics were as varied as the personal relationships that exist between individual women and their doctors. Initially, when the escort service was operating on a volunteer basis, Dr Robert Scott was the physician providing services to the Morgentaler clinic. Scott's motivation for providing abortion services was an individualistic one relating to his personal feelings about what constituted good medical care. As one activist explained, 'Dr Scott sees himself primarily as a doctor and not as part of the pro-choice movement.' As such, he was willing to allow the escort service to operate during periods of extreme patient harassment, but he did not see it as a clinic priority in the allocation of resources. It was significant that less than a month after Scott's resignation from the Morgentaler clinic, agreement was secured to make escort coordination a staff function. In February 1985, OCAC's Coordinating Committee reported that 'the escort service hopes to be functioning soon, with the idea that OCAC will set the political tone and the clinic will do the administrative work.'

The change in the escort situation after Scott's departure signified the difference between the relationship of OCAC to the original Morgentaler clinic and its relationship to the clinic that Scott soon opened. Whereas, in both instances, ultimate control was in the hands of the owner of the clinic, the owners differed in their understanding of the political needs of the movement and their role in the movement. Politically, Morgentaler had a sense that he was participating in (or leading) a struggle for a cause, whereas Scott approached the problem as one of providing a medical service that he, as a professional, felt was necessary.

The problem of having to provide the requisite support for abortion clinics (without the opportunity to participate in the decision making about how the service would be provided) was highlighted when, soon after his resignation from the Morgentaler staff, Scott revealed his intention to open another clinic in Toronto. OCAC's response to this illustrates its political commitment to turning decisions made by others into opportunities for building the movement:

'There are benefits to the movement in this decision in that it dramatizes the existing problem with access and strengthens the access in the province. However, there are also significant problems for us. This is not just another doctor providing abortions. It is another clinic and one where we do not have any control. He has never really consulted with us. He has informed us. We do not know answers to some important questions: Will it heighten the anti-choice activity? Will it need escorts? What will he be charging?' ...

'I see this as a positive step. It would be better somewhere else but there is a good political argument for its opening. The access in Toronto has been cut and it is harder to get an appointment at the Morgentaler clinic' ...

'I feel that we can use this. Harbord Street Clinic is not exactly what we want either, but it is a step towards it.' (OCAC meeting, April 1986)

The different relationship with Scott posed organizational problems for OCAC, and the degree of support that OCAC would have to provide the Scott Clinic was discussed again at a general meeting immediately after its opening:

'While we need to give support, it is more difficult because of the different relation involved. Scott does not want escorts at this point. He feels that the clinic should be defended politically rather than physically. Also, given our escort resources, we have to be circumspect' ...

'Despite our lack of control, we have to keep the access issue in mind. One of the losses of the amalgamation of hospitals has been a cutback in abortion at the Western Hospital. We have to be careful in not saying that we are not too happy regarding the opening of this clinic' ...

'I see this as a step forward, but we have to clearly differentiate between our relation with this clinic and the one we have with the Morgentaler clinic ... Dr Scott is unlikely to want OCAC's help. He is an individualist' ...

'We *have* to provide the support. The government knows that Scott is isolated and we have to make it clear that if they bust this clinic, they also take on the whole women's movement. We have to be able to back it up with an alliance of organizations ... If we don't defend, we will lose everything. There have been attempts before to divide the movement and isolate us from the rest of the movement. We can't let that happen now' ...

'The opening of the clinic is a positive thing but the bad thing is that its operation is out of our control.' (OCAC meeting, May 1986)

OCAC did not operate outside the patriarchal relations that shape the lives of all Canadian women. Yet despite the fact that the decision-making power was outside its hands and despite the lack of visibility of its efforts, those most active in the movement had a healthy respect for their power to influence events. Their meetings were often devoted to discussions of how to change OCAC's position from one of reaction to one of initiation. Although the movement was not always successful in using a given reality in order to change that reality, OCAC's activities often did succeed in opening up new and sometimes unexpected opportunities for extending its base of support.

The events surrounding the defence of the Scott clinic illustrate the degree to which OCAC was able to turn that decision to its advantage. In an attempt to ensure that the government did not close down the clinic, OCAC members moved to organize a 'mass press conference' of the various organizations and groups that supported a pro-choice position. In this they were successful in obtaining statements from sixty-one organizations, forty of which sent representatives to the press conference. In the process of getting these groups to attend, the issue had to be debated in a whole range of organizational forums where such discussions had not previously been held. In these various discussions, organizational support could be secured only when the links between abortion and the specific concerns of each organization were made. In discussing the press conference, one member of the Coordinating Committee said that it 'allowed us to lay the groundwork for a response to any future charges at the clinic. The ability to organize the current level of support has been a culmination of years of work. This is particularly true with regard to the NDP and the position which Rae took at the conference. While we need systematic follow-up, public commitment has spread to include the Scott clinic as well as the Morgentaler one. It is likely that the degree of support we garnered will have some influence on government action against the clinic. While it is likely that there will be a charge, we can be hopeful that a raid and removal of equipment will not occur' (OCAC meeting, May 1986).

The amount of time and energy required to defend patients and keep a clinic open, together with the lack of direct control over the decision making, frequently raised new dilemmas for the women in OCAC. Believing that the struggle was a national one, they had organized speaking tours and meetings with activists from other provinces in order to discuss requirements for the opening of new clinics. The question of opening new clinics in other provinces in order to bring added pressure on the state was seen as politically necessary. However, OCAC was also very much aware that the movement's experience in Ontario and Manitoba indicated the need for a political superstructure: women's groups had to be sufficiently organized to ensure that the necessary supports were in place before a clinic was opened. It was evident, however, that Dr Morgentaler was less aware of the degree of movement energy that went into keeping the clinics operating. At times, his actions suggested that he accepted the general perception that it was his performance that forced the abortion issue to be addressed. The downplaying of the movement's activities had already strained his relations with women activists in Quebec, and OCAC members were cognizant of the problems this created in building links with other parts of the country. One activist reported to a general meeting: 'Henry is seen as a personal problem by the women's movement in Quebec. He has never given them credit and they resent that he has given interviews in which he says he didn't get any support. They feel it to be insulting that they mobilized and he doesn't give this any credit' (OCAC meeting, May 1985).

It was not only a lack of credit that was the problem. The relative invisibility of movement activity frequently placed the movement in a reactive position. Morgentaler was in the habit of making public statements about where he would open next, a habit that caused great consternation within the movement. Reporting to the general membership on discussions held at a number of binational[2] strategy meetings, members of the Coordinating Committee elaborated this concern on a number of occasions:

There are occasionally different strategy positions taken by Henry and the pro-choice movement generally with regard to the opening of more clinics. The general feeling at the meeting was that the movement will be diffused by a new struggle at this point. There is a general lack of understanding by Henry as to just how crucial the underlying support provided by the women's movement is, that this is not just a matter of his individual effort. It was felt that we need to attempt to end the isolation of the various struggles across the country first. (OCAC meeting, January 1985)

We discussed the pros and cons of opening new clinics in each province, the lessons learned from Ontario and Manitoba, how to strike the right balance between our short- and long-term goals, the necessity to be solidly based within the woman's movement, the need to strengthen local coalitions so that success is not aimed at a single issue ...

We felt that this meeting was basically an advisory or educational one for Henry. We stressed the two factors that needed to be involved in where we would open next: the need [for the service] and the positive support to win in court. The second is the most important since successes are required to build upon. It was very instructive for Henry to hear someone from Halifax say that this support was not there. It was hard to tell what kind of impact this had on him but it was instructive. (OCAC meeting, May 1985)

The difference in the movement's relations with the Morgentaler and Scott clinics also characterizes other forms of gender relations under capitalist patriarchy. While, ultimately, the person who controls the purse also controls the context, within this context individual men have approached the personal needs of their partners in more or less positive ways. They may or may not inform them of their decisions; they may or may not ask their opinion; they may or may not consider the effect of their decision on mutual needs; they may or may not take for granted what will be required to carry out the decision. The degree of benevolence or sharing of power that individual men exhibit certainly affects the autonomy of the women to whom they relate. The same can be said of the

2 The term 'binational' was used to refer to the coordination of pro-choice mobilizing in Quebec and in English Canada. The use of this terminology was a symbolic stressing of the group's political support for Quebec self-determination.

individual reactions of doctors. For instance, those who refused to perform abortions or who used women as pawns in pursuing the interest of
their profession were certainly different from those who put the basis of
their own power on the line. Moreover, for those who display willingness
to put their own freedom at risk, the decision making involved may be
undertaken in more or less collective ways. Dr Scott, in his response to
the personal needs of his women patients, was certainly different from
those doctors who insist on making abortion decisions for their patients;
and Dr Morgentaler was certainly different from Dr Scott in his response
to political needs.

As different as these individual reactions of doctors are, at issue for the
feminist movement is the 'right' of doctors (or men) to decide if and
when they will share their powers of decision making. The systemic control of women remains even when such a right is not exercised by the person who has the power to do so. The medical monopoly on the definition
of reproductive needs and the unwillingness of doctors to share this
power was a much greater challenge for the Canadian pro-choice movement of this period than the ability to secure a paternalistic response to
its requirements. Almost invariably, when the movement appeared to be
gaining ground in its political demands for reproductive decision making, provincial governments undercut its momentum by stepping up hospital access. The Morgentaler clinics eroded the state's practical ability to
dichotomize autonomy and access in the sense that they allowed a woman
to define what her circumstances required and then provided the medical response she needed to carry out her decision.

While understanding the importance of a unity of autonomy and
response for women seeking abortions at the personal level, Morgentaler
was sometimes deficient in sharing the decision making when the political needs of the movement were at stake. The political power he could
draw on was derived from a public consciousness that equated his name
with the abortion cause. The persistent media reinforcement of a congru-
ence between the abortion problem and the actions and decisions of
Morgentaler helped to render the movement's activities invisible, thus
perpetuating a perception of its insignificance. As one OCAC activist put
it, 'The profile of Morgentaler allows the movement to disappear. We see
the importance of increasing our visibility but it is very difficult to do so.
The grass-roots support, the hard slogging work of the movement, is not
news. While this could be dealt with in columns and editorializing, the
focus here is also on Henry.'

Although news items did sometimes focus on the more visible activities of the movement, the headlines generally referred to Morgentaler. Unlike the reporting of the opposition (generally referred to in headlines as 'pro-life' or 'anti-abortion'), the headlines in the major newspapers overwhelmingly linked the report of abortion-related issues to Morgentaler's name. Although this personalization is a standard media procedure (Gitlin 1980), Morgentaler's identity as a male and as a medical doctor ideologically severed any association between his actions and the objectives of the women's movement. Moreover, references that linked him to the pro-choice movement portrayed the movement in a supporting role. The movement did indeed support Morgentaler's activities, but in selectively ignoring the fact that Morgentaler's actions supported the movement's activities, such references distorted the interdependence of the relationship. In turn, the image of Morgentaler as a benefactor of 'the women of Canada' reinforced social-code assumptions about men and doctors dispensing welfare to women. While compelled to deal with this reality, OCAC consistently sought to turn public perceptions to its benefit and in the process to influence the perceptions themselves.

In November and December 1985, OCAC discussions turned to a press conference that was to be held in conjunction with the anniversary of the clinic's opening. Dr Nikki Kolodny, an active member of OCAC and a committed supporter of the broader reproductive goals of the women's movement, had recently begun to perform abortions at the clinic, and it was hoped that her presence would counter the perception of Morgentaler as the sole actor in the abortion drama. In their deliberations, the activists discussed whether it would be advisable to have Morgentaler attend the anniversary event:

'Nikki's beginning at the clinic is a politically important step. We now have a doctor who is part of the women's movement and we want to give this event a lot of attention. Although this was announced at the annual NAC meetings, this was not picked up by the media. Nikki herself has made it clear that this is not a personality thing and that it is still OCAC that is the moving force. We need to publicize her new role within this context' ...

'If we have Morgentaler speaking, we would be more likely to get press coverage and we need this since we lost the initiative of highlighting the date to the anti-choice groups. On the other side, to have Morgentaler means that the media will be less likely to focus on Nikki' ...

'The problem is that his attendance will ensure press coverage but it will change the focus from movement activity ... Henry and the clinic are so intertwined in people's minds that the news media do not separate them in their reports' ...

'We could have Henry attend but say what we want him to say, that is, he should make the major statement but the statement should focus on Nikki's starting to work at the clinic ... It would also help to have representatives from various groups as speakers. This would indicate the nature of the support we are now able to get.' (OCAC meetings, November and December 1985)

The decision to enlist Morgentaler's help in establishing illegal clinics was not viewed by OCAC activists simply as a way of getting around the choice/access polarity that the state had structured. The clinic strategy was carried forward in a manner that can be described neither as straightforward activity nor as passive reactivity. It involved OCAC in an active mediation of the inconsistencies and contradictions that were created by a context within which it had little control but was able to influence outcomes. In the process of identifying the parameters of the political environment, these activists negotiated among themselves about what decisions were politically possible, but as they did so they reiterated and reflected on their socialist-feminist principles of organization. In most discussions, these principles were raised, but they were never viewed as absolutes that would determine any particular decision or strategy. Rather, they provided both a guide for action and a justification for short-term deviation in the pursuit of long-term goals. The degree to which the organization was successful in using immediate solutions to further more revolutionary aims was directly related to its ability to provide a bridge between different but interrelated struggles.

Building, Consolidating, and Preserving Relationships

Because capitalism and patriarchy reinforce one another – each allowing for the legitimation of unequal relations within one by the other – any attempt to achieve change in both capitalistic and patriarchal relations can mean that the immediate priorities of socialist and feminist groups will come into contradiction. From OCAC's perspective, networking with other feminists and socialists was an important goal, but it was a goal frequently shaped by conflicting priorities.

Despite the interdependent nature of the concerns of labour and women's groups, there were times when the conflicting priorities of the allied groups presented the organization with no satisfactory alternative. The available alternatives were at least partially determined by the

the federal-provincial division of powers. As already noted, the 1969 amendments to the Criminal Code that structured abortion decision making through the medical profession falls under federal jurisdiction, whereas the right to legislate on health matters is a provincial power. For OCAC, this division meant that the attempt to build a bridge between institutionalized and grass-roots groupings (of both feminists and socialists) was complicated by the need to build links with women's groups and with unions both locally and nationally.

Because alliance building was such an important underpinning of the clinic strategy and so important for the achievement of long-term socialist-feminist objectives, OCAC was often in a position of mediating the conflicting priorities of other groups as well as those posed by its own set of objectives. Both on an individual basis (through adjunct activities of OCAC members) and on an organizational level (through organizing mutually supportive discussions and activities) OCAC spent a lot of time and energy in grass-roots organizing. It took every opportunity to speak or write about its perspective in its effort to illustrate the commonality of purpose between OCAC and other groups that sought to promote the interests of women or labour. Frequently, this activity occurred at a level that was not publicly visible, and it did not fit well into the paradigms utilized by the public media. In one sense, success in turning media attention to OCAC activities was helpful in promoting mobilization since, as one member put it, 'visibility of support builds opportunities for further visibility'; but in another sense, the frame that bounded the movement's visibility could alter the public's perception of the struggle, thus marginalizing its efforts. The challenge for OCAC activists was to make the support they were building visible, but to do so in a way that would promote their main objectives in integrative rather than oppositional terms.

Making visible the interconnection between inequalities of sex and class meant that a major priority for OCAC was the building of links with labour organizations. A problem with turning labour support at the grass-roots level into public support was, as one OCAC activist stated, 'the time it takes for the union wheels to turn,' and this was further complicated by the internal requirements of the clinic strategy. For example, at an October 1985 consultation meeting with the Ontario Federation of Labour's women's committee, OCAC had decided to organize solidarity weeks in which different unions would serve as escorts to the clinic on different days of the week. A large number of union women signed up to do escort duty, and the plan was then expanded to include the recruiting of escorts from women's groups and student groups as well as labour. By plugging the proposed project into an existing service, OCAC hoped to attract a broader base of people to direct involvement with the pro-choice movement and 'to publicly show the broad support that the movement has from different sectors of society.' Because media attention would be sought on those days that involved the participation of well-known personalities, the escort duty provided by these celebrities would be limited to a symbolic show of group support that would simultaneously highlight the ongoing service being provided to women coming to the clinic. At the same time, the escort experience itself could be expected to firm up grass-roots commitment, thus influencing abortion-related decision making by the groups taking part.

After several months of planning, the 'solidarity week' project was suddenly cancelled as a result of OCAC's responsibility for supporting the ongoing operation of the clinic. Although OCAC still felt the necessity to bring to public attention the breadth of support it was building, the clinic staff were worried about escalating a conflict that had been waning. As the Coordinating Committee reported, 'Dr Scott has suggested that the anti-choice demonstrators are currently low-key and demoralized. His feeling is that something like this now could only serve to recharge their batteries. He does not want to reopen the conflict. We feel that, at this time, we have to respect Dr Scott's wishes' (OCAC meeting, January 1986).

Although defence of the clinic and concern for the women patients who used the service were often at odds with broader political objectives, the juxtaposition of national and local abortion politics frequently presented an even more serious problem for OCAC decision making. The building of local networks with labour and women's groups and the need to build links nationally with activist pro-choice groups in other provinces were inextricably interwoven, but they also had the potential to come into conflict and to make competing claims on the organization. One planned project – involving local networking at both grass-roots and institutional levels – was overturned by events that occurred in Manitoba and by a refocusing of the local struggle to the national level. Conversely, attempts to shift the focus to the national scene were hampered by events occurring locally.

At a March 1985 meeting, OCAC decided to hold a 'walk-a-thon' in Toronto with the combined objectives of replenishing financial coffers and building up the movement. The Coordinating Committee presented the project as one that could bring people into the movement who had not previously participated in pro-choice demonstrations. It would also attract media attention, thus addressing the ongoing marginalization that the group was experiencing. Most importantly, leading OCAC activists viewed the project as a vehicle for establishing and reinforcing links with other sympathetic groups. Such groups could become involved either by being walkers or by providing group sponsorship for walkers. On the other hand, fear was expressed that the mass-action component of the organization would be 'watered down' by the political neutrality associated with walk-a-thons. To counter this possibility, it was suggested that OCAC's major thrust should be to keep the political component front and centre in all publicity. Proponents of the project argued that an emphasis on the political objectives of the movement would distinguish the OCAC event from traditional walk-a-thons, which were organized for the express purpose of raising money. In this sense, the event would be presented as a quasi-demonstration in support of the clinics.

Despite the opportunity to bring together politically diverse groups under a banner of pro-choice unity, some activists argued that because of its political nature, the walk-a-thon would have to be staged with great care. If silent supporters were to be enticed into playing a more active role in future, it was important not to alienate participants who had conventional expectations. A balance would have to be struck somewhere between marginalization and depoliticization. The planning for the walk-a-thon raised new discussions about where OCAC's priorities should be placed. Members explored at length the pros and cons of prioritizing trade union involvement or of concentrating attention on building a grass-roots base within particular neighbourhoods. During the planning stage, the event was viewed as having 'the potential to become one of the group's largest actions,' with the result that the process proved to be internally valuable. Discussions of the details allowed for a clarification of immediate priorities while educating new members about the group's broader political goals. However, the local character of the planned event, coupled with major new developments in Manitoba, resulted in the walk-a-thon being called off.

During the period in which the Toronto walk-a-thon was being initiated, Dr Morgentaler was planning to reopen his clinic in Winnipeg. The clinic had been closed – except for counselling and referral services – since the police raids in the summer of 1983. Although Morgentaler was facing abortion-related charges in Manitoba, the attorney general was not proceeding with them, pending the appeal of Morgentaler's Toronto acquittal. The decision to reopen the clinic provided a catalyst for renewed activity by opposition forces in Manitoba. On 7 March 1985, in a bid to stop the reopening, '[t]hree Catholic bishops led more than 2,000 anti-abortion demonstrators – including schoolchildren, priests, nuns and nurses – in a march on the Manitoba Legislature' (*Toronto Star*, 8 March 1985). The marchers were seeking to persuade the Manitoba attorney general to grant an injunction that would prevent Morgentaler from carrying out his intentions. Less than a week later, the president of the Manitoba College of Physicians and Surgeons resigned in protest over a licence granted to Morgentaler to practise in Manitoba. In his resignation, he stated that it would be 'inconsistent for me to remain as president of the college which would renew a licence to a surgeon who has openly professed his intent to flout the law, who has not given assurance that he would abide by the college regulations which his clinic previously contravened, and who would destroy life simply on demand' (*Globe and Mail*, 14 March 1985).

The following week, the anti-abortion crusader Joe Borowski called on anti-choice supporters to 'embark on a path of "non-violent civil disobedience," even though it may land some of them in jail' (*Globe and Mail*, 22 March 1985). In a further effort to stop the opening, the anti-abortion group League for Life applied for a court injunction. Although this move was frustrated when the court postponed its hearing, it added to the general climate that caused the entire pro-choice movement to feel that it was under siege.

Morgentaler reopened his Manitoba clinic on the morning of 24 March 1985. Six hours later it was raided by the police, and medical equipment was once again impounded. Morgentaler publicly vowed to reopen as soon as the equipment could be replaced. The obstacles mounted, however, as the Manitoba College of Physicians and Surgeons once again suspended Morgentaler's licence to practise in the province, this time on a temporary basis. The college stressed that the temporary suspension was necessary to discover if sufficient legal evidence existed for revocation. The college registrar, Dr Morrison, was publicly quoted as stating, 'It appears from the newspapers that (Morgentaler) may have broken our bylaws but we have to have proof that will stand up in court.' He was also quoted as saying 'that at the time the licence was renewed, it did not permit the Montreal doctor to perform abortions' (*Toronto Sun*, 28 March 1985). Despite the medical barrier placed in his path, Morgentaler reopened the Winnipeg clinic on 31 March. He defended his professional position by arguing that the college had acted improperly in suspending his licence because it had not given him an opportunity to appear before the hearing. Once again, the clinic was immediately raided by the police and the equipment impounded. This time the police added a new twist, cautioning Morgentaler's lawyer (who was in attendance during the raid) 'that he could be charged with aiding and abetting an indictable offence' (*Toronto Star*, 1 April 1985). Morgentaler responded publicly that this was not only an act of intimidation by the Winnipeg police but that the NDP attorney general was personally responsible for the continued harassment.

The Government of Canada now had three sets of charges pending against the clinic, two from the raids in March 1985 and one from the raid in June 1983. Although these charges were stayed, pending the appeal of the Toronto charges, Morgentaler was still before the courts in Manitoba. Following the latest Morgentaler act of defiance, the Manitoba College of Physicians and Surgeons won an injunction prohibiting him from practising medicine until the matter could be settled at trial. The judge who granted the injunction, Judge Dewar, had acted as legal counsel for the college prior to his appointment to the bench. Furthermore, when Dr Morgentaler launched his appeal against the injunction, two of the judges who would be hearing the appeal were generally considered to be biased against the pro-choice movement: Justice Joseph O'sullivan was chairman of the Roman Catholic Grey Nuns' Youville Clinic, and Justice Alfred Monnin had affixed his signature two years earlier to an anti-abortion petition protesting the Morgentaler clinic (*Globe and Mail*, 6 and 20 April 1985).

Back in Toronto, the developments in Manitoba changed the direction of OCAC energies. On 2 April 1985 the Coordinating Committee reported to the membership meeting:

While the response of the Coalition in Winnipeg has been good, there is not a sense of public outrage in that community over what is going on. This is not a good situation. The NDP government is getting away with continued harassment and, at this point in time, there has not been a large response to their actions either in Winnipeg or across the country. This is a serious problem for us. If the Winnipeg clinic is successfully closed, or if the problems of the clinic continue to be seen as an issue of Henry Morgentaler on a solitary crusade, we have cause for concern. We could be faced with a serious attack here as well but beyond this, it is a serious attack on the movement as a whole. The Coordinating Committee feels that OCAC has not responded quickly enough nor followed through. We feel, in retrospect, that we should have immediately called a press conference involving union leaders and Ontario New Democrats to speak against the actions of their counterparts in Manitoba. We feel that a lot of us have been too focused on other things which have absorbed our time and turned our attention from what is happening nationally. We are also tired.

Canada is a difficult country in which to organize a truly binational movement. This has been a major concern of ours for some time and Winnipeg now gives us a focus to organize around. It also points out the weaknesses that need to be addressed. The decision to withdraw from the walk-a-thon at this point is a difficult one because it involves a very different kind of organizing. Those of us on the Coordinating Committee feel, however, that to continue to focus on the walk-a-thon, given the developments in Manitoba, would not be a correct strategy. Nevertheless, we feel that we need a wide-ranging discussion on this from the entire coalition. It should also be noted that we have another time problem because of the upcoming provincial election. While organizing for this will not be as extensive as it was during the federal election, we still have to organize a pro-choice voice. Our recommendation, therefore, is as follows: we should spend all of our time and energy for some kind of support to the Winnipeg coalition and to strategizing for a binational meeting of activists from across the country.

A lengthy discussion followed. While there were differences about possible strategies, it was clear that there was a general consensus that there should be a change of direction. The following comments, made by some of those present at the meeting, demonstrate the basis for this consensus:

'It is important to assess why we wanted to do the walk-a-thon in the first place in relation to the current situation we face. While our objectives for the walk-a-thon are still valid, we must remember that it would be basically a Toronto event. It is important to realize that Ontario cannot be the political centre. The whole question of outreach and of solidifying our base is still important, but the binational struggle is clearly the priority at the present time. I agree with the Coordinating Committee's recommendation. I feel that it is crucial to organize the binational strategy and to provide some support action for Winnipeg' ...

'I think that there are two factors which change the situation politically. While the Ontario election is only three weeks long, it is important that our movement take on the government and counter the voice of the anti-choice movement. It also would appear that the NDP in Manitoba is vulnerable to this at this time. There is outrage within the NDP ranks in Manitoba over the actions of their elected representatives ... I think that it is important that we link up with women in the NDP on this issue' ...

'I think that the Coordinating Committee's analysis is essentially correct and I agree with postponing the walk-a-thon. We need to talk concretely about what we can do. I would propose that we link up with positive action within the NDP ranks and put pressure on both the Manitoba and Ontario wings of that party' ...

'The reason that we are pinpointing the NDP is that we are really associating with the "movement" within that party. We would be working within the NDP to challenge an action taken by an NDP government. The danger is often in the tendency to mobilize those who are already active and to fool ourselves that we are organizing a mass movement. But, on this issue, it appears to be correct to link up with the challenge to the Manitoba NDP' ...

'We also need to discuss what the postponing of the walk-a-thon does to our own needs regarding the hiring of an organizer, especially since Henry now thinks all money should go towards purchasing new equipment.'

Out of this group discussion came the decision to redirect organizational efforts towards getting Ontario NDP and union leaders to protest the actions taken by the Manitoba government. In addition, it was decided to organize a press conference that would focus on statements from national NDP and union leaders to the effect that their groups likewise deplored the actions of the NDP government in Manitoba. The consensus within OCAC was that the most effective pressure that could be put on the Manitoba government would come from within its own political ranks; it was this pressure that was to be mobilized. The consensus on strategy pointed the group in a new direction, but the national focus it entailed would depend on the strength of its support from local trade unions and the NDP.

The ability of OCAC to mobilize local support in the challenge to Manitoba authorities was directly hampered by the timing of the Ontario provincial election. At the next general meeting of OCAC (April 1985), the seriousness of the Manitoba situation for the movement as a whole was again stressed, though the meeting was informed that 'we have been unable to organize a press conference since all trade union leaders and NDP leaders feel this would hurt the Ontario NDP during the election. The problem with the NDP people's response is the current election.' Because of the Ontario election, it now appeared that a joint press conference was not going to be feasible. The Coordinating Committee felt, however, that a public petition might be worded in such a way as to get the required support from NDP and union leaders: 'The Coordinating Committee is proposing that we take out a full-page ad in the *Winnipeg Free Press*, that we get the names of prominent people, for example from both the trade unions and the NDP and write it as an appeal to the government of Manitoba, not denunciatory but as an appeal that the current actions reflect badly on the party. We would suggest that the Manitoba government take control of the clinic and make it a women's reproductive clinic. We think this could make the national news. If we are going to do this, we need to begin soliciting prominent people from each province to lend their names' (OCAC meeting, April 1955).

The membership of OCAC expressed its ambivalence over whether the petition strategy should call for a clear denunciation of the Manitoba government or whether local support had to be appeased:

'I see the whole situation as very precarious. I do not see an ad which "appeals" as being sufficient. We are clearly on the defensive and we need to say more than that we are disappointed!' ...

'If we want the NDP and trade union people to cooperate, it cannot be an attack. This is a tactical decision. We need to denounce the Manitoba government in such a way that NDP supporters can be a part of it. This is a serious problem in that those [NDP supporters] in Ontario do not see this as an attack against the whole movement and not just in Manitoba. This makes it very difficult for us to build solidarity with Winnipeg as well. (Ibid.)

At this point in the movement's history, the lack of a national strategy was proving to be a problem for local network building, and, conversely, the lack of sufficient local commitment hampered the movement's ability to show solidarity with the national struggle. For OCAC leaders, the events surrounding the Winnipeg clinic reaffirmed the need for a dual vision of mobilization.

As the OCAC activists turned their energies towards what was happening in Manitoba, their initial strategy centred on pressuring the political candidates in Ontario. Although the provincial election hampered their efforts, it provided a new opportunity for securing public promises from political actors. The pressuring of Ontario politicians was helped by a Statistics Canada report, released early in April 1985, which showed that while hospitals were not legally required to establish abortion committees, the existence of such committees clearly did not mean that women had access to abortion services: fewer than one-third of Canadian hospitals had established therapeutic abortion committees, and less than 15 per cent of those with committees had performed 73 per cent of all abortions in Canada during 1983. Moreover, of the 257 hospitals with committees, 50 had not performed any abortions during that year. In the wake of the report and under pressure from pro-choice forces, all three parties in Ontario proclaimed their support for reducing inequities of access – the Conservatives by 'encouraging' hospitals to improve the equality of access (*Toronto Star*, 7 April 1985), the Liberals by asking district health councils to assure equal access (*Globe and Mail*, 4 April 1985), and the NDP by reaffirming its traditional position of providing access based on the decision of a woman to terminate her pregnancy.

In the general discussions of how OCAC should address the election campaign (in view of the actions of Manitoba's NDP government), there was a clear tension between members about how the Ontario NDP candidates should be questioned. Were they friend or foe? If friend, where was this support when it was most needed? Many expressed the opinion that the NDP was little different, in practice, from the old-line parties; but it was also clear that OCAC's approach to it had to be different because, on paper, the NDP clearly supported OCAC objectives, even though it was an NDP government that was behind the harassment of the pro-choice movement in Manitoba. The following remarks are extracted from the OCAC discussion of election strategy.

'All three parties are the same in some ways. The Tories and the NDP have both betrayed women, albeit in different provinces. We need to push the NDP to disassociate themselves from Pawley's government' ...

'It is not fair to say that all three are the same. Miller [Conservative] and Peterson [Liberal] have both come out in favour of access, but Rae [NDP] has clearly said that this will not help the situation. We could ask the Conservative and Liberal candidates, "In light of your leader's positions, how would you see access being improved?" and, since the NDP has come out as pro-choice, "Do you disassociate yourself from the Manitoba NDP?" What those of us who are worried about it is that – in the way questions are posed – the attack will be on the NDP, thus antagonizing those who are supporting us' ...

'But we need to point out that many of us are their political supporters as well, and that we expect them to follow through on NDP policy' ...

'I do not think we should focus on attacking one party. This would be a tactical error, but we do need to ask, "Are you going to stand by policy?" and "How do you feel about Manitoba's actions?"' ...

'The focus should be on the fact that it is Manitoba that is not following policy – Would they fight to maintain their policy if elected? – and point out that what they actually do when under fire is important.'

The events in Manitoba and the subsequent lack of outrage among the movement's political supporters highlighted the fragility of the alliances that OCAC had built with institutionalized groups. The lack of response from leading individuals within the NDP and labour unions proved disappointing and frustrating for OCAC activists. Without a commitment to the pro-choice cause by mainstream groups, achieving public visibility becomes a matter of manipulation rather than a calling forth of mutual concern. This pattern of frustration with 'friends and supporters' is not a new experience for most women. OCAC was experiencing what many women have experienced from supposedly sympathetic socialist groups, at the political level, and from supposedly sympathetic feminist men, at the personal level. When supporting women's needs proves to be politically or personally problematic, such support often dissolves.

In making change, individual women and women's groups do not always find a Morgentaler among those who profess their support for women's particular needs. This wavering support in turn frequently causes individual women and women's groups to put more effort into building networks with other women. While most women have a basis for unity in their inability to command supportive resources from those with social power, they are not a unitary group economically, racially, or politically. Solidarity thus requires an ongoing reciprocal concern for varying needs and priorities. Consequently, networking with other women's groups has more than its share of inherent tensions and conflicting responsibilities. One particular issue of 1985–6 illustrates the ongoing difficulty that OCAC experienced in attempting to bridge the gap between feminists and socialists, institutional groups and grass-roots movements, in a context over which it had minimal control.

'The Manning Issue'[3]

In the year following Manitoba developments and the Ontario election, OCAC's major objectives involved establishing a network of pro-choice activists in different parts of the country. At the institutional level, these efforts were directed towards strengthening ties with women's groups that had a national base (for example, NAC and CARAL) and using this base to establish networks of a more activist nature than those that

3 The following events depict the manner in which OCAC experienced the professional choices of Morris Manning, the lawyer who defended Dr Morgentaler in the appeal courts. Since these events took place well before the rise of the Reform Party in Canada, led by Preston Manning, there was no ambiguity in the minds of OCAC members concerning the phrase 'the Manning issue.' Unlike the liberal position of Morris Manning, Preston Manning's right-wing political philosophy concerning family issues was discursively prefigured by Crown arguments at the Supreme Court (see chapters 9 and 10).

characterized the parent organizations. Despite this renewed focus on strengthening OCAC's connection with institutionalized women's groups, the organization did not abandon its activist orientation. It did, however, turn its socialist focus more towards grass-roots organizing within the women's committees of local trade unions and towards building a new solidarity with local immigrant women's groups. Attempting to build support at two levels simultaneously (institutional and grass-roots, local and national), coupled with a lack of control of the legal struggle, led to a crisis within the organization during 1985 and 1986.

In the latter part of 1985, OCAC faced a strategic crisis that brought together, in one major issue, many of the usual contradictions and inconsistent alternatives posed by the clinic strategy. This issue, which I term 'the Manning issue,' concerned the conflicting priorities of institutionalized women's groups and women at the grass-roots level within unions. An examination of this crisis illustrates the difficulty of organizing local networks of supporters within union and women's groups while attempting to build a national movement based on socialist and feminist objectives. The issue also illustrates the interconnectedness of socialist and feminist objectives as well as the inconsistent alternatives that are posed by a dual networking strategy. While the various emphases and loyalties of trade union women and women in the established women's movement were often mutually reinforcing within OCAC, they also presented the OCAC activists with some very difficult choices. Although OCAC was able to initiate action designed to overcome systemic conflicts between productive and reproductive struggles, its efforts were constrained by the lack of decision-making power that arose from the clinic strategy.

During September 1985, pro-choice supporters began to express concern about the professional activities of Morgentaler's lawyer, Morris Manning. This concern first surfaced when the Morgentaler legal case was before the Ontario appeal court. Manning had successfully presented the case before the lower court (securing a jury acquittal), had later argued the case before the Ontario Court of Appeal, and was now awaiting the judgment of that court. The 'Manning issue' would continue to be a factor after the Ontario Court of Appeal ruled against Morgentaler, when Manning was preparing and presenting an appeal at the Supreme Court of Canada.

The root cause of the crisis was a clash between the legal conception of 'choice' and the political meaning of the term as it was understood within the reproductive-rights perspective of OCAC. However, it was not the manner in which Manning argued for a woman's 'right to choose' that elicited OCAC concern; it was the fact that in addition to representing Morgentaler (and, by extension, the interests of women in the pro-choice movement), Manning was also involved with a number of cases that were considered to be in direct opposition to labour interests. Manning's actions and the way they were interpreted began to have an effect on the movement-building efforts of OCAC as well as on its attempt to redefine ideologically the nature of 'choice' along the lines of reproductive-code assumptions.

The initial case at issue involved a constitutional challenge by Merv Lavigne, an engineering instructor, against the Ontario Public Service Employees Union (OPSEU). Financially backed by the right-wing National Citizens' Coalition (NCC), the case challenged the right of unions to use compulsory dues to support political activities. Since 1945, when the Rand formula had instituted the principle of compulsory dues check-off (regardless of membership in the representing union), Canadian unions had been free to use these funds to implement decisions taken collectively by the union membership. Now, Lavigne and the NCC were arguing that individuals who disagreed with the principles of various organizations and political parties were being forced to subsidize them through the union check-off system. This, they argued, was in violation of the Charter right of 'freedom to associate' or not to associate.

Although the Lavigne case did not entail a direct challenge to the Rand formula requirement that if an individual is in a union shop, he or she must pay union dues, it was seen by most union leaders as part of a concerted attempt by the NCC to delegitimate unions and turn their relationship with management into one of fragmented individualism. In its financing of Lavigne's court case, the NCC was said to be calling into question a century of union social and political activism (Deverell, *Toronto Star*, 13 July 1986). The implications of the case went beyond the relations involved in negotiating contracts, and many union leaders were 'haunted by the vision that this case may be but a small tremor in a much larger Charter shake-up of traditional labour-management relations' (*NOW*, 17–23 July 1986). As the labour reporter for the *Toronto Star* argued, 'When the coalition inveighs against the curtailment of "individual liberty" by compulsory union dues, as it has in the recent Lavigne case, it is pursuing a much broader agenda. It wants workers to be free of unions altogether' (*Toronto Star*, 13 July 1986).

The broader reproductive-rights definition of 'choice' to which OCAC subscribed did not imply a limitation on collective struggle. Within the frame of reference of a reproductive code, the autonomy of individuals is directly dependent on, not in opposition to, the collective responses that they receive from others. Unlike the liberal interpretation of 'choice,' the socialist-feminist variant includes the collective resources that 'provide the context in which individuals can shape and control their lives' (Adamson, Briskin, and McPhail 1988:155). It was these collective resources that were under attack in the court challenge to depoliticize unions. In commenting on the Lavigne case, labour historian Desmond Morton stated, 'The inherent North American tendency to support individuals against the group is fatal when the whole nature of trade unionism is groupism and collective strength against what may be one individual. It may be Conrad Black but you need all the members of the union to make the slightest impact on one individual' (quoted in *NOW*, 17–23 July 1986). OCAC members were as concerned with the implications of this legal challenge as union activists were, but their public opposition was hampered by their own legal battles, which were being orchestrated by Manning.

In his approach to the labour cases that he was representing, Manning addressed the issues in terms of an opposition between individual freedom and collective power, not unlike the way he perceived a woman's, or a doctor's, right to choice. Philosophically, the basis of his various legal challenges, including both productive and reproductive challenges to the law, was a civil libertarian one – that the Charter was a fundamental protection of the rights of individuals from encroachment by collective interests, regardless of whether those interests were represented by state or civil-society institutions. The approach Manning was taking in the labour case was similar to that pursued in his defence of Dr Morgentaler – choice being a matter to be decided between doctor and patient in a private relationship – but this was not the meaning that OCAC was attempting to convey in its political statements.[4]

---

4 The relationship between Morris Manning and the pro-choice movement was always an indirect one. While some pro-choice activists may have regarded Manning as their 'hired gun,' his arguments at the Morgentaler hearings were designed to translate facts about abortion in Canada into categories that were already implicitly understood by the court. As I have illustrated in part 3 of this book, the position taken by Manning was directed towards defending the liberty rights of Dr Morgentaler, a defence that hinged on the argument that the law actually hampered doctors from carrying out their mandated responsibility to determine which pregnant women would be considered deserving of welfare rights. Whether pro-choice objectives might have been injected into legal discourse – pushing the boundaries of debate beyond the traditional dichotomy of choice and access – cannot be determined by Manning's legal work. The events depicted in this section suggest, however, that his ideological position was in harmony with the legal paradigm's depiction of the normal legal subject as an autonomous individual.

In early September 1985, some concern was expressed by OCAC members about Manning's other 'choice' activities, though the conflicting loyalties that would eventually arise were not at first apparent. At this point, the OCAC reaction consisted of a 'strongly worded letter' to Manning indicating the group's displeasure about his involvement in the power struggles between management and workers. Although, Manning's professional activities were viewed as distasteful, the full implications that they would have for OCAC's socialist-feminist objectives were not immediately grasped. The political relevance was initially obscured by what was occurring in the legal arena and the perceived need to politicize this process.

On 1 October 1985 the Ontario Court of Appeal handed down its decision in the Morgentaler appeal. Not unexpectedly, the decision went against Morgentaler. While a new trial had been ordered by the Court of Appeal, the decision would now be appealed to the Supreme Court of Canada. Manning had indicated that he expected a somewhat better chance for success at this level. There was some question by activists about whether, given his position on the union issue, Manning should continue to represent the pro-choice movement, but the major focus at the October meeting involved a discussion of the best way to respond to the appeal court's decision. Nevertheless, at this time there was some indication that the Lavigne issue was beginning to have an effect on visible union support for the abortion cause.

In their report to the meeting about events occurring at a Canadian Labour Congress (CLC) women's conference, the OCAC members who had attended noted the various ways in which union women were demonstrating positive support for the pro-choice cause. The vast majority of the women at the conference had signed a pro-choice petition to be sent to the CLC president, Cliff Pilkey, applauding him for his support of pro-choice activities and encouraging him to continue in this direction. A variation of this position had come out of a workshop in the form of a resolution that linked the abortion issue to affirmative action for women and called for concrete union support of the Morgentaler clinic. Despite this show of support, however, the OCAC members expressed their unease at the apparent attempt of the conference chair to block the resolution from coming to the floor of the convention. Although the resolution eventually did get moved and passed, the OCAC activists believed that the leadership was trying to keep the issue from being debated. In discussing the resolution with trade union women, OCAC elicited the information that a major problem with the resolution was its inclusion of a call for political and monetary support of the Morgentaler clinic. The OCAC members were told, 'This raises the whole issue of labour union fees going to support the fight for abortion services and the leadership does not want this raised.'

By the end of October, members of the OCAC Coordinating Committee had held a meeting with representatives of women's committees from a number of Ontario unions. They came away from this meeting convinced that the problem was of a more serious nature than they had formerly believed. The union women were pressing OCAC members to meet with the Canadian Abortion Rights Action League (CARAL) to suggest firing Manning or, at the very least, to dissociate the pro-choice movement from the positions taken by Manning in his legal attack on unions. The members of the Coordinating Committee accordingly met with CARAL representatives to discuss the situation, but they found that although the issue was considered disturbing, CARAL did not view it as serious enough to warrant drastic action. The CARAL members informed OCAC that they had already written a letter to Manning stating that they did not like his position but that, nevertheless, he would continue to represent the pro-choice interests in court. The Coordinating Committee feared (with good reason, as subsequent events would prove) that Manning's activities had the potential to occasion either a split between OCAC and CARAL or between OCAC and its supporters in the women's committees of local trade unions.

The discussion of the general OCAC membership following the report of the Coordinating Committee illustrates the importance this issue was to have for several months:

'This position [of CARAL] has undercut our negotiations. We are trying to go step by step. It is a ticklish issue. We need to persuade CARAL of the seriousness of continuing to be represented by Manning' ...

'The union women will undoubtedly ask CARAL to fire Morris ... We want to try to work out a conciliation. The labour unions are unanimous that he should be fired. We have persuaded them that it isn't fair to ask us to come to a decision yet, that we need to talk to CARAL first. They feel that their credibility is at stake and that this issue will be used by not just the anti-choice but by the whole anti-feminist strain within the unions' ...

'I think we need to know what our bottom line is. Is OCAC ready, in the final analysis, to recommend the firing of Manning? I am concerned that we do not provoke a split with CARAL. We have no mandate to fire Manning at this point' ...

'We have not yet taken a position regarding firing Manning ... We need to have a discussion ourselves. We decided at the last meeting to (1) meet with union women, (2) put immediate pressure on Manning, and (3) to prepare leaflets for union distribution which make our public disassociation clear. We need to make clear that this disassociation is not for the press but an OFL leaflet. We do not want a firm position at this time from OCAC. Rather, we [on the Coordinating Committee] want the authority to proceed to do what appears best, to have some flexibility ... This is a serious situation and could blow up. We want a mandate but we don't want to provoke any split where this is unnecessary. We are in a position that this issue is more serious within the labour unions than we had thought, on the one side, and, on the other, CARAL has, with their letter, undercut our ability to negotiate' ...

'This is the most dangerous point that we have ever been at. Our goal is to keep a strong movement, but we also need to stick to principles' ...

'I think it is hard for us to come to a consensus right now. We are feeling our way around to see which is the worst evil. We need to see how bad it is first. '

Which was the worst evil? During the next few months, Manning's other legal activities were to challenge OCAC's organizing principles further. By mid-November, OCAC members were feeling even greater pressure to deal with the issue, for Manning had now taken on another anti-labour case. This time he was representing an employer who was challenging the right of unions to post bills in the workplace. It was becoming clearer to OCAC activists that the advocate who represented their case in the legal arena was operating from a very different ideological conception of liberty rights than they did. Nevertheless, within the parameters of the legal code, Manning was acting appropriately. According to the assumptions of value neutrality, one can detach oneself from a social context in order to make neutral judgments. From a feminist (or socialist) perspective, this was precisely the problem of entering the legal arena: the abstract rules of neutrality allowed Manning to evade responsibility for his actions and rendered his ideological position invisible. Although it was useful for engaging the power of the law, the concept of 'choice' now threatened to harm the cause rather than further it. Manning's particular perspective was now a factor in the subordination of the political struggle to the legal challenge. The intent of the legal fight was being turned upside down. All the warnings of those who had criticized the clinic strategy seemed about to come to pass.

In contrast to OCAC's political understanding of the enabling power of 'choice,' the individualizing rhetoric of these Charter challenges stressed the hegemonic belief that the autonomy of individuals can be achieved by legally limiting the powers of the collective. What became important was the way in which the concept of 'choice' could be individualized in order to restrict and limit the activity of those who challenged unequal power relations. By conceptually tying his other Charter challenges to the Morgentaler case, Manning was ideologically attacking the broader political understanding of the pro-choice movement. In the process, he was undercutting the ability of OCAC to build networks between different movements. The feminist challenge was being redefined in terms of the legal discourse, and its radical potential was being absorbed in a way that threatened to undercut union support for the pro-choice cause. The relevance of arguments criticizing the use of legal strategies was being confirmed as the individualizing discourse of the legal arena was now being turned back on the movement in the political arena.

Despite the commonality of interests between the union movement and the women's movement, it looked as if the Manning issue might destroy the working relationship between them. The OCAC activists were, on the one hand, threatened with being defined out of the abortion struggle altogether; a break with CARAL would sever their link with the institutionalized challenge to the paternalism of the therapeutic abortion committees, and the institutionalized wing of the labour movement had already demonstrated the fragility of its support. On the other hand, to break with the women's committees within the trade unions would mean that the 'choice' struggle would be drawn too far inside a hegemonic framework that pitted collective interests against individual ones. The United States experience had already made clear the problem inherent in 'winning' an individual right of choice without also gaining access to collective supports. The available options appeared to be equally unthinkable. The following report of the members of the Coordinating Committee shows how the dilemma was posed to the general membership:

A union delegation has met with CARAL. The union women were very articulate and persuaded the CARAL representatives of how serious they perceive the situation. However, CARAL has not been convinced to change their current position of 'censoring but unwilling to disassociate.' There was no rancour in the meeting between these two groups. Everyone understood the point of view of the other side and the need to be responsive to the base of support on each side. But there is a feeling by CARAL that Manning cannot be let go, that 'he is the lawyer who won the case for us' ...

Manning is not willing to back down. He sees himself as a crusader and is very unlikely to be persuaded. The feeling within the unions is that he will become the lawyer used by anti-unionists to bring Charter provisions to smash the unions. We have been very cautious on this issue. We do not know if the majority of our movement is supportive of the labour movement. There is a potential here for a very large split in the movement we have been building ...

It now appears that an impasse has been reached; while it is not yet 'public,' this is likely to happen. Therefore, the Coordinating Committee is recommending that we ask Henry to get another lawyer as a gesture of support for the solidarity shown us over the past number of years by the unions. While it is still our goal to get rid of Manning without splitting the movement, it is now necessary to come down on one side or the other. We should do so publicly as a gesture of solidarity with those in the union movement who have supported us so strongly for the past three years – a reciprocal show of support.

The discussion following the Coordinating Committee's report and recommendation attempted to clarify whether the current OCAC position was a 'public' or 'private' one. A consensus was arrived at that OCAC would recommend to Morgentaler that he get a new lawyer but that this would remain a 'non-public' position in the sense of not going to the media with it. This decision allowed the issue to be placed in a holding pattern until January 1986, when Manning took on another anti-labour client. This time, Manning's clients were the scabs in a strike involving Visa and mailroom workers against the Canadian Imperial Bank of Commerce.

The strike action of the Union of Bank Employees was viewed as a major labour challenge to all Canadian banks rather than as an isolated labour dispute. Despite much union organization, Canadian banks had managed to remain largely union-free, and this strike was seen as a key struggle. Union officials claimed that, in general, 'banks have assigned batteries of lawyers to ensure that negotiated agreements always represent little more than the minimum required by law and bank policy' ('Insight,' *Toronto Star*, 15 January 1986). In this case, the Canadian Labour Congress was arguing that the Bank of Commerce 'is employing the same tactics at the table involving Visa and mailroom workers ... and the congress wants an end to it' (ibid.). The strike was seen within the labour movement as one that had the potential to result in either 'an imposed settlement that may draw more members to the bank union – or set back Canada's entire labor movement' (ibid.). Because of the perceived importance of this strike, the strikers were getting monetary support from the United Auto Workers and the Canadian Union of Postal

Workers while the Canadian Labour Congress was allocating strike pay of 'more than three times the amount many unions pay' (ibid.). Those on the picket lines were distinguished by the fact that most of them were female, and many of these women regarded sexism to be a major issue in the relations between management and workers. While the Visa strike was important to the labour movement generally, the women's movement saw it as a women's strike, in every sense.

The Visa strike was thus considered important for both the feminist and the labour struggle. With this in mind, members of the Coordinating Committee reached a consensus that they could 'no longer work in any fashion with Manning as the pro-choice lawyer' (OCAC meeting, 14 January 1986). They outlined their recommendations as follows:

The plan is for Judy and several labour women to travel to Montreal to visit Henry and to 'lean' on him. If he refuses to fire Manning, we believe that OCAC should disassociate themselves in a public way. This is seen as going one step further. But it is important to remember that Morgentaler hires, the pro-choice fund pays and OCAC has no direct power ... We felt that CARAL might find this a step too far – it is a women's strike – and that they might now come on board as well. However, while they say that they are offended, they are still not willing to say that Morris must be dropped. The general feeling is that to drop Morris would damage the case. Arguments from other lawyers do not support this. While CARAL is convinced that Manning won the case and is indispensable, other legal opinion is that it is not uncommon to change lawyers to go to the Court of Appeal. A different strategy is needed anyway. (Ibid.)

The discussion at the meeting was an elaboration of the feelings of outrage many of the women felt. At a strategic level, there was some dissension about whether this was a time to take the initiative in going to the media – 'to frame and say our reasons why as opposed to journalists framing it in an irrelevant way' – or whether this was a time when taking the initiative would be politically unwise. If the issue should go public, the fear was that the media frame would not present the political implications as OCAC perceived them but would pose the issue within the discourse of libertarianism. As one member put it, 'Manning is a lawyer, lawyers do not take value positions about their clients, and, in any event, he should have freedom of choice.' Posed in this way, OCAC could not win. If the general public accepted this version, they might also support the abortion cause but in a manner that would ultimately be restrictive for achieving any real change in the nature of reproductive relations. On the other hand, a rejection of the right of lawyers to make such individualistic choices could then undercut the pro-choice movement's own legal challenge.

Members present at this January meeting raised questions about the effect a dissociation might have on the whole legal campaign. Concern was expressed that going public with the issue would involve risking a clear split with CARAL and with Morgentaler. Because OCAC had generally provided the spokespersons for the clinic, it grappled with the question of what its political position should be if Morgentaler did not agree with the necessity of firing Manning. Ideologically, the OCAC women felt that it was not possible to split with Morgentaler because 'in the eyes of the public Morgentaler is the movement; he represents the pro-choice movement.' Without the Morgentaler connection, ideological marginalization was inevitable; and without the CARAL connection, much of the binational character of the group's political organizing would disappear. Although OCAC had begun building its own pro-choice network with other grass-roots activists across the country, the majority of these links were accomplished under the auspices of its association with CARAL. Many pro-choice women situated in cities across Canada had only CARAL to work through, and a split with the institutionalized pro-choice movement that CARAL represented would ultimately mean a set-back in national organizing. If the group was cut off from the clinic strategy, its political activities would be effectively marginalized. The events in Manitoba earlier in the year had clearly indicated that national networking with other pro-choice groups was as important as that within the local trade union circles. Without a broad-based group equally willing to support demands for a repeal of the federal law and to demand the provision of state-funded abortion services throughout the country, choice and access could continue to be polarized through the tossing of the issue back and forth between the federal and provincial levels of government.

How could the OCAC members afford to opt for either alternative? How publicly visible should they make the strategic differences between themselves and the institutionalized wing of the movement? To initiate a public split with those who represented the movement in the eyes of the public – Dr Morgentaler and CARAL – would significantly set back the organization of a national pro-choice movement. On the other hand, not to go public would undermine all the grass-roots work that had been done within the women's trade union committees. OCAC had always stood by the primary principle of mobilizing trade union women, and its political credibility within the union movement would be at stake if it appeared to waffle on this commitment. The fear was expressed that if the issue was raised at the CLC without OCAC having taken a strong public position, OCAC would be placed in a reactive and defensive position.

The key to the dilemma was Dr Morgentaler. If he could be prevailed upon to see the political need to fire Manning, it was felt that CARAL would go along with this. Because Morgentaler had agreed to take on the fight in Ontario on the understanding that the movement would raise the funds required for a legal battle, this was one area in which OCAC felt it might exert at least a symbolic influence. Although it did not directly control the pro-choice defence fund, its activities significantly affected the financial ability to mount the ongoing legal challenge. The meeting decided that OCAC would stop working for the defence fund until Morgentaler found another lawyer and that he would be prevailed upon to do so.

By February, members of the Coordinating Committee had met with Dr Morgentaler in an attempt to persuade him of the seriousness of the situation for the movement as a whole. As a result of this meeting, Morgentaler agreed to dissociate himself publicly from Manning's position of 'choice' in the labour struggle, but he would not agree to a firing. Even so, this compromise was enough to avert the crisis that OCAC activists had feared. Morgentaler's public announcement proved to be sufficient for the labour women to ward off criticism within their unions. For the moment at least, OCAC was able to avoid a public split with either camp. The compromise allowed it to bridge the gap between the currents expressed in institutionalized trade unionism and institutionalized feminism.

The difference in the philosophical positions of Manning and the movement was to become much clearer during the Ontario doctors' strike of 1986 when Manning, in his support of a doctor's right to extra-bill, publicly took a position that was at odds with the pro-choice movement. Manning interpreted the provincial government's decision to end extra billing as an attempt 'to do away with the ability of a willing patient and a willing physician to contract for services' and 'to end free enterprise in the physician-patient relationship' (*Canadian Lawyer*, May/June 1986:43–4). Like his position on union organizing, his position on the doctors' strike was one that abstracted relations between groups out of their existing context of power, and it had similar implications. As Hutchinson and Petter noted in their critique of Manning's position in support of extra billing, 'If Manning's constitutional arguments were accepted at face value, governments would be obliged to do away with laws establishing minimum wages and imposing unemployment insurance schemes upon employers' (*Canadian Lawyer*, September 1986:42–3). This, of course, is exactly the kind of concern that union groups were expressing about Manning's professional decision to champion anti-union causes.

Based on the legal-code assumption of autonomous individuals, Manning's positions were ideologically consistent, but his general perspective was directly at odds with OCAC's political objective of challenging unequal power relations within both production and reproduction. Taken together, Manning's choice of clients constituted a significant threat to OCAC's ideological objectives, because it conveyed the idea that a collective response to need is an exceptional and not an essential component for achieving individual autonomy. As such, it reinforced the legitimacy of the legal paradigm rather than providing an effective challenge to its logic.

If Manning's involvement with the union issue had threatened to split the pro-choice movement, the situation was different when the doctors' strike arose during the following year. On this issue, union and women's groups were uniformly allied against the medical profession, and their collective mobilizing on the issue allowed for a joint challenge to systemic medical power as well as to the individualistic legal discourse that justified it. That in this instance they were able to do so should not be seen as unrelated to the work performed by OCAC during the earlier crisis over Manning's union activities. They were able to coordinate a concerted challenge to the medical establishment during the doctors' strike *because of* their earlier efforts to mediate the conflicting demands of the two movements. While this work was decidedly political in nature, it was also reproductive labour in the sense that it created the conditions whereby power could be exercised.

13

Integrating Personal Experience and Collective Action

Feminism is not simply the female viewpoint, and it does not flow automatically from women's experience ... The importance of women's specific life experience is not that it endows women inevitably and automatically with an alternative set of values, but that it provides a material basis from which to forge them. (Miles 1985:59)

A politic of building sisterhood on the basis of difference is expressed organizationally in the women's movement, not through large homogeneous political organizations, but rather through alliances and coalitions. (Briskin 1990:47)

Personal Experience and the Problem of Choice

One of the criticisms of the Canadian pro-choice movement (emanating from within the women's movement itself) focused on the gulf that separated the subjective motivations of women who sought to terminate unwanted pregnancies from the rhetoric used by the pro-choice movement. These critics called for a recasting of the abortion debate in terms grounded in women's personal experiences (McDonnell 1984; Clement 1983; Cole 1983). Without this shift in discourse, they argued, women could not be mobilized in sufficient numbers to bring about a restructuring of the way abortion services could be secured. For example, in addressing the Ottawa Planned Parenthood organization during 1985, McDonnell reiterated the fundamental point made in her book *Not an Easy Choice: A Feminist Re-examines Abortion* (1984). She contended that 'many people who advocate a woman's freedom of choice have failed to talk about the complexity of abortion or offer emotional support' (*Ottawa*

Citizen, 23 May 1985). Basically, her position was that the pro-choice movement, in its attempt to make political gains for women, had strayed too far from the 'personal is political' roots of feminism itself. While she noted that 'choice' was a convenient slogan for tapping into society's overall emphasis on individualism, she maintained that the pursuit of this legal liberty right gave the general public the impression that pro-choice activists considered moral questions about responsibility to be an unimportant aspect of the debate. McDonnell thus concluded that the pro-choice movement would be unable to 'mainstream' its perspective to the majority of women until it clarified the connection between the morality that informs a woman's nurturing work and society's restrictions on abortion services.

An examination of public discourse reveals both the truth of McDonnell's argument and the problem with it. Where experience has taught women the value of nurturing and responsibility for others, and where cultural explanations pose such activities in a framework of opposition between self and other, 'choice' easily becomes the public metaphor for the loss of human caring values and the embracing of pure individual self-interest. An example of the patriarchal nature of this social-code discourse is provided in George F. Gilder's popular book *Sexual Suicide* (1973). Gilder argues that society is committing suicide when it encourages women to abandon their traditional roles. It is, he maintains, the feminine virtues that humanize men by limiting their natural aggression. Thus, if social morality is to be maintained, these female characteristics must be protected, not undermined. If the care women provide for others is turned into another market commodity, human values of empathy and compassion will be lost forever, leaving a society based solely on relationships of loveless competition.

The logic of this conservative reasoning provides an experiential grounding for anti-choice forces to argue that collective values and nurturant activities will be entirely eliminated from the social fabric if traditional gender relations are not defended. What makes such traditionalism salient is that it reflects social-code assumptions about the 'true' nature of men and women, and thus is already part of the context in which women interpret debates about the morality of abortion. Moreover, although the fear of losing human values of care and nurture is based on a hegemonic distortion of reproductive experience, the nature of hegemony is such that its discourse reflects current practices. Women do make choices that are not solely determined by external forces, and men do give little legitimacy to the particular needs of women. In the absence of alternative discourses, the translation of this asymmetrical relationship into theories of natural gender difference transforms a woman's strength into an ideological weapon that she may wield against the interests of her sex.

The fear, exploited by the anti-choice forces, is that, unrestrained, women might actually choose self-interest over their traditional nurturing values and that, conversely, men might be prisoners of a biological make-up that prevents them from freely choosing activities of empathy and compassion for the needs of others. Although McDonnell was certainly not supporting the notion of natural sex roles, she was arguing that pro-choice activists were not giving enough credence to the distinctive morality of women. To argue for choice, where such a right is interpreted as a lack of care for others, is to ground one's freedom on the very terrain of 'male selfishness' that is feared by women who suffer the most from this selfishness. As a leading Toronto anti-choice activist put it, 'Women (feminists) think they've gained so much. But they haven't changed men one iota. Because men won't change. It's in their nature' (Laura McArthur, quoted in the *Globe and Mail*, 29 January 1985).

If, ideologically, men can be made to appear inherently unable to respond to the needs of others, then the anti-choice forces can gain ground by appealing to women to continue in their socially assigned role as preservers of caring values. The anti-choice position becomes the argument that appears to be based on women's experience: on the one hand, it stresses the responsibility for others that is central to the reproductive code but, on the other hand, it portrays female responses as a passive reaction, an interpretation central to the social code. Within this interpretive frame, the defence of traditional gender roles can be especially appealing to women who depend on societal structures to protect them from the men in their lives, however inadequate these structures may be in actual practice.

McDonnell's criticisms are therefore partially correct: the terms of the public abortion debate do not reflect the total experience of women who choose to terminate their pregnancies, but they do reflect a selected portion of that experience. However, my observation of the dilemmas facing the Ontario Coalition for Abortion Clinics (OCAC) suggests that a focus on personal experience is not in itself sufficient to break through hegemonic discourse. Because reproductive experiences are structured within patriarchal relations and explained within the terms of those relations, social structures and social discourse reinforce each other. If change is to be brought about, the argument about women's experience within patriarchal capitalism needs to be understood as including their political experiences within patriarchal capitalism.

A full understanding of the manner in which women's experiences are socially created and explained (rather than biologically determined) requires an understanding of the patriarchal nature of the process through which change itself is structured. It is impossible to have a complete picture of the hegemonic process without understanding the ways in which women's political efforts to change reproductive relations have themselves been shaped by hegemonic discourse. Without such comprehension, the work of those who seek social change continues to be conceptually understood as lying outside the power dynamic that discourse structures. What I am arguing is that an understanding of the dynamics of creating social change, or of maintaining a patriarchal order, requires a theoretical grounding in the political experiences of those movements that seek to change the relations of patriarchal capitalism, including the way those experiences are shaped by their particular relationships with other groups or individuals.

An examination of the experiences of the OCAC activists demonstrates that although the feminist criticisms of the pro-choice movement (for example, McDonnell's) are accurate – as far as they go – they are inaccurate in their assumption that the pro-choice activists had not thought through the negative implications of their particular strategies and endeavoured to counteract them. OCAC had consistently stressed the problematic nature of focusing on abortion as a single issue involving the removal of legal constraints on individual autonomy. The decision to highlight a legal right to choice was not a matter of short-sightedness on the part of activists within the organization. Their policy statements and internal discussions make it clear that they understood choice in the reproductive (empowering) sense of collective concern for individual needs.

Although OCAC's perspective was derived from reproductive-code morality, the problem of introducing the reproductive-rights perspective into the public consciousness was a political problem that required more than a focus on experience alone. What was not understood by the feminist critique of the pro-choice strategy was, first, the sheer difficulty of breaking through a frame that dichotomizes autonomy and responsibility and, secondly, the degree to which pro-choice activities were geared to accomplishing this breakthrough. Without a simultaneous twofold attack, any particular strategy can be accommodated within the status quo. Unless hegemonic boundaries are challenged and resisted, 'practice simply ends up working within the confines of what is already there. The problem is that the degree of change possible within these confines is quite limited' (Adamson, Briskin, and McPhail 1988:180). The major problem with McDonnell's criticism, and with those who affirmed it, was not the inaccuracy of the analysis; it was the failure to grapple with the contradictory nature of simultaneously focusing on the personal experiences of women in conditions of unequal power and politically changing those same relations of power.

The socialist critics of the pro-choice strategy (for example, Nichol) understood more clearly the need for a broader political analysis than personal experience alone can provide, but their analysis did not reveal the way in which political change in relations of *production* is prevented through a continuation of patriarchal *reproductive* relations. By maintaining that any improvement in the position of women can be made only through prioritizing issues according to their apparent class content and their direct relation to the productive sphere, and by arguing that the abortion struggle has to be grounded in the struggles of women in the workers' movement, these critics left unexamined the hierarchical relationship between productive and reproductive life as well as the role of reproductive labour in reproducing this relationship.[1] Because this analysis discounts the experience of women, it unwittingly contributes to the continuation of the ideological split between public and private, which in turn structurally imposes experiences by gender.

In practice as well as theory, the OCAC activists were all too aware that their concepts (including a collective understanding of the concept of choice) could be co-opted into dominant discourse in ways that worked against their overall political objectives. The Manning issue had reconfirmed the kinds of distortion that could occur when their slogan of 'choice' was appropriated and explained within the framework of social and legal discourse. It also illustrated, however, the tension that exists within the need both to develop short-term strategies that provide access to the political and ideological arena and to attend to the long-term objective of changing the structural and ideological underpinnings of that arena. The ongoing challenge, which many OCAC activists understood, was to find ways to enter the public political arena of ideological discourse without being assimilated into that discourse.

---

1 Class reductionism arranges issues of sex and class in an 'internal hierarchy of issues, with those issues having the most apparent class content at the top and those with the least at the bottom. One gets many points for helping to organize a support picket for striking women workers, but few for putting together a lesbian conference' (Weir, quoted in Adamson, Briskin, and McPhail, 1988:130n29).

As a short-term strategy, 'choice' offered a means by which OCAC activists could penetrate the dominant discourse, thus preventing the kind of marginalization that usually results from speaking in the 'different voice' of feminine experience. On the other hand, as long as the individual and the collective were posed in oppositional terms – as they were in the public arena – the movement's rhetoric could be interpreted in individualistic ways that undercut the more revolutionary objective of changing moral consciousness at the public level. The inherent dilemma of attempting such change in both sexist ideology and patriarchal structure often led to perceptual inconsistencies as OCAC attempted to speak on both levels at once. As one activist put it, 'We can't keep talking "reproductive choice" when they are talking "murdering babies." We need to address this distortion. Nevertheless, there is a different way of speaking when we are trying to convince the general public of the "rightness" of the issue as opposed to the political mobilizing of our women supporters' (OCAC meeting, 19 February 1985). In the process of choosing strategies that would capture the current concerns of women while changing the context within which those concerns arose, the OCAC activists were attempting to avoid the problems of marginalization that result from either abstract political analysis or isolationist alternatives to the status quo. In attempting to keep from being defined out of the political struggle, however, they faced – at the other extreme – the risk of institutionalization and the loss of ability to make any significant change in the relations of either production or reproduction (Adamson, Briskin, and McPhail 1988).[2]

What is required at the level of theory is not a unitary focus on either political principles or concrete experience but an unveiling of the way in which women's political choices and motivations are themselves both structurally shaped and actively resisted. This unveiling reconnects the personal and political lives of women, illuminating some very radical possibilities for social change. To illustrate this potential, as well as the ten-

---

2 See Adamson, Briskin, and McPhail (1988) for a discussion of this 'strategic dilemma' common to feminist practice. They discuss the two extremes of marginalization and institutionalization in their insightful analysis of the women's movement in Canada. Their description of the socialist-feminist dilemmas is very similar to that which I observed within OCAC. I have liberally used their material to illustrate how OCAC's internal dialogue involved grappling with the political options of mainstreaming and disengagement and the attendant risks of marginalization and institutionalization. At the same time, I disagree with their conclusion that radical feminism is implicitly essentialist, arguing that women's political decision making under patriarchal capitalism parallels that noted by radical feminism at the personal level of experience.

sions involved, it is useful to describe two distinct but connected events that were planned by OCAC during 1985 and 1986. These events expose some of the contradictions inherent in socialist-feminist practice, including the problems and the opportunities that result from them.

Tribunals: The Politicization of Personal Experience

If the challenge to patriarchy is to be maintained, public-level discourse and the patriarchal structures that support it need to be actively resisted and politically undermined by discourses that capture both the similarities and contradictions of women's personal and political experiences. One of OCAC's major campaigns during 1985 and 1986 exemplifies a practical attempt to retain the personal roots of the political struggle for legal abortion services. This 'personal is political' emphasis grew out of specific political problems that arose from the split of the legal and medical aspects of reproductive control along a federal-provincial axis. The allocation of jurisdiction over health matters to the provincial level of government and of criminal law to the federal Parliament allowed the state to toss the ball from one court to another, continually forcing the pro-choice advocates to stress either choice or access at the expense of the other.

During a cross-country speaking tour that Dr Morgentaler and an OCAC spokesperson made in 1984, regional activists in different provinces began to express the need to build a unified national movement. They felt that only a national movement could effectively speak with one voice in calling for a change of the federal law and that, with a national movement, one could ensure that actions taken in one province would not undermine those taken in another. OCAC's goal in getting together with sister activists in other provinces was to discuss problems common to all regions while finding ways to support those provinces that were facing specific problems arising from particular political contexts. The specific impetus, for what was to become a national campaign concerned with personal experiences, developed out of discussions about opening clinics in all parts of Canada rather than first solidifying the gains made in existing clinics. During the early part of 1985, discussions at OCAC meetings thus began to focus on the need to coordinate coalitions across the country and to develop ongoing strategy sessions between activists in different provinces. The attack on the Winnipeg clinic in April 1985 had served to refocus the energies of Toronto activists. As one OCAC member stated, 'While the whole question of outreach and of solidifying our local base is still important, the binational struggle is clearly the present priority.'

The first formal meeting between regional groups of activists was held in May 1985, in conjunction with the annual meeting of the Canadian Abortion Rights Action League (CARAL). The activists came away from this meeting excited about the new chapters of CARAL which were being formed throughout Canada and which appeared to them to be merging the more radical grass-roots groups with the traditional lobbying orientation of CARAL. They believed that the enthusiasm expressed at the meeting indicated that there was a committed movement of women across the country, all of whom were eager and anxious to coordinate their separate activities into a strong national force. The meeting also brought into clear focus the specific dilemmas being faced in each province. Provincial struggles for access to medical services were deflecting energies from the national struggle to overturn the abortion law. At the same time, the fragmentation of the movement's forces and the difficulty of ensuring medical access highlighted the importance of legal change. For example, Quebec women attending the meeting described how the lead which their province had taken was now being eroded. At Ste-Therese, Quebec, a number of anti-choice people had been elected to the board of the local health clinic and were threatening to stop the performance of all abortions within their venue. The Quebec activists perceived that the precariousness of their provincial compromise was predicated on its illegal status. They were thus anxious to begin building links between labour and women's movements and to begin exploring strategies for joining with the English-Canadian movement in its attempt to overturn the federal law.

At the initial meeting of activists from across the country, it was decided to adopt a plan for a series of mock court tribunals to be held in each province, ending with a national action in Ottawa. Although the tribunals were to take on a somewhat different character in each part of Canada, they were seen as a way of helping to build a broad movement with a unified focus. The tribunal theme would be way of 'putting the law on trial,' using the actual life experiences of women in each province as evidence for indicting the federal legislation. The national theme of criminal legislation was intended to coordinate provincial efforts and provide the basis for an Ottawa action, while each area would have the autonomy to organize in a way that would best provide solutions to regional problems.

The planned tribunals were aimed at connecting and politicizing the personal experiences of women who had undergone abortions in a variety of contexts. In coordinating the tribunals, OCAC opted for a 'super-organizing role,' channelling information and ideas between the different groups in each region. In placing the bulk of their energies into this coordination of provincial and national issues, the OCAC activists hoped the events would, first, highlight the way in which the national law enabled provincial governments to control women's productive lives in different ways; secondly, publicly illustrate the political nature of women's personal experience of abortion; and, thirdly, be a mobilizing and empowering strategy for the movement as a whole.

The tribunals began in January 1986 in Vancouver, and it was expected that the final, national event, in Ottawa would be held in May. Those who chose to speak at the tribunals recounted their feelings of anxiety and their reasons for seeking the abortion procedure, but just as telling were the many women who had too much to lose by speaking publicly about their personal experiences. In some provinces, the ideological climate and structures of oppression were such that testimony could not be given directly by any of the women who had undergone abortions. For the most part, the stories of poor and immigrant women were recounted through their counsellors.

The Toronto tribunal, sponsored by OCAC, is an example of the attempt to politicize the personal world of women. At this tribunal, which was held in March 1986, women gave testimony about their personal abortion experiences in a variety of contexts: at the hands of illegal abortionists (pre-1969), in hospitals through the therapeutic abortion committee (TAC) process, and in a Morgentaler clinic. To stress the interconnectedness of reproductive and productive struggles, eleven members of the jury posed as various personalities (political figures, labour leaders, and physicians) who represented groups responsible for the medical, economic, and social needs of women. The twelfth juror was the audience. The verdict here, as from other tribunals, was to be sent on to Ottawa.

The tribunals brought together the personal and the political in a truncated version of the consciousness-raising (CR) groups of early feminism during the 1960s and 1970s: 'By encouraging women to speak about what were apparently "personal" problems, and by discovering the common character of these experiences, the CR process played a key role in exposing the institutionalized, entrenched oppression of women in our society' (Adamson, Briskin, and McPhail 1988:204). The testimonies given by the witnesses at the Toronto tribunal were both 'personal' and 'subjective,' but they were placed within the 'political' context of the power relations reproduced by 'objective' law. In other words, the frame was not that of the dominant discourse of the status quo; rather, it high-lighted the oppressive effects of societal structures as they currently existed. The critique of the law was meant to resonate with the personal experience of women but to do so within a structure that would fuel the struggle for change. The events the women related actually happened to them and, despite the diversity of the accounts, 'there was one striking continuity in their testimony – all considered the law to discriminate against women, and all demanded its repeal' (Ferguson, *Toronto Star*, 2 March 1986).

As a number of contemporary feminists have noted, the early consciousness-raising groups revealed the political nature of personal issues for the women involved, but they did not in themselves provide a political avenue for social change. The same was true of the tribunals: the problem remained of penetrating the public consciousness while speaking within the framework of women's experience. The approximately 250 members of the Toronto audience were mostly female and apparently already committed to a pro-choice position, and the media did not cover the event as news in the same front-page sense as events that concerned the clinic, the court, or the pronouncements of Morgentaler. As in other provinces, the coverage of the tribunals in Ontario did not go beyond the local news media, and even here there was no explicit connection made with the subordinate status of women as reproductive workers. Focusing on the personal was not enough to penetrate the arena where ideological definitions of the reproductive experiences of women are explained and culturally transmitted. The movement's counterhegemonic explanations of women's experiences remained cut off from mainstream social dis-course.

The marginalization of the tribunal strategy did not come as a com-plete surprise to its OCAC organizers. Although OCAC had consistently attempted to pose the problem of 'choice' in terms that would resonate with the personal experience of women at the private level, the media had habitually presented abortion-related stories either as instances involving an individual championing a cause (Morgentaler) or as instances of the victimization or irresponsibility of individual women. Within the media framework, the 'abortion problem' was generally severed from the con-text of women's lives, and abortion services were seldom portrayed as a resource that was required by responsible members of society. Although abortion events have always been considered newsworthy when they are connected to dilemmas faced by political actors in the public sphere, the same does not hold true for women in the private sphere.

Suspecting that media coverage of the tribunals would be limited, OCAC had hoped to build on the private abortion experiences of individual women and to broaden their public effect in a number of ways. For one, OCAC planned to use videos of the mock court proceedings in future educational forums. More importantly, individual tribunals were expected to mobilize pro-choice supporters for the main national event in Ottawa. The objective of bridging the gap between private personal experience and public collective action by bringing together the personal experiences of women from different provinces into a national mass action was expected to elicit sufficient political pressure to influence both government activity and the Supreme Court decision. The major goal of the campaign was collectively to politicize the personal reproductive experiences of individual women by stressing how these experiences were socially determined by state action and inaction. Unfortunately, the national action that was to be the culmination of the campaign's efforts was sidetracked by events which OCAC could not control but in which it actively participated.

The Ottawa Action: Mobilizing a Unified Struggle

All the tribunals organized across Canada were developed with a sensitivity towards local realities, but they were never intended to be simply a documentation of the various personal indignities suffered by women in their respective provinces. By linking discrete instances (involving both legal and illegal medical intervention) under a common theme of legal oppression, the tribunal organizers planned to turn the personal abortion experiences of Canadian women into a public political strategy that would put pressure on the federal government and the Supreme Court. By demonstrating the links between the personal and the political, between gender inequality in personal reproductive relationships and gender inequality in public productive ones, the organizers of the strategy hoped to expand the parameters of the public debate on abortion. By mobilizing around the actual experiences of women, the more radical reproductive-rights discourse of grass-roots activism could be injected into the institutionalized struggles concerning liberty rights.

As Adamson, Briskin, and McPhail (1988:251) have argued, 'the more difficult part of the dilemma [between being institutionalized and being marginalized] is often that of marginalization.' OCAC's connection with the National Action Committee on the Status of Women (NAC) was its main bulwark against such marginalization. While the public face of NAC is essentially a liberal one (demanding change in terms of existing ideologies), the OCAC activists reasoned that the growing number and range of NAC's member groups not only made it a more effective political voice but also gave it the potential to be shaped in more radical directions. Although most of the new member groups could hardly be considered revolutionary, the demands they were making for their own improvement involved such a fundamental change in society that it would inevitably require some form of revolutionary change (Rowbotham 1972:246).

OCAC's relationship with NAC involved 'pushing' the radical potential within NAC's liberal strategies and within the grass-roots organizations without being absorbed into the mainstream discourse of the institutionalized process. Initially, the idea was to have each of the regional groups come together in Ottawa in conjunction with NAC's annual general meeting in May 1986. Connecting the final tribunal with this meeting would facilitate travel for many women, who would otherwise be unable to attend. The timing could also be expected to extend the usual media coverage of the activities of the institutionalized organization to the grass-roots movement, where activities are more easily marginalized. In February, however, the NAC executive rejected the idea, passing a resolution against any such event being held within a week on either side of its meeting dates.

The NAC executive reasoned that too close an alliance between the tribunals and the annual general meeting would steal media attention away from a whole range of concerns on which it hoped to lobby politicians; it would also allow media coverage to reduce NAC's demands to the single issue of abortion. Since the proposal to hold the major tribunal in conjunction with NAC's annual general meeting had arisen during discussions with activists attending NAC's earlier mid-year meeting, some OCAC activists argued that the decision of the NAC executive was undemocratic in that it overrode the decision making of grass-roots members. In their eyes, a passive acceptance by OCAC of NAC's decision would be a form of co-optation subverting the radical intent of the earlier grass-roots decision.

Although OCAC did make some effort to change the decision of the NAC executive, NAC's official position remained firm. In discussing the effect of this decision, activists in OCAC's Coordinating Committee stressed the point that NAC's political credibility was an important resource for mobilizing any national action and that it was certainly better to have NAC 'on side' than to lose potential support over issues of timing. The Coordinating Committee's approach to the issue of potential institutionalization was similar to the way it understood the legal strategy of using the medical expertise of Dr Morgentaler to challenge the legal right of doctors to make reproductive decisions: it was a necessary step in coping with short-term realities and was not a co-optation of principles in the long term. Despite the dissatisfaction expressed by many of its members, the Coordinating Committee concluded that any attempt to push ahead without NAC's official approval would cause rifts that ultimately would be detrimental to the achievement of pro-choice objectives.

By March, it was clear to all members of OCAC that the national tribunal could not go ahead in May without NAC's approval. Events had been occurring in Quebec that changed the size and nature of the proposed Ottawa action while increasing the possibility of linking English-Canadian and French Quebec pro-choice forces into an unprecedented binational movement. As reported in CARAL's spring issue of *Pro-Choice News*,

A truly momentous occasion was the founding conference for a new coalition on abortion rights, held in Montreal on February 8, 1986. Over 100 organizations took part including representatives from women's health centres in Montreal, Quebec City, Hull, Trois-Rivières and Sherbrooke: women's shelters; union and student organizations, women's committees; the Quebec Women's Federation and its regional committees; the YWCA; the Quebec NDP Women's Caucus; and many others, to respond to what the women of Quebec felt to be the urgent necessity to form a broad, militant Quebec coalition which would regain the offensive in the abortion rights struggle.

The new coalition had been initiated by Quebec women who had attended the OCAC-sponsored meetings in Toronto, and a public abortion tribunal was a major plank in the strategies proposed at their founding meeting. As coordinator of the tribunal events, OCAC had maintained an ongoing contact with Quebec activists, and the two groups had discussed strategies for focusing the various provincial struggles on the national arena. The link between the two movements was strengthened by the attendance of OCAC representatives at the founding convention of the new Quebec coalition, and they had been asked to make a presentation to that conference. When reporting to their own membership, the OCAC members who had attended this 'momentous occasion,' explained what they thought the new coalition would mean for the pro-choice movement as a whole: 'It will push us forward. Quebec is starting at such an advanced level. They have an existing infrastructure that is much better than other parts of Canada ... This coalition is a great victory; without it, we couldn't have a binational strategy or movement. They are stronger than us because this coalition is broadly based on the labour movement. It is also important in that it is province-wide. We can't underestimate the importance of this. It gives us leverage to pressure our own unions' (OCAC meeting, March 1986).

In the wake of the problems with NAC about the timing of the national tribunal in Ottawa, the Quebec coalition proposed that the original rally be replaced with a major Ottawa demonstration that would link trade union support with the various women's groupings (NAC, CARAL, OCAC) as well as with the Quebec coalition. It initially proposed that the event be timed for June 1986. At several meetings in April 1986, the OCAC members wrestled with their ability to cope with the direction in which they were being taken as a result of the success of their binational efforts. Their discussions illustrate their understanding of the contradictions posed by the oppositional aspects of their struggle:

'A tribunal alone is felt to be too low-key. The key, however, is Quebec. The only way we can organize federally is to have Quebec involved. But can we find the energy to do it?' ...

'If it was just OCAC, we couldn't do this, but being part of a larger coalition of NAC, CARAL, unions, is a different thing. The Quebec movement is labour-based, which gives us the leverage to go to our unions here for their support' ...

'I see this as an important tactic in our goal of binational unity, but it is not the only *tactic*. It has tremendous logistical problems, especially with regard to transportation. Our current public support has dwindled' ...

'People come out in defence of the clinic, but we can't mobilize around the upcoming court decision. We need to have a focus for our activities, a spark. But we will need a full commitment if we take it on' ...

'It would mean putting off some other things regarding access. We need to balance national and regional movement strategies. We have to be careful not to neglect the local movement. The opposing view, of course, is that it would provide a means to mobilize locally at the same time' ...

'It is easier to mobilize in Quebec. It is not the same thing in Ontario. It is not in our history in the same way. Also, we need to ask if this is the right time politically to do this' ...

'We need time to think this through, how to integrate our other focuses. This has to involve more than just Ontario and Quebec. The question is how to integrate those things we have already begun' ...

'In another sense, this is an extension of what we are already doing: building a binational movement, establishing labour-union links, focusing on the federal law, etc. An Ottawa action can integrate all these objectives.'

The discussions at the April meetings also focused on the old problem of whether the personal could be effectively brought into a mass political strategy and, if so, how it could be done in a way that would not dilute the interconnection of the abortion issue with other problems of gender inequality:

'We have to find a way to incorporate the tribunals so this action is not detached from our former work ... Should we have a tribunal as well as a demonstration? We would lose momentum if we have two events, but I think we have to make it clearly understood that there is a connection, particularly for those who do not know or understand the experiences of these women' ...

'Demos build the movement and give people a sense of their own power. Tribunals don't affect people in the same empowering way' ...

'There has to be a link up with the tribunal; that is what will distinguish this demonstration from other demonstrations ... It is very important to use the tribunals, and the representation from across the country that this involves, but we can't do this at a rally. The impact of the personal would be lost' ...

'How do we integrate the repeal of the abortion law and free-standing clinics with the wider problems of contraception, forced sterilization, day care, etc.? ... Perhaps we could think about ways to get the testimonies out beforehand, maybe a booklet to labour leaders to follow up on' ...

'We need a balance between abortion rights and the broader context. If we make it too broad, then we lose the impact. I would hesitate to have a "shopping list" of demands. We can make our points in speeches but, tactically, we should not do so in our demands on the government' ...

'I feel that it is important to bring up the broader context in some way because forced sterilization is the other side of the coin for Native women. Also, with regard to birth control, we are always hearing from the other side that this is the alternative so we should take it up. We need to illustrate that this is not women's irresponsibility but a lack of contraceptive options' ...

'If we make it too broad, then we water everything down. We need to mobilize regarding choice and then educate. We can't mobilize on reproductive freedom' ...

'I agree. Some demands would keep people away. There can be a risk in raising broader sexuality and labour demands. We do not want to narrow our support' ...

'I feel that the reproductive rights perspective should inform our political position but it may not be tactically the time to do it' ...

'We could link the action to the abortion caravan of fifteen years ago and involve these people' ...

'This could be a way to get beyond how others have seen us as a single-issue group. I am concerned, however, that we do it in stages and not go too big politically at first.'

Before making any final commitments on the particular form of the Ottawa action, OCAC members met with representatives from NAC, CARAL, and some of the women's committees in the union movement. They also discussed the idea informally with their various feminist contacts in the broader women's movement in Toronto. The initial meetings elicited optimism about the real possibility of mounting a national action that would unite groups that had previously advocated different tactics and strategies. Both NAC and CARAL indicated their support and commitment for the proposal. During the next few months, meetings were held between the different groupings to ascertain what would be needed and what kinds of support could be given. The following comments at general OCAC meetings held in April and May 1986 indicate the level and extent of support that was being gauged:

'Many of the those feminists critical of the clinic strategy see this as "a women's march for choice," with broad links to birth control and forced sterilization, raising the possibility of a much broader mobilization' ...

'The OFL women's caucus is not unsupportive, but they have qualified their support based on whether they can actually command any union resources' ...

'The CLC women would like to broaden demands, but it is clear that the focus would be on abortion. They are going back to their groups to see what kind of commitments they could get. They also feel that more time is needed because of the Lavigne case. It is hard to get a more militant stance at this time' ...

'At the CARAL AGM, it was obvious that there is more activism evident in the regions, an activism that appears to have been affected by the tribunals. As well, the American speaker at the meetings emphasized that the numbers that came out in Washington resulted from a lengthy period of grass-roots movement building' ...

'NAC is supportive and have passed a resolution to that effect, but union people are saying, "What does that mean?" We need to decide what we need and then get it committed. We need to talk about transportation and getting bodies there and then make it absolutely clear that we need commitments.'

The major problem the group faced was how to get the various trade unions to commit to the project. Working through the women's groups within the unions would not automatically lead to a commitment of the needed resources. Time was necessary to get the required support. Coordinating meetings had to be held between the different groupings to ascertain just what could be given by whom. Because of this need for organizational time, the ad hoc committee (composed of representatives from the different groupings) moved at one of its meetings 'that the Pan-Canadian action in Ottawa be proposed for Spring 1987. Each representative was to take back to her respective group the proposal for a spring action in Ottawa which will focus on abortion and our demands but be seen within the larger political context of women's demands' (strategy meeting minutes, 3 May 1986).

The OCAC members thus changed the date from the fall of 1986 to the spring of 1987 in order to allow time for the ad hoc committee to mobilize and build the action broadly across the country. However, they agreed that it was still necessary to build on the momentum of the tribunal campaign and to carry through the theme that the federal law oppressed women. As well, despite the change of date for the major action, there was a continuing organizational commitment to carry out the original plan for a tribunal in Ottawa in the fall of 1986. This was considered necessary in order not to 'risk losing energy from the tribunal campaign' (strategy session minutes, 3 May 1986). The Ottawa tribunal was to be organized locally by the Ottawa pro-choice group, though OCAC would assist wherever possible. The tribunal in the national capital was to be much reduced in scale from its original design, but it would still allow for a public action in conjunction with the Supreme Court appeal hearings. By reducing the scale of the action, OCAC would be able to put its energy and time into mobilizing labour support for the major spring action, and the link between the regional tribunals and the upcoming spring demonstration would remain intact.

Meetings continued to be held between representatives of the various groups involved in planning the demonstration, and at the same time OCAC continued to juggle its various priorities and to respond to such things as the Ontario medical strike and attacks on the clinics. The proposed event was next discussed at a general OCAC special meeting called in July 1986. At this meeting, the planning committee revealed that a lack of committable resources in Ontario might present an insurmountable problem for the kind of action the membership had envisioned. Members of the ad hoc committee reported that the Quebec coalition was still enthusiastic and was mobilizing effectively in that province; at the same time, it was apparently becoming frustrated with the lack of a similar mobilization in Ontario. The major difficulty for the Ontario activists was securing a concrete commitment from labour to provide material resources. With the Lavigne case before the Ontario Supreme Court, neither monetary nor visible political support could definitely be counted on. This state of indeterminacy was firmed up when the Ontario Supreme Court brought down its ruling: compulsory union dues were not to be used in support of political causes. Nobody was certain what this ruling would entail, but for the moment it was clear that extensive labour support for the demonstration was unlikely to be secured.

The labour union position affected the enthusiasm of other supporting groups. As the Coordinating Committee reported, CARAL was 'not enthusiastic about coming on board without a labour commitment.' Nevertheless, it was generally believed that CARAL would give its endorsement and support to any creative or dramatic action that would promote the abortion cause, and it was suggested that if a major demonstration in Ottawa was not feasible, an action could be organized that would be a repeat of the Abortion Caravan (sponsored this time by CARAL, NAC, and OCAC). Some concern was expressed, however, that a caravan had the potential to divert the focus away from Ottawa and the federal government. Like the regional tribunals, a caravan might fragment media attention into a series of regional abortion issues rather than putting pressure on the federal government to repeal the law. However, it was felt that the major problem was OCAC's lack of ability to command resources at a time when the organization was overextended on other fronts. The basic question considered by the membership was whether sufficient numbers could be mobilized to support any major event without the labour movement's official backing.

'The problem is how to build outside Quebec without resources. I don't think that CARAL would put on full-time staff. OCAC does not have a full-time coordinator and doesn't have the volunteer power at this time. We are currently in a fight to defend the clinic and need our resources to support staff ... The key to the action is staff. We can't get dollars from NAC because of the way money is allocated' ...

'It's more than staff. We need money for buses, and our time and resources would be needed even with staff' ...

'We could organize an ad hoc committee so that it is not all on our shoulders, but where does this ad hoc committee come from? This alone would require mobilization' ...

'It is important that we support the alliance with Quebec. I do not feel that we can realistically say no' ...

'I don't agree that we can't say no. It would be irresponsible on our part if we took it on and then couldn't do it. We are in a different position than Quebec. Can we afford to put part of our coordinating committee into this action and then have them drown in the ongoing crisis? We also have dollars to consider – if the clinics get busted again, then we need more money for defence. If we don't get busted, we won't be able to mobilize if the public thinks we will win at the Supreme Court.'

Despite the concerns expressed about the lack of resources, the decision taken at the July meeting was to have a caravan beginning from both coasts and ending at the national rally in Ottawa, which would be timed to coincide with that city's tribunal and with the Supreme Court hearings in October 1986. It was agreed that further attempts would be made to itemize exactly what would be needed, what kind of fund-raisers would be feasible, what unions and other organizations would give 'in kind,' and what type of ad hoc committee could be put together to promote the action.

The OCAC ad hoc committee continued to meet and to talk with the new Quebec coalition over the summer months. During this time, it became apparent that OCAC's initial enthusiasm for the possibility of a joint action had led it to downplay the problems which the Quebec movement was having in its own province. Facing new and sustained attacks on clinics that had been in operation for years, the women in the Quebec coalition were concerned that they might not be able to find the additional energy and resources for a major fall action. In August 1986 the Coordinating Committee called another special meeting of the OCAC membership to discuss the increasingly bleak chance of being able to get any meaningful support from labour in the way of resources:

'The upshot is that to go through the steps required to go to the locals, the CLC women's committee couldn't make a decision before the fall and the action had to be postponed until the spring. However, it is looking worse and worse for any kind of union support. CARAL are also hostile to a fall action. They feel this would be disastrous with regard to our case at the Supreme Court. Ottawa also does not appear to want to move their tribunal date and they do not feel that they can handle both a tribunal and a major demo at the same time. Quebec is now also concerned that there is no concrete support from the OFL. The situation is that both Ottawa and Quebec are now leery and we would need their full support' ...

'To focus on a quick demo would not allow us to build the grass-roots support needed for a national action and we would still have an Ontario focus. One of the main objectives was to build this grass-roots support nationally and a fall date will foreclose that objective' ...

'We need an October action. The reason for our current small numbers relates to a lack of any recent actions' ...

'NAC will give some labour if we put out the call. We could move to the spring but we need to have a decision so we can talk to people. We can't continue to vaguely check it out' ...

'This is our opportunity to strike a new level of activism with Quebec. We can't afford to say anything but yes. The more we rehash it, the vaguer it becomes' ...

'I think that we should use the time from now until spring to try and bring labour on board but to go ahead regardless' ...

'The dynamics may be very different with Quebec if we do not at least get the support of NAC and CARAL. They may feel very differently if it is just OCAC' ...

'We can't pre-empt the CLC discussion, but as soon as CLC meets, then we should organize who we have to call.'

After extensive discussion, the meeting once again moved the date of the action from October 1986 to June 1987. The Ottawa tribunal was to go ahead in October, but on a much reduced scale, reflecting the fact that most of its organizing would now fall on the Ottawa pro-choice group. It was also agreed that regardless of whether labour support was forthcoming, OCAC should prepare to put the call out for support from the women's movement.

Despite the motion carried at the OCAC meeting, within the ad hoc committee it was increasingly clear that the initial enthusiasm of the early meetings had dampened considerably. This was largely because of the difficulty in organizing at a time when the issue had been diverted into the courts; some supporters in CARAL were leery of doing anything that might antagonize the Supreme Court. This fear surfaced again in early September when the Ottawa tribunal was cancelled by its local hosts. Morris Manning had cautioned the Ottawa group that the mock trial might be seen as contempt of court if it was performed while the hearings were taking place. Similarly, CARAL and Dr Morgentaler had expressed concern that the tribunal could have an adverse effect on the judges hearing the appeal. The feeling by this part of the movement was that activities should be kept as low-key as possible while the matter was before the court. The cancellation of the Ottawa tribunal had a further effect on the ability of the ad hoc group to garner support for planning and organizing a national Ottawa action, even though this event had been postponed until the spring of 1987. In mid-October, the OCAC Coordinating Committee came to the general OCAC meeting with a recommendation that the proposed action be postponed indefinitely:

Our decision has been made because support and momentum has been lost. The months of work have not been enough to get people-power and resources. What did come out of it was a suggestion from Quebec that we meet once a month to organize a structure that would allow for this to happen when conditions are better. The feeling from the last meeting was that it would not be constructive to continue to meet regarding the action itself but to begin to meet on an ongoing basis to build the support necessary. Their objection to proceeding at this time is not to an action per se but is a different reading about what should be done ...

The position we now take is that we remain politically committed but that we have to have a hard discussion regarding what is possible at this time. The trade-union support was not there at this time. Without this, we do not have enough energy and resources for a large national action. Before we can do this, we need to build locally. There is a feeling that just because we are not in a position now would not mean we wouldn't be in five months' time. This is not really a defeat but a tactical and responsible decision with regard to our possible success. The link forged between Quebec and English Canada is an incredible step forward. The main agenda item of the meetings has changed. It is now not 'when' but 'what needs to be done.' (OCAC meeting, October 1986)

The action did not die easily, nor did the members immediately concur with the recommendation of the Coordinating Committee. This was not the first time that political strategies had changed and events had been cancelled, but just as there is a difference in personal abortion experiences according to the context in which such decisions are made, there was a difference in the way OCAC perceived this termination. In the past, planned projects had been cancelled because other priorities and responsibilities clearly required the group's energy and commitment. While it had never been easy to let go of any project that had claimed time and energy, the group's previous decisions had been taken on the thesis that its responsibility lay elsewhere. This time the decision making context was different, and the action was not aborted without a great deal of painful deliberation:

'I think the support is there. It just needs to be organized. If this is seen as a political necessity, then resources of time and money can be found ... If we have lost momentum, how do we regain it? One of the things which did mobilize the movement in the early 1970s was the Caravan' ...

'This is not the same thing as a rally in Toronto. We would be looking at a major mobilization. Without the trade unions, *we* can't do it. They are on the defensive in their own arena. If the union isn't behind us, if Quebec has too much

happening on their own turf, if Ottawa can't host, then we can't do a major mobilization of this kind now' ...

'How would the response of unions be any different if we organize to push
later rather than now? ... There is a frustration among our supporters that nothing is happening right now. If we build the action, then the pressure is on for the
support to come out' ...

'The sense that I am getting is the resources of the various organizations is
unavailable, yet the grass-roots support is there. So surely, if this is our major political goal, we could mobilize. The trade union women would at least support even
if they could not organize' ...

'When speaking about their major action, activists in the United States emphasized the need to organize as an essential factor in success. The ability to mobilize
is essential' ...

'I do not think this is just a question of our size. This hasn't changed. Do we
now feel that our original goal was an unrealistic one, or have conditions
changed?' ...

'We have always thought politically that it is a good goal. But, as we went along,
our outreach efforts for concrete needs – buses, advertising, etc. – led to answers
that the required support was not there. We have not been able to garner the
physical material resources and we need to work towards that' ...

'I wish I had a film of what was going on in the early 1970s. The faces have
changed, but the same issues have arisen. The same arguments: no labour support, no CARAL, no host in Ottawa. We had only 300, 400 women but we felt it
was a success. It was better than no one saying anything. We just felt that we had to
do it' ...

'We cannot have a binational action on our own. We could build the event
smaller but then we have to look at what our role is' ...

'We also have to understand where we are at right now. To organize consciousness on the issue is difficult at this time. The United States women understood
that they were under attack. This is not so in Canada. We at OCAC believe that we
are in crisis, but since the clinic is open and operating, others do not perceive this
in the same way. For example, our union supporters were not out to the demo last
week. We need to understand why' ...

'It was always the case that we would only go ahead if the resources were available. Meetings have been held all over and doors have been closed all over. It may
seem to be an abrupt ending but we have always held the view that we would
support the idea politically but that we would only go with it if the support and
resources were there. It is not really an abrupt shift. The conditions are not there.
We can't wish it or impose it on the other groupings' ...

'Some things that have been said here concern me. The women in the women's committees [of the unions] are under siege. This is not a surprise. So what do we do to help? Let's not use it as an excuse not to do something else' ...

‘It is a shame to let the opportunity go after we have been involved for such a long time. We lose the sense of how we can "make the difference."'

The above comments represent only a fraction of a lengthy discussion, but they demonstrate that the termination of the planned activity was a difficult decision. The Ottawa action had been seen as an opportunity to highlight the political nature of the personal experience of abortion as well as its interconnectedness with the whole range of women's political and economic concerns. This political priority had not changed, but there was clearly not the kind of support required to carry it out. For those who were most committed to change through mass mobilization, the loss elicited feelings of powerlessness and frustration.

The loss of a project that had commanded so much time and commitment (and had held out the promise of uniting the many different factions involved in the movement) led to an internal re-examination of the organization's objectives and priorities. At a meeting held in late October 1986, the Coordinating Committee addressed the membership in a way that echoed its answer to the earlier criticisms about the decision to employ an illegal clinic strategy but also illustrated how this earlier decision affected current options:

There is a feeling in the Coordinating Committee that more discussion is required regarding the decision to cancel the Ottawa action and to be able to come to some conclusion regarding our priorities for the future. We feel that the key question was whether OCAC should press for calling for an immediate action in Ottawa. It is important to keep in mind that OCAC has not lost its commitment to mass action. There is no change in this. What we felt was that, given our political assessment of where we are at, this was not the right time. However, the decision to call the action was taken in a general meeting, and the decision to halt the action must come from here as well. What the Coordinating Committee was trying to assess was whether there was enough energy at this time to actually carry the action through. We made a tactical decision. In looking back at the last six months, we evaluated the response from the trade union movement, from CARAL and NAC, and the women's movement generally. We also looked at the U.S. experience, the size of the demo, the paid staff, the national structure, the different traditions re a march on the capital. In the U.S., there was a real consciousness of crisis regarding the taking of rights away. This did not exist here. A lot of women don't perceive the crisis as long as the clinics are operating. In order to mobilize, we felt the need for a 'spark' – essentially why the clinic strategy began, to provide a spark for mobilizing. We are not backing away from the mass-mobilization strategy or being influenced by reformist groups as some feel. If we organize for when the Supreme Court decision comes down, we have a potential for a large action rather than the lower-keyed one that we could mobilize now. As well, we are not in a position to call for the action in a vacuum. We could go back and push the various groups but we do not think this is a good strategy. We feel that it would be better to go back and build a consciousness of the need for a strong public action. Therefore, we are presenting a motion that we not call for an Ottawa action at this time.

In discussing the motion, the women at that meeting attempted to articulate for themselves the current political context and whether this context called for a period of consolidating past gains or whether it called for an even greater amount of pressure on the state. Since the Morgentaler case was before the Supreme Court of Canada, this could be seen as a time when energies could be replenished or as one that required even more sustained effort to keep the issue alive in the public consciousness:

'The Supreme Court decision will shape the dynamics of the movement for some time. Whichever way it goes will require a continuing political pressure on the federal government. The paradox of the clinic strategy is its success in building consciousness about the problem, but its culmination in the courts limits the potential of movement-building. The legal arena is abstract for most people' ...

'While the period will be slower than the focus on street action, it is an important time for getting ready and will allow us to build the movement for the next stage. We need to get the message of a reproductive-freedom perspective out to a broader base' ...

'We need to know more regarding the reasons for why the support for the Ottawa action was not there, particularly with regard to CARAL. Were the legal implications important? Was there an idea that we would jeopardize the Supreme Court decision?' ...

'CARAL would have been more tentative with regard to the timing coinciding with court deliberations but this was not the main problem. We also were under a misconception as to the actual numbers which Quebec could mobilize and bring out at this time' ...

'I am not sure in what form, but I think it would be an error not to act before the Supreme Court decision comes down. One of the designs of the court is to demobilize and my fear is that is what is happening. We are being demobilized despite what we know. The big question is whether we move before the decision or wait to react to it' ...

'I think this is an opportunity to do the work we have always wanted to do rather than just to react. We could take the time to build the movement so that when the time comes to react, we will have a broad base. I do not see this as not doing anything' ...

'I am not convinced that the task of this period is consolidation. I feel we will be even more demobilized if we do not have an offensive strategy now. I feel that now is the time to build on the strengths that we now have and not to consolidate' ...

'I do agree that we need an offensive strategy. The problem with our efforts to coordinate the Ottawa action was that in attempting to convince everyone else what was required, we only demobilized ourselves' ...

'I think that we have been fixated on what was the best possible tactic, but the art of politics is to know *when* to move. We in the Coordinating Committee began to feel that to push the action, regardless of how good a tactic it was, would be irresponsible at this time. We are not necessarily reducing our action-oriented strategies if we let go of the Ottawa action. We see this as only one aspect of our political strategy. What has come out of these meetings over the past six months is an increased commitment to and awareness of the need for a pan-Canadian movement' ...

'I still feel that the only way we can have some impact on the Supreme Court is to have some kind of an action *before* the decision comes down. I think the main thing is to put the pressure on. I am not sure how to do but I think we have to have some kind of action' ...

'The Supreme Court knows that there is more support for the pro-choice position than ever before, but it is important for us to focus on the fact that the struggle will not be over even if we win in court. We have to raise the public consciousness on that point. We have to stress the wider reproductive freedom perspective' ...

'We also need to take into consideration the upcoming proposals coming from the provincial government. We need to prepare to argue against extending access only in hospitals. We need a broader consciousness about the difference between access in clinics and access in hospitals. While the provincial government proposals for increasing hospital access is a direct reaction to our strength, it also undercuts our longer-range goal.'

The deliberations of OCAC in the fall of 1986 reflected the range of contradictory alternatives that are part and parcel of the process of change. The political work the members were engaged in provides an example of a process designed to mediate the inevitable tension between

moral vision and practical reality. The moral vision that guided their decision making was a socialist-feminist one in that it gave priority neither to
the feminist objective of undermining the patriarchal denial of choice
nor the capitalist denial of resources. At the same time, they were frequently confronted with the practical reality of patriarchal capitalism,
where options are structured in 'either/or' terms. In challenging the gendered discourses and practices of both law and medicine, the process
itself helped these women understand (sometimes imperfectly and often
painfully) that political strategies could not be delineated in advance of
their need or without considering those who would be most affected by
the choices of any particular strategy. The main contribution of the initiation and dropping of the Ottawa campaign was to challenge the hegemonic process itself. Here, as in other campaigns, the victories won were
victories of mobilization. Moreover, this change in ideological environment was embedded in the actual process of struggle rather than resulting from any particular decision or strategy.

The Personal and Political Faces of Care

The activities OCAC engaged in can be characterized as caretaking work:
they were oriented towards empowering women with particular needs
without appropriating the definition of need. In their attempt to bridge
the separation of choice and access – as they were structured through the
medical-legal relation – the women of OCAC internally mediated the
contradiction between themselves and others and between theory and
practice in much the same manner as that described by Gilligan (1982) in
her study of women faced with the contradictions of making personal
reproductive choices. Like women who provide personal acts of care,
these political activists were continually called on to mediate between the
standards of their beliefs and practical reality. The choices they made
during their struggle to mobilize a mass action were not always those they
would have made if they had had greater control of the resources needed
to achieve their goal.

The context in which the OCAC decisions were made was rife with
contradictions, but the activists involved did not experience any contradiction between their choice of strategies and their overall socialist-
feminist vision of a moral order. Nor did they view their choices as
pragmatic deviations from the basic aim of eradicating class and gender
hierarchy. The challenge for the OCAC activists, like that for most
women, was to pursue strategies that would address current dilemmas

without compromising future opportunities for the achievement of the broader moral vision to which they subscribed. The invisibility and distortion of OCAC's political work allowed its critics to interpret its motivations within the master discourses of hegemonic rhetoric. While various criticisms of OCAC strategies were often theoretically or logically 'correct,' this correctness depended on abstracting the decisions from the context in which they occurred. To reinject strategic directions into the discussions that surrounded such decision making is to illustrate that despite the fact that most OCAC activists were avowedly socialist feminist, their decisions could not always be made according to the commonly accepted principles of either socialism or feminism. The contingency of principles according to particular contexts did not mean, however, that the socialist-feminist values themselves were discarded. Rather, the operative strategy was to change the context to make it more amenable for the achievement of the broader vision.

14

Conclusion: The Contradictions

When you watch a light show you see one coloured pattern created by the slides in a projector disintegrating in the very moment in which it appears distinctly and immediately to be altering its relationship to all the other colours which are themselves going through the same process according to their own unique pattern. Revolutionaries now have to accommodate themselves to organizing in the midst of a gigantic three-dimensional light show. (Rowbotham 1972:28)

It is impossible to grasp fully the mechanics of how colours change in this 'three-dimensional light show' without understanding how each colour interacts with the whole range of other colours. Equally hard to document is the effect of any particular interaction on those who observe the show. But the most difficult aspect of describing the process of social change concerns the way interaction is itself bounded by the consciousness of the audience. What makes the job of drawing conclusions about this light show so difficult is that any new description has the possibility of altering the pattern, because each interpretation changes the boundaries of consciousness. Paradoxically, within this interpretive dilemma lies the potential for revolutionary groups to participate in choreographing the show.

As difficult as it is to document cause and effect in the changing consciousness of a public audience, there is little doubt that discourses about abortion and the meaning of the practice have altered dramatically in the past twenty years. This change is certainly related to broader changes in the position of women within society, but it has been most apparent among those with the greatest exposure to the ongoing drama of clinic attack and defence. Media attention in the cities where illegal clinics operated helped turn what was once a private and unmentionable secret into a commonplace topic of debate. A less abstract and more enduring change in the political understandings of women has come out of the practice of defending the clinics. In areas where the clinic struggle became a daily reality, women took to the streets more spontaneously and in increasing numbers as each new crisis arose. With each 'set-back,' more and more women became aware of new threats to their own autonomy; with each 'victory,' they were imbued with a new sense of the political possibility of changing relations that give low priority to women's needs. With each new involvement, more and more women began to speak about and believe in their power to create new ways of living. The mobilization of supporters to the pro-choice cause brought with it a shift in ideological boundaries that forced political and legal actors to react, and the responses of the state and the courts in turn altered the parameters by which public consciousness was bounded.

To analyse theoretically the strengths and weaknesses of any particular political position or legal strategy is not an easy task. Within a context in which patterns shift and meanings change, it is outwardly difficult to find theoretical consistency between the political stance and the actions of those at the centre of the movement. Nevertheless, as Rowbotham (1972) has noted, theoretical consistency often comes out of dogmatism, and dogmatism cannot cope with contradiction. It is contradiction and the struggle to mediate contradiction that provide the most accurate theoretical base for understanding both the choices made by the Ontario Coalition for Abortion Clinics (OCAC) and the importance of these decisions in shifting the social relations of reproduction. More than one contradiction is central to the maintenance of the status quo, but each contradiction interacts with the whole range of other contradictions and each alters its relationship to the others that 'are themselves going through the same process according to their own unique pattern' (Rowbotham 1972:28). Just as one can specify the primary colours of a light show, one can analytically separate out a number of primary contradictions, but the moment one begins to describe them, they shade into those with which they interact.

The presence of contradiction means that it is difficult to make conclusive statements about the success or failure of any particular strategy for the broader political agenda of socialist feminism. There can be no doubt that the activities of OCAC did influence the institutional structures that project 'patterns of colour' onto the screen. By mobilizing grass-roots support into highly visible protests, OCAC challenged traditional discourses and put pressure on the government and other institutions to respond (Adamson, Briskin, and McPhail 1988:191). OCAC discovered that although strategic options and political goals are analytically separable, they do not act in isolation from one another. For theorists, this interaction raises a maze of issues and problems that make definitive answers as impossible as they were for the activists themselves. Yet as OCAC also discovered, each new resolution of competing demands raises its own set of contradictions. Because each 'victory' or 'failure' brought with it a new set of contradictions, the possibility of new alliances was created even as the old ones were threatened.

While institutional responses frequently had contradictory implications for OCAC, each response did open a new space for struggle. Thus, to consider the process of OCAC decision making within the context of patriarchal capitalist relations is to highlight the contradictions that these relations promote and the process by which they can be used either to stifle dissent or to mobilize it. Moreover, to consider how OCAC activists not only coped with contradiction but attempted to turn it to their advantage is to step out of the mind-set that demands abstract 'either/or' conclusions into one that illuminates a *process* for politically making social change.

The Contradiction between Discourse and Practice

As long-term activists in the pro-choice movement discovered, the way an issue is posed at the public level is a strategic problem that cannot be ignored. The struggle for reproductive freedom is already structured and perceived in terms that take for granted a knowledge about the nature of women and the work they perform. The language of public discourse concerning abortion has mirrored the equations and assumptions of legal and moral thought. While most media interpretations of the abortion struggle are important in shaping new attitudes, they still retain their hegemonic character, implicitly posing the commitments of each side within a moral framework that assumes an opposition between individual agency and responsibility for others. While a woman's right to choose the former and reject the latter is a part of the discourse, the basic dichotomy of classical philosophy remains. On the absolutist side, 'life' is an abstraction that exists over and above conscious human volition: to be 'pro-life' is understood as absolutely upholding maternal responsibility in the abstract, and the term implies maternal duty to this natural fact. To be 'pro-choice' implies the primacy of human volition in seeking one's own purposes according to particular circumstances. The equation of self-interest and human volition is not always fully articulated, but it is implicitly understood as the motivational factor behind the seeking of abortions.

The events and issues discussed in the previous chapters illustrate the powerful constraints that interpretive frames place on decision making. At the political level as well as the personal, our 'experiences and relationships do not exist apart from the discourses about them,' and reproductive practices can no more exist independently of their conceptualizations than productive ones can. Such practices, and the relations they entail, 'are constituted by the discourses in which we think them. These discourses will be interpreted differently in different historical, political, and social contexts,' but so long as the categories themselves are gendered, the powerless can only struggle from within the prison of this discourse (Greenberg, introduction to Frug 1992:xviii).

The walls of our ideological prison are held together by gendered interpretations of what it means to act like a man or woman in any particular relationship, and they are no less strong because they are flexible or because the prisoners take part in their construction. The juxtaposition of gender with particular linguistic concepts means that the moral commitments underlying one's decisions are likely to be associated with the characteristics of 'masculine' autonomy or 'feminine' responsiveness, regardless of the actual sex of the decision makers. Within our various cultural discourses, 'real' actors are defined in masculine terms and women are generally perceived as being dependent on the benevolent responses of others. The supportive activities that women provide may be (and often are) acknowledged, but they cannot be used as currency in the securing of resources. In practice, however, the attention given to the welfare of a particular other is not an exceptional requirement of 'feminine' victims but is a prerequisite for both human agency and human relationship. Despite the supposed superior independence of men and boys, all human beings develop and grow only within relationships that are attentive to their particular needs, and a continuance of this autonomy is achieved through their power to gain access to a mode of labour that is generally (but not essentially) performed by women.

The significance of attention as a resource is veiled by viewing it through a lens that differentiates according to the gender of the giver and receiver (cf. Hochschild 1983). Patriarchal assumptions concerning the nature of women turn responsive activity performed *by* women into a natural and universal support for human liberty (the norm), while activity that responds *to* their needs becomes welfare (the exception). From a vantage point centred in women's experience of caring for others, the disadvantaged status of women springs from their *relative* lack of access to and personal control of the very resources that their work has traditionally provided for others. At the same time, the *relative* exclusion of men from the performance of reproductive labour (in all its facets) serves to recreate systems of thought that are differentiated by gender (Schaef 1981).

Legal and social codes can interact to recreate master discourses, not because they exclude women or the 'feminine' characteristic of care but because they misrepresent the relationship between men and women while claiming that the misrepresentations are gender neutral. Such discourses are constructed from the standpoint of those who take the responses of women to be a universal resource while simultaneously understanding objectivity to be a practice that excludes the definitions of those who care for and about others. This type of reasoning indicates a blind spot concerning the form of other-oriented labour that allows abstract reasoning and independent judgment to take place (Smith 1987, 1979; cf. Matsuda 1986).

There is a dilemma for all subordinate groups in the gendered dichotomy of freedom and responsibility that characterizes legal reasoning: for a subordinate to exhibit a need for the response of another is to mark him or her as incapable of the self-interested agency that choice requires, but a response given to a dominant person will also imply a lack of agency on the part of the responder. 'In the dominant discourse, much of compassion is taken as nonauthoritative, marginal pleadings for mercy – gestures of the subordinate' (Jones 1988:121); but, conversely, the showing of compassion by an authoritative figure ideologically reaffirms the powerlessness of the subordinate.

The reality of reproductive work belies the equations and dichotomies of our cultural discourses. The performance of this work cannot be explained by a conceptual framework that dichotomizes liberty and welfare, especially where these abstractions are respectively equated with pursuit of self-interest and responsiveness to others. When satisfactorily performed, activities intended to empower others, in any aspect of life, involve much more than nonvolitional subjective reaction. Empowerment of another requires that the other retain the right to participate in the definition of his or her own needs within particular contexts, and the subjectivity of the one who performs responsive labour can never be solely that of self-interest. Such work requires a concentrated and conscious attention to the priorities and interests of the one to be empowered. Although conceptually separated, the relationship between autonomy and responsibility at the level of material reality is one of interdependence, and women are actively involved in performing the tasks that allow legal and medical benefactors to choose between being responsive or 'objectively' withholding their care.

It is the exclusion of reproductive discourses, not women or reproduction, that allows the law to justify the continued subordination of women and the work they perform. It is only because the responses that all human beings require for independent action are perceived as noncontingent and universally available that Rawls's 'man in the original position' is able to contemplate his needs in the abstract. The contradiction is that a maintenance of an interpretive code that assumes a natural asymmetry of gender characteristics must have social institutions that selectively impose responsiveness and then define that imposition in gendered terms. The imposition of responsibility for others is mystified, in circular fashion, by the assumption that any responsiveness by women is only a natural backdrop for the real activity of masculine benefactors.

The contradiction between master discourses and reproductive practice presented the pro-choice movement with the option of challenging common assumptions about the nature of abortion or of addressing practices that prevented attention to immediate needs. To address one source of oppression only strengthened the other. It was the attempt to make sense of the contradiction between practical reality and ideological interpretation that led the OCAC activists to explore political options that would allow them not only to cope with dichotomized practices in the short term but to create a more enduring change in the longer term. They needed strategies that would be relevant for coping with existing practices but that would also promote new opportunities for achieving their theoretical goals in the long term. The development of illegal clinics grew out of political analysis, and mobilizing to challenge the law opened spaces for challenging discourse at the level of public debate. At certain times, working within this contradiction meant placing an emphasis on entering ideological discourse – stressing the need to extend autonomy of choice to women – whereas, at other times, the establishing of networks for challenging the structural distribution of resources took precedence.

In choosing strategies that would address both ideological and structural change, the OCAC activists and their decisions could not be described in terms familiar to philosophical discourse. Liberty (choice) and welfare (access) were equally important goals, and attention to context did not erode the group's fundamental commitment to socialist and feminist principles. But the ideological context in which they sought revolutionary change transformed these political motivations into the discursively gendered categories they were resisting. To understand the ongoing importance of OCAC's socialist-feminist principles in terms that break out of the oppositional framework of master discourses, it is necessary to consider both the ideological and the structural context in which the decision to establish and support illegal abortion clinics was made.

The options available to North American women in the 1970s included an abstract right to liberty without a concern for particular need or the equally abstract right to be taken care of without the freedom to define one's own need. In the United States, women had won the symbolic right of choice without a corresponding right to medical services (access) while, in Canada, women enjoyed a symbolic right to these services (access) without the corresponding right to choose. In the absence of socialized medicine, the freedom from state interference won by American women proved to be illusory for those lacking monetary resources or social power. By contrast, despite the presence of a universal medical system in Canada, the 1969 amendment to the Canadian Criminal Code gave the Canadian medical profession the right/responsibility to determine the reproductive needs of its pregnant patients. The legitimation of the medical profession as the appropriate judge of a woman's need achieved a similar end result for low-income Canadian women as did the vastly different law south of the border. The difference in the laws meant different things for different women, but the commonality was that physicians consistently acted as ideological gatekeepers, defining the parameters of response to reproductive need.

Following the 1969 amendment, the Canadian pro-choice movement struggled to mediate the contradiction between medical access and legal choice that was legislatively constructed and was reflected in the federal-provincial distribution of powers. Medical practice and legal ideology buttressed each other in such a manner that to gain ground in the struggle for equal medical access (regardless of class) eroded the legal right of choice (on the basis of gender) and vice versa. The various intersections of legal and medical policies within each country meant that the medical profession was legally granted the power either to restrict choice by regulating access or to restrict access by regulating choice.

Abstract principles (relating to the choosing of either class- or gender-related strategies) were of little help to the Canadian pro-choice movement. Choosing one or the other did not challenge the ideological and structural interaction that was the root of the problem. Regardless of the particular type of reproductive control that American and Canadian courts defined as legitimate, a conceptual dichotomy between individual autonomy and access to collective resources was upheld and reproduced by the interaction of law with medicine. The illegal clinic strategy (although ideologically 'incorrect' in an abstract sense for both feminists and socialists) was a way of challenging the medical control of access and the legal restrictions on choice. The selection of this strategy did not, however, mean that the ideological visions of feminism and socialism were unimportant factors. Rather, in OCAC's simultaneous challenge to classist and sexist structures and the ideology that justified them, socialist-feminist principles were vitally important. They provided a guide that helped OCAC members steer between the pitfalls of co-optation and marginalization (Adamson, Briskin, and McPhail 1988). By weighing the principled vision of socialist feminism with the reality actually faced, the organization made conscious attempts to choose strategies that would exploit the weakness in the class-gender contradiction of the moment, without being absorbed into one side or the other. This decision-making process met with greater success at some times than at others. Whatever the outcome of any particular decision, however, the process itself generated new avenues for socialist and feminist resistance.

The Contradiction of the Personal and the Political

Master discourses do not capture the actuality of the lived reality of women or men. One might even say that male reality has been distorted the most because our understanding of men's lives is more likely to overlook the effect which their relationships have on their public identities. Gender is a relational practice, however, and our distortion of men's lives has a greater impact on what women (including women in political groups) are able to choose or accomplish in their lives. An examination of the work of OCAC demonstrates that the ideological framework of our language captures women's political activity within its boundaries as surely as it captures their personal activity. Discourses that imply that motivations can be characterized in the 'either/or' terms of self or other, choice or need, individual freedom or responsibility to others, provide a frame for the work of the women's movement as surely as they do for the work of individual women within personal relationships. It is therefore possible to make some significant comparisons between the way individual women make personal decisions about abortion and the political choices made by OCAC without also implying that these similarities relate to any essential difference between the sexes.

Although there are significant differences between the political outcomes of caring activities carried out collectively within a social movement and those that are carried out by individual women acting in isolation, the choices made and the context in which they are made can be shown to be similar in intent and in kind. At the personal level, women who contemplate a moral dilemma have been shown to understand implicitly that their actions are important for the creation of human value and that a person's responsibility towards another has to be adjusted to particular situations. As Gilligan has argued, such situation-specific responses do not mean that these women are necessarily reacting passively to external events or to the moral dictates of others. Similarly, at the political level, OCAC activists understood (both implicitly and explicitly) that their actions were important for creating the conditions by which women could exercise a greater degree of reproductive freedom. As they considered the effect of their decisions on their own goals and on those of interrelated others, they did so within situations which they often had little part in defining. Yet their inability to control the definitions did not mean that they were passively reacting either to the dictates of circumstance or to the dictates of absolute principles. In their attempt to bridge the separation of choice and access – as these were structured through the medical-legal relationship – the women of OCAC internally mediated the contradictions between self and other and between theory and practice in much the same way as women make their personal reproductive choices. The dialogue between OCAC members facing difficult choices illustrates the same kinds of ambivalence that are said to characterize the internal dialogue that individual women have with themselves as they grapple with moral dilemmas.

The activities that OCAC engaged in can be characterized as caretaking work. Although our culture understands activism and caretaking as an oxymoron, the work of OCAC is an excellent example of caretaking as it is implicitly understood by most women whose vocation includes the nurturing of others; its aim was to empower women with particular needs without appropriating the definition of need. The work cannot be understood in terms of legal- or social-code reasoning, because it involves a form of care 'where morality has neither been relativized out of the window [teleology] nor been seen simply as the reflection of an "essential" human condition [deontology]' (Waugh 1989:169). The similarity between personal and political caretaking extends beyond the motivations of the workers to include the implications of the actual performance of caretaking work in our society. The consequences of OCAC's decision to engage in providing support for pregnant women were similar in kind to those experienced by individual women who care for the needs of others. While OCAC's activities kept the abortion clinics alive, its ability to use clinic resources to achieve its own political goals had to be presented in terms that would appeal to the doctor who owned the clinic. An asymmetry of care and authority was the norm, and OCAC coped with this dilemma by considering the effect of its options on related others.

One might say that OCAC spoke in 'a different voice' from that of traditional politics, but it is important to note that this difference is not one that can be understood within the terms of a discourse that characterizes female nurturing as the absence of conscious action or regards female powerlessness as the result of victimization alone. Although OCAC made choices within a context that it did not control, its various reactions were hardly passive responses to external demands. Rather, its shifts in strategy indicate an active attempt to intervene in the decision-making process in order to change the relations themselves. The constraints OCAC faced in realizing this goal resulted not so much from hostile acts as from a lack of access to ideological and cultural resources, including those controlled by state authorities and OCAC's own supporters.

OCAC's decision making belies the gendered notion that agency and empathy, self and other, feeling and cognition, are polar opposites. The values with which OCAC operated were 'female values' emanating from reproductive experience, but these were not the same as the feminine virtues of conventional discourse. They were values that retained the visionary and activist edge of socialist and feminist theory even as they were applied in contexts that required giving priority to the need of a related group or individual. In actively promoting the opportunity for women to define their own reproductive needs and the resources necessary to exercise such choices, OCAC's support of the clinic strategy focused attention on the contradictions women face within capitalist patriarchy, giving priority neither to the feminist objective of undermining the patriarchal denial of choice nor to the capitalist denial of resources.

Understanding the patterned similarities between the manner in which women make personal decisions about abortion and the political choices made by OCAC is important because it reaffirms Gilligan's point that the differences in the moral development of men and women points to a problem with moral theory and not with women. It is language that defines caring activities in gendered terms, not the acts themselves: the discursive opposition of self and other distorts pro-choice motivations by positioning them at the active 'masculine' pole while, at the other pole, caring is associated with femininity and is defined as a passive reaction involving self-sacrifice and a submission to duty. While the dominant discourse distorts the nurturing activity of individual women by equating such work with passive reaction and dependency, the distortion of the aims and objectives of the pro-choice movement is one that poses 'the seeking of choice as a self-serving form of activism' (Fee and Finkelstein 1986:364). These parallel discourses reproduce the gendered dichotomy of liberty and welfare, and render invisible the agency of all those women who choose to respond to the needs of others while seeking to influence those who deny them access to the same advantage. In turn, the intersection of gender with law makes the stereotype of women as passive nurturers in some part true – if only contingently and temporarily.

To understand the similarities and differences between caretaking in the private and political realms does more than challenge the power of master discourses; it also helps us rethink the nature of power as it is conceptualized in law and the relevance of feminist discourse for the particular ways this power is exercised in practice. Both feminists and socialists have, on occasion, spoke of law as a body of abstractions without reference to the material world of gendered practice. Because productive and reproductive labour are essentially interdependent but conceptually separated, legal regulation of abortion can allow some women the autonomy necessary to undertake reproductive responsibilities while preventing any general challenge to the power structure itself. By supporting medical services that would give women the opportunity to define their own reproductive needs and the resources needed to exercise such choices, OCAC did not give priority to undermining either the patriarchal denial of choice or the capitalist denial of resources. These women understood the interdependence of these denials, but without the alternative discourse of a socialist-feminist vision, the strategies they chose at particular times would have been more easily subsumed under either the choice or access poles of the interpretive dichotomy. Instead, the illegal clinic allowed the pro-choice movement to mount an overt challenge to the discourses of both patriarchy and capitalism.

Despite the fact that most OCAC activists were avowedly socialist feminist, their decisions could not always be made according to the commonly accepted principles of either socialism or feminism. But while the various criticisms of their strategies were often theoretically or logically 'correct,' the correctness depended on abstracting the decisions from the context in which they occurred. When particular contexts forced decisions that appeared to counter the group's principles of organization, socialist-feminist theory was not discarded; rather, the operative explanation was that 'in such situations as this, the theory does not hold up' (Scales 1986:1396) and, more importantly, that this particular strategy is now needed if we are to change the context in the direction necessary to make our vision a more viable goal. As one activist put it during a group discussion of an organizational response to an external demand, 'If we choose to do this, it is also important that we emphasize that we are choosing a particular strategy at a particular time and that we are not abandoning our principles concerning mass-action.'

The political work of this group of women provides an example of a feminist process designed to mediate the inevitable tension between moral vision and practical reality. Notwithstanding the criticism from feminist and socialist quarters, the OCAC women did not themselves experience a contradiction between their choice of strategy and their overall socialist-feminist vision of a moral order. Nor did they view their choices as pragmatic deviations from the basic aim of eradicating class and gender hierarchy. Cohen's (1990) statement that 'it is possible to recognize the contingency of our values and language and yet remain wholly faithful to them' was given substance by the process through which OCAC arrived at particular decisions. In challenging the gendered discourses and practices of both law and medicine, these women understood (sometimes imperfectly and often painfully) that political strategies could not be delineated in advance of their need or without considering those who would be most affected by the use of any particular strategy.

The decision to fight reproductive control in the legal arena did not mean that OCAC was shifting its emphasis from the larger political struggle of attacking patriarchy in the 'real world.' As the Crown arguments at the Morgentaler hearings demonstrate, the gendering of liberty and welfare within legal theory does not exist in isolation from the real world of gender relationships in which men are viewed as autonomous actors, women as responsible nurturers, and doctors as objective decision makers. Legal theory and legal practice both intersect with institutionalized relations and cultural explanations to ensure that, normally, men and men's groups retain the autonomy to make decisions – whether to respond or not, and how responses will be forthcoming – while the same context ensures that women and women's groups continue to provide the necessary supports.

Legal theory is shaped by gendered practices within the broader social context, and, in turn, legal rulings play an important role in recreating the gender stereotypes of social discourse. 'Law and gender are not two separate, unrelated systems. Each is constitutive of and defined by the other' (Greenberg, introduction to Frug 1992:xxiii). Because law is gendered in both its theory and its practice, it has an important role in constructing our personal and political identities as women and men. Where women respond to another in the other's own terms, thus creating the conditions for independence, the responses are perceived as a part of the essential character of the woman herself and not as something she has consciously undertaken. Based on this cultural belief in the natural determinism of woman's responsiveness, the law then specifies that the people she supports with her work are entitled to a protection of their liberty rights. Conversely, however, a woman's need for a reciprocal response reaffirms her natural dependence, thus permitting a limitation on her right to define the nature of the response that she requires. Where men control economic resources, they will remain the primary subjects of law, and women will be entitled to the welfare they require in order to provide supports for their 'benefactors.' At the political level, patriarchal ideas about dependence also interact with the logic of capitalism. Thus, while the pro-choice movement's activities provided the necessary supports for keeping the Morgentaler clinics operating, the lack of visibility of the movement's work and its lack of a legitimate voice in institutional decision making created similar relations of nonreciprocity between OCAC and those who were considered to be the 'real' political actors in clinics, political parties, and unions.

Despite the parallels between the political and personal lives of women, the contradiction between discourse and practice also creates a contradiction between the outcomes of personal and political acts of resistance. Although the personal and political relationships of women are similar with respect to definitional power and material resources, attempts by individual women to bridge the choice/access dichotomy in their personal lives can actually undermine the collective struggle at the political level. For example, the Canadian law meant that individual women seeking control over their reproductive lives were forced to participate in a process that reinforced the common belief that being pro-choice was a self-serving act and that requiring an abortion was a mark of defective femininity, thus increasing the difficulty of the movement to mobilize on behalf of all women. Similarly, any increase in access to hospital abortions made life easier for individual women but made political efforts of mobilization more difficult. While the illegal clinics were intended to be a means of bypassing this contradiction between discourse and practice, giving some women both choice and access, the responses required to keep a clinic operating passed the problem along to the political level: its existence frequently restricted OCAC's ability to make completely autonomous political decisions or to receive the support it needed from other allied groups.

The ability of OCAC to develop political alliances and to influence individual doctors was bounded by institutionalized relations that were based on both class and gender. Within this frame, those who owned the clinics, led the political parties, or ran the unions were the 'benefactors,' and, as such, they legitimately retained all decision-making power concerning the allocation of resources. Within this frame, the political responses of the women's movement that enabled the decisions of doctors, politicians, and union leaders to be put into practice were a form of indirect currency that gave the movement the space to put forth its case for resources to be allocated to its concerns, but the direct authority remained with the 'real' actors. Without access to political or medical resources of its own, the decision to support a legal challenge made OCAC dependent on the choices of those who did control these resources. However, one cannot generalize from the structural dependence that surrounded the clinic's operation in order to make conclusive statements about the use of law as an instrument for preventing or creating real social change. Just as dependence is experienced differently by individual women according to the particular nature of a personal relationship, there were distinct differences in how OCAC experienced its lack of decision-making power according to the alliances that had been developed and the willingness of these allies to respond.

It is not possible to make conclusive statements about the progressive or regressive nature of legal strategies, because the nature of change is affected by the degree to which legal power is actually exercised or not exercised in any particular instance. Because men (as a group) have the structural power of choice, individual men have the option of choosing to use this power to undermine the basis of the power structure itself. Morgentaler's willingness to respond to women on their own terms was an important component in the struggle for reproductive freedom, even though it did not itself constitute such freedom. Of course, one can say the same thing about the actions of individual men in their relations with individual women. At the personal level, women know that there is a difference between one man and another, despite the structural nature of the relations themselves. At the political level, OCAC understood that there was a difference between Dr Morgentaler and Dr Scott, as well as a more significant difference between clinic doctors and those working through the legal TAC process.

To generalize about gender inequality in theoretical terms does not preclude variation within particular sets of relations. The willingness of those with power to respond to women on their own terms is an important component in the struggle for equality. While doctors and legislators in general enjoy a greater measure of choice about whether or not to act on behalf of others, how they choose to respond is as important for achieving female independence as women's willingness to respond to human need has been for male independence. At the same time, however, the dilemmas facing the OCAC activists would suggest that to focus on generalizing the personal experience of women concerning care is not in itself sufficient to break through hegemonic discourse. An articulation of personal experience as that experience gets interpreted within social discourse unwittingly contributes to the problems that political movements have in addressing the concerns of women in general. The solutions to the problem of gender inequality lie not in overcoming the willingness of women to provide for others but in attacking both the institutionalized lack of reciprocity between the sexes and the discourses that mystify our understanding of dependence and independence.

Socialist critics of the pro-choice strategy more clearly understood the need for a broader political analysis than personal experience alone can provide, but their critique of the Canadian pro-choice movement did not reveal the way in which political change in the relations of *production* is prevented by the continuation of patriarchal *reproductive* relations. By maintaining that any improvement in the position of women can be made only through prioritizing issues according to their apparent class content and their direct relationship to the productive sphere, the socialist critics left unexamined the hierarchical relationship between productive and reproductive life, as well as the role of reproductive labour in reproducing that relationship. Whenever theoretical analysis discounts the importance of reproductive labour for the creation of power, it unwittingly contributes to the continuation of the ideological split between public and private, which in turn structurally imposes experiences by gender.

If the feminist challenge to patriarchy is to be maintained, public-level discourse and the patriarchal structures that support it need to be actively resisted and politically undermined by discourses that capture both the similarities and contradictions of women's personal and political experiences. A fuller understanding of the manner in which women's experiences are socially created and culturally distorted (rather than biologically determined) requires an understanding of the patriarchal nature of the process through which change is structured. What is required at the level of theory is not a unitary focus on either political principles or concrete experience but an unveiling of the way in which women's political choices are both structurally shaped and actively resisted. This unveiling reconnects the personal and political lives of women, illuminating some very radical possibilities for social change.

The Contradiction between Universality and Specificity

Within what has loosely been termed postmodernism, there is a tendency to reject all generalist categories (including class and gender) as totalizing fictions and to focus primarily on multiple differences and site-specific explanations. In their emphasis on the local and on discontinuity, postmodernists have frequently implied a wholesale rejection of universality and continuity. For example, feminist contentions about the centrality of gendered experience in the creation of subjectivity and about a system of moral thought that is primarily understood by women (a woman's culture) are perceived by many postmodernists as discursive fictions that need to be deconstructed and opposed. Moreover, by privileging language as the constitutive factor in the construction of subjectivity, they have challenged the Marxist and feminist positions on the specificity of perspective that arises from differential class and gender experiences.

An examination of the relationship between abortion practices and the subordination of women, historically and comparatively, discloses a variety of different kinds of social relations as well as site-specific justifications for how and why human reproduction should be regulated, and a comparison of the manner in which reproductive power is regulated across time and between countries demonstrates that the form patriarchy takes is historically specific. In each instance, however, the differences are encompassed within a patterned relationship between law and medicine – within the relationship between a woman's legal right to reproductive choice and her access to the medical resources that would allow choice to be exercised. For academics to focus only on endless variety according to shifts in policy across time and place is to miss the way that hegemonic discourse structures a patterned subordination by shifting an issue from one pole of a discursive dichotomy to another; in the case of abortion, by shifting the discourse from issues of abstract liberty (legal choice) to issues of concrete gender welfare (access to medical and political resources).

Familiar to all pro-choice activists, the dichotomy of choice and need has roots that extend back into the opposing theoretical positions of classical thought. Moreover, changes in the nature of the legal paradigm that were intended to promote social justice for women as well as for other powerless groups have, in fact, continued and strengthened the gendered nature of traditional reasoning. Although contemporary reforms seek to incorporate an ethic of responsibility into the legal paradigm, the responsibility to respond to the needs of powerless groups remains tied to an authoritarian rule. Despite Rawls's sophisticated attempt to devise a method for arriving at social justice for all, he has made the same two key assumptions about human nature and human reality that classical thought did – that human beings are essentially self-interested, and that whatever responses are required for human agency to be activated are naturally accessible on a universal basis. Within this gendered frame, an admission of dependence allows the state to provide resources according to the law's definition of need and the kind of response to be given. The paternalistic rhetoric of protection represents the limits of care that the state must provide and does not challenge the gendered assumptions that are inherent within the model itself. Unlike the reproductive code, where response to another's need considers the concerns or motivations of the one in need, contemporary legal reasoning continues the classical tradition of an essential (and gendered) dichotomy between autonomy and responsiveness. In providing a rationale for practices of either masculine justice or feminine care, contemporary law may treat women like men or men like women, but the gendered nature of the discourse is retained in a stronger form. Thus, the reforms in law provide no real change in the power structure; they simply provide a standard that differentiates between normal and exceptional subjects on the basis of their powerlessness.

The argument that women are written out of law is misleading. The writing out has occurred only at the surface level; the activities that women perform in providing for the welfare of others in order that they may assert agency is a subtext without which the legal text has no meaning. Law is gendered, not because it excludes the responsibility ethic but because it addresses the need for care from within a framework that is already organized according to a justice logic that relies on gendered categories. While it is intended to address situations in which the state should provide resources in exceptional cases, contemporary legal reasoning reaffirms the erroneous belief that normal human beings can exist without sustenance and outside relationship. The 'impartial' reasoner in legal circles is the ideal male who 'stands outside of and above the situation about which he reasons, with no stake in it,' adopting an attitude about possible events as though he and his deliberations were outside and above the conclusions he will reach (Young 1988:60).

The classifications used in the feminist literature to describe and contrast the ethics of care and justice frequently retain the kind of conceptual opposition between justice and care that contemporary legal theory has carried over from classical thought. Those who have debated the social-change value of Gilligan's revamped model of moral development have paid too little attention to the *relationship* between justice and care within both theory and practice. Without this focus, care and justice retain a conceptual independence that is at odds with the more relational reasoning attributed to women. As Young (1988:39) suggests, the insights of Gilligan's respondents implicitly deny the oppositions as an accurate reflection of their experience. One can therefore say that it is the gendered nature of the discourse that eliminates choice from reproductive activity and not the manner in which women actually undertake the work of caring for others.

To take up the challenge of deconstructing totalizing discourses is to understand that the work of women who seek social change is shaped within the power dynamic that language structures; but, more importantly, it is to understand that women's work also shapes that power dynamic. Without an understanding of the ways in which the political efforts of women shape and are shaped by hegemonic discourse, any theorizing (including most variants of postmodernism) will remain within its boundaries. While stressing the importance of master discourses in the production of cultural hegemony, I want to distance myself from the conclusions of those theorists who consider the deconstruction of master discourses to be the main or only task of radical theory. If we are to learn anything from the experience of women, it is that freedom is not just freedom from oppression; freedom also has a positive aspect that is related to the attention one receives from others. Because there is no essential nature of those who give care or take it, human relations vary from site to site, yet the language that describes these relations will continue to recreate gendered interpretations unless we illuminate the continuity of theory that misrepresents itself as gender neutral.

Women have never been actually excluded from the master narratives of modernist theorizing, for although human identity has been constructed from a male standpoint, *the narratives themselves have depended on work undertaken by women but depicted as a universal resource devoid of human agency*. Moreover, to the degree that a particular narrative successfully masquerades as a gender-neutral depiction of human reality, the capacity of the discourse to impose gender-differentiated forms of labour is reinforced. For theory to continue to ignore the manner in which women's work has been central to and invisible within the discourses that create our understanding of human subjectivity would be to continue to create, within language, women who remain outside the power dynamic. To dispense theoretically with that which has been taken for granted within modernism (namely, the universality of reproductive labour as a gendered activity) is to reproduce within postmodern theory the same conceptual dichotomy between individual autonomy and collective welfare that has existed within both classical and modern forms of thought. On the other hand, to take the position that the theories we develop are an important aspect of social change is to understand that the construction of a morally responsible theory compels us to consider the negative *political* implications of making gender a non-issue.

Unmasking our own power resources and identifying how we participate in the creation of power, which in turn is alienated from us, would seem to be as important as demonstrating how male power is used against us. The construction of a counterhegemonic moral vision must recognize that the meanings women impute to their various experiences of caring and being cared for have been different from men's, and that these experiences are more than a matter of victimization that can be alleviated by negative strategies alone. As Sawicki (1988:179) has argued, there are inadequacies in current feminist conceptions of power in that they are concerned only with repressive models of power: '[W]e find a negative view of freedom, that is, freedom is freedom from repressive norms.' If we are to construct more liberating discourses, we need to search out and identify those activities that represent the other face of power.

While theories that include an articulation of women's work and women's power are important for constructing new forms of moral discourse, there is an inevitable tension between the theoretical development of a broad moral vision based on the need to care for others and strategic support for the various practices by which women are able to assert agency within oppressive contexts. The decisions that feminist groupings make as they collectively seek to care for others without damaging their own integrity can provide us with a glimpse of how the tension between moral standard and political strategy might be mediated. The political work of the women in OCAC is but one example of a feminist process that continually mediates between moral vision and practical reality.

The Fundamental Contradiction: Care and Autonomy

The opposing traditions within classical thought stressed either individualistic rights or social duties. The primary good of rights philosophy was the promotion of individual liberty in the pursuit of self-interest according to the demands of specific situations. The primary good of duty reasoning was the promotion of absolute rules that would ensure the welfare of the collective. Both, however, took for granted that self and other are opposing concepts, that, given a choice, the nature of human beings is to promote their own interests at the expense of others. In each, human volition is associated with self-interest and determinism with concern for others. Ideas about gender are thus deeply rooted in our culture, and we 'are accustomed, if not reconciled to categorizing characteristics according to the masculine/feminine paradigm' (Frug 1992:80) The result is that the individualistic and active aspects of teleology are associated with all that is masculine while the communitarian and passive aspects of deontology are associated with the feminine.

Contemporary legal reasoning has attempted to mediate the liberty/welfare dichotomy of these gendered positions by specifying universal standards by which any legal subject would be entitled to claim liberty or welfare. If the traditional discourse of rights and responsibilities has been socially interpreted along gender lines, the contemporary method of legal reasoning purportedly offers men and women equal chances to claim liberty or welfare, the critical factor for determination being the independence or dependence of the legal subject. Viewing itself as outside that which it regulates, this form of legal discourse does not acknowledge the gendered nature of its method or the manner in which its standards recreate in practice the individualistic picture of human nature that our culture already assumes. For this reason, many have viewed law as simply an ideological instrument, available only to those men who already have power. As such, all attempts to convince powerless groups to pursue legal challenges is seen as part of law's power to co-opt revolutionary struggle.

My description of the events involving OCAC confirms the premise that struggles in the legal arena can co-opt revolutionary change and sub-due dissent, but the power of the law is double-edged. The law's power to enforce consent depends on transforming challenges into its own frame of reference, and, in this, the criticisms of legal strategies are all too cor-rect – as far as they go. However, merely criticizing the use of law as a vehicle of social change is deceptive. OCAC's concern for women who had an immediate need for abortion services and who did not have access to these services meant that the activists also had to take into account the implication of not engaging the law. To refrain from doing so would not only affect the individual women who required but could not get an abor-tion; it also meant that those who could legally secure this medical service were participating in the creation of myths that ultimately oppressed all women. What was needed was a strategy that would not only respond to the practical problems of individual women but would address problems of abortion discourse as well. What was needed was a strategy that would not only deconstruct the myths behind such discourse but would provide a practical base for the construction of alternative discourses. By support-ing the illegal abortion clinics, OCAC was partially able to satisfy existing needs while simultaneously providing an opening for discussing the social value of providing for women's needs as women themselves define them.

Legal strategies that remain within the law's own frame and use its terms of reference do not help to empower those without resources. The seeking of equal rights of noninterference does not further the cause of general female emancipation, because it does not address the dispropor-tionate access women have to the kind of care they provide for others. Moreover, it transforms demands for reciprocal care into terms that con-note instantaneous convenience and a lack of concern for others. How-ever, to refrain from participating in ideological struggles within the legal arena is to ignore the fact that the law's emphasis on abstract autonomy is itself determinate. When an active concern for the needs of another is simply one choice that independent individuals may consider in the abstract, nonpaternalistic forms of responses to powerless groups are hard to come by. 'In a world where everyone looks after themselves, and where mutual concern is merely an extension of self-interest, people are wise to place primary value on liberty' (Matsuda 1986:625). Thus, patriar-chy intersects with capitalism, because cultural understandings involving gender do affect the way in which individuals can be mobilized to chal-lenge institutional structures.

Although women have their lives shaped by the degree of access they have to supportive resources, it is equally true that the ability to challenge nonreciprocity is itself shaped by the ideological framework of dominant discourses, including law. Because the basis for the ambivalence that women feel in carrying out reproductive tasks is mystified by the terms of the debate, personal resistance is co-opted and political dissent can be fragmented. The discourse in which a woman's moral dilemmas are discussed transforms a woman's strength into an ideological weapon that she may wield against the interests of her sex. This strength can, however, be equally useful in promoting the collective interests of women. To turn this strength into a political force, we need to construct and publicly articulate a feminist theory that takes care and responsibility for others to be an indispensable factor of 'normal' social relationships.

The feminist ambivalence concerning the postmodernist rejection of grand theory is well founded, for if we are going to construct an alternative reality, we have to elaborate theories that explore the moral implications of whatever subjectivities we are creating through our discourse. One can see in some postmodernist theory the same desire to displace the material experience of women as is found in classical and modern reasoning – a desire to transcend the human individual's dependence on the caring response of another through the 'substitution of intellectual categories and formal "impersonal" structures' (Waugh 1989:20). Thus, while we need to be concerned with disrupting discourses 'where subjectivity, the norm of human-ness, is male' (Waugh 1989:11), this deconstruction can be only one part of the overall struggle for female emancipation. Equally important are the efforts we direct towards the creation of a form of discourse that will capture the specificity of human experience without sacrificing the universal need of human beings for the caring attention of others. Such a discourse is not incidental to the political project of structuring relations of mutuality. It is a necessary resource.

The problem of gender inequality is not just that most women are forced to care and some men are free to be independent; because discourse is itself gendered, we internalize distorted definitions of caring and independence that downplay the relationship between them. Women who consider the meaning of woman to be 'one who cares for others' may strive to fulfil this role by stressing the self-sacrifice of their lives, while those who define care in terms of a conventional and rejected notion of femininity seek to avoid stressing the importance of care within their lives. The problem with either option is that one's subjectivity is measured according to a norm that does not incorporate the reality of human reproduction or the work of empowering others. This gendering of language not only affects female subjectivity. Men who consider the meaning of man to be 'one who is independent' may strive to fulfil this role by stressing their ability to refrain from empathizing with the needs of others and by downplaying the real importance of the support they receive from others.

Our moral paradigms and our discourses inevitably enter into the choices we make in practice. Within a moral paradigm that relies on the gendered asymmetry of autonomy and care, women are included as taken-for-granted carers, yet we cannot get the care we require without affirming the gendered logic of the discourse itself. In stressing the importance of theoretical constructions in constituting various kinds of discursive subjects, I do not mean to suggest that our subjectivities are wholly the result of symbolic explanations, for 'if individuals were wholly constituted by the power-knowledge regime Foucault describes, it would make no sense to speak of resistance to discipline at all. Foucault seems sometimes on the verge of depriving us of a vocabulary in which to conceptualize the nature and meaning of those periodic refusals of control that, just as much as the imposition of control, mark the course of human history' (Bartky 1988:82). Because we have a material grounding for the construction of a counter-hegemonic discourse, master discourses can never be wholly determining of the scope of resistance or of the dreams envisioned.

The feminist movement does have a mobilizing base within reproductive experience. Every woman who has ever been involved in creating human life or a human relationship intuitively understands that the outcome is dependent on the process through which she actively integrates the responses she requires to meet her own needs with her commitment to her relationship with others. It has been less well understood, however, that particular strategies or techniques are not as important for creating social change as the political process that promotes individual agency and commitment to others. More important than the choice of any particular strategy is a movement's intent and capacity to mobilize individuals to respond to the social needs of particular others. Strategies must remain flexible enough to cope with particular situations, but one's political theory must be coherent enough to resonate with the experience of those who understand the importance of care.

The construction of a counterhegemonic moral vision with the capacity for mobilizing women on a large scale must recognize that the meanings women impute to their various experiences of caring and being cared for are more than a matter of ideological victimization. Without this understanding, we shall continue the tradition of viewing women and our interpretations as being outside the history of subordination about which we are theorizing. We need to construct new theories of human being, but we also must be clear about our responsibility for the effects that our theory will have on the lives of individuals. While postmodernists are correct in their contention that there is no basic essence of human subjectivity for us to discover, it is also true that we shall continue to create certain kinds of human subjects through the knowledge-power spiral of discourse and practice.[1] Although all theories are in some sense myths (Lauter 1984), feminists cannot evade the responsibility for reconstructing a new human subjectivity by articulating more comprehensive explanations of human reality. As Hartsock argues, 'we need to engage in the historical, political and theoretical process of *constituting ourselves as subjects as well as objects of history* ... [T]he point is to develop an account of the world which treats our perspectives not as subjugated or disrupted knowledges, but as primary and constitutive of a different world' (Hartsock 1990:171; emphasis added).

The equation of caring work with the essence of women – rather than with the essence of humanity, where it properly belongs[2] – is part of a discourse of disempowerment. The danger of stressing the importance and value of care lies within the hegemonic framework itself and not in the nature of the work or in the ethical system that accompanies its performance. While we cannot ignore the fact that the prevailing definitions of care and nurturance have served to constitute us as subordinate and powerless subjects whose responsible choices disempower rather than empower us, our only option is not to reject the moral commitments of those who do respond to the needs of others. What is needed to break out of this frame is a fuller articulation of what activities may be thought about as 'care for others' – as well as what these activities mean to those who engage in them.

---

1 To the degree that any individual, male or female, *chooses* to respond to the need of another by performing the tasks that empower that other, I would argue that they have not been wholly constituted by the knowledge-power spiral of liberal discourse.

2 It is not women, their work, or their values that require change if gender equality is to be achieved; rather, it is our theoretical lack of understanding about the degree to which care is an integral resource for the exercise of all social power. It is care for the needs of particular human subjects that is the background condition for all human agency, and it is the equation of women with natural responsiveness that has relegated them to this background.

To elaborate care from a position that does not essentialize means identifying the range of sites where the tasks that empower others are disproportionately borne by women yet are rendered invisible through discourses that identify the 'real' activity of the site as the activity of dominants. It means identifying care in public sites as well as private ones (Hochschild 1983; Armstrong and Armstrong 1983; Stehelin 1976). Rather than equating caring work with the welfare part of the agency/ response dichotomy, we should theoretically articulate a broader range of activities that do provide responses to the need of another in the other's own terms, specifying the various conditions that empower or disempower the worker. Instead of disdaining responsive work as the reaction of powerless subjects, we need to think more deeply about the forms of work that can be conceptualized as caring labour and the relevance these tasks have for the creation of human agency. We need to stress the responsive nature of activist work that is undertaken by the feminist movement as well as the agency that is involved in the acts of care by individual women. Redefining care, by identifying the relationship between caring activity and empowerment or disempowerment, allows us politically to challenge the conception of women as natural servants of humanity while affirming the values of those who have served.

Only when we unhook caring activity from its implicit signification of femininity and powerlessness will we be able to articulate fully the part that attention or non-attention to particular needs plays in the creation of power differences between different groups of women as well as between men and women. By specifying those activities based on 'responsive autonomy,'[3] we destabilize hegemonic opposition and equations. More importantly, in formulating a discourse in which care is both a necessary component in the development of human subjectivity and a work that may be chosen, we may begin the difficult task of articulating alternative discourses that can support reciprocal relationships. What I am suggesting is that we need to search out and identify those activities that represent the other face of power. To make visible women's role in the creation of power is to shift the theoretical focus from a 'deficiency model,' where women are deemed lacking, to a critique of the nonreciprocal nature of policies or laws that conceptually and structurally separate the liberty rights of most women (and some men) from attention to their welfare needs. To reorient our culture's theoretical explanations con-

3 See Nedelsky (1989) and Pepinsky (1987) concerning redefinitions of the relationship between autonomy and responsiveness.

cerning care is to make visible the diverse ways in which women have cared for and empowered others, as well as the ways in which discourse has defined these activities in different terms from the responsive work that is undertaken by men. Such discourses serve to construct human beings who define themselves and their activities in gendered terms. To expand our definitions of caring to include their empowering aspects can provide us with 'an alternative conception of the subject as constructed through *relationship*, rather than postmodernism/poststructuralism's anti-humanist *rejection* of the subject' (Waugh 1989:12).

Our aim as feminists must be to affirm theoretically the various kinds of supportive activity that we, as women, perform in diverse circumstances, and to demand of our society a similar concern for all needs that do not fit a universal norm. Perhaps the biggest challenge we face is the construction of discourses that can embrace difference and the need for different forms of care in different contexts; that is, how we care for those of different classes and races in a way that permits them to define the care they need. Again, it seems to me that there is, within the experience of women, a material base for the development of theoretical guidelines. Gilligan (1987:25) has described a mature care ethic as '"respect for people in their own terms" rather than assuming "one set of terms"' (Daly 1989:5, citing Gilligan 1987:25). Caring responsibly, within a moral paradigm oriented by care, means responding to others according to specific circumstances *as those circumstances are understood by the others* (Code 1988; cf. Pepinsky 1987). To care within a context depends on a strategic definition of the trait, asking what it means for this other if we do or do not provide care in this particular situation. When care is understood in this way, the important focus for responsible strategizing is a consideration of how to attend to those who are different so that we really hear what they say they need.

If theoretical explanations will inevitably enter into the discourse that shapes our subjectivities, we are right to be wary of constructing yet another totalizing discourse. But to be faithful to broad conceptual categories does not necessarily mean that specific differences between people or circumstances have to be ignored in practice (Cohen 1990). In fact, it is our strategic attention to the support of difference within our daily practices that can make the attainment of a counterhegemonic discourse possible. By examining the value of our own skills to care for those whose needs are different from our own, feminist theory can create counter-hegemonic discourses in which response to need is not just something required by victims and subordinates, and in which participation in the creation of knowledge/discourse will not be viewed as the prerogative of those who already control resources. In empowering (caring for) both ourselves and others, feminists need to develop theories that describe those social relations where agency and responsiveness are structured reciprocally and to contrast them with the disempowering situations where they are not.

The totalizing tendency of hegemonic discourses can best be avoided not by abstaining from the creation of common visions but by encouraging political practices that are flexible enough to address the variety of ways in which subordinate relations are reproduced. While we need to develop broad forms of moral reasoning, any dogmatic adherence to these theoretical constructs will be as politically paralysing as having no moral theory at all. Although counterhegemonic explanations of reality are desperately needed by those who resist subordination, we must take care not to prefigure the form that resistance will take in diverse situations. Where attention to diversity is important is in the strategies we choose both to respond to the needs of particular others and to create discursive space for those whose experience of care is different from our own. All decision making occurs in a changing context where the capacity to choose any particular strategy over that of another is dependent on gaining access to the ideological and material resources which women help create but do not control. Since the context within which individuals respond to others will vary (often on the basis of class and race), we have to create a space where different experiences of care and resistance can be articulated. Any theory that does not incorporate the motivations of those who act in particular situations will ultimately, if unwittingly, participate in the construction of repressive discourses.

As feminists, we have seen that an ethic of care can contribute to subordination by failing to address the degree to which different groups have access to the power that care bestows. To counter this lack of mutuality, we need to foster a truly democratic construction of the concept, one that includes the voices of those who have experienced care in different or contradictory ways.[4] Inclusion of those whose realities are dissimilar is of vital importance if we are to discontinue the discursive tradition of articulating reality from a centred standpoint. 'The least dangerous way to dis-

---

4 Although 'caring is the constitutive activity through which women achieve their femininity' (Graham 1983:17), there is no one femininity because there is no one experience of care. As I have sought to demonstrate, masculinity (in the guise of humanity) has also been constituted through acts of care, but our language has obscured this fact.

cover whether and how specific practices are enslaving us is not to silence and exclude differences, but rather to use them to diversify and renegotiate the arena of radical political struggle' (Sawicki 1988:90).[5] When opportunities to speak of such differences are not enabled or attentively supported, any theory (no matter how liberal or postmodern) can become another totalizing ideology. If discourse and practice are interwoven, there is no veil of ignorance for us to stand behind or apolitical ground on which to stand.

Conceptually, there is an inevitable tension between the theoretical development of a broad moral vision based on the need to care for others and strategic support for the various practices by which women are able to assert agency within oppressive contexts. Our strategies can never be as abstract as our theories or moral visions must be, and the idealized subjects we construct will continue to live in a fictionalized world. In recognizing that our theories will never be total or complete, but are nonetheless necessary, we are recognizing that our identity and our perspective of reality is a function of our 'place in the social field at a particular time, not given. They are constantly open to change and contestation' (Sawicki 1988:184). At the level in which we live our daily lives, however, we are continually called upon to mediate between moral standard and practical reality, and the decisions that feminist groupings make as they collectively seek to care for others without damaging their own integrity can provide us with a glimpse of how the tension between moral standard and political strategy may be mediated.

The feminist aim, like the postmodernist one, must be to destabilize the discursive categories that subordinate, but our agenda must be a broader one. In beginning the never-ending task of constructing the kind of world we want to create, we cannot dismiss the power of discourse, but neither can we ever be satisfied with a theory that focuses only on ideological constraints. When we look for theoretical similarities within the experience of women while encouraging opportunities to express the concrete differences that varying contexts require, I think we will come to understand that the creation of discursive space requires more than the removal of impediments, ideological or otherwise. Reproductive experience teaches us that human agency is not inherent but is created by

5 Too often, when women have attempted to articulate their experience with the contradictions of agency/dependence within caregiving, they have had their words distorted in a way that confirms the dominant equation of responsiveness with powerlessness. Within this framework, some feminists hesitate to speak about their own need for care or their own desire to respond to others.

responses to particular material needs. Such work does not spontaneously occur once impediments are removed or deconstructed. By unveiling our own motives for the responsive work that we perform, we are
simultaneously articulating alternative concepts of selfhood and ethical
relations: we are opening a space for describing the kinds of relations
that are necessary for meeting the particular and historically specific –
but unexceptional – needs of many different kinds of people. By combin-
ing a broad gender analysis that integrates human agency and human
responsiveness with diverse strategies across and within multiple sites, we
can collectively work to destabilize the hegemonic discourse that is currently stabilized by our individual acts of care.

Ultimately, the pro-choice activities that I have described in this book
were important in overturning the Canadian law on abortion, but as great
as this victory was, OCAC activists never expected that such an outcome
would mark the end of their struggle. It did, however, move it into a new
ideological space. The struggle is ongoing, and, as feminists, our task is to
continue the work. Interpretation is a political tool that we can use to dis-
close or create a space for change within established discourses, and each
time we use these spaces to promote strategies that reconnect agency and
responsiveness, we will once again be faced with the reality of our own
power as social beings. In our everyday practices, we do create relations of
domination and subordination, but we can also choose to create a reality
where no form of oppression is 'natural.'

References

Adamson, Nancy, and Anne Molgat. 1986. 'NAC '86: Who's In and Who's Out?' *Cayenne* 2, no. 4

Adamson, Nancy, and Susan Prentice. 1985. 'Toward a Broader Strategy for Choice.' *Cayenne* 1, no. 3

Adamson, Nancy, Linda Briskin, and Margaret McPhail. 1988. *Feminist Organizing for Change*. Toronto: Oxford University Press

Adamson, Walter L. 1978. 'Beyond "Reform or Revolution": Notes on Political Education in Gramsci, Habermas and Arendt.' *Theory and Society* 6, no. 3

Adler, Nancy E. 1979. 'Abortion: A Social-Psychological Perspective.' *The Journal of Social Issues* 35, no. 1

Allatt, Patricia. 1981. 'Stereotyping: Familism in the Law.' In *Law, State and Society*, ed. Bob Fryer et al. London: Croom Helm

Appleton, Susan Frelich. 1981. 'Beyond the Limits of Reproductive Choice: The Contributions of the Abortion-Funding Cases to Fundamental-Rights Analysis and to the Welfare-Rights Thesis.' *Columbia Law Review* 81, no. 4

Ardener, Shirley. 1977. *Perceiving Women*. London: Dent

Arditti, Rita. 1980. 'Feminism and Science.' In *Science and Liberation*, ed. Rita Arditti, Pat Brennan, and Steve Cavrak. Montreal: Black Rose Books

Arditti, Rita, Renate Duelli Klein and Shelley Minden, eds. 1984. *Test-Tube Women*. London: Pandora Press

Armstrong, P., and H. Armstrong. 1983. 'Beyond Sexless Class and Classless Sex: Towards Feminist Marxism.' *Studies in Political Economy* 10

– 1984. *The Double Ghetto*. Toronto: McClelland and Stewart

As, Berit. 1981. 'A Five-Dimensional Model for Change: Contradictions and Feminist Consciousness.' *Women's Studies International Forum* 4, 1

Bart, Pauline. 1981. 'Seizing the Means of Reproduction: An Illegal Feminist

Abortion Collective – How and Why It Worked.' In *Women, Health and Reproduction*, ed. Helen Roberts. London: Routledge & Kegan Paul

Bartky, Sandra Lee. 1975. 'Toward a Phenomenology of Feminist Consciousness.' *Social Theory and Practice* 3, no. 4 (Fall)

– 1988. 'Foucault, Femininity, and the Modernization of Patriarchal Power.' In *Feminism and Foucault*, ed. Irene Diamond and Lee Quinby. Boston: Northeastern University Press

Bartlett, Katharine, and Rosanne Kennedy. 1991. *Feminist Legal Theory*. Boulder, Colo.: Westview Press

Beagan, Brenda L. 1990. 'Jargon, Myth and Fetishes: Language Use and New Reproductive Technologies.' *RFR/DRF* 18, no. 4

Beard, Mary. 1976. *Women as Force in History: A Study in Traditions and Realities*. New York: Collier Books

Belenky, M.F. et al. 1986. *Women's Ways of Knowing: The Development of Self, Voice, and Mind*. New York: Basic Books

Bertelson, David. 1986. *Snowflakes and Snowdrifts: Individualism and Sexuality in America*. Lanham, Ind.: University Press of America

Bleier, Ruth. 1984. *Science and Gender: A Critique of Biology and Its Theories on Women*. New York: Pergamon Press

Blishen, Bernard R. 1969. *Doctors and Doctrines*. Toronto: University of Toronto Press

Blum, Larry, et al. 1976. 'Altruism and Women's Oppression.' *Women and Philosophy*, ed. Carol C. Gould and Mark W. Wartofsky. New York: G.P. Putnam's Sons

Boggs, Carl. 1976. *Gramsci's Marxism*. London: Pluto Press Limited

Bordo, Susan. 1986. 'The Cartesian Masculinization of Thought.' *Signs* 11, no. 3 (Spring)

– 1990. 'Feminism, Postmodernism, and Gender-Scepticism.' In *Feminism/Postmodernism*, ed. Linda J. Nicholson. London: Routledge

Bouchier, David. 1984. *The Feminist Challenge*. New York: Schocken Books

Boyle, James. 1985. 'The Politics of Reason: Critical Legal Theory and Local Social Thought.' *University of Pennsylvania Law Review* 133 (April)

Bridenthal, Renate, and Claudia Koonz, eds. 1977. *Becoming Visible: Women in European History*. Boston: Houghton Mifflin

Briskin, Linda. 1989. 'Socialist Feminism: From the Standpoint of Practice.' *Studies in Political Economy* 30

– 1990. 'Autonomy, Integration and Legitimacy: A Comparative Analysis of Socialist Feminist Practice in Canada, the United States and Western Europe.' Working paper presented at the Law and Society meetings, Learned Societies Conference, Victoria, B.C., (May)

Brophy, Julia, and Carol Smart. 1981. 'From Disregard to Disrepute: The Position of Women in Family Law.' *Feminist Review* 9

Buechler, Steven M. 1990. *Women's Movements in the United States*. New Brunswick, N.J.: Rutgers University Press

Butler, Judith. 1990. 'Gender Trouble, Feminist Theory, and Psychoanalytic Discourse.' In *Feminism/Postmodernism*, ed. Linda J. Nicholson London: Routledge

Cain, Maureen. 1986. 'Realism, Feminism, Methodology and Law.' *International Journal of the Sociology of Law*. 14

– 1990. Realist Philosophy and Standpoint Epistemologies or Feminist Criminology as a Successor Science. In *Feminist Perspectives in Criminology*, ed. Lorraine Gelsthorpe and Allison Morris. Philadelphia: Open University Press

– 1994. 'The Symbol Traders.' *Lawyers in a Postmodern World: Translation and Transgression*, ed. Maureen Cain and Christine B. Harrington (Eds.) New York: New York University Press

Cain, Maureen, and Christine B. Harrington eds. 1994. *Lawyers in a Postmodern World: Translation and Transgression*. New York: New York University Press

Chafetz, Janet Saltzman. 1988. 'The Gender Division of Labor and the Reproduction of Female Disadvantage.' *Journal of Family Issues* 9, no. 1

Clement, Connie. 1983. 'The Case for Lay Abortions.' *Healthsharing* (Winter)

Code, Lorraine. 1988. 'Experience, Knowledge and Responsibility.' In *Feminist Perspectives in Philosophy*, ed. Morwena Griffiths and Margaret Whitford. Bloomington, Ind.: Indiana University Press

Cohen, Stanley. 1984. 'The Deeper Structures of the Law or "Beware the Rulers Bearing Justice": A Review Essay.' *Contemporary Crises* 8

– 1985. *Visions of Social Control*. New York: Basil Blackwell

– 1990. 'Intellectual Scepticism and Political Commitment: The Case of Radical Criminology.' Monograph of lecture given at the Willem Bonger Institute of Criminology, University of Amsterdam, 14 May

Cole, Susan G. 1983. 'Doctor Power: The Real Abortion Issue.' *This Magazine* 17, no. 2 (June)

Collins, Anne. 1985. *The Big Evasion: Abortion, the Issue That Won't Go Away*. Toronto: Lester & Orpen Dennys

Collins, Larry D. 1982. 'The Politics of Abortion: Trends in Canadian Fertility Policy.' *Atlantis* 7, no. 2

Currie, Dawn. 1988. 'Re-thinking What We Do and How We Do It: A Study of Reproductive Decisions.' *Canadian Review of Sociology and Anthropology* 25, no. 2

Daly, Kathleen. 1989. 'Criminal Justice Ideologies and Practices in Different Voices: Some Feminist Questions about Justice.' *International Journal of the Sociology of Law* 17

Davis, Nanette J. 1985. *From Crime to Choice: The Transformation of Abortion in America*. Westport, Conn: Greenwood Press

De Jong, Katherine. 1985. 'On Equality and Language.' *Canadian Journal of Women and the Law* 1

Delorey, Anne Marie. 1989. 'Joint Legal Custody: A Reversion to Patriarchal Power.' *Canadian Journal of Women and the Law* 3

Derber, Charles. 1979. *The Pursuit of Attention: Power and Individualism in Everyday Life*. Oxford: Oxford University Press

Deverell, John. 1986. 'Union Dues Ruling a Dilemma for Labor.' *Sunday Star* (July 13)

Di Stefano, Christine. 1983. 'Masculinity as Ideology in Political Theory: Hobbesian Man Considered.' *Women's Studies International Forum*. 6, no. 6

– 1990. 'Dilemmas of Difference: Feminism, Modernity, and Postmodernism.' *Feminism/Postmodernism*, ed. Linda J. Nicholson. London: Routledge

Donnison, Jean. 1977. *Midwives and Medical Men*. London: Heinemann Educational Books

Donzelot, Jacques. 1979. *The Policing of Families*. New York: Pantheon

Doyal, Leslie. 1985. 'Women and the National Health Service: The Carers and the Careless.' In *Women, Health and Healing*, ed. V. Olesen and E. Lewin. New York, London: Tavistock

Duff, R.A. 1976. 'Absolute Principles and Double Effect.' *Analysis* 36, no. 2

Easlea, Brian. 1980. *Witch-hunting, Magic and the New Philosophy. An Introduction to Debates of the Scientific Revolution 1450–1750*. Brighton: Harvester Press

– 1981. *Science and Sexual Oppression*. London: Weidenfeld and Nicolson

Egan, Carolyn. 1984. 'Socialist Feminism: A Challenge to Marxism.' *Fireweed* 19

– 1985. 'The Right to Choose.' *Our Times*. (June)

– 1987a. 'Sexual Politics.' *Rebel Girls Rag* 1, no. 3

– 1987b. 'Toronto's International Women's Day Committee: Socialist Feminist Politics.' *Feminism and Political Economy: Women's Work, Women's Struggle*, ed. Heather Jon Maroney and Meg Luxton (eds.). Toronto: Methuen

– 1988. 'Abortion Rights Won Through Women's Struggle.' *Rebel Girls Rag* 2, no. 2

Ehrenreich, Barbara. 1984. *Hearts of Men: Flight from Commitment*. Garden City, N.Y.: Anchor Press

Ehrenreich, B., and D. English. 1973. *Witches, Nurses and Midwives: A History of Women Healers*. Old Westbury, N.Y.: Feminist Press

– 1978. *For Her Own Good: 100 Years of Experts' Advice to Women*. Garden City, N.Y.: Anchor/Doubleday

Eichler, M. 1983. *Families in Canada Today*. Toronto: Gage

Eisenstein, Zillah. 1988. *The Female Body and the Law*. Berkeley: University of California Press

Elshtain, Jean Bethke. 1982. 'Feminist Discourse and Its Discontents: Language, Power and Meaning.' *Signs* 7, no. 3

English, Deirdre. 1981. 'The War against Choice: Inside the Antiabortion Movement.' *Mother Jones.* (February/March)

– 1983. 'Romantic Love and Reproductive Rights.' In *Perspectives on Women in the 1980s,* ed. Joan Turner and Lois Emery. Winnipeg: University of Manitoba Press

Ericson, R.V. 1985. 'Legal Inequality.' *Research in Law, Deviance and Social Control* 7

Ericson, R.V., Patricia M. Baranek, and Janet B.L. Chan. 1989. *Negotiating Control: A Study of News Sources.* Toronto: University of Toronto Press

Falik, Marilyn. 1983. *Ideology and Abortion Policy Politics.* New York: Praeger Publishers

Farrell Smith, Janet. 1984. 'Rights-Conflict, Pregnancy, and Abortion.' In *Beyond Domination,* ed. Carol Gould. New Jersey: Rowman & Allanheld

Fee, Elizabeth. 1983. 'Women's Nature and Scientific Objectivity.' In *Woman's Nature: Rationalizations of Inequality,* ed. Marion Lowe and Ruth Hubbard. New York: Pergamon Press

Fee, Elizabeth, and Ruth Finkelstein. 1986. 'Abortion: The Politics of Necessity and Choice.' *Feminist Studies* 12, no. 2

Ferguson, Ann. 1983. 'On Conceiving Motherhood and Sexuality: A Feminist Materialist Approach.' In *Mothering: Essays in Feminist Theory,* ed. Joyce Trebilcot. New Jersey: Rowman & Allanheld

Ferguson, Ann, and Folbre, Nancy. 1981. 'The Unhappy Marriage of Patriarchy and Capitalism.' In *Women and Revolution,* ed. L. Sargent. Boston: South End Press

Finch, Janet, and Dulcie Groves. 1983. *A Labour of Love: Women, Work and Caring.* London: Routledge & Kegan Paul

Findlay, Deborah. 1986. 'Medicine's Construction of Women's Reproductive Health.' Paper presented at the CSAA meetings of the Learned Societies Conference, Winnipeg

Fineman, Martha L.A. 1994. 'Feminist Legal Scholarship and Women's Gendered Lives.' In *Lawyers in a Postmodern World: Translation and Transgression,* ed. Maureen Cain and Christine B. Harrington. New York: New York University Press

Fishman, Pamela M. 1978. 'Interaction: The Work Women Do.' *Social Problems* 25, no. 4

French, Marilyn. 1985. *Beyond Power: On Women, Men, and Morals.* New York: Summit Books

Frohock, Fred M. 1983. *A Case Study in Law and Morals.* Westport, Conn.: Greenwood Press

Frug, Mary Joe. 1992. *Postmodern Legal Feminism.* New York: Routledge, Chapman, and Hall

Gavigan, Shelley. 1981. 'Women, Law and the State: The Case of Abortion.' MA thesis, Centre of Criminology, University of Toronto

– 1986a. 'On "Bringing on the Menses": The Criminal Liability of Women and the Therapeutic Exception in Canadian Abortion Law.' *Canadian Journal of Women and the Law* 1

– 1986b. 'Women, Law and Patriarchal Relations: Perspectives within the Sociology of Law.' In *The Social Dimensions of Law*, ed. Neil Boyd. Scarborough, Ont.: Prentice-Hall

– 1987. 'Women and Abortion in Canada: What's Law Got to Do with It?' In *Feminism and Political Economy: Women's Work, Women's Struggle*, ed. Heather Jon Maroney and Meg Luxton. Toronto: Methuen

– 1990. 'No Man's Land?: Men's Intervention in Abortion and Pregnancy.' Paper presented at the Law and Society sessions, Learned Societies Conference, Victoria, B.C. (May)

Gellatly, Mary. 1988. 'I. S. Challenged.' *Rebel Girls' Rag* 2, no. 3

Giddens, Anthony. 1981. *A Contemporary Critique of Historical Materialism.* Los Angelos: University of California Press

Gilder, George. 1973. *Sexual Suicide.* New York: Quadrangle/New York Times Book Company

Gilligan, Carol. 1979. 'Women's Place in Men's Life Cycle.' *Harvard Educational Review* 49, no. 4

– 1982. *In a Different Voice: Psychological Theory and Women's Development.* Cambridge, Mass.: Harvard University Press

– 1987. 'Moral Orientation and Moral Development.' In *Women and Moral Theory*, ed. E. Kittay and D. Meyers. Totawa, N.J.: Rowman and Littlefield

– 1988. 'Remapping the Moral Domain: New Images of Self in Relationship.' In *Mapping the Moral Domain*, ed. Gilligan, Janie Victoria Ward, and Jill McLean Taylor. Cambridge, Mass.: Harvard University Press

Gilligan, Carol, and Jane Attanucci. 1988. 'Two Moral Questions.' In *Mapping the Moral Domain*, ed. Gilligan, Janie Victoria Ward, and Jill McLean Taylor. Cambridge, Mass.: Harvard University Press

Gilligan, Carol, and Pollock. 1988. 'The Vulnerable and Invulnerable Physician.' In *Mapping the Moral Domain*, ed. Gilligan, Janie Victoria Ward, and Jill McLean Taylor. Cambridge, Mass.: Harvard University Press

Gilligan, Carol, Janie Victoria Ward, and Jill McLean Taylor, eds. 1988. *Mapping the Moral Domain.* Cambridge, Mass.: Harvard University Press

Gitlin, Todd. 1980. *The Whole World Is Watching.* Berkeley: University of California Press

– 1984. 'Making Protest Movements Newsworthy.' In *Media Power in Politics*, ed. Doris A. Graber. Washington, D.C.: CQ Press

Gordon, Linda. 1976. *Woman's Body, Woman's Right: A Social History of Birth Control in America*. New York: Penguin

Gordon, Linda, and Allen Hunter. 1977–8. 'Sex, Family and the New Left: Anti-Feminism as a Political Force.' *Radical America* 11, no. 6

Gordon, Maggie, and Shelley Gavigan. 1975. 'The Prosecution of Dr. Morgentaler.' *Canadian Dimension* 10, no. 8

Graham, Hilary. 1982. 'Coping: Or How Mothers Are Seen and Not Heard.' In *On The Problem of Men*, ed. Scarlet Friedman and Elizabeth Sarah. London: Women's Press

– 1983. 'Caring: A Labour of Love.' In *A Labour of Love*, ed. J. Finch and D. Groves. London: Routledge & Kegan Paul

Gramsci, A. 1971. *Selections from the Prison Notebooks*, ed. Quinton Hoare and Geoffrey Nowell-Smith. London: Lawrence and Wishart

Greenhouse, Linda. 1982. 'Medical Groups Opposing Curbs in Abortion Law' and 'Excerpts from Akron, Ohio, Abortion Law.' *New York Times*, 31 August, sec. A

Greer, Edward. 1982. 'Antonio Gramsci and "Legal Hegemony."' In *The Politics of Law*, ed. David Kairys. New York: Pantheon Books

Griffin, Susan. 1983. *Woman and Nature: The Roaring inside Her*. Markham, Ont.: Fitzhenry & Whiteside

Guillaumin, Colette. 1982. 'The Question of difference.' *Feminist Issues* 2 (Spring)

Gusfield, J. 1981a. *The Culture of Public Problems*. Chicago: University of Chicago Press

– 1981b. 'Social Movements and Social Change: Perspectives of Linearity and Fluidity.' In *Research in Social Movements: Conflict and Change. A Research Annual*, ed. Louis Kriesberg. Vol 4. Greenwich Conn.: IAI Press

Hale, Sylvia M. 1989. 'Male Culture and Purdah for Women: The Social Construction of What Women Think Women Think.' *Canadian Review of Sociology and Anthropology* 25, no. 2

Harding, Sandra G. 1984. 'Is Gender a Variable in Conceptions of Rationality? A Survey of Issues. In *Beyond Domination*, ed. Carol C. Gould. New Jersey: Rowman & Allanheld

– 1987. 'The Instability of the Analytical Categories of Feminist Theory.' In *Sex and Scientific Inquiry*, ed. Sandra Harding and Jean F. O'Barr. Chicago: University of Chicago Press

– 1990. 'Feminism, Science, and the Anti-Enlightenment Critiques.' In *Feminism/Postmodernism*, ed. Linda J. Nicholson. London: Routledge

Harding, Sandra G., and Merrill Hintikka, eds. 1983. *Discovering Reality: Feminist*

Perspectives on Epistemology, Metaphysics, Methodology, and Philosophy of Science.
Dordrecht, Holland: D. Reidel Publishing

Harrington, Christine B. 1994. 'Outlining a Theory of Legal Practice.' In *Lawyers in a Postmodern World: Translation and Transgression*, ed. Maureen Cain and Christine B. Harrington. New York: New York University Press

Harrison, B.W. 1983. *Our Right to Choose*. Boston: Beacon Press

– 1984. Article in *Making the Connections: Essays in Feminist Social Ethics*, ed. Carol S. Robb. Boston: Beacon Press

Hartsock, Nancy. 1983. 'The Feminist Standpoint: Developing the Ground for a Specifically Feminist Historical Materialism.' In *Discovering Reality*, ed. Sandra G. Harding and Merrill Hintikka. Dordrecht, Holland: D. Reidel Publishing

– 1984. *Money, Sex and Power*. Boston: Northeastern University Press

– 1990. 'Foucault on Power: A Theory for Women?' In *Feminism/Postmodernism*, ed. Linda J. Nicholson. London: Rougledge

Heinsohn, Gunnar, and Otto Steiger. 1982. 'The Elimination of Medieval Birth Control and the Witch Trials of Modern Times.' *International Journal of Women's Studies* 5, no. 3

Herland, Karen. 1986. 'Abortion Coalition in Quebec Pushes for Legislation.' *Herizons* 4, no. 4

Hochschild, Arlie Russell. 1983. *The Managed Heart: Commercialization of Human Feeling*. Berkeley: University of California Press

Hubbard, Ruth. 1983. 'Have Only Men Evolved?' *Discovering Reality*, ed. Sandra G. Harding and Merrill Hintikka. Dordrecht, Holland: D. Reidel Publishing

Hubbard, Ruth, and Marian Lowe, eds. 1983. *Woman's Nature: Rationalizations of Inequality*. New York: Pergamon Press

Hutchinson, Allan, and Andrew Petter. 1986. 'Charter's Core Values Don't Belong to Property Owners.' *Canadian Lawyer* (September)

Jackman, Martha. 1989. 'The Protection of Welfare Rights under the Charter.' Paper presented at Law and Society sessions, Learned Societies Conference, Quebec City

Johnston, D. Kay. 1988. 'Adolescences: Solutions to Dilemmas in Fable: Two Moral Questions, Two Problem-Solving Strategies.' In *Mapping the Moral Domain*, ed. Carol Gilligan, Janie Victoria Ward, and Jill McLean Taylor. Cambridge, Mass.: Harvard University Press

Jones, Kathleen. 1988. 'On Authority: Or, Why Women Are Not Entitled to Speak.' In *Feminism and Foucault*, ed. Irene Diamond and Lee Quinby. Boston: Northeastern Press

Jong, Erica. 1981. *Witches*. New York: Harry N. Abrams

Kaufmann, K. 1984. 'Abortion, a Woman's Matter: An Explanation of Who Controls Abortion and How and Why They Do It.' In *Test-Tube Women*, ed.

Rita Arditti, Renate Duelli Klein, and Shelley Minden. London: Pandora Press

Kellner, Douglas. 1981. 'Remarks on Alvin's Gouldner's *The Two Marxisms.*' *Theory and Society* 10, no. 2 (March)

Kellough, Gail. 1990a. 'The Abortion Controversy: A Study of Law, Culture and Social Change. Doctoral dissertation, University of Toronto

– 1990b. 'The "Ideological Ceiling" of Male Culture.' In *Gender, Sexuality & Social Control*, ed. Bill Rolston and Mike Tomlinson. Bristol: European Group for the Study of Deviance and Social Control

– 1992. Pro-Choice Politics and Postmodernist Theory. In Organizing Dissent: Contemporary Social Movements in Theory and Practice (William Carroll, Ed.). Toronto: Garamond Press

Kelly (Kelly-Godol), Joan. 1977. 'Did Women Have a Rennaissance?' In *Becoming Visible: Women in European History*, ed. Renate Bridenthal and Claudia Koon. Boston: Houghton Mifflin

– 1984. *Women, History and Theory*. Chicago: The University of Chicago Press

Kett, Joseph F. 1981. 'American and Canadian Medical Institutions 1800–1870.' In *Medicine in Canadian Society: Historical Perspectives*, ed. S.E.D. Shortt. Montreal: McGill-Queen's University Press

Kirzner, Ellie. 1986. 'Labouring under the Charter.' *NOW Magazine* (17–23 July)

Kohlberg, L. 1981. *The Philosophy of Moral Development: Moral Stages and the Idea of Justice: Essays on Moral Development.* San Francisco: Harper & Row

Lake, Randall A. 1986. 'The Metaethical Framework of Anti-Abortion Rhetoric.' *Signs* 11, no. 3

Larner, C. 1984. *Witchcraft and Religion: The Politics of Popular Belief.* Oxford: Basil Blackwell

Lasch, Christopher. 1977. *Haven in a Heartless World: The Family Besieged.* New York: Basic Books

Lauter, Estella. 1984. 'Steps toward a Feminist Archetypal Theory of Mythmaking.' *Women as Mythmakers*, ed. Lauter. Bloomington, Ind.: Indiana University Press

Lees, Sue. 1994. 'Lawyers' Work as Constitutive of Gender Relations.' In *Lawyers in a Postmodern World: Translation and Transgression*, ed. Maureen Cain and Christine B. Harrington. New York: New York University Press

Lucas, Roy, and Lynn I. Miller. 1981. 'Evolution of Abortion Law in North America.' In *Abortion and Sterilization*, ed. Jane E. Hodgson. Toronto: Academic Press

Luker, Kristen. 1984. *Abortion and the Politics of Motherhood.* Berkeley: University of California Press

Lyons, Nona P. 1983. 'Two Perspectives: On Self, Relationships and Morality.' *Harvard Educational Review* 53, no. 2

- 1988. 'Two Perspectives.' In *Mapping the Moral Domain,* ed. Carol Gilligan, Janie Victoria Ward, and Jill McLean Taylor. Cambridge, Mass.: Harvard University Press

Macdonald, R.A. 1982. 'Postscript and Prelude – The Jurisprudence of the Charter: Eight Theses.' *Supreme Court Law Review* 4

McDonnell, Kathleen. 1984. *Not an Easy Choice: A Feminist Re-examines Abortion.* Toronto: Women's Press

MacKinnon, Catherine, A. 1982. 'Feminism, Marxism, Method, and the State: An Agenda for Theory.' *Signs* 7, no. 3

- 1983a. 'Feminism, Marxism, Method and the State: Toward Feminist Jurisprudence.' *Signs* 8, no. 4

- 1983b. 'The Male Ideology of Privacy: A Feminist Perspective on the Right to Abortion.' *Radical America* 17, no. 4

- 1987. *Feminism Unmodified: Discourses on Life and Law.* London: Harvard University Press

McLaren, Angus. 1981. 'Birth Control and Abortion in Canada, 1870–1920.' In *Medicine in Canadian Society: Historical Perspectives,* ed. S.E.D. Shortt. Montreal: McGill-Queen's University Press

McLaren, Angus, and Arlene Tigar McLaren. 1986. *The Bedroom and the State: The Changing Practices and Politics of Contraception and Abortion in Canada, 1880–1980.* Toronto: McClelland and Stewart

McQuaig, Linda, et al. 1983. 'Stop Signs and Detours in the Way of Abortion.' *McLean's* (July 25)

Manning, Morris. 1985. 'The Morgentaler File.' *Canadian Lawyer* (October)

- 1986. 'Constitutional Heartbeats and the Extra-Billing Dispute.' *Canadian Lawyer* (May)

Marcus, Isabel, et al. 1985. 'Feminist Discourse, Moral Values, and the Law: A Conversation.' *Buffalo Law Review* 34

Marieskind, Helen I., and B. Ehrenreich. 1975. 'Toward Socialistic Medicine: The Women's Health Movement.' *Social Policy* 6, no. 2

Marshall, Barbara L. 1988. 'Feminist Theory and Critical Theory.' *Canadian Review of Sociology and Anthropology* 25, no 2

Martin, Sheila L. 1985. 'R. v. Morgentaler et al.' *Canadian Journal of Women and the Law* 1

- 1986a. 'Canada's Abortion Law and the Canadian Charter of Rights and Freedoms.' *Canadian Journal of Women and the Law* 1

- 1986b. 'The Reluctance of the Judiciary to Balance Competing Interests: R. v. Morgentaler in the Ontario Court of Appeal.' *Canadian Journal of Women and the Law* 1

Matsuda, Mari J. 1986. 'Liberal Jurisprudence and Abstracted Visions of Human

Nature: A Feminist Critique of Rawls' Theory of Justice.' *New Mexico Law Review* 16

Mensch, Elizabeth. 1982. 'The History of Mainstream Legal Thought.' In *The Politics of Law*, ed. David Kairys. New York: Pantheon Books

Merchant, Carolyn. 1983. *The Death of Nature*. Markham, Ont.: Fitzhenry & Whiteside

Michelman, Frank I. 1973. 'In Pursuit of Constitutional Welfare Rights: One View of Rawls' Theory of Justice.' *University of Pennsylvania Law Review* 121

– 1979. 'Welfare Rights in a Constitutional Democracy.' *Washington University Law Quarterly* 3

Miles, Angela. 1982. 'Ideological Hegemony in Political Discourse: Women's Specificity and Equality.' *Feminism in Canada: From Pressure to Politics*, ed. Angela Miles and Geraldine Finn. Montreal: Black Rose Books

– 1985. 'Feminism, Equality, and Liberation.' *Canadian Journal of Women and the Law* 1

Miller, Jane Baker. 1986. *Towards a New Psychology of Women*. 2d. ed. Boston: Beacon Press

– 1987. 'Preface.' *Canadian Women's Studies* 8, no. 4

Mills, Chris. 1985. 'Strategy for Choice: An Interview with Judy Rebick.' *Cayenne* 1, no. 2. (Feb)

Mitchinson, Wendy. 1979. 'Historical Attitudes Toward Women and Childbirth.' *Atlantis* 4, no. 2, pt. II (Spring)

– 1988. 'The Medical Treatment of Women.' In *Changing Patterns: Women in Canada*. ed. Sandra Burt, Lorraine Code, and Lindsay Dorney. Toronto: McClelland and Stewart

Mohr, James. 1978. *Abortion in America: The Origins and Evolution of National Policy 1800–1900*. New York: Oxford University Press

Morgan, Robin. 1984. *The Anatomy of Freedom: Feminism, Physics, and Global Politics*. Garden City, N.Y.: Anchor Books/Doubleday

Naffine, Ngaire. 1987. *Female Crime: The Construction of Women in Criminology*. Sydney: Allen & Unwin

Nedelsky, Jennifer. 1989. 'Reconceiving Autonomy: Sources, Thoughts and Possibilities.' *Yale Journal of Law and Feminism* (Spring)

Noonan, John. 1970. *The Morality of Abortion: Legal and Historical Perspectives*. Cambridge: Harvard University Press

O'Brien, Mary. 1981. *The Politics of Reproduction*. London: Routledge

– 1982. 'Feminist Theory and Dialectical Logic.' In *Feminist Theory: A Critique of Ideology*, ed. N.O. Keohane, M.Z. Rosaldo, and B.C. Gelpi. Chicago: University of Chicago Press

– 1983. 'Reproductive Labour and the Creation of Value.' *Atlantis* 8, no. 2

– 1984. 'Hegemony and Superstructure: A Feminist Critique of Neo-Marxism.' *Taking Sex into Account*, ed. Jill McCalla Vickers. Ottawa: Carleton University Press

Overall, Christine. 1986. 'Reproductive Ethics: Feminist and Non-Feminist Approaches.' *Canadian Journal of Women and the Law* 1

Penelope, Julia. 1986. 'Language and the Transformation of Consciousness.' *Law and Inequality* 4

Pepinsky, Hal. 1987. 'Violence as Unresponsiveness.' *Justice Quarterly* 4

Petchesky, Rosalind. 1984. *Abortion and Woman's Choice: The State, Sexuality and the Conditions of Reproductive Freedom.* New York: Longman

– 1985. 'Abortion in the 1980s: Feminist Morality and Women's Health.' In *Women, Health and Healing: Toward a New Perspective*, ed. Virginia Olesen and Ellen Lewen. New York: Tavistock Publications

– 1987. 'Foetal Images: The Power of Visual Culture in the Politics of Reproduction.' In *Reproductive Technologies: Gender Motherhood and Medicine*, ed. Michelle Stanworth. Minneapolis: University of Minnesota Press

Polan, Diane. 1982. 'Toward a Theory of Law and Patriarchy.' In *The Politics of Law*, ed. David Kairys. New York: Pantheon Books

Powell, Marion. 1987. *Report on Therapeutic Abortion Services in Ontario. A Study Commissioned by the Ministry of Health.* Toronto (27 January)

Rawls, John. 1971. *A Theory of Justice.* Cambridge, Mass.: Cambridge University Press

Reasons, Chuck. 1989. 'Law, State and Economy.' *Journal of Human Justice* 1, no. 1 (Autumn)

Richards, David A.J. 1981. 'Rights, Utility, and Crime.' In *Crime and Justice*, ed. Norval Morris and Michael Tonry. 3. Chicago: University of Chicago Press

Rifkin, J. 1980. 'Toward a Theory of Law and Patriarchy.' *Harvard Women's Law Journal* 3

Robinson, Betty D. 1979. 'Women and Class Consciousness: A Proposal for the Dialectical Study of Class Consciousness.' *Insurgent Sociologist* 8, no. 4

Rose, Hilary. 1983. 'Hand, Brain and Heart: A Feminist Epistemology for the Natural Sciences.' *Signs* 9, no. 1

Rowbotham, S. 1972. *Woman's Consciousness, Man's World.* Harmondsworth, England: Penguin Books

– 1974. *Hidden from History: Rediscovering Women in History from the 17th Century to the Present.* New York: Random House

– 1982. *Beyond the Fragments: Feminism and the Making of Socialism.* London: Alyson Publishers

Rubin, Eva. 1987. *Abortion, Politics and the Courts.* Westport, Conn: Greenwood Press

Rubin, Gayle. 1975. 'The Traffic in Women: Notes on the Political Economy of Sex.' In *Toward an Anthropology of Women*, ed. Rayner Reiter. New York: Monthly Review Press

Ruddick, Sara. 1982. 'Maternal Thinking.' In *Rethinking the Family*, ed. Barrie Thorne. Longman: New York

– 1984. 'Preservative Love and Military Destruction: Some Reflections on Mothering and Peace.' In *Mothering: Essays in Feminist Theory*, ed. Joyce Trebilcot. New Jersey: Rowman & Allanheld

Samek, Robert A. 1982. 'Untrenching Fundamental Rights.' *McGill Law Journal* 27

Sarvis, Betty, and Hyman Rodman. 1974. *The Abortion Controversy*. New York: Columbia University Press

Sawicki, Jana. 1988. 'Identity Politics and Sexual Freedom: Foucault and Feminism.' In *Feminism & Foucault*, ed. Irene Diamond and Lee Quinby. Boston: Northeastern University Press

Scales, Ann C. 1986. 'The Emergence of Feminist Jurisprudence: An Essay.' *The Yale Law Journal* 95

Schaef, Anne Wilson. 1981. *Women's Reality: An Emerging Female System in a White Male Society*. Minneapolis: Winston Press

Shortt, S.E.D, ed. 1981. *Medicine in Canadian Society: Historical Perspectives*. Montreal: McGill-Queen's University Press

Smart, Carol. 1981. 'Law and the Control of Women's Sexuality: The Case of the 1950s.' In *Controlling Women*, ed. Bridget Hutter and Gillian Williams. London: Croom Helm

– 1986. 'Feminism and Law: Some Problems of Analysis and Strategy.' *International Journal of the Sociology of Law* 14

– 1987. 'There Is of Course the Distinction Dictated by Nature: Law and the Problem of Paternity.' *Reproductive Technologies*, ed. Michelle Stanworth. Minneapolis: University of Minnesota Press

– 1989. *Feminism and the Power of Law*. London: Routledge

Smith, Dorothy. 1979. 'A Sociology for Women.' In *The Prism of Sex: Essays in the Sociology of Knowledge*, ed. Julia A. Sherman and Evelyn T. Beck. Madison: University of Wisconsin Press

– 1987. *The Everyday World as Problematic*. Toronto: University of Toronto Press

– 1988. 'Institutional Ethnography: A Feminist Method.' In *Gender and Society*, ed. Arlene Tigar McLaren. Mississauga, Ont.: Copp Clark Pitman

Smith, Kenneth D., and Harris S. Wineberg. 1970. 'A Survey of Therapeutic Abortion Committees.' *Criminal Law Quarterly* 12

Snider, Laureen. 1992. 'Feminism, Punishment and the Potential of Empowerment.' Revised paper of that presented at 'Women and the Law' conference, Mount Gabriel, Quebec, in July 1991

Stehelin, Lilliane. 1976. 'Sciences, Women and Ideology.' *The Radicalisation of Science*, ed. Hilary and Steven Rose. London: Macmillan Press

Stone, Lawrence. 1977. *The Family, Sex, and Marriage in England: 1500–1800*. New York: Harper and Row

Stuard, Susan Mosher. 1976. *Women in Medieval Society*. University of Pennsylvania Press

Sydie, R.A. 1987. *Natural Women, Cultured Men*. Agincourt, Ont.: Methuen Publications

Ursel, Jane. 1984. 'Toward a Theory of Reproduction.' *Contemporary Crises* 8

– 1992. *Private Lives – Public Policy: 100 Years of State Intervention in the Family*. Toronto: Women's Press

Valverde, Mariana. 1985. *Sex, Power and Pleasure*. Toronto: Women's Press

– 1990. 'The Rhetoric of Reform: Tropes and the Moral Subject.' *International Journal of the Sociology of Law* 18

Wallsgrove, Ruth. 1980. 'The Masculine Face of Science.' In *Alice through the Microscope*. Brighton: Women and Science Group

Waugh, Patricia. 1989. *Feminine Fictions: Revisiting the Postmodern*. London: Routledge

Weil, Simone. 1951. *Waiting on God*. London: Routledge & Kegan Paul

West, Robin. 'Jurisprudence and Gender.' *University of Chicago Law Review* 55, no. 1

Whitbeck, Caroline. 1984. 'A Different Reality: Feminist Ontology.' In *Beyond Domination*, ed. Carol C. Gould. New Jersey: Rowman & Allanheld

White, R.D. 1985. 'Legal Problems and Social Issues,' Paper presented at annual meeting of the Western Association of Sociology and Anthropology, Winnipeg (14–16 February)

Williams, Raymond. 1973. 'Base and Superstructure in Marxist Cultural Theory.' *New Left Review* (November/December)

– 1977. *Marxism and Literature*. Oxford: Oxford University Press

Yeatman, Anna. 1990. 'A Feminist Theory of Social Differentiation.' In *Feminism/Postmodernism*, ed. Linda J. Nicholson. New York and London: Routledge

Young, Iris Marion. 1988. 'Impartiality and the Civic Public: Some Implications of Feminist Critiques of Moral and Political Theory.' In *Feminism as Critique*, ed. Sayla Benhabib and Drucilla Cornell. Minneapolis: University of Minnesota Press

Index

225; hierarchical structure of, 176, 206, 214; individualism underpins patriarchal, 147, 176; liberal democracy's uneasy coexistence with, 214; personal service moves into the marketplace under, 37, 49; reinforces patriarchy, 228, 276, 288, 290, 298; social arrangements under, 102; socialist-feminist critique of, 131; women's political struggles under, 213, 217, 228, 254, 256 n2, 276, 280, 287–8, 298

CARAL. *See* Canadian Abortion Rights Action League

'The Case for Lay Abortion,' 209

Centres de Santé des Femmes, 184

certificate of vehicle roadworthiness, 149, 153–4, 156–7, 165

Chafetz, Janet Saltzman: cited, 36; quoted, 37

CLC. *See* Canadian Labour Congress

Clement, Connie: cited, 251; quoted, 209–10

Code, Lorraine, cited, 303

Cohen, Stanley: cited, 303; quoted, 19, 289

Cole, Susan G., cited, 211, 251

College of Physicians and Surgeons of Manitoba, 197, 232–3

College of Physicians and Surgeons of Ontario, 183

Collins, Anne: cited, 77–8, 179, 181, 183, 185; quoted, 78, 177–8, 196

Collins, Larry D.: cited, 78–9, 109, 179; quoted, 76–7, 178, 180

Committee for the Establishment of Abortion Clinics (CEAC), 184–5

Community Health Clinics (Montreal), 208

Connecticut v. Menillo, 72

conservatism, 24, 103, 105, 165–6, 252

contraception: abortion as, 136; control of the knowledge of, 51–4; Criminal Code regulation of, 54, 76; current need for reliable, 38, 265–6; medieval, 46–9; nineteenth-century Canada, 55

courts, 274; abstract rulings of, 70; crown attorneys describe role of the, 163–4; decisions of U.S., 71–4, 81–2; differentiate between individuals, 151; evaluate broader state intervention, 60; identify women's with family interests, 145; Manitoba, 232–3; overturn jury verdicts, 178; regulation of abortion enters the, 13, 88–90, 120–49, 151–3, 156–69, 171, 217, 233, 279. *See also* law; legal code; legal theory

Criminal Code (1892), 54

Criminal Code, 1969 amendment, 77, 229; abortion funding under the, 186; contradicts equality of law, 13, 81, 151–3; Crown defends, 145, 169, 201; exception to universality of health care, 13, 79–81, 123, 171; falsifies public understanding of abortion, 116–17, 182; foetal rights in the, 122–3, 151–3, 155, 157; furthers interests of state and medical profession, 90, 162; hegemonic process at work in the, 156, 161, 171–2; legal and social codes interlock in, 12; legalizes contraceptives, 76; legalizes informal abortion practice, 76, 78, 108, 116, 142 n4; Morgentaler challenges the, 15, 178, 181; purpose as stated by the Crown, 107, 119, 123–4, 127, 136, 143, 146; strengthens power of medical pro-

Morison, Dr J.B., 232
Morton, Desmond, quoted, 241
Munro, John, 178

NAC. *See* National Action Committee
on the Status of Women
Naffine, Ngaire, cited, 27
National Action Committee on the
Status of Women (NAC), 188–9,
227, 238, 261–4, 266, 268, 270, 273
National Citizens' Coalition (NCC),
240
natural law, 21–4, 61, 65–6, 103, 124,
130, 163, 169
Nedelsky, Jennifer, cited, 302 n3
New Democratic Party of Canada, 191,
235, 238
New Democratic Party of Manitoba,
191–4, 196, 233–7
New Democratic Party of Ontario, 185,
187, 224, 233, 235, 237
New Democratic Party of Quebec, 263
news media, 56, 77–8, 177, 185, 188–
90, 202, 217–19, 223, 226–33, 246–7,
260–2, 268, 278–80
Nichol, Nancy, 207–8, 210, 213, 215,
255
Noonan, John, cited, 46–8
North America, colonial, 9, 44, 51,
53–4, 80
Not an Easy Choice, 251
NOW, 240–1

O'Brien, Mary: cited, 94; quoted, 30,
117
OCAC. *See* Ontario Coalition for Abortion Clinics
Ontario: abortion, 186–7, 190, 220;
doctors' strike, 188–90, 197, 200,
214, 249–50, 267; medical profes-

sion's position of power, 185–90,
197, 199–201; NDP supporters, 236;
news reporting, 189–90, 218, 227–
30, 232–3, 260; OCAC's shortage of
help in, 267; OCAC successes in,
218; political process of opening an
illegal clinic in, 181, 201, 204, 215,
249; possible loss of transfer pay-
ments, 187; provincial election
(1985), 187, 234–8; Roman Catholic
Church anti-abortion actions, 219;
unions' women's committees, 243;
women's health movement, 182–4,
199, 215
Ontario Coalition for Abortion Clinics
(OCAC), 253, 297, 306
anti-abortionists work against, 218–
20; disputes content of *The Struggle
for Choice*, 207 n1; escort program,
220–2, 224, 229–30; founded, 7, 185,
215; fund raising, 219; hurt by split
of feminists and socialists, 211, 228,
238; 'Manning issue,' 238 n3, 239–
50, 255; organizes activists locally
and nationally, 6–7, 16, 214, 219–24,
229–31, 238–9, 248, 257–60, 263–4;
reacts to doctors' strike, 188–90,
250; relations with Morgentaler and
Scott, 216, 221–8, 230, 249, 291–2;
relations with NAC, 262–3; relations with the labour movement,
228–31, 238–9, 242–50, 266–7, 269–
73; socialist-feminist principles of,
205, 217, 228–9, 241–2, 244, 257,
276, 284–5, 287–9; strategic decisions of, 6, 16, 19, 184, 203–5, 207–8,
213–24, 228–31, 233–9, 243–50, 254–
6, 256 n2, 257–77, 279–80, 283–91,
298; supports self-determination
for Quebec, 225 n2